THE MOFFAT PAPERS

1919–1943

JAY PIERREPONT MOFFAT

about 1933

The Moffat Papers

SELECTIONS FROM THE DIPLOMATIC JOURNALS OF

JAY PIERREPONT MOFFAT

1919–1943

Edited by

NANCY HARVISON HOOKER

With a foreword by

SUMNER WELLES

HARVARD UNIVERSITY PRESS

Cambridge, Massachusetts

1956

FOREWORD

During the years of my service in the Department of State it was my privilege to be frequently closely associated with Pierrepont Moffat in the conduct of American foreign policy. He served for a protracted period and with notable distinction in the key position of what was then termed Chief of the Division of European Affairs; he accompanied me as my chief assistant when President Roosevelt sent me to Europe as his personal representative in the spring of 1940; and I was in the closest touch with him during the time he served as American Minister to Canada, a service so tragically terminated by his untimely death in 1943. I know of no man who came up through the ranks of the Foreign Service with whose work I am personally familiar who impressed me as having in his latter years greater knowledge, a wiser and more balanced judgment, or a greater devotion to the highest interests of this country.

These papers of Pierrepont Moffat, which include the diaries that he so sedulously kept as well as a few notes from personal letters bearing upon world affairs, comprehend the years of his official activity. They cover that deplorable and sterile era between the two world wars during a part of which time Pierrepont Moffat was stationed in Switzerland near the seat of the League of Nations. Subsequent to his transfer to the Department of State he was, of course, afforded a better vantage point for knowledge and observation. During this stage his papers present a brilliantly qualified technician's inside view of how American foreign policy was formulated and the methods by which it was carried out.

I have studied these papers very carefully, partly because of my friendship for their author, and partly because they represent in my judgment an exceptionally important historical document which throws much light upon the diplomacy of our times. I believe that every student of international relations and every citizen who seeks intelligently to follow the trend of our current foreign policy will find these papers of the utmost value as a means of clarifying his own views as to the nature of our errors of omission and of commission in the past, as to where our national foreign policy took the right course or went astray. It is my conviction that a book of this character, written by an authoritative observer, offers much for the enlightenment of American public opinion.

SUMNER WELLES

ACKNOWLEDGMENTS

Many times the family and friends of Pierrepont Moffat have helped with this book, and it is a pleasure to thank them. Mrs. Jay Pierrepont Moffat and Mrs. R. Burnham Moffat submitted to numerous interviews, and they and Mr. Abbot Low Moffat read the manuscript. Some questions which arose about the chapter on Poland were cleared up by Mr. John Campbell White. From among those who worked with Mr. Moffat in the Department of State, Mr. Adolf A. Berle, Jr., former Assistant Secretary of State, gave access to his own private papers and was exceptionally helpful. Former Secretary of State Cordell Hull, former Assistant Secretary of State John D. Hickerson, Ambassador Lewis Clark, Ambassador Rudolf Schoenfeld, Minister Theodore Achilles, Ambassador John Farr Simmons, and Mr. J. Graham Parsons were of great assistance. Certain parts of the book have benefited from the help of the Canadian Ambassador to the Netherlands, Mr. Thomas Stone, Mr. Ellery Sedgwick, former Polish Ambassador Jan Ciechanowski, Colonel Elbert Farman, Mr. J. Fred Rippy, Mr. E. Taylor Parks, Mrs. Dorothy Forbis Behen, Miss Katherine Hall, and Miss Winifred Ver Nooy. The Department of State permitted access to all the official records which were requested, and the manuscript was read in the Department.

To five people a particular debt of gratitude is owed. Through the initiative of former Ambassador Joseph C. Grew, the papers of Mr. Moffat were given to me to edit. His wise advice and unfailing kindness have been a constant aid.

The former Under Secretary of State, Mr. Sumner Welles, wrote the excellent foreword to this book.

Mr. Walter Johnson, Chairman of the Department of History of the University of Chicago, was both friend and teacher. Having taught me much about history and historical research, he continued to give his counsel generously in the preparation of these papers.

Mrs. Lydia Crouse Harvison skillfully typed much of the manuscript and assisted in the proofreading.

And during the two years that the book was in preparation my husband, Richard J. Hooker, gave more advice and encouragement than any other person, as with continuing good humor he shared the problems of editing.

NANCY HARVISON HOOKER

Contents

THE MOFFAT PAPERS

1919–1943

INTRODUCTION

In the late autumn of 1917 a young man named Pierrepont Moffat sailed from New York to become the private secretary of the American Minister at The Hague. He began a great adventure, which not only led across the submarine-infested ocean between Europe and America in 1917 but which carried him through twenty-five years of one of the most dramatic periods in American history. He rose through the lower ranks of the American Foreign Service to top posts in Australia and Canada and to the key position of chief European adviser in the Department of State before the outbreak of World War II. Few modern careers are so well chronicled. A keen and dispassionate observer, he diligently recorded his work and his times.

The diplomatic career which Jay Pierrepont Moffat began in 1917 was one he had chosen many years earlier. Born on July 18, 1896, in Rye, New York, the son of a well-known lawyer, R. Burnham Moffat, and of Ellen Pierrepont Moffat, he had been given the name of his ancestor John Jay, the first Chief Justice. It was, perhaps, the stories that he was told as a child about the Jays and other branches of his family — the Pierreponts, the Livingstons, the Constables, the Lows — that first interested him in a career of public service. He later wrote that such stories had "instilled not only a knowledge of history, but an intense pride in the United States" and "gave an unconscious feeling that one had almost proprietary interest in its well-being and a traditional urge to participate in public service." [1]

By the time he was an adolescent he had decided definitely that he wanted to be a diplomat. At Groton and the other private schools to which he went, he excelled in languages and history and was consistently first or second in his class. In 1915 he entered Harvard to begin even more serious preparations for his career.

But it was less his long-range planning that determined the circumstances of his entry into the Foreign Service than the fact that the United States became involved in World War I in April 1917.

[1] Moffat papers, undated note, probably written during the 1930's.

Pierrepont Moffat had chosen sides long before American entry: "Personally I feel that not only our honor as a country, but our honor as a civilized nation is at stake, and that the firmest measures — yes, war — must be shown, if Germany does not immediately change." [2] But in the same letter he expressed the fear that a tubercular condition, which he had recently overcome, might prevent him from being accepted as a soldier. When he was, in fact, rejected as unfit for army service, he watched impatiently as his Harvard friends left for the war.

He soon decided to get some form of civilian war work. He obtained a letter of introduction to Hugh Gibson of the Department of State, and in mid-November 1917 he went to Washington. Although he found there were no jobs open in the Department, by chance he met the sister-in-law of John W. Garrett, the American Minister at The Hague. He explained to her why he had come to Washington, and she offered to find out if Mr. Garrett needed a private secretary. Within ten days a telegram arrived asking Mr. Moffat to come to the Netherlands to be Mr. Garrett's private secretary.

Pierrepont Moffat began his diplomatic career and his diary simultaneously on December 1, 1917, the day on which the telegram arrived. Ten days later he sailed for the Netherlands. Here he found that the Legation was a meeting place for news from both Germany and the United States, and the swift movement of events corresponded with the excitement and enthusiasm with which he had undertaken his duties. Although he was not in a position of great responsibility, he began to record his own ideas on problems faced by the Minister, to analyze public opinion, and to learn some of the work of a diplomat.

He had, however, entered diplomatic life through a back door, in an unsalaried position without official rank, and his years at The Hague were only an apprenticeship, while he waited to take the written and oral examinations which were prerequisites for admission to the Foreign Service. In 1918 he took the written examinations at The Hague, and the following year he returned to Washington for the oral examination. When he passed this, first in his class, he spent a short training period in the Department, and in September 1919 was assigned to Warsaw as Third Secretary of Legation.

[2] Jay Pierrepont Moffat to Ellen Pierrepont Moffat, May 15, 1915.

From August 2, 1921, when he was sent to Tokyo, until he was posted at Berne in 1927, his record of his career is very sketchy. As Second Secretary in Japan he had hoped to find "another active post, where vital issues were at stake," but a brief account, written some years later, reveals that he remembered best the people, the customs, and the places and not the political problems. He recalled with pleasure the evenings in Tokyo, when from the top of Atago Yama "you could see myriads of lanterns illuminating the street booths, with people walking to and fro in the cool of evening in their loose hanging kimonos," the trips to Nikko and around Fuji, the Imperial Chrysanthemum Party, his amazement at his first geisha party, and his amusement at the Imperial Duck Hunt where "the weapon was a butterfly net; the sporting costume . . . a frock coat and top hat." [3] During the second winter in Japan his health reached a low ebb, and the doctor ordered him home.

After his recovery he was sent in the autumn of 1923 to Constantinople as Second Secretary to the American Commission. Although in Turkey he must have witnessed the remarkable strides toward modernization which that country was making under Kemal Atatürk, he kept no written record of these years.

In 1925 he was brought back to Washington to become the first protocol officer at the White House. Acting as a sort of social arbiter for the capital — his friends dubbed him "Pierrepontifex Moffaximus of Protocol" — he found little incentive to write about what he once described as "a bad post and worse than that a dull post." He had to make out the lists for all the official receptions, dinners, and informal musicals and to decide questions of protocol that were often more harrowing than an international crisis. Although this had often been mistaken to be the major duty of a diplomatic officer, it was a part of the life which Pierrepont Moffat had little heart to make a full time job.

Yet there were advantages to the life in Washington. An eligible bachelor was much in demand, and he was less lonely than he had been in Tokyo and Constantinople. One autumn day in 1925 he lunched at Blair House, where the guests included his good friend, Mrs. Joseph C. Grew, the wife of the Undersecretary of State, and her seventeen-year-old daughter, Lilla. This was his first meeting with

[3] Moffat papers, undated account of the assignment in Japan.

Lilla Cabot Grew, his future wife. Two years later he began to escort her around Washington, and their engagement was announced in June 1927. On July 27, 1927, Lilla Grew and Pierrepont Moffat were married before a small family group at Hancock, New Hampshire.

When he was assigned in September 1927 as First Secretary in Berne, Switzerland, he began his diary again. There were, however, few troubled spots in the relations of the United States with Switzerland, and the most challenging part of his work concerned the problems that arose with the League of Nations. Personally these years were most happy. Hugh Wilson, the Minister to Switzerland, was an old friend, and the business of the Legation was light enough to permit the officers to enjoy the cosmopolitan and cultural atmosphere of Berne and Geneva. And to the Moffats' delight their first child, Edith, was born in 1929.

It is with Pierrepont Moffat's return to Washington in 1931, as he assumed increasingly responsible positions, that the diary excerpts printed in this book begin. In 1932 Mr. Moffat became Chief of the Division of Western European Affairs, acting as the principal adviser to the Secretary of State on matters dealing with West Europe and on disarmament questions in particular. But the rise of the totalitarian states, and of Nazi Germany especially, lessened the chance for effective action along these lines. "There is a certain futility," he wrote in 1935, "in expending year after year every ounce of energy in chasing what I fear is a will-o'-the-wisp, namely European disarmament under present conditions." [4]

So it was with a degree of relief that he accepted in the same year his transfer to Australia as Consul General. Here for two years he dealt with the unsettled trade relations of the United States and the Commonwealth.

In the summer of 1937 he was appointed the Chief of the newly created Division of European Affairs, an expanded version, entailing tremendous duties, of his former position in the Department. He remained in this crucial position during the *Anschluss*, the fall of Czechoslovakia, Munich, and the outbreak of World War II, and his diaries are among the best contemporary records yet published of the inner workings of the Department of State during this time of crisis.

When Pierrepont Moffat was transferred to Ottawa in June 1940

[4] Jay Pierrepont Moffat to Joseph C. Grew, January 27, 1935.

as Minister to Canada, the press pointed out that the choice of such a competent minister illustrated "the growing responsibilities of the position." [5] In the field again he undertook the task of coordinating the United States–Canadian defense efforts, both before and after Pearl Harbor. One newspaper reported that it had heard "no word except the warmest praise for Minister Moffat from every Canadian we cross-examined." [6]

December 1942 brought a severe cold wave to Ottawa, and an attack of phlebitis forced him to stay in bed. He was not a complete invalid, and he carried on the routine matters of the Legation from his house, talked with friends, and observed all the traditions of Christmas. After the holidays his condition became worse and necessitated an operation which at first seemed a success. He continued to improve until suddenly, on Sunday morning, January 24, 1943, a coronary embolism ended his life.

The death of the forty-six-year-old Minister was a great blow to the American Foreign Service, which he had served with distinction for twenty-five years and in which his future prospects were so bright. Most of those who knew his work agreed that he was the outstanding American career officer of his generation of officers, and President Roosevelt had described him as "one of our finest public servants" who represented "the very highest qualities of our Foreign Service."

He had brought to his work not only high ideals, but a brilliant and disciplined mind, an arresting personality, and an ability to work hard and with a minimum of error. His devotion to the Foreign Service led him to develop positive and well-considered views of the role of a responsible officer. Such an officer, he thought, must be "dispassionate in his judgment" and cultivate "an understanding and tolerance for the ways of others, and an ability to comprehend not only other points of view but the reasons for such points of view." He must subordinate himself and his personality for the greater effectiveness of his work: "He must realize that his value, and hence his success, will in the long run depend not upon individual brilliance but on an ability to make himself a valued if not indispensable member of his team." And as an adviser he must render "loyalty to the Government, loyalty to the Service, and loyalty to a Chief." [7] This was not only a creed

[5] The *Philadelphia Bulletin*, May 29, 1940, p. 10.
[6] *New York Daily Mirror*, February 2, 1941, p. 24.
[7] Jay Pierrepont Moffat to Wilbur J. Carr, January 15, 1935.

but also a code of behavior to Pierrepont Moffat. A man of absolute integrity, "there was no one in the Foreign Service," wrote Sumner Welles, "who had his capacity, his loyalty, and devotion." [8]

Only those who knew him well caught glimpses of the idealism that lay behind his work, but casual acquaintances and colleagues were aware of his ability. He was one of the youngest men ever to reach such high posts in the American Foreign Service, and he had the reputation in the Department for a broad general knowledge, encyclopedic information about specific problems with which he was dealing, conscientious study, and careful organization and expression of thoughts.

The quarter-century during which he served was a dramatic time, which can be described poignantly in the pages of diplomatic history. The diplomat, as one peculiarly charged with responsibility for foreign affairs, was often in a position to report intimately on the international problems and crises that disrupted this period. And Pierrepont Moffat kept records that could stand as models for objective reporting.

During twenty-five years in the Service he accumulated about fifty-two volumes of diaries, memorandums, letters, speeches, and miscellaneous writings. Of this collection the diaries and memorandums, which amount to about one half the total number of volumes and contain around ten thousand typewritten pages, are the most valuable part for the historian.

The Moffat papers presented have been treated as a primary source of diplomatic history. They do not form a biographical study in the accepted sense of those words, nor has an attempt been made to expand them into the story of the international relations of these twenty-five years. It has been assumed that their major importance is as an intelligent, reliable, contemporary record of a part of our perishable past, and that extensive editing would not enhance their value. When introductions have been inserted, it has been to add only enough general information to set the stage for the chapter and enough specific material to make the chapter comprehensible. All bracketed matter in the text has been inserted by the editor. The few misspellings that oc-

[8] Sumner Welles to Lilla Grew Moffat, January 1943.

curred in the original text have been corrected, but errors in grammar or punctuation have not been changed unless they obscured the meaning of the text.

The diaries extend chronologically from December 1917 to May 1940, with lapses in the period before 1927. Between 1917 and 1931 Mr. Moffat kept only five small volumes of diary, and no part of these is included in this book, because of limitations of their interest and of space. Within the years from 1931 to 1943, with which this book is concerned, he wrote fifteen volumes of diary, and when he suspended the diary in 1940, he began to keep "memorandums of conversations," of which he had written approximately two and one-half volumes by 1943.

At first the diary seems to have been mainly a personal record of his new and exciting career. But after his marriage in 1927 it served the additional purpose of providing a channel for diplomatic and family news. Mr. Moffat regularly exchanged his diary with his father-in-law, Mr. Grew, who was also a veteran diarist. The diary was rarely shown to anyone else, except when Mr. Moffat went to Australia and sent copies to several friends in the Department of State.

The diaries and memorandums are typewritten. Until 1931 Mr. Moffat laboriously typed the entries himself, but after his assignment to the Department he had secretarial help. As soon as he reached his office each morning he dictated the diary of the preceding day to his secretary. With few exceptions most of the material printed here was written within a day or two of the events described.

Another fact that contributes to the reliability of these diaries was Mr. Moffat's training as a Foreign Service Officer in the value of accurate reports and records. "Upon their accuracy," he wrote, "must depend many major decisions in the field of economics, finance, and national defense." [9] His reputation in the Department for factual and objective reporting was unexcelled by anyone.

Only the chapter on Poland contains material which was not written soon after the events described, and for this reason it differs from the rest of the book in both style and content. Mr. Moffat wrote it in 1942 as the first, and only completed, portion of what was to

[9] Moffat papers, October 28, 1940.

have been a volume of memoirs. Poland was his first assignment as a Foreign Service officer, and this exceptionally interesting, and often exciting, account of his experiences there from 1919 to 1921 provides an appropriate beginning for this book.

The papers from which this book has been taken have been deposited in the Harvard College Library.

WARSAW

November 1919 – March 1921

"From the wrecks of the three Empires, the new Poland sprang"

When Pierrepont Moffat entered the Foreign Service, World War I had just ended. An era had perished in the war, but Wilsonian idealism held hope that the corpse of that era might soon be transported to a more heavenly sphere. This better world was to be the goal of diplomats, statesmen, and men of good will for two decades, and the twenties were punctuated by Locarno, the Kellogg-Briand Pact, and disarmament conferences.

Mr. Moffat's first assignment was as Third Secretary of Legation in Warsaw, Poland, the state which had been reborn during the peace settlement. In 1795 the Polish State ceased to exist. Dismemberment had begun twenty years earlier, and in the passing of those years the greed of Austria, Prussia, and Russia had completely destroyed Poland. Only in the customs and language, the hearts and minds of the Polish people did the country live, until at the end of World War I Poland was allowed once again to become a political entity.

The job of reconstructing the Polish State was enormous. The internal problems of establishing the normal operation of a state whose people had been molded and divided for over a century by different cultures were equalled in difficulty only by the task of defending Poland from external enemies.

In the spring of 1919 I returned to America to take my examinations for the diplomatic service. They were not as much of an ordeal as I feared, and I was fortunate enough to pass in first of my group with a grade of 90.65. Before being sent to our posts we were given a few weeks training in the State Department during the summer months. In those days the Department was still like a club: the outsider was regarded with a faint air of suspicion, but a member, even a junior, was treated with absolute trust. With rare exceptions, the day's work ended at 4.30; an occasional afternoon off for golf was considered normal, and no one raised a disapproving eyebrow at generous weekends. Naturally, my work was pretty routine in character, making summaries of despatches for Bill Castle [special assistant in the Department of State], keeping the minutes of interdepartmental meetings, and the like; but I did have access to most of the telegrams, particularly those relating to the new states in Europe. For the most part they told of a series of clashing nationalistic ambitions, which neither hunger, nor poverty, nor revolutionary mutterings served to quell. But our forcing policy was at a standstill; there was little the United States could do until the Senate had ratified or rejected the Treaty of Versailles and the League of Nations. . .

Late in September I was posted to the Legation in Warsaw. It is hard to recapture in memory all the excitement of the next few weeks. Poland sounded infinitely remote and faintly exotic. True, I had taken a course in Slavic history under Professor Lord [of Harvard University], and I had more than once read Sienkiewicz's great trilogy *With Fire and Sword*, *The Deluge*, and *Pan Michael*.[1] But of modern Poland I knew nothing. I recall my impatience to be off. An enforced delay of some weeks due to a longshoremen's strike in New York; an uncomfortable crossing on a transport amid heavy autumn gales; two or three rather hectic days in Paris; a long, slow journey across Central Europe in the courier train; a first sight of emaciated faces and hungry stares; long hours looking out over plains of unutterable dreariness, where the sticky brown mud was waging a winning battle with the early snow; a sudden passage, without preliminary warning in the shape of suburbs, into the heart of a large and active city; at long last I had reached Warsaw and set foot on the lowest rung of the ladder called career.[2]

I was lucky in drawing Hugh Gibson as my first chief. He was only thirty-six at the time, the youngest minister in our service. President Wilson had promoted him to Warsaw over the heads of a score of seniors at the joint instance of Mr. Hoover and Colonel House. Mr. Hoover had gauged his abilities in Brussels during the early days of the War, when as secretary Gibson had done most of the work

[1] Henryk Sienkiewicz, *With Fire and Sword* (Boston: Little, Brown & Co., 1890), *The Deluge* (Boston: Little, Brown & Co., 1891), *Pan Michael* (Boston: Little, Brown & Co., 1893).
[2] Mr. Moffat arrived in Warsaw on November 6, 1919.

for which Brand Whitlock [American Minister to Belgium] received public credit;[3] Colonel House had subsequently used him on roving errands as a political intelligence officer. He had a scintillating mind and a razorlike wit, fortunately tempered by a keen sense of fun. He knew Europe as did few Americans; he was on terms of intimacy with the key men in a dozen Foreign Offices; his use of French was not only fluent, but so accurate that he could convey shaded meanings. Many a time he had to tell his Polish friends some unpalatable truth, but the happy knack of wrapping it up with a quip or a jest enabled him to convey his message without leaving a sting. He quickly became a prime favorite with Polish society, and no gathering was complete without "our dear Gibson." He had not yet married, but he knew his world well enough to understand the importance attached by the Poles to outward show. He had accordingly rented for our Legation the historic Blue Palace with its sixty rooms and its priceless collections.[4] His means however were slender and he found the upkeep a strain until someone suggested a happy arrangement, equally advantageous to all, whereby he invited the two secretaries of the Legation to occupy available apartments in the Palace, and in return to share the running expenses of the establishment, prorated according to the size of their official salaries.

The evening of my arrival Hugh Gibson and Arthur Lane, the first Secretary, took me to Fukier's, a diminutive restaurant built over the entrance to one of Europe's great wine cellars. After we had eaten a roast duck and consumed a bottle of Burgundy, which gastronomically speaking laid the proper foundation, our host brought us up a bottle of golden Tokay, its heavy incrustations testifying to its venerable age. "*Hongaria natum, Polonia educatum,*" this old Tokay of Warsaw, which is matured in casks and not even bottled for sixty years, is the prince of dessert wines. It does not travel even for short

[3] Mr. Hoover had been Chairman of the Commission for Relief in Belgium. For his comments on Gibson and Whitlock see Herbert Hoover, *The Memoirs of Herbert Hoover, Years of Adventure 1874–1920* (New York: The Macmillan Co., 1951), pp. 206–207.

[4] In his diary of November 6, 1919, Mr. Moffat wrote about the Blue Palace: "It is a splendid old palace of the Zamoyskis, with a large garden in the back. It contains treasures of every conceivable sort, some splendid oil paintings, and a library full of the rarest manuscripts, for one of which the British Museum offered half a million dollars. I have a large room on the ground floor with a good bathroom–dressing room which contains a large sunken tub into which one descends by three or four marble steps."

distances, and thus is little known, but he who has once tasted it does not forget.

We sat late into the night before an open wood fire, sipping the Tokay, while Hugh Gibson talked to us about Poland. He wove a veritable tapestry with pictures of war and famine and plague slowly fading into the task of reconstruction. Two central figures dominated his theme: Pilsudski and Paderewski, Chief of State and Prime Minister. In the clash of their personalities, as in the clash of their political beliefs, could be found the symbols of the inner struggle that was agitating Poland. Pilsudski represented change; Paderewski, the established order. Pilsudski was always a Slav; Paderewski a citizen of the world. Pilsudski believed in the inevitability of war; Paderewski trusted in the finer arts of diplomacy. For a few brief months Poland had hoped that the two men could work in double harness, but this was not to be. Oil and water would not mix. If Poland were to have unity, one would have to displace the other. . .

No race in Europe dreaded the outbreak of war more than did the Poles. Such a war would be fought over Poland's broad plains. Polish cities would be sacked, Polish supplies would be confiscated by hard-pressed commissaries, Polish citizens would be held hostage. Worse still, there were few Polish families where there was not divided allegiance. A war would mean cousin pitted against cousin, sometimes brother against brother, in each instance fighting for an alien overlord.

Thus when fighting at last broke out in the summer of 1914, the Poles for the most part saw nothing but darkness and disaster ahead. Only a few, like Pilsudski, were gifted with longer vision. Pilsudski sensed that with Poland's three hereditary foes locked in a death struggle, there was a chance, albeit a small one, that they might mutually destroy each other. He urged that Polish support should be thrown against the strongest and most relentless, which his every instinct told him was Russia. He therefore organized a Polish legion for the Austrian army, which by the end of 1916 comprised two battle-worthy divisions. But when in March 1917 the first revolution overthrew Czardom, Pilsudski intuitively knew that the scales had shifted, and that henceforth not Russia but Germany was Poland's most potent enemy. Taking counsel of no man, and acting in cold blood, he resolved on the hardest maneuver in modern warfare; encouraging his fighting force to shift from one side to the other. His attempt failed. The Germans would undoubtedly have shot him but for fear of goading Polish feeling, already disaffected, beyond the breaking point. Instead, they locked him up in the grim fortress of Magdeburg, where he languished the last eighteen months of the war, brooding upon events, and preparing himself against the day of his liberation and of Poland's destiny.

The armistice ended Pilsudski's captivity, and he made his way, a free man, to Warsaw. The city was in confusion and without a master. Pilsudski with his instinct for command assumed charge. He disarmed and expelled the remaining Germans, took over the powers of the Regents,[5] authorized the election of a Parliament, and set to work to create a Polish army. His acts were immediately ratified by the force of public opinion. The left turned toward him because of his revolutionary background; the right acclaimed him because he imposed public order.

As much as possible he avoided the limelight, preferring to dominate the scene from off-stage. When, a few months later, Paderewski, fresh from his triumphs in the United States, was received throughout Poland with unparalleled ovations,[6] Pilsudski asked him to head the Government as Prime Minister while he himself would remain outside the political arena as Chief of State. To Paderewski the words "Chief of State" meant the equivalent of a constitutional monarch, who reigned but did not govern, and who was bound by the advice of his ministers. To Pilsudski the words "Prime Minister" meant the western equivalent of a Grand Vizier, who took orders from the Chief of State, and by assuming nominal responsibility, protected him from the consequences of a mistake.

This difference of opinion was accentuated by divergent cultural outlooks. Pilsudski knew little of the Western world and viewed it with deep suspicion; Paderewski regarded it as the region of promise,

[5] After the Central Powers had conquered much of Russian Poland, the Germans established a military government at Warsaw and the Austro-Hungarians set up a military government at Lublin. In mid-October 1917 the Kaiser and the Austrian Emperor appointed a Regency Council of three men. Although the Regents subsequently were permitted to establish certain formalities of Polish self-government, the German and Austrian military governors continued dominant. But the collapse of the Central Powers enabled the Regents to take steps in October 1918 toward the creation of a national government, which could treat with the Associated governments concerning the boundaries of an independent Poland.

[6] Paderewski arrived in Warsaw on January 3, 1919.

where help for Poland must be sought and found. Not merely material assistance in the form of guns and ammunition or even credit, but help in the form of encouragement, advice and guidance. Hugh Gibson's sympathies were strongly with Paderewski, alike on personal and political grounds, though as time passed it had become clear that he lacked the attributes of political leadership.

His genius had many facets. Quite apart from his music, he was an outstanding linguist, orator, and diplomat. With the outbreak of the war he had dedicated all his gifts to Poland. His patriotism was like a burning brand that illuminated his every action. He transmuted into a Polish triumph each personal success that he won. He was able to dramatize the tragedies of Poland's past, the anguish of the war years, and the possibility of redressing historic wrongs by the recreation of a Polish state. He healed the rifts in the groups of Poles living abroad, and became the spokesman of united committees. His views were moderate. He made no exaggerated territorial or ethnic claims. His vivid personality and crystal clear character made a deep impression on many, including President Wilson and Colonel House. In fact, the thirteenth of the Fourteen Points which read, "An independent Polish state should be erected which should include the territories inhabited by indisputably Polish populations, which should be assured a free and secure access to the sea, and whose political and economic independence and territorial integrity should be guaranteed by international covenant," [7] was in no small measure Paderewski's handiwork. . .

As Prime Minister, Paderewski kept for himself the portfolio of Minister of Foreign Affairs and divided his time during the spring and early summer of 1919 between Warsaw and Paris. In the galaxy of statesmen who assembled at the Peace Conference, Paderewski was one of the stars of first magnitude. He stated Poland's case fairly and convincingly. He was constantly pressing for action, but never to the point of antagonizing. If he could not get everything he wanted, he neither sulked nor threatened; instead, he expressed gratitude for what he had in fact received. His technique was refreshing. There is a story of those days which I like to believe is not apocryphal. He and

[7] The fourteen points were enumerated by President Wilson in a speech before a joint session of Congress on January 8, 1918. Woodrow Wilson, *President Wilson's Foreign Policy*, ed. James Brown Scott (New York: Oxford University Press, 1918), pp. 354–363.

Beneš [Eduard Beneš, Czechoslovakian Minister of Foreign Affairs] were arguing before the Supreme Council about Teschen. Beneš had advanced a reasoned argument on the economic need of Czechoslovakia for coal. Paderewski rose for rebuttal, speaking slowly and with dramatic emphasis. "Mr. Beneš," he said, "has shown that for Czechoslovakia, Teschen means coal, coal, coal; I tell you that for Poland, Teschen means Pole, Pole, Pole. Mr. Beneš asked for half of Teschen; I ask for all of Teschen. Which, O Solomon, is parent of this child?" [8]

With the signing of the Treaty of Versailles, Paderewski reached the apogee of his career. From the great popular ovations, in which the public cheered him in a sort of rhythmic litany, he recharged his batteries of energy and inspiration. But he could not, alas, repeat in Poland the successes he had won abroad. He could more accurately gauge the reaction to a given problem in the United States or France, than in his native Poland. He had lived too long abroad, and his fellow Poles fell short of his idealization. He made a series of blunders, chiefly in the choice of his collaborators. He was himself so transparently honest that he could not bring himself to question the motives, much less the integrity of others. Slowly he lost the confidence of the public, though never its affection. His opponents, once they discovered his Achilles' heel — that while he throve under adulation, he wilted under criticism — threw shaft after shaft of venom in personal, as well as in political attack. He felt hurt, baffled, discouraged.

And now, concluded Hugh Gibson, Pilsudski had whispered that the moment had come for Paderewski to go.

Our evening at Fukier's ended and we walked back through dark cold streets to the Blue Palace. As we passed the Zamek, the old castle of the Polish Kings, we saw the lights in Paderewski's rooms blazing brightly.

A day or two later he sent for Hugh Gibson and told him that he was on the verge of giving up and leaving Poland, but that his final

[8] Paderewski and Roman Dmowski were the chief Polish delegates to the Peace Conference. Teschen was a district in southeastern Silesia, to which Poland advanced claims based mainly upon ethnological and linguistic arguments and Czechoslovakia put out claims of an economic and historic nature. On July 28, 1920, a decision of the Ambassadors' conference divided the Duchy of Teschen between Poland and Czechoslovakia. H. W. V. Temperley (ed.), *A History of the Peace Conference of Paris*, IV (London: Henry Frowde & Hodder & Stoughton, 1921), 348–364.

decision would depend on the reception accorded a policy speech he was planning to make in the Diet the following afternoon.[9] With no little trepidation we drove out to the long low building in the Frascati gardens which housed the Assembly. From our seats in the Diplomatic tribune we could watch the expressions of the deputies seated at low desks, crowded closely together, a narrow aisle separating the Conservatives from the radical groups. Peasants were numerous and came in their national costumes, and there were enough women deputies to be noticeable. When, after some preliminary business, Paderewski arose, the house was so still that one could hear a pin drop. Not being able to understand a word he said, I was able to concentrate on the technique of his oratory. At first his words were received with marked coolness. Soon by a chauvinistic reference he won a round of applause. Then, having broken the ice, he proceeded to play upon his audience, using all the tricks of eloquence, speaking now loudly, now dropping his voice to a whisper, first scolding and then pleading, exhorting and then explaining, and finally pounding the rostrum before him, not with his fist but with his fingers outstretched as if striking a crashing chord. He sat down nearly exhausted while the Diet burst into a spontaneous storm of applause. Five minutes later, however, it voted to adjourn rather than to pass an immediate vote of confidence.

Paderewski had scored a success, but not an overwhelming victory. The intrigues against him began again with doubled force. He sought advice from a dozen friends and emerged confused by the welter of conflicting counsel . . . we heard whispers that Madame Paderewska was alarmed by reports reaching her that a well-known medium had visions that if Paderewski remained in office, he would be murdered. One day she would be in the depths of despondency and urge Paderewski to order his special train. The following day she would be encouraged by some trifle and forget her previous urgings. Paderewski was so sensitive to environment that he was subconsciously affected by Madame Paderewska's moods. More than once the ministers of Great Britain and the United States felt called on to counteract her influence by reminding Paderewski that in threatening to resign he was thinking more of his own peace of mind than of Poland's welfare. Paderewski would agree, but the effect would soon wear off

[9] Paderewski spoke before the Diet on November 12, 1919.

and again he would be tortured by doubts and indecision. It was not that he was a weak man, but he was fighting in an unfamiliar arena and he had been irreparably hurt.

The final phase came when Pilsudski took matters into his own hands. Three nights in a row he drove the length of Warsaw's main avenue from the simple whitewashed Belvedere where he lived, to the great lavishly decorated Zamek, and sat for hours staring straight into Paderewski's eyes, relentlessly beating down his will power. The third night he drove back with Paderewski's signed resignation in his pocket. The following morning the Paderewskis moved out of the Zamek. . .[10]

Poland at the time was neither at war nor at peace. Except for occasional local clashes where Polish and Soviet troops were massed against each other, there was as yet no actual fighting. But an unfought war was being waged, with the Bolsheviks employing every resource of propaganda to stir up dissension within Poland and to paralyze the

[10] Paderewski resigned on December 9, 1919, but he did not leave Poland until February 1920. Mr. Moffat's diary of February 8, 1920, gives a friendly and amusing account of Paderewski's departure: "At last Paderewski has left for Switzerland and a difficult process it was. He has postponed his departure innumerable times, his private car meanwhile waiting in the station at the cost of 1200 francs a day. The minister went over to the Bristol to bid him goodbye. He waited a minute and then Paderewski staggered in, looking a wreck, his hair disheveled, great lines under his eyes, in fact almost unrecognizable. 'Oh, my dear Minister,' he groaned, 'I am dead, I am dead. What time do you think I got up? At ten o'clock.' 'Why that's nothing,' said the Minister, 'I got up earlier than that myself.' 'No, no, you do not understand, ten o'clock yesterday; I was writing important letters and documents all last night, and before I got to bed this morning people came in again, and then the politicians, and then my friends, and then these good, kind ladies who are trying to help me packed all my letters in the bottom of one of my trunks, and Oh me, Oh my, I don't know where I am.' So the minister wished him a good trip and said good-bye at once, whereupon Paddy wept tears and kissed him on both cheeks and a happy time was had by all. It seems that later on he missed some other letters, and entered the room where the packing was going on with rage in his heart; but when he saw the 'good, kind ladies' working, he relented, and gave vent to his feelings by saying in English, which they could not understand, 'Oh, to hell with all helpers.' Then having gotten it out of his system, he was as equable as before. At length the hour of the train approached. The hurry and flurry grew worse; things were lost, only to be refound, and ten minutes before train time they started out. At the station was a large crowd, but it was well policed and the actual getaway was fairly easy. The last time they left, however, all their luggage was left behind, and five minutes before the train pulled out six people got aboard whom Madame Paderewska had invited to travel with them on their private car and then forgotten all about. There were not enough beds to go around; whereupon Paddy said he would sleep upon the floor and give up his bed; at that everybody protested, and just as they were in the midst of the discussion, the train stopped as it discovered that the baggage car had been left behind and it took three hours to send a locomotive back to fetch it."

Government. The diplomats at Paris and Versailles wanted a Poland strong enough to prevent the virus of Bolshevism spreading to the "uninfected" states of Europe, but the country they actually set up was sorely handicapped. They gave neither men, nor money, nor directives. They did not even lay down the final frontiers, and much of Poland's energy which should have been otherwise [employed], was consumed in trying to extend her territory. This was particularly the case in the East, where the members of the Supreme Council could not agree on a boundary between Poland and Russia. True, they had drawn a line across the map and called it a "minimum line." To all land lying westward, Poland was given an unchallenged title, but the door was not closed to a later award of territory to the East. Such a compromise was courting trouble. Polish troops were already far to the East of the minimum line, and its provisional nature was advanced by certain Polish groups as an argument for insisting on the frontiers of 1772 as they existed before the First Partition, by others for "liberating" the Polish landlords in Podolia and Volhynia, and by still others for putting the maximum distance possible between the Russian army and the city of Warsaw.[11]

To make matters worse, the French and British were giving the Poles contrary advice. The French, through their minister Monsieur Pralon, lost no opportunity to proclaim that Poland was Europe's champion against the powers of destruction, that any measures she might take were licit, and that France would assist as soon as she could with equipment, munitions, and credits. The British, through Sir Horace Rumbold, an old-time diplomat who concealed an unusually acute intelligence behind a monocle set in an expressionless face, kept reiterating that Poland's only salvation lay in attempting to make peace with the Soviets; if war should none the less ensue, Poland could count on more support than she could possibly hope to obtain as an aggressor; meanwhile in default of arms and credits, the only thing Britain had to offer was disinterested advice. It is not surprising that French influence was the more potent in Warsaw.

[11] The Supreme Allied Council had determined Poland's southeastern frontier provisionally on November 20, 1919. The eastern frontier was further extended by another decision of the Council on December 8, 1919. At the close of 1919 Polish troops had advanced approximately two hundred fifty miles east of this line. W. P. and Zelda K. Coates, *Six Centuries of Russo-Polish Relations* (London: Lawrence & Wishart, 1948), p. 99; Leszek Kirkien, *Russia, Poland and the Curzon Line* (Edinburgh: Caldra House Ltd., 1945), pp. 22–23.

During the course of the winter months, the counterrevolutionary armies of Kolchak and Denikin succumbed, and the Bolsheviks thereby became free to concentrate against Poland virtually all their armed strength. Pilsudski calculated that he had until April to complete the organization of his army. He shrewdly discounted all promises of Allied aid, and once snapped out that it would be time enough to talk about this, when some equipment had actually reached Polish soil. Nevertheless in January he authorized his new Foreign Minister Mr. Patek to go to London to make one final attempt at persuading the British to reverse their policy and to supply the Poles with military stores.

Mr. Patek was a close friend of Hugh Gibson and frequently dined at the Legation. He was one of the leaders of the Warsaw bar, and had made his reputation by defending in the Russian courts Polish patriots who were charged with political crimes. A little man, with flashing eyes and fierce mustachios, inclined to strut, he had an overweening confidence in the persuasive power of his eloquence. Unfortunately this was a gift that was largely wasted on the British. He was politely received, given full opportunity to present his case, but returned — as Pilsudski had foreseen — empty-handed. As a parting thrust, Lloyd George had told him that if Poland decided to take the initiative and attack the Bolsheviks, the inevitable result would be the resurrection of a national spirit in Russia. This prophecy must have rankled, for some months later in the only conversation I ever had with Pilsudski (third secretaries have scant opportunities for consorting with a chief of state) he went out of his way to tell me that a national spirit had been reborn in Russia the day the last effective counterrevolutionary army had collapsed, and that it had been artificially fostered by the Bolsheviks ever since.

After his return from London we saw little of Mr. Patek. He seemed too busy to spend even an occasional evening at the Legation. He was closeted for hours at a time with Marshal Pilsudski at the Belvedere, and we heard rumors that he had been seen more than once in the strange company of Petlura, the brigand chieftain of the Ukraine.

Meanwhile, the men at the front were enduring in stolid silence all the miseries of a northern winter. The ranks kept up their spirits by checking off the days before the coming of spring; the officers, with so much to do and so little time in which to do it, prayed that the cold weather, which permitted training and prevented fighting, might drag on beyond its normal season. Drill, drill, drill, day in and day out. Slowly, almost imperceptibly, what had been an amorphous mass of half-trained individuals was welded into a cohesive fighting force. What it lacked in equipment, it made up in eagerness and unity of purpose.

Colonel Farman, our Military Attaché, was impressed. So too was General Carton de Wiart, the chief of the British military mission. They told Hugh Gibson that in their judgment the Polish army was superior to the Soviet army. Its training, if elementary, had been on orthodox lines; its morale was high; it would fight with patriotic fervor. On the other hand the Bolshevik forces, even if they did outnumber the Poles, were dispirited, war-weary, and confused by the divided authority of military officers and political commissars.

Early in April Hugh Gibson was called back to Washington for consultation. I accompanied him as far as Berlin, spending a day in Posen and a few hours at a frontier town which had the unforgettable name of Stench-am-Oder. We reached Berlin in the late afternoon and were soon at the Opera listening to a flawless performance of "Fidelio." The following day I spent at the Embassy, where Ellis Dresel as Commissioner [American Commissioner to Germany] headed a picked staff which included Hugh Wilson, Fred Dolbeare, Allen Dulles and Reggie Foster.

Their report was ominous. Germany was rife with social and political unrest. The Ruhr was in revolt, and in all the big cities the rumblings of revolution could be heard. The conflict of interest between the proletarian and peasant, between Red and Green, was nearing the danger mark. So tense was the situation that if the Soviets succeeded in establishing a common frontier with the Reich, Bolshevism would probably flare up across Germany as far West as the Rhine. The impending campaign between Poland and the Soviets might well determine the future social order in Europe.[12] The men

---

[12] The new Communist regime in Russia was anxious to carry communism into all western Europe. The obvious path lay through Poland. Bernard Pares, *History of Russia* (3d ed. rev.; New York: Alfred A. Knopf, 1937), p. 483, has written: "Militant international Bolshevism urgently required contact with revolutionary Germany, and this could only be won over the body of Poland."

of Moscow knew the stakes for which they were playing and would throw in their last resource to win that common frontier. Were the Poles grimly in earnest? Could they be counted on to hold the Bolsheviks at bay?

After the chill despondency of Berlin, Warsaw seemed positively buoyant. Our friends told us that "great events were in the making." In a few days Poland would launch an all-out offensive. She could not wait to be overrun, she must strike before the Bolsheviks were ready and force Moscow to offer a just and lasting peace. If the Western world thought that Poland was imperialistic and planning to annex the Ukraine, Mr. Patek had a surprise in store. A few days later he revealed his secret: a treaty with the brigand, Petlura, who was thereby legitimized as the head of an independent Ukraine.[13] The Polish army would help him liberate his territory, set up a viable government, and would then retire. By this treaty Mr. Patek counted on chalking up three successes: he would win foreign approval for a "preventive attack"; he would create a buffer state between Poland and the Soviets; and he would acquire indirect control of the resources of the rich Ukraine, for during the years of its immaturity it would have to lean heavily on Poland for its security. It all seemed delightfully simple to my Polish friends; and they were still naïve enough to believe that it would seem equally simple in Berlin and London and Washington.

With the diplomatic stage thus set, military operations began. Polish legions marched proudly eastward. Soviet resistance was easily, much too easily overcome, and in a few short weeks the White Eagle was flying over the citadel of Kiew.[14]

Warsaw went wild with enthusiasm. Pilsudski was given a triumphal entry into the city. There were parades and fireworks. Patriots burst into public speech and their allusions to the days when the Polish overlords ruled from the Baltic to the Black Sea were no longer covert. But Bolshevik counterattacks were already beginning. A flotilla of river boats, secretly massed in the hidden reaches of the Dnieper steamed slowly toward Kiew from the Southeast, while new Soviet forces drove down the railroad from the North. The Poles beat off

[13] A treaty was signed by Poland and the Ukrainian Independent People's Republic on April 23, 1920.
[14] Kiev, or Kiew, was occupied on May 7, 1920.

these attacks, but only by throwing in their reserves. The staff became worried about its lines of communication, which were long and exposed, and telegraphed Warsaw for additional units.

For a month the Kosciuszko squadron [15] had been where the fighting was thickest. Flying at all times and in all weathers, it had carried out a variety of missions, and was even accepted on equal terms by its rivals, the cavalry.

One still evening late in May, just as darkness fell, a Kosciuszko pilot burst unceremoniously in at headquarters with an alarming report. He had been on a routine flight, south and east of the walled city of Uman, where in other times the cameled caravans from the east had rested in its Oriental khans. Just before turning back, he had noticed some miles ahead long columns of dust rising over the broad highroads. Flying low to determine the cause, he had come upon a new Bolshevik army: horsemen, eight abreast, stretching as far as the eye could see. He had counted ten, twenty, thirty thousand of them, moving in a compact mass. They wore sand-grey uniforms, with astrakhan caps, and for weapons each man carried a sabre, and had a carbine slung across his back. They were headed northwest, with the obvious intention of outflanking the entire Polish army at Kiew.

At the head of his Cossacks Budienny, like a modern Bogdan, was sweeping into the Lower Ukraine.

Thus far I had been following the Polish-Soviet war from afar. It was exciting, but it was unreal. I was now to see it at closer range, in fact, at very close range indeed. It happened in this wise.

General Carton de Wiart was sending two British officers to Kiew on government business. They were Captain Maule, his aide-de-camp, and Colonel Graham, a railroad expert. He had given them his private car, and as it accommodated two more, he had invited Paul Dukes, the correspondent of the London *Times*, and then, happening to run into me, he asked if I too wouldn't like to make the trip. "You won't be wasting your time," he said, "you'll see the Ukraine, you'll see an army at or near the front, and you will have two or three days in Kiew while my officers are transacting their business."

We left Warsaw the day after the Kosciuszko pilot had discovered

[15] The Kosciuszko squadron was an aviation unit of the Polish army, which had been organized by and made up of American veterans of World War I.

Budienny's army. No hint had as yet reached Warsaw that anything was seriously amiss. We rolled eastward, across the Bug, down past Kowel, through Rowno, and on toward Szepetowka . . .

As our train pulled into Szepetowka station, Maule and Graham immediately sensed that there was something wrong. The station platform was crowded with a seething mass of humanity, joining furtively in little groups, separating, and looking apprehensively down the railroad track toward Berdiczew as if expecting some imminent trouble from that direction. While Colonel Graham went to find the stationmaster, Maule, Dukes and I mingled with the crowd. Suddenly I heard my name called:

"Moffat, what in the name of all that's holy are you doing here?"

A small man, in overalls, covered with oil and dirt, and staggering with exhaustion, drew near. I had to look twice to recognize Merian Cooper [of the Kosciuszko squadron].

"Come aboard, wash up, have some food and drink, and then tell us what's gone wrong."

Cooper needed no second urging. His story was not told consecutively, but we were able to piece it together. Budienny's army, the proletarians on horseback as they called themselves, had advanced with incredible speed. The Cossacks ate as they rode, and by commandeering peasant carts to which they tied their unsaddled mounts, rode as they slept. Despite the warning given by the squadron, the Poles had only forty-eight hours in which to prepare for the shock. Budienny had struck at the railroad junction of Berdiczew, far behind the front lines, and had severed all communications between the Polish army at Kiew and its base by way of the southern route. Fortunately the northern railroad via Korosten was still open. It was a magnificent cavalry raid, one of the greatest in history, surpassed if at all — added Cooper who was a southerner — only by those of Jeb Stuart. But still it was only a raid, and the Poles would be able to restore order in a few days. The trouble was that the raiders had come up in such numbers that they were spreading over the entire Ukraine like locusts. Groups would detach themselves from the main columns, travel through woods and gullies, and fall upon unsuspecting Polish commands.

He himself had barely escaped capture. The squadron, in pursuance of orders, had fallen back from Biela Tserkov to Novograd

Volynski. Only Fauntleroy, Crawford [members of the Kosciuszko squadron] and he had remained attending to last minute tasks, and were preparing in leisurely fashion to follow when the sun had risen high. Fauntleroy had gone aloft on a reconnaissance flight, but within a few moments had returned, circled over the airport, and fired twice, a signal that danger was so close as to admit of no delay. At the same time leaning out of his cockpit he had waved toward the southeast. Cooper and Crawford jumped into their respective planes, but the engines had not been properly warmed. He saw Crawford's plane taxi across the field, rise a few feet, and then crash. He could not stop to see anything more for at this moment Bolshevik horsemen appeared in sight. He opened the throttle of his plane, only to experience the anguish of feeling his engine sputter and die. He set a match to the plane, emptied his revolver into the gasoline tank to add fuel to the flames, and plunged into some nearby woods. He had been on the road since early morning. From time to time he had been given a lift on some peasant's cart, but he thought that he had been on his feet a total of ten or twelve hours. Poor Crawford, it was doubtful whether he could have escaped; it would be incredible luck if both of them had reached safety. Meanwhile, could he sleep? If Crawford turned up, would we tell him that Cooper was with us? He didn't think the Bolos would get as far as Szepetowka that night, but in any event there was nothing we could do about it. His voice grew thicker and thicker, and the first thing we knew he had fallen asleep in the middle of a sentence.[16]

Colonel Graham came back with much the same news about Budienny. He told us that the line ahead could not possibly be repaired for several days. We would therefore retrace our steps in the morning as far as Kowel and continue to Kiew via the northern line. The car would be shunted for the night on to a siding a quarter mile or so away. There was always the possibility of a sudden Bolshevik raid on the station; if that occurred it would be just as well not to be too close. No one knew just where Budienny's main forces were. There had been a complete breakdown of Polish communications. All he had been able to learn for certain was that three hours ago, the Bolos

[16] For another account see Kenneth Malcolm Murray, "The Kosciuszko Squadron," *Poland*, VI (August, 1925), 467–469, 494–498; *ibid.* (September, 1925), pp. 532–534, 555–558.

had not yet appeared at Polonnae, the next station down the railroad in the direction of Berdiczew.

Our car was soon hauled back to the siding where we spent the night. As a precaution we darkened the car. All through the night there was desultory rifle fire nearby, though whether it was peasants shooting at marauding stragglers, or hungry stragglers threatening peasants, we never knew. In happier days Szepetowka had been the station for Count Joseph Potocki's fabulous estate of Antoniny, and we tried to picture it as it must have looked with coaches and four drawn up for the laughing and carefree guests arriving from St. Petersburg, and the fourgons to transport the servants and the mountains of baggage.

About midnight Paul Dukes who was restless and worried, made his way back to the station. Knowing the language he hoped to pick up the latest rumors, if nothing more. Almost the first person he saw was an earnest individual talking English, trying to make a weary stationmaster who knew only Polish understand his questions by repeating them over and over, each time more slowly, but each time a trifle louder.

"I say," said Dukes, "you're not Crawford, are you?"

"Yes I am. Why?"

"Because we've got Cooper with us, safe and sound asleep in a car a few hundred yards up the track. Better come along."

When Crawford reached the car, Cooper opened one eye, muttered, "Thank God," and went sound asleep again. But at half-past four, with the first streaks of light, Cooper was awake, shook Crawford into consciousness, and the two of them disappeared on their trek to find the squadron at Novograd Volynski.

About nine o'clock a long train was assembled and started back toward Kowel. The countryside, that early June morning, was smiling. The wheat was waving green, and the great fields of sugar beets were laid out in mathematical nicety. The villages had a certain air of prosperity, and behind small woods we could see the country houses of the gentry, many of them still standing despite the surges of war which had passed over this particular countryside three or four times between 1914 and 1918.

The news of Budienny's raid had already spread over the countryside. At each station men and women who had special reasons to fear the Bolsheviks were storming the train. We noticed one poor white-haired woman, obviously a lady, trying in vain to find a place large enough for herself and her few possessions, the most important of which was a large basket containing her pet cat. We invited her to share our car. She was Countess X; her estate was a few miles out of Rowno; her son-in-law was sending her to relatives in Warsaw, but he himself had so much to do in saving what he could and in hiding the rest, that he had not been able to spare the time to come to the station to see her properly installed on the train. Having thus explained the situation, and expressed real gratitude for our hospitality, her worldly instincts came into play, and for an hour she talked to us in the most polished French about the latest novels, the plays in Paris, in short about everything in the world except her own troubles and misfortunes.

It was after midnight when we reached Kowel, and no train was scheduled to start eastward till late in the morning. We therefore had a sound sleep, our last for several nights.

The railroad from Kowel to Kiew being broad gauge, we had to abandon General Carton de Wiart's private car, and the best that could be offered us was a dilapidated fourth-class coach, with broken windows, whittled wooden benches, and an underfed population of bedbugs and lice. We took over a blanket apiece, a little food, and two bottles of whiskey. The coach was coupled onto a long troop train which we were told was to rush reinforcements to Kiew. "Rushing" in those parts did not preclude a stay of six hours in the Kowel station, or a maximum advance of fifteen miles in any one hour.

We passed the Stochod river where the broad marshes, rather than the skill of the Austrians had halted the Brusilov offensive in 1916.[17] We made out row upon row of barbed wire, still standing, the remains of corduroy roads, and the individual shelters built up above the level of the ground water which human ingenuity had evolved as a substitute for trenches. From the marshes we passed into forest land, nor did we see the open plain again until we came within a few miles of Korosten the following morning.

[17] Beginning on June 4, 1916, the Russian general, Aleksey Brusilov, had led an offensive on the southeastern front against the Austrian army. B. H. Liddell Hart, *A History of the World War 1914–1918* (Boston: Little, Brown & Co., 1935), pp. 272–274.

Korosten is a junction of some importance where the east–west road running from Kowel to Kiew is intersected by the north–south road running from Moghilew to Zitomir and Berdiczew. The station was filled with Polish troops. Colonel Graham went to consult the stationmaster and did not return for a full hour. He looked very serious.

"We can't go on to Kiew as planned for the bridge over the Teterev some forty miles ahead was blown up last night. There is only one way left to enter Kiew. That is to proceed south by train to Zitomir and try to find automobile transportation there. Zitomir was raided by Budienny yesterday, but I am assured that the Poles have recaptured the town and are now occupying it in force. I don't see how Kiew can be held much longer, but until it is evacuated Maule and I must carry out orders and try to reach the city. The military are preparing a special train for us which should be ready about noon."

The train consisted of a tank car filled with water, calculated to explode any mines that might have been set under the track; an open car, with two machine guns mounted behind several cords of wood, stacked high as a protective shield; the locomotive, facing the wrong way (so that it backed the entire distance to Zitomir); our coach; and a caboose carrying thirty to forty armed soldiers and three or four officers.

Thus prepared for trouble our train pulled out of Korosten and with frequent halts for consultations between the engineer and the Polish officers aboard, we covered the ninety miles to Zitomir. Instead of finding the town held "in force" by the Poles, we found it deserted, with neither side in occupation. What had been the station was merely a mass of glowing embers; the station yard was in confusion; and some twenty or more civilians, who had been hanged in open-doored box cars and not yet cut down, bore eloquent testimony to the recent passage of the dread Budienny.

The only official in evidence was the stationmaster. He almost wept tears of joy at seeing our locomotive, and promptly informed us that it could pull out at least forty empty box cars and thus save them for the Poles. As it was Poland's war, Poland's rolling stock, and Poland's locomotive, we could not gainsay him. We asked how long it would take to assemble the train. Three hours. "But don't worry," he continued, "Budienny rests his horses during the heat of the day.

He has raided the town twice, but each time at dusk, between nine and ten o'clock. It is only five now and you should be able to get away by eight."

To while away the time the four of us walked over to the town. As is so often the case in Russia, the railroad station was a mile or so away. The reason for this was graft, the insiders buying up at cheap rates the land between the town and the site selected for the station, and holding it for speculative profit.

Zitomir was a ghost city. Not a solitary soul was abroad, and as a measure of rude precaution, rough planks had been nailed across front doors and ground windows. As we walked along the deserted streets, our footsteps reverberating in the silence, we could see through cracks and peepholes the whites of human eyes following our progress. We could sense the terror to which the populace was prey.

In the center of a large square we stopped to hold a council of war. I remember advocating an immediate return to the station, in order to be near the only available means of retreat. It was always possible that the train would be assembled more quickly than expected, and I for one did not put it beyond the engineer to maroon us in Zitomir if he had a chance to make good his own escape. Maule and Graham told me that I was arguing like a civilian. The station was the most dangerous locality in the vicinity. If Budienny should make another raid, it was the first place his Cossacks would overrun. While we were still discussing matters, we heard an automobile dashing up the street at high speed. Instinctively we all looked for the nearest cover.

It turned out to be a Red Cross car, and its occupants spoke English. They told us, with a fine sense of the dramatic, that Kiew had been evacuated,[18] that they had watched the White Eagle being lowered from the Citadel, and the Polish troops march out as if on parade, with General Rydz-Smigley, his bride riding a pillion behind him on his charger, bringing up the rear. Where were the Bolsheviks? We walked back to the station resolved to make the Polish officers leave with as much rolling stock as had been gathered together, and no more.

Even this turned out to be difficult. With one single locomotive to do the shunting, and only a few untrained soldiers to man the switches,

[18] Kiev was evacuated by Polish forces on June 13, 1920.

the tracks had become clogged. Colonel Graham watched the inefficient handling with growing indignation, until he could stand it no longer, when he stepped forward, assumed charge, barked out orders through a Polish officer who volunteered as interpreter, and slowly, very slowly, brought order out of chaos. By the time a train of reasonable length had been assembled, it was close to nine o'clock, and the sun was sinking below the horizon.

The engineer was at the throttle, we had all climbed aboard, and were waiting for the wheels to begin turning, when suddenly a man, wearing parts of a Polish uniform dashed into the station, waving a piece of paper, and shouting to the engineer not to start the train. He told us that he had been sent posthaste by the colonel of a Polish regiment stationed some three miles back of Zitomir. The colonel had received a wire that reinforcements were being sent down by train from Korosten. As the line was single track, with only occasional sidings, our train was on no account to leave the station. Was the message a true order, or was it a decoy to facilitate our capture? Opinion among the Polish officers was divided, and precious minutes passed while they palavered. Did the messenger carry any credentials? No, the colonel had given him the message, nothing more. As a bold half-measure, the officers finally decided to run the train as far as the next station, some eighteen kilometers up the line, even at the risk of having to back the entire distance if we met the troop train on this stretch of track. Further plans could be held in suspense for the time being.

It was nearly half-past nine when we finally pulled out of Zitomir. Maule produced some whiskey, which we drank neat, and never before or since has drink tasted better. With each passing mile our spirits rose, and although the train was fired on during the night as we steamed through a thick copse of trees, we reached Korosten safely at dawn. There had never been a plan to send reinforcements by rail from Korosten. The messenger had been a Bolshevik agent, and the Polish soldiery were loud in their laments that by not bringing him along they had missed the pleasure of shooting him for a spy. From Korosten it took us two days to reach Brest-Litowsk, where I had a chance to visit the citadel and see Trotsky's famous words "No war — no peace" scribbled on the whitewashed walls of the fortress,[19] and

[19] Leon Trotsky, the Soviet Commissar of Foreign Affairs, issued an official state-

another half-day to reach Warsaw. My dominant impression was that a large city conveys a comfortable sense of security.

A month later the Polish front collapsed. Warsaw became a vantage point from which to watch two concurrent dramas.

The first drama was purely military. For six weeks [20] the Bolshevik flood flowed relentlessly westward till it reached the very city limits of Warsaw. It seemed as though nothing could save the city and for three days all Europe watched with bated breath. The fall of Warsaw was to be the signal for uprisings in Germany, Austria and Northern Italy. The outlook for European civilization was in many ways as dark as when the Hun stood before Chalons, or the Saracen before Tours. And then occurred the "miracle of the Vistula." The tide was not merely stayed, but turned back. A few days more and the Bolshevik army in its turn collapsed, the victorious Poles advanced to reoccupy the Eastern lands, and the groups in Europe that were on the point of revolting slowly subsided to await either improving conditions or a more propitious day.

The second drama was political and diplomatic. An onlooker could sense enough of the plot to see that all the characters were agreed in wanting to create a new dike against the westward spread of Bolshevism. But so intent was each in seeing that the dike was built according to his particular specifications that Paris was still bickering with London, and in London Lloyd George was still bickering with the Foreign Office, when the battle of the Vistula disposed of the issue. The inability of France and England to fuse their efforts even in time of crisis was not forgotten in Eastern Europe for many a long year.[21] The United States made only one appearance on the stage:

---

ment on February 10, 1918, from Brest-Litovsk that although the Russian delegation was unable to sign a formal treaty of peace with Germany, the state of war with Germany was ended. James Bunyan and H. H. Fisher (eds.), *The Bolshevik Revolution 1917–1918, Documents and Materials* (Stanford University, Cal.: Stanford University Press, 1934), pp. 509–510.

[20] Mr. Moffat is referring to the period from about July 4 to mid-August 1920.

[21] At the Paris Peace Conference France and Great Britain held different views about the organization and aims of the Polish State. France, because of her long friendship with Poland and in the belief that Germany was a threat to both countries, supported Polish plans for expansion. But Great Britain opposed Polish aims in many major areas, "from a deeply rooted belief that if Poland was to be strong both internally and externally it was necessary that self-determination should be the guiding principle of the settlement." H. W. V. Temperley (ed.), *A History of the Peace Conference of Paris*, VI (London: Henry Frowde & Hodder & Stoughton, 1924), 238–240.

this was during the last act, just before the curtain fell, when the Secretary of State, Mr. Bainbridge Colby, interrupted the dialogue to read a statement of what America thought about Bolshevism, bowed to the audience, and made an unapplauded exit.[22]

During these crucial weeks, the Legation at Warsaw reported fully day-to-day developments; it gave useful advice to the eight American relief organizations that were functioning in Poland;[23] and at the appropriate moment it evacuated all American citizens from Warsaw. So vivid were the events of July and August 1920 that today, after the lapse of twenty-two years, the story is still etched in bold lines on the tablets of my memory.

It started one afternoon early in July when Colonel Farman, our Military Attaché, came to the Chancery to tell us of the defeat of General Szeptycki's army group on the northern front.[24] The General had for some time been rumored to be discouraged about his position. He had whispered too widely his fears that his lines could not be held in the event of an attack in force. But never in his most pessimistic mood had he foreseen that within the space of a few days the enemy would succeed in separating the Polish and Lettish armies, in capturing Minsk, in forcing the evacuation of the North Pripet region and in turning the Polish retreat into a rout.

The Polish Government reacted to this news by swinging from an unjustified optimism to an exaggerated pessimism. Frantic appeals were sent to the Allies for help, and to reinforce them the Prime Minister, Mr. Grabski, was despatched to Spa where a reparations Conference was conveniently in session.[25] Lloyd George dominated

[22] On August 10, 1920, Mr. Colby sent to the Italian Ambassador at Washington a lengthy statement of attitude of the United States toward the Russian advance into Poland and the Russian question in general. U. S. Department of State, *Papers Relating to the Foreign Relations of the United States, 1920* (Washington: Government Printing Office, 1936), III, 463–468.

[23] The best account of American relief organizations in Poland is given by H. H. Fisher, *America and the New Poland* (New York: The Macmillan Co., 1928), pp. 161–318.

[24] The Polish armies in the North, commanded by General Stanislas Szeptycki, were inferior in numbers and equipment to the opposing Russian troops of Mikhail Tukhachevsky. On the night of July 6–7, 1920, the Russian general led his troops across the Beresina and began into Polish territory a steady advance which proceeded without interruption for almost a month. Robert Machray, *Poland 1914–1931* (London: George Allen & Unwin, 1932), pp. 148–149.

[25] The Conference of the Spa, which took place from July 5 to 16, 1920, had assembled to consider the disarmament of Germany and the deliveries of coal to Germany

the conference, and Lloyd George had no liking for the Poles. He brushed the French delegate aside, summoned Mr. Grabski to his rooms, and browbeat him into accepting then and there a set of stern conditions. The clash between the two men must have been pathetically one-sided: to overcome the prejudices of the masterful Lloyd George, the Poles had sent a round-shouldered and myopic ex-Professor, whose whole career had shown him to be stubborn when he should have yielded, pliant when he should have stood firm. By his own admission, he made no attempt to set forth the role that Poland had played in staving off Bolshevism; he made no threat to "open the front" if Europe did not assist; he did not even verify if Lloyd George was speaking for the French as well as the British Government. Instead he agreed to an armistice based on the withdrawal of Polish troops to the "minimum line" laid down by the Peace Conference, a bare 120 miles east of Warsaw, and to meet Soviet negotiators in London and arrange peace terms under the aegis of the none too benevolent Lloyd George. Only if the Bolshevik armies crossed the "minimum line" would Allied help be forthcoming.

Grabski returned to Warsaw trembling. He knew that if he made public the conditions he had accepted, he would receive short shrift from his chauvinistic countrymen. We half-suspected that he hoped the Soviets would refuse the armistice so as to free him from his undertakings.

It was a week or two before the Bolsheviks replied to Lloyd George.[26] The answer was sent by wireless from Moscow to London, and as it was *en clair* had been intercepted by the Poles and given to

due under the Treaty of Versailles. On July 10 the Polish Prime Minister, Ladislas Grabski, gained a hearing at the Spa. He agreed that the Poles would give up all ideas of conquest, would refer all questions in dispute to the Supreme Council, would withdraw Polish forces to the Curzon Line, and would send delegates to a Peace Conference in London at which Russia, Poland, and various border states should be present. The next day, July 11, 1920, a note was sent to Soviet Russia embodying the Polish concessions and intimating that if, despite these proposals, Russian troops advanced into Poland, the Allies would feel obliged to aid Poland. Machray, pp. 151–152; Temperley, VI, 319–320; S. Konovalov (ed.), *Russo-Polish Relations* (Princeton, N. J.: Princeton University Press, 1945), pp. 68–70; Arnold J. Toynbee, *Survey of International Affairs 1920–1923* (London: Oxford University Press, 1925), pp. 13–14; Stanislaw Grabski, *The Polish-Soviet Frontier* (New York: Polish Information Service, n.d.), pp. 7–9.
[26] The Soviet reply of July 17, 1920, declined to accept the proposals for attending a conference in London, holding that "the past attitude of the British Government in the conflict . . . can hardly be considered as a reason for assuming the role of

Sir Horace Rumbold and General Carton de Wiart. It was a rambling message, later termed "incoherent" in London and "impertinent" in Paris. But its purport was clear: The Soviets did not desire to discuss with the British the question of war or peace with Poland. I have not forgotten the first reaction of my British friends on reading the text. They refused to believe that it was an official communication addressed to His Majesty's Government; probably it was merely a bit of propaganda put out for home consumption. But London soon confirmed its authenticity, declining to take umbrage at its tone and telegraphed Sir Horace Rumbold that its essential feature was a not unreasonable demand that Poland should make a direct application to Moscow for an armistice.

Sir Horace at once drove to the Belvedere where the Council of National Defense was sitting and urged the Poles to despatch the requisite telegram that very evening. Each hour's delay might make the Bolsheviks, intoxicated with daily victories, less inclined to accept.

Yet neither that evening, nor all the next day was the request for an armistice sent. The Council was engaged in what was termed "an essential preliminary," the creation of a coalition cabinet, and thirty hours were unprofitably spent in haggling over who would or who would not be given the various portfolios. Finally the peasant Witos, the socialist Daszynski, and the Prince Sapieha were agreed upon as Premier, vice-Premier and Minister for Foreign Affairs.[27] Only then were two telegrams sent off, the first to Chicherin [Georghy Chicherin, Soviet Commissar for Foreign Affairs], the second to the Commanding General of the Red Armies. The Bolsheviks were by now at the gates of Grodno.

The time had come to make plans for evacuating the American colony. There were no diplomatic relations between Washington and Moscow, and stories of ill-treatment meted out to Americans in Soviet territory seemed to be well authenticated . . .

The Polish authorities when approached became exercised at the mere thought of evacuation. The Minister of Railroads told me that

---

mediator." Russia also stated her desire to open "direct negotiations" with Poland and her willingness to agree to a more favorable frontier with Poland than that suggested by the Supreme Council in 1919. Jane Degras (ed.), *Soviet Documents on Foreign Policy*, I (London: Oxford University Press, 1951), 194–197.

[27] The Government of National Union under Witos took over power on July 24, 1920.

any concerted exit of Americans would produce a panic in Warsaw. The Government had not yet envisaged the possibility of moving the capital. Were we not acting prematurely? Would we not withdraw our request for rolling stock? Under questioning he had to admit that with each day's delay there would be fewer and fewer railway carriages available. At last I got a contingent promise of a special train to take the Americans to Danzig, though the Minister made it clear that no luggage or heavy effects could be transported. One freight car would be reserved for the chattels and records of the Legation, but that was the limit of what he could do. I spent a good part of the next day trying to rent some barges to float heavy luggage down the river. Normally they held eighty tons each, though the extreme low water in the Vistula due to a prolonged drought made it inadvisable to load them so heavily. The various American relief organizations and the Legation agreed to pool their requirements, and the contracts were drawn up and signed several days before any other Legation even so much as suspected the existence of a river barge . . .

Meanwhile Lloyd George, with his inveterate distrust of the professional diplomat, decided that perhaps Sir Horace Rumbold was being unduly pessimistic. In any event he would welcome a report from an emissary of his own choosing. He would therefore send a special mission, with high-powered civil and military representatives, and the French could be counted on to do likewise. This was action, or at the very worst could be construed as action.

The British mission was headed by Lord D'Abernon, the newly appointed Ambassador to Berlin.[28] He was a banker trained in the devious bypaths of Levantine finance. He was later conspicuously successful in Berlin in the days when his talents could be devoted to adjusting the reparations imbroglio. But in Poland, he was plunged into the vortex of a major crisis without any background, either political or psychological, and did what many a lesser man would have done, either reported what his master desired to hear, or did not report at all. It was Sir Horace Rumbold whose political analyses, though unpopular at the time, showed true political acumen.

The French mission was headed by Ambassador Jusserand, Ambassador to Washington, who happened to be in Paris on leave. He was a wise old man, a curious blend of the cynic and the idealist. He

[28] The mission arrived in Warsaw on July 25, 1920.

saw from almost the first day that only the soldiers could influence the course of events. The role of a diplomat, particularly a French diplomat, was to see that if Poland survived the crisis, France would get as large a measure as possible of the credit. He therefore effaced himself in favor of his principal military adviser General Weygand, and accented his role as chief of staff to the redoubtable Marshal Foch. For the rest, he kept urging Paris to send munitions and more munitions, and above all to put pressure on the Czechs who because of Soviet sympathies were showing reluctance to let them pass. Lord D'Abernon, on the other hand, took scant notice when Sir Reginald Tower, the interallied High Commissioner at Danzig, declined to force the German stevedores to unload supplies for Poland, justifying their stand on the ground that it was due to an industrial dispute and not to political bias.

By July 27th or 28th the Bolshevik armies again started their advance. Evidently the advices from Soviet agents in Britain had been reassuring. To be sure His Majesty's Government was adopting an increasingly ominous, not to say minatory, tone in official communications, but to counterbalance this, a group of labor leaders styling themselves the "Council of Action" was beginning through the voice of Mr. Ernest Bevin to suggest the possibility of a general strike if Britain risked involvement with the Soviets. The public at large showed little sympathy with the attitude of either the Government or the Council of Action. The average Englishman was apathetic and war-weary. Eastern Europe seemed far away; the Poles by their incursion into the Ukraine had forfeited any claim to British support; the alarm of the French could be written down to emotionalism. "No adventures" was the order of the day.

Lloyd George sensed the popular mood, and making it his own, brushed aside the warnings of his Foreign Office, the appeals of his French Allies, and the gloomy forebodings of Winston Churchill.[29] Thenceforth the policy of the British Government was to be one of

[29] Mr. Churchill has recalled his apprehensions of this summer in Winston S. Churchill, *The Aftermath, The World Crisis, 1918–1928* (New York: Charles Scribner's Sons, 1929), pp. 273ff. He foresaw the possibility of a "complete Polish collapse," and he was afraid that an internal communist revolution might occur in Poland or the communist armies might overrun the country. "Would it be the policy of the British Government to remain impassive in the face of such an event, which may be conceivably near?" he had asked.

inertia. The Red cavalry appeared at the gates of Lomza; London took the news in its stride, and the Red cavalry promptly pushed still deeper into Polish territory. Positive help to Poland was never actually refused; it was merely never forthcoming. The Poles swallowed their resentment, but from that moment on, watched British policy with a jaundiced eye. French influence waxed as that of the British waned. Soon Weygand was the only foreigner whose advice was sought, and more important, followed.

Nothing could now be seen that was to save Warsaw from its doom. Certainly a day at the front with Colonel Farman left me profoundly discouraged. We motored out to Brest-Litowsk on August 2nd. Long before we reached its outskirts we passed village after village filled with tired, dispirited troops, a few of them digging shallow meaningless trenches, most of them merely watching with resigned empty faces the hundreds of peasant carts, which seemed to be the only commissariat, moving either toward or away from the front line. Of motor transport we saw none. The roads were so bad that twice our car stuck in the dried ruts. We called at General Haller's headquarters and spoke with his Chief of Staff. At best he talked of holding the line of the Bug, but even while we were speaking word came in that the river had been forced. We returned convinced of the need to order out the American colony, and to move the Legation records.

Jack White [John Campbell White, Chargé d'Affaires of the American Legation at Warsaw] called in the heads of the various American groups and told them in unmistakable terms that the time had come for the evacuation to begin. Two hundred places were reserved on the Danzig train the following night. But to our chagrin, many declined to go, selfishly declaring that they wished to be the last to leave. We warned them that if they waited too long, they might never get a place on the train. If panic should grip the city, the station would be stormed, and such trains as pulled out would be packed to the limit by humans who had the physical strength to beat their way in, with others riding on the roof or clinging to the outside steps. In vain. All too many preferred to believe that somehow the magic words "American citizens" would suffice to hold against all comers the compartments that were to be reserved.

Meanwhile I went upstairs and started burning documents. For four hours on a summer day I stood before a huge open hearth, feeding papers to the flames, neither too fast nor too slowly, and breaking up the glowing ash with a heavy poker. Let no one who has not done as much belittle the fatigue. We then packed the remaining office files in numbered containers and loaded them on the freight car that had been assigned us, where they remained under guard pending the decision of the Government to transfer the capital to another Polish city.

Paradoxically, the nearer the Bolshevik armies thrust, the more calm and indifferent the Polish ministers seemed to grow. First they had hinted that they would leave if ever the Bolsheviks captured Grodno; later, if they reached Lomza; and now, if they reached Modlin, barely thirty miles away. With few exceptions the diplomats had instructions to follow the Government. Yet if the Government did not leave in short order it might well be too late to leave at all . . .

The last desperate week had arrived. The Bolshevik armies driving from the north and east were fast closing in on Warsaw. Further south Budienny's cavalry was moving on Lwow, tempted by its rich booty. The Armistice delegation at Russian insistence had been replaced by a peace delegation,[30] which was busily trying to locate the body with which it was supposed to conduct negotiations. Refugees from the east were pouring into the city with lurid tales of Bolshevik atrocities. Every Polish officer carried a tablet of poison as in the event of capture, death was preferable to torture. The landlords were no longer safe as in many regions the peasantry was in a ferment, stirred up by infiltrating Soviet agents. (The term fifth column had not yet been coined.) Dzerzynski, master of the dread Cheka [31] was not far from Warsaw, waiting to take it over and purge it of counter-revolutionary elements.

And as the refugees poured in from the east, there began the great exodus toward the west. Nearly all who had funds abroad, or had any liquid assets, or relatives in Posen, fled before the approaching

---

[30] In late July Poland asked Russia for armistice terms. In negotiations at Minsk the Russians offered very severe conditions, but the Polish military recovery led to the rupture of the Minsk talks. Peace negotiations were resumed at Riga in September and produced an armistice on October 12.

[31] "Cheka," the Extraordinary Commission for the Suppression of Counter-Revolution, was established by Lenin on December 20, 1917. A terroristic political police force, it was the precursor of the "G.P.U."

Reds. Those who remained, like old Count Joseph Potocki, were few. He spent those days of anguish repairing his palace and rehanging his masterpieces. He had fled from the Bolsheviks before. This time if they came he would meet them at the front door, and fall with his house and his order.

But the great mass of the people could not flee. They would have to accept the dictates of fate. Was Poland, after two brief years of life, doomed to perish? Had she, united after her hundred and fifty years partition among three military empires, merely to fall under one single overlordship, and an anti-Christian one at that? There was little the people could do, but they could always pray. And so that last Sunday [August 8, 1920], in answer to a spontaneous urge, Warsaw devoted the day to public supplication. From dawn until dusk long processions of men and women marched through the streets of the city, bearing the religious banners and sacred relics from one church to another, chanting the old and well-beloved Polish hymns. A look of fervor glowed in every face. The city was praying for a miracle.

The next day martial law was declared and curfew imposed. Life became grim. Prices were skyrocketing and the poor were already having difficulty in finding nourishing food . . . Lord D'Abernon and Monsieur Jusserand decided that the moment had come to seek safety in Posen. They rationalized their decision which seemed to many Poles like desertion, by stressing the need of maintaining uninterrupted communication with their governments. They were sorry that the Polish Government was not moving with them, the atmosphere of Warsaw was too tense, they felt, for coldblooded decision, but they could always offer advice to Prince Sapieha by long-distance telephone. Their special train pulled out of the darkened station shortly before midnight [during the night of August 13–14, 1920], carrying all but eight of the resident diplomatic corps.

When we returned to the Legation, Jack White and I reviewed our own situation. We had instructions from Washington not to risk capture by the Bolsheviks for fear we might be held as hostages. On the other hand, our mere presence in Warsaw after the others had left was an encouragement to the Poles, and we felt that American prestige would be enhanced by our remaining until the very last moment. But what was the very last moment, and how could we determine it?

We finally decided to remain until the Poles blew up the two great bridges crossing the Vistula between Warsaw and its suburb Praga. If we happened to be away from the Legation, the sound of the explosion would in any event reach us, and we could make our way to an agreed rendezvous just to the west of the city, where our automobile with the one remaining American clerk carrying the cipher book would meet us.[32]

It had been a long day and bed was welcome. It seemed as though I had barely fallen asleep when I was roused by Farman who came into my room saying, "You had better get up. It's no longer a question *if* we leave the city but when. The Bolos took Radzymin shortly before dawn and are now inside the city limits. The Poles are counterattacking and may succeed in delaying matters for a few hours, but the game is up."

All day we went listlessly about our business, expecting each minute to hear the air shattered as the great steel spans of the two bridges were blown from the piers and sent crashing into the river. But the long day dragged to a close and the bridges still stood. When darkness fell, we climbed to the roof of the Blue Palace and gazed out, just as the besieged in earlier wars had done, over the Praga plain to where a vast semicircle of campfires proved that the enemy was already investing the city.

A still longer day followed. Early in the morning, it was rumored that Radzymin had been recaptured; later, that it had been lost a second time. But at least the Poles were resisting. Could the city after all be saved? We tried to work, but it was a meaningless shuffling of papers. Our thoughts were far afield. From time to time we would telephone one of the remaining colleagues and barter tidbits of information. A few Polish friends dropped in seeking comfort, their heads held high, but their eyes betraying the anguish they felt.

It was not until after seven o'clock that we left the Legation, bound as usual for our evening meal at the club. To our surprise the Great Square was roped off, but lined up within the cordon we could see row upon row of unarmed soldiers, standing sullen and sweating in the August heat. We looked again and sure enough, the uniform

[32] On August 8, 1920, the Warsaw Legation telegraphed the Department of State that John Campbell White, Mr. Moffat, and one Polish clerk were remaining in the capital until the Polish ministers left. U. S. Dept. of State, *Foreign Relations, 1920*, III, 387.

they wore was Bolshevik. The sight thus vouchsafed of a thousand prisoners taken that morning in battle could mean only one thing — a sizable Polish success. The news spread like wildfire. In a matter of minutes the nearby streets were crowded. Onlookers who approached skeptically, with discouraged steps, straightened up and walked home erect. There was a song of hope that night in every Polish heart.

During the hours of darkness, the Soviet troops that were investing Warsaw began their retreat. Daylight revealed that Radzymin, Zegrze and Serock had been abandoned. The Poles advanced, at first incredulous, then confident, and finally exultant. Bolshevik morale crumpled, their retreat turned into headlong flight. Harassing them day and night, cutting off groups here and there, the Poles never paused until their inexorable compulsion had driven the enemy back into the dark forests of White Russia and onto the distant plains of the Ukraine.

Historians will continue their sterile debate as to whether Pilsudski or Weygand was the author of victory. There was a deeper cause. At the very moment when all seemed lost, there came a transformation in the Polish spirit, born of a realization that if Warsaw fell, there could be no survival for the Polish state, no future for the Polish race. Fired by an idea, the Poles gained an ascendency in morale and this they retained through the remaining weeks of the war.

Let it be admitted that Pilsudski and Weygand, be it one or the other or both, profited brilliantly from Soviet errors. Budienny was particularly at fault, for tempted by the high booty of Lwow, he dallied for several days before the city, ignoring repeated orders from Tukhachevsky to move northwestward toward Warsaw with the utmost despatch. The result was that when battle was joined under the walls of the capital, not only were Budienny's Cossacks a hundred miles away, but there was a gap between the two converging Soviet armies near Deblin, the very point where the last Polish reserves were massed. Two forced marches diagonally northeastward through this gap brought them directly behind the Soviet forces that were already engaged with the Poles at Radzymin. This maneuver climaxed what Lord D'Abernon not inaptly termed the "Eighteenth Decisive Battle of the World" . . .[33]

---

[33] The Polish–Soviet peace treaty was signed at Riga on March 18, 1921. D'Aber-

From the wrecks of the three Empires, the new Poland sprang into being. German Posen, Austrian Galicia, and the Russian area of "Congress Poland" [34] fused into a single state. There was unity of language — it had been kept alive and pure in Polish homes despite five generations of bondage — and there was unity of religion, but little else. There was not even unity of character. During those generations the Russian Poles had been taught to conspire, the Austrian Poles to compromise, and the German Poles to fight back. This meant inefficiency in the Departments, the formation of cliques and a jealous scrutiny of all promotions. The difficulties of forming an administration, of unifying three financial systems, three judicial systems, and three sets of military traditions at times seemed almost insuperable.

Fortunately, the Pole is by nature sanguine. He lives in the present. He has the happy faculty of closing his eyes to gathering storm clouds and concentrating on transient sunshine. Although he subconsciously sensed the dangers threatening the country from without and within, the average Pole preferred not to think about them, but to taste the unfamiliar pleasures of national independence and to enjoy in anticipation the prosperity that he felt destiny held in store. He gave free rein to enthusiasm, to buoyancy, to optimism. The future at long last was his, and it called for festivity. Each class made merry in its own way.

Never had Warsaw known such a "season" as the winter of 1919–1920. The great families, Potockis, Radziwills, Lubomirskis, Sapiehas, after having lived in the country for decades, made a point of returning to Warsaw and reopening their palaces. With their eighteenth-century standards, they felt that they were testifying to their faith in Poland's stability by making its capital for one brief winter the most brilliant in Europe. The impact of three emotions, reaction from the privations of the past, pride in the present, and an anguished, if suppressed, fear of the future, combined to create an urge for exaggerated gaiety . . .

The real strength of Poland came from the fields and the forests. The love of the soil was instinctive in every Pole, and from living

---

non's account of the period is given in his book, *The Eighteenth Decisive Battle of the World* (London: Hodder & Stoughton, 1931).

[34] At the Congress of Vienna in 1815 a part of Poland was set up as the "Kingdom of Poland" with Czar Alexander of Russia as its king. In 1832 "Congress" Poland, as it is known, was done away with, and the territory was incorporated with Russia.

near the soil he derived all that was finest in his make-up. It was not until I had paid a number of visits in the country, that I began to sense the true worth of my Polish friends. Life was still feudal, but it was devoid of sham.

Landlord and Peasant had made common cause during the partition in resisting alien overlordship and in keeping Polish nationalism alive. This had welded a strong bond between them, despite the gulf between the perfectly appointed castle and the poverty of the thatched villages outside the castle gate. The gulf was so great that not even in imagination was it bridged. The more lavish the castle and its invariable hunt, the greater the pride of the peasants.

I recall spending the week between Christmas and New Years with the Henry Potockis. This was a large eighteenth-century manor house built over the remains of an old fortress, the walls of the ground floor thus being twenty feet thick. It was set in a vast forest which was subdivided into eighty sections, where cutting and replanting were carried on in regular rotation. There were no near neighbors. Friends and cousins would harness their carriages and drive over from a distance to remain two or three days. We never sat down at table fewer than thirty or forty, the generations mixing with perfect freedom. Here for the first time I tasted some old Polish dishes, such as soup made of the hot blood of goose heavily spiced, and drank miod or distilled honey (the ancient mead of the British).

There were some ten thousand peasants on the estate, happy enough, loyal enough, but not to be tempted beyond a point. Each morning Count and Countess Henry Potocki would go to the front hall at nine o'clock to receive one by one any petitioners from the estate who lined up at the entrance. Each man or woman was free to come with his wish or his grievance. To one they would give a few coins; to another a calomel pill; a third would be sent away with a scolding; a fourth would come to announce the birth of a child and go away with congratulations and a small present. And thus it went on for an hour or more. In the afternoon Countess Potocka would go out in a light sleigh to visit the sick and infirm in their thatched huts. The system worked, and it would work so long as the landlords were willing to give so much of themselves . . .

Another visit I made was to Lancut, the fairy-tale château of Alfred Potocki. No description could do justice to the house or to the princely state with which it was maintained. For untold generations each owner had added to the house until it had become a veritable museum. We never dined twice in the same dining room. Once we ate from the plates carried by Napoleon on his invasion of Russia and abandoned during the retreat. We had coffee in a drawing room where the furniture and pictures came from Versailles, bought by an ancestor during the French Revolution. There were galleries, halls of sculpture, an orangerie, even a theatre. I asked how it was that the house remained undamaged through the vicissitudes of war. The answer was that there was no river nearby, for in open warfare the worst fighting always occurs near a river crossing. But a more probable reason is to be found in the fact that the Potockis, and the Radziwills with whom they intermarried, were connected with both the Austrian and the Russian courts, and that when one branch of the family was driven out, another branch took charge of the property on their behalf. Lancut even survived the invasion of 1939. The story goes that when the German motorized columns were approaching, an elderly friend tried to persuade Countess Betka Potocka to flee. "Why should I?" she answered, "I'm not afraid of any German living." And when the enemy took possession they found the chatelaine in the rose garden calmly snipping off the heads of her roses. These Polish aristocrats had *"panache."* They were living in a bygone world, mistaking the gesture for reality, but they were governed by a code, and that code included intense loyalty to friends and unflinching defiance of foe . . .

Theoretically, communism embodied a conception of life far more advanced than our own system, yet in practice it was reviving the Dark Ages. It required an act of faith to see a happier world growing out of the misery and torture and carnage that followed wherever the early Bolsheviks trod. And yet we instinctively knew that the Polish way of life, twentieth century feudalism however benevolent, was doomed to die. Not so our Polish friends. To them Bolshevism was sheer evil. It was anti-Christ. The memory of relatives massacred, of houses burned over their heads, of properties torn from them was too near, too vivid. It confirmed them in a super-conservatism, a resistance to reform. They resolutely closed their eyes to the fact that the world about them was changing, that new ideas were afloat, and that different standards were prevailing. They were satisfied with their world, and ready to die in maintaining it. The two decades that followed were therefore socially stagnant, and politically unreal.

My mind might rebel at their ideas, yet I liked the Poles as I have liked few races. They have a positive gift for friendship, a gift that once bestowed is yours for life. I made a host of real friends during my two years in Poland, many of whom I did not see for another twenty years. Yet in each case we started again just where we had left off. What was still theirs was to be shared, be it only a cup of coffee in the hall bedroom of a dingy boarding house. The ups and downs of fortune never affected the friendship of a Pole.

In March 1921 I went home to be present at the wedding of my sister and Jack White.[35] While in the United States I received orders transferring me to Tokyo.

[35] Mr. White had met Elizabeth Barclay Moffat when she and her mother visited Pierrepont Moffat in Warsaw in 1920.

II

WASHINGTON

July 1931 – March 1933

"The home front is tending to crumble"

During the nineteen-twenties Pierrepont Moffat moved quickly from post to post. Two years in Tokyo from 1921–1923 as Second Secretary were followed by another two years at the same rank in Constantinople. From 1925 to 1927 he was in Washington working on protocol matters at the White House, and in 1927 he was sent to Berne, Switzerland, as First Secretary of Legation.

In Switzerland he had an opportunity to handle many of the problems of relations between the United States and the League of Nations, particularly those relating to disarmament. Since the end of World War I, when the treaties of peace had imposed strict limitations upon the fighting forces of Germany, Austria, Hungary, and Bulgaria, the League had been struggling with the question of disarmament. The Allied nations had stated that the disarmament of the defeated Central powers was only a step "towards that general reduction and limitation of armaments . . . which it will be one of the first duties of the League of Nations to promote," and the League had set up the Permanent Advisory Commission on disarmament in May 1920. This was followed in 1921 by the Temporary Mixed Commission, which was itself replaced in 1924 by the Coordination Committee. The failure of these various groups to deal with the problem satisfactorily was due to its complexity. Not only were there technical considerations involved, but also the fears and antagonisms which had always shaped foreign policy among the nations influenced the disarmament question.

In 1925 the League decided to make a fresh start. It established the Preparatory Commission for the Disarmament Conference which, it was hoped, could in a year's time agree upon a draft treaty. This treaty would then become the basis for discussion at a general disarmament conference. But the delays and difficulties which confronted the Preparatory Commission were much the same as those which faced the earlier committees. France insisted that security must precede disarmament, and cast wary eyes on Germany. Germany, disarmed by others, insistently pressed others to disarm. Great Britain felt that disarmament and security must be achieved together but was unwilling to break the common front with France. The Soviet Union could quite often be found differing with any majority view. Italy, antagonistic to France, became increasingly sympathetic with German aspirations as the fascist movement developed in Germany. And the United States pursued its course in the disarmament meetings aloof from European political considerations.

Finally in 1930 the Preparatory Commission agreed upon a draft convention, and a general disarmament conference was called to meet at Geneva in 1932. Pierrepont Moffat, who had attended three sessions of the Preparatory Commission in 1927, 1929, and 1930, was recalled from Berne to Washington to prepare for American participation in the Geneva Conference.

Since the Peace Conference at Paris there had been no more important international gathering than the scheduled Geneva Disarmament Conference. Throughout 1931 it was the focus of negotiations among and preparations in most of the countries of the world. Even the United States welcomed "the opportunity to cooperate with the other nations in a common effort to reduce the menace and to lighten the burden of armaments." [1]

Tuesday and Wednesday, September 8 and 9 [1931].

The Secretary returned to Washington on Tuesday morning [2] and after attending Cabinet meeting and making his report to the President, he plunged right into disarmament matters. He sent for Pierre Boal [Chief of the Division of Western European Affairs] and myself on Wednesday morning to talk over the general line he would take in press conferences regarding disarmament matters. The day before, Grandi [Dino Grandi, Italian Minister for Foreign Affairs] had proposed at Geneva an arms suspension to last at least during the Conference at Geneva. The details of the proposal were not at all clear but the French press had already begun to knock the project. Mr. Stimson decided that he would, for background purposes only, inform the press that we were distinctly sympathetic to the idea. He did not wish to make a public statement for fear of embarrassing any conversations which might be proceeding at Geneva. He also ran over certain other points which he wished to emphasize: that in contradistinction to the preparations for the London Conference [of 1930] with which the United States was immediately and vitally

[1] Mr. Moffat drafted this American note of acceptance on July 8, 1931.
[2] Henry L. Stimson had just returned from a two months' visit in Europe.

interested,[3] the difficulties lying before the Disarmament Conference are largely a series of bilateral European political problems. Even if the entire United States army and fleet were eliminated, these European problems would not be benefitted one iota. Our chief interest, therefore, in the preparations for the Conference, is to help the other nations in making advance preparations for the Conference in respect to their individual problems much as we had to do before the London Conference last year. . .[4]

October 20 [1931].

H.R.W. [Hugh Wilson, American Minister to Switzerland] went over and had a conversation with the President at the White House, in which he outlined the conclusions regarding what we could do to save the European situation which he, Hugh Wilson, and Ted Marriner [Counselor of the American Embassy at Paris] had jointly worked out. Without going into the details of the conversation as reported by H.R.W., I gathered two or three impressions which confirmed what I had previously been told: (1) that the President is viewing the entire problem from an exclusively American angle; he feels that the public is angry at what steps we have taken to cooperate with the rest of the world;[5] (2) he does not exclude the possibility of divorcing American economy from world economy, and getting on as best we can by ourselves; (3) he has a strong personal animus against France and French policy. . .

The prospects of real achievement at the Geneva Disarmament Conference became perceptibly less bright when, on September 18, 1931, the

[3] However remote from the American national interest seemed many of the tasks facing the Disarmament Conference, the United States, bounded by two oceans and apprehensive of growing Japanese naval strength, felt deep concern over the specific problems of naval limitation which had been treated at the London Conference.

[4] A summary of the Secretary's views as given to the press on September 9 and 10, 1931, is printed in U.S. Department of State, *Papers relating to the Foreign Relations of the United States, 1931* (Washington: Government Printing Office, 1946), I, 441, 522–523.

[5] Mr. Hoover felt that steps taken to cooperate with the League of Nations during the Manchurian crisis had been very unpopular in some quarters. *The Literary Digest* cited unfavorable comments in such papers as the *New York Evening Post*, the *Chicago Tribune*, and the *New York Daily News*, but estimated that "the applause for the Hoover-Stimson policy . . . seems to be a bit louder and more wide-spread than the booing and hissing." Herbert Hoover, *The Memoirs of Herbert Hoover, The Cabinet and the Presidency 1920–1933* (New York: The Macmillan Co., 1952), p. 371; *The Literary Digest*, October 24, 1931, p. 6.

Japanese army moved into Manchuria.[6] Most of the European powers were immediately concerned with the Sino–Japanese dispute, because it came within the scope of the Covenant of the League of Nations. Since the United States was a signatory of the Nine-Power Treaty and the Kellogg-Briand Pact, the conflict also involved American interests and obligations. The quest for disarmament seemed in vain, as the antagonisms of some of the nations considering the reduction of arms erupted into open warfare.

November 6, 7 and 8 [1931].

Hugh Wilson and Ted Marriner, both having spent three days trying to get into the Secretary's office, finally took their troubles to Klots [Allen T. Klots, Special Assistant to the Secretary of State], who said he would tell the Secretary that they wanted to talk with him about the make-up of the American Delegation. The Secretary very petulantly replied that of course it was important and he did not understand their not coming in to see him about it. Eventually it was arranged that Marriner would go out to "Woodley" at about six o'clock and discuss the matter there. Events in Manchuria are obviously affecting the situation so far as the Administration is concerned, and unless the situation calms itself we may find ourselves faced with a passive instead of an active participation in the Conference.[7] Thus the Secretary, who had at one time thought of heading the Delegation, was now inclined to believe that it would be a mistake but did not wish to shut the door definitely on the possibility. The result was that there would be no actual selection of the delegates nor announcement until the situation regarding Manchuria clarified, which may mean weeks, if not two or two and a half months.

He approved the idea of appointing two assistant delegates, namely, Rogers and Hugh Wilson, whose appointment would be announced ahead of the Conference, and who would start the interde-

---

[6] A brief summary of the events of the night of September 18–19, 1931, and its antecedents is given in Arnold J. Toynbee, *Survey of International Affairs, 1931* (London: Oxford University Press, 1932), pp. 430–447.

[7] The Japanese army had begun to move to the far north of Manchuria in late October. From November 4 to 6 a battle took place between Japanese troops and those of the Chinese General Ma Chan-shan. By mid-November General Ma's forces had been dispersed. On November 18, 1931, Secretary Stimson called in the Japanese Ambassador to tell him that the United States regarded such action as a violation of the Kellogg-Briand Pact and the Nine-Power Treaty. Henry L. Stimson, *The Far Eastern Crisis* (New York: Harper & Bros., 1936), pp. 70–75.

partmental technical conferences.[8] He also approved in principle the idea of an Advisory Committee to enable the various shades of American opinion to have a chance to say their say. Finally he agreed to summon Admiral Pratt [William V. Pratt, Chief of Naval Operations] and ask him to select a navy contingent.

On the whole a rather satisfactory talk, but it was obvious that for the moment at least his mind was on Manchuria and that he regarded disarmament as of distinctly secondary importance. . .

November 14–15 [1931].

A return of Indian summer gave us a chance to motor Edith [9] to the Zoo and through Rock Creek Park. She enjoyed every minute, but could not help refraining, after the Cadillac, from commenting on the Chrysler as "la toute petite auto de Daddy." In the evening we went to see Lynn Fontanne in "Reunion in Vienna," a very bright but very broad comedy, the likes of which certainly could not have been shown in this country a few years ago. Our enjoyment was heightened by sitting directly behind the Chief Justice and Mrs. Hughes, the former of whom enjoyed himself to the full, while the latter sat rather rigidly throughout most of the last two acts. . .

December 4 [1931].

We have had our meeting with the Army and Navy concerning the air clauses of the Convention this afternoon. As I foresaw, there was no disposition on the part of either Army or Navy to make the slightest contribution toward allaying the fears of the world by agreeing to a limitation other than numerical of the air forces. They took the position that our needs of defense were so special that we needed a large number of heavy bombers to protect our coast from invasion, and to sink the hostile troop transports some two or three hundred miles off our coast. . . Suffice it to say, however, that having now run over the draft Convention,[10] we find that the Army is willing to

[8] Mr. James Grafton Rogers, Assistant Secretary of State, was not sent as a delegate, when the final selection of the delegation was made. U.S. Dept. of State, *Foreign Relations, 1931*, I, 534–535.

[9] The Moffats' first child, Edith Alice Pierrepont Moffat, had been born on October 14, 1929, in Berne, Switzerland. Since there are not many personal references in the Moffat diaries, some have been left for their interest and the light they cast on Mr. Moffat and his activities outside the Department.

[10] The Sixth Session of the Preparatory Commission for the Disarmament Confer-

reduce our forces to 2½ times their present size; that the Navy is willing to reduce its expenditures from $340,000,000 to a mere $600,-000,000; and that neither is willing to reduce in any way our aviation. On the other hand, I think that these meetings have done far more good than the written record would show. Everyone has had a chance to speak his mind fully in a gathering where even the most extravagant claims were received with unfailing good humor. As soon as the delegates are appointed I think that they will be prepared to view the problem far more realistically. . .

January 4 [1932].

This morning Ted Marriner, Boal and myself went out to spend the morning with the Secretary at "Woodley." He was taking the day off and decided to devote the morning to disarmament and the afternoon to the Far East. The Far East, however, kept intruding upon our discussions in the way of telephone calls or documents being brought in. There is no question but that it is the Secretary's real interest.[11]

At first he took up the draft instructions that we had prepared, but laid them down again and asked for an oral report as to what were the principal problems to be decided. He indicated that having been brought up in the Anglo-Saxon school, he dreaded codification of principles and liked to leave decisions until circumstances made it essential for them to be reached. Basically he wondered at the purpose of our armed forces. Had the theory of offensive-defense gone by the board? Did the Kellogg-Briand Pact so change human nature that only the defense of one's actual territory was essential? He said that he, for one, was by no means sure.[12] He had had to un-

---

ence had agreed upon a draft convention concerning armaments, which was to be the basis for discussion at the Geneva Disarmament Conference in 1932.

[11] On the evening of January 4, 1932, Mr. Stimson laid before President Hoover his plan to send notes to China and Japan stating that the United States did not intend to recognize any *de facto* situation or "any treaty or agreement entered into between those governments, or agents thereof, which may impair the treaty rights of the United States or its citizens in China, including those which relate to the sovereignty, the independence, or the territorial and administrative integrity of the Republic of China, or to the international policy relative to China, commonly known as the open-door policy." The identical notes were delivered to the Japanese Ambassador and the Chinese Chargé d'Affaires on January 7, 1932. Stimson, *Far Eastern Crisis*, pp. 95–99. U.S. Department of State, *Foreign Relations of the United States, 1932*, vol. III, *The Far East* (Washington: Government Printing Office, 1948), pp. 7–8.

[12] Secretary Stimson's views on disarmament have been summed up by him: "His

learn a great deal of what was considered axiomatic in his youth, and did not have very clear-cut convictions as to the new order. He then asked how we had gotten along with the Army and Navy and when we told him that they were in opposition to almost any form of reduction, much less limitation, he remarked that with the Army it was essential to convince Secretary Hurley [Patrick Hurley, Secretary of War], who would then convince the Generals; while with the Navy it was necessary to convince the Admirals who would then convince Secretary Adams [Charles Francis Adams, Secretary of the Navy].

As far as the Army is concerned, the Secretary simplified the problem enormously. He said that our Army was of one-half the size of the German Army in proportion to its population, and that it was so small that obviously no one could cavil at it. We pointed out that it was necessary to decide a basis for Army figures. Was this the present size of the Army or the National Defense Army of 280,000 men? [13] The Secretary replied that he would leave that to General Dawes [Charles G. Dawes, American Ambassador to Great Britain and Chairman of the American delegation to the Disarmament Conference], who after all, would have to assume the major responsibility. . .

Changing from his rather petulant tone to a very earnest and convincing bit of argument, the Secretary said that when it came to navies the guiding principle of our Delegation must be that the superiority on the seas of the Anglo-Saxon nations must not be imperiled. In other words, he felt that the greatest gauge of peace was the fact that the continental powers could not devote the necessary strength to build up to and rival the great peace-loving naval powers. For this reason he felt that the British, from their own point of view, were making [a] tactical mistake in asking for a reduction in the size of capital ships.

With the air problems we reached even fewer conclusions, and

---

own conviction was that armaments were less a cause than a result of international insecurity, and he was not optimistic about the prospects for disarmament unless and until the major political difficulties of Europe should have been materially eased." Henry L. Stimson and McGeorge Bundy, *On Active Service* (New York: Harper & Bros., 1948), p. 266.

[13] The National Defense Act of June 4, 1920, had provided for a Regular Army in peacetime not to exceed 280,000 enlisted men and 18,000 officers. But as of June 30, 1932, there were only 119,889 enlisted men and 13,153 officers in the Regular Army.

merely had occasion to outline the Army's view on gas warfare. We were interrupted for the last time by Hornbeck's [Stanley K. Hornbeck, Chief of the Division of Far Eastern Affairs] telephoning . . . and so left after having arranged for the Secretary to receive the four delegates tomorrow at 12. They will lunch with the President, continue, if they desire, their informal discussions in the afternoon, and hold a full dress meeting with the Army and Navy advisers on Wednesday morning at 12.

January 5 [1932].

. . . By being on the hill I missed the morning meeting of the delegates, to whom Mr. Stimson made an extemporaneous address, which showed that our 2½ hours yesterday at "Woodley" had not been in vain. He is a curious man in that while talking to him you have a feeling that he has not gathered the point you are trying to make, only to find it come out anywhere from a day to a week later, rephrased, redressed, but seized in all its details. Following this meeting, the delegates went over to the White House, where they were invited to lunch with the President. I am told that the President, in his conversation, brought out four main points: (1) That armies must be split into two parts — (a) an absolute minimum necessary for the maintenance of internal order; (b) further troops. Relativity between nations should only apply to these further troops. (2) Navies, on the other hand, are relatively without police function and any *pro rata* cut or any extension of the life of existing treaties which would have the same effect would be welcome. (3) As to aviation he felt that the difference between civil and military aviation was constantly growing less, as the speed of civil planes was being increased. (4) As far as budgets were concerned, he felt that any budgetary cut in so far as it affected the armies should not touch the internal order army, but merely such sections of the army as were over and above this minimum force.

An afternoon session of the Delegation was held at 3.30, General Dawes in the chair. He looked older than when I last saw him, but displayed a good deal of energy when he spoke in his high, rasping voice with underslung pipe always between his teeth. At his right sat

U.S. Bureau of the Census, *Statistical Abstract of the United States, 1933* (Washington: Government Printing Office, 1933), p. 144.

Senator Swanson, with an unlighted cigar, interrupting the conversation from time to time with jocular remarks. On his left sat Norman Davis [financier], slouched in the chair, occasionally speaking in a low, measured voice, which commanded attention. The fourth member, Miss Woolley [Mary E. Woolley, president of Mount Holyoke College], sat silently most of the time. She only spoke on one subject, and then to ask a few questions which utterly disconcerted the Navy. If I had had my eyes closed I should have imagined it was Margaret Perry [Mrs. Moffat's aunt] speaking both as to intonation and as to the direct way in which she approached a problem. The meeting really accomplished nothing. Dawes invited both the Army and Navy experts to tell him the results of their studies, and when they had finished talking for an uninterrupted hour, he sat back and said, "Well, if this is a sample of what we are going to listen to for six months, the Lord help us. I am an expert in only one thing, and that is in other experts. My experience in conferences has taught me to pay no attention to them. Give them their head for a while, and then reach your own conclusions." "Years ago," he continued, "I read a book on the breakdown of the Atom. I did not understand a word of it, but I kept on reading. Finally, in the last chapter when it came to conclusions, I did get what the author was driving at and was glad I had read the text because it gave me added confidence. That is your purpose as experts. If, in our own country and among our own people, we cannot simplify the problem more than you have done, what will it be like when we are faced with 63 delegations?" General Dawes then went on to quote Lord Cecil, who, he said, was now hopeful of accomplishing something in only two fields, namely, aviation and submarines. These, he said, were peculiarly British problems, but the fact remained that if we went after a limited achievement we would have a better chance of success than otherwise. . .

January 8 [1932].

Today General Dawes left for Chicago and threw a bombshell into the camp by announcing his resignation as Ambassador to Great Britain and as delegate to the Conference at the conclusion of the general discussions. As he phrased it, he would "leave the technical negotiations to others." Later I gathered from Mr. Rogers that while they had known for some days that he was going to resign as Ambassador, they had all understood that he would take on and keep the job as Chairman of the Delegation. The reasons motivating his action are shrouded in considerable mystery. Probably it is a combination of reasons having to do with: (1) assisting the unhealthy banking situation in the Middle West; (2) helping at the World's Fair; (3) combating the growing anti-Republican feeling in the State of Illinois, et cetera.[14] The man has extraordinarily quick comprehension, but to my mind he carries scorn of detail and accuracy to such a point as to be a great liability. . .

January 15 [1932].

The confusion daily increases. The newspapermen are convinced that General Dawes was not going to sail but would remain behind to take the head of the Credit Corporation. On the other hand, he informed Ted Marriner at 12 o'clock that he was going. Finally the Secretary got him on the telephone at the White House and asked him point-blank whether or not he actually planned to go. His reply was evasive, from which we have drawn our own conclusions. Meantime Mr. Pepper [George W. Pepper, lawyer and ex-senator from Pennsylvania] declined an appointment as delegate. At about half-past three a letter came in from the Secretary of War violently protesting against accepting any form of budgetary limitation.[15] In view of the fact that he had told the Secretary two days before that if his advisers brought up any new arguments against it he would come over with the Chief of Staff [Douglas MacArthur] and General Simonds [George S. Simonds, Assistant Chief of Staff], Mr. Stimson feels that they have not played quite square with him. Finally, just as he was most incensed by this, the telephone bell rang and the President directed the Secretary to appoint Mr. Goldsborough, the son of the Senator from Maryland [Phillips Lee Goldsborough], to the Delegation, for personal reasons. When the Secretary asked what were his

[14] Mr. Dawes says that he resigned, because he wished to become president of the Reconstruction Finance Corporation. Charles G. Dawes, *Journal as Ambassador to Great Britain* (New York: The Macmillan Co., 1939), p. 432.

[15] The Chairman of the American delegation was authorized to say in his opening speech: "We are prepared to consider a limitation of expenditure on matériel as a complementary method to direct limitation, feeling that it may prove useful to prevent a qualitative race, if and when quantitative limitation has been effected." U. S. Department of State, *Foreign Relations of the United States, 1932* (Washington: Government Printing Office, 1948), I, 30.

qualifications, the extraordinary reply came through that he was 26 years of age and had had hard luck.

January 16 [1932].

. . . Here we are within 96 hours before the Delegation sails with the make-up of the Delegation itself still open, without any instructions, with no authorization from Congress, no appropriation, consequently no travel orders issued, and what is still more extraordinary nothing to do about it. . .

January 18 [1932].

Today everything which started at sixes and sevens smoothed out. The President finally decided on the make-up of the Delegation and went back to our original recommendation of eight weeks ago, namely to make Mr. Stimson the titular head with Gibson [Hugh Gibson, American Ambassador to Belgium] the acting head. This, however, will not be announced until General Dawes' retirement is made public. Then in the late afternoon and after considerable haranguing and sniping, the House authorized our appropriation for the full amount of $450,000. To be sure it will still be necessary to get the appropriation itself through, but this is a distinctly less important proposition.

Finally the Secretary signed the "letter of guidance" to Hugh Gibson, on which we had been working for three whole weeks.[16] Marriner and Tuck [S. Pinkney Tuck, technical adviser to the Disarmament Conference] left for New York and the actual getaway will take place with less confusion than might be imagined. . .

Fifty-nine nations were represented at Geneva when the Conference for the Reduction and Limitation of Armaments opened on February 2, 1932. For three weeks the delegates met in plenary sessions, which were devoted to organization and to the exposition of the main theses on disarmament. Country after country affirmed its willingness to disarm and explained the best way to achieve this for itself and others. France underplayed her insistence on security before reduction of armaments; Germany advanced her claims in nonprovocative terms. Indeed all the participants were so earnest in their attachment to the general principle of disarmament, that it seemed possible that the specific technical and polit-

[16] *Ibid.*, pp. 1–12.

ical problems might be solved in the committees and subcommittees to which the delegates dispersed on February 24.[17]

In Washington, once the American delegation had left, the tension and strain in the Division of Western European Affairs eased. The problems were now ones of coordination and communication, focusing in the first phase of the conference on the preparation of Hugh Gibson's opening speech. The President, the Departments of State, War, and Navy had to modify, advise, and agree upon measures, as the situation changed daily in Geneva.

On February 9, Mr. Gibson outlined the nine-point proposal of the United States in regard to disarmament:

1. The draft convention should be used as the basis for discussion, but supplementary proposals could also be considered.
2. The terms of the Washington and London Naval Treaties should be extended.
3. The figures on naval tonnage, however, should be reduced from the levels agreed to at Washington and London, as soon as all parties have entered this framework.
4. Submarines should be abolished.
5. Civilian populations should be protected against air bombardment.
6. Gas and bacteriological warfare should be abolished.
7. Armed forces should be computed on the basis of the effectives necessary for policing plus a defense body.
8. Aggressive arms, such as tanks and heavy mobile guns, should be specially restricted.
9. Limitation of expenditure might be considered as a complementary measure to direct limitation.[18]

January 21 [1932].

. . . In the afternoon Mr. Rogers sent for me to say that the President was distinctly worried by the flood of pacifist protests which had been reaching him from all over the country as a result of newspaper despatches appearing in the past week to the effect that the United States would take a passive role only at the Conference rather than assume leadership.[19] He wanted the Secretary to prepare an opening speech for Mr. Gibson which would counteract that

[17] William T. Stone, "The World Disarmament Conference," *Foreign Policy Reports*, VIII (May 11, 1932), 60–66.

[18] U. S. Dept. of State, *Foreign Relations, 1932*, I, 29–30.

[19] President Hoover had said on January 5, 1932, that the conference "would be of less than primary concern" to the United States. And it was known that the dominant current of thought in the Department of State held it to be Europe's place to take the first positive step in the conference. Stimson and Bundy, *On Active Service*, pp. 266–267; Arnold J. Toynbee, *Survey of International Affairs, 1932* (London: Oxford University Press, 1933), p. 202.

sentiment. Mr. Rogers and I talked it over at some length, but to me at least, the task seemed like eating your cake and having it, as words alone would not satisfy the pacifist groups and there seems no intention of taking any action to meet their wishes. However, their influence is so strong that something must be done to make them feel that the administration is in earnest. I spent most of the evening trying to draft a short statement from the Secretary to be included verbatim in the Gibson speech which would give a tone of leadership without holding out false promises. . .

January 27 [1932].

The President again reminded the Secretary about the part of the opening Gibson statement which he still wishes to have prepared here. Mr. Rogers completed his draft this morning which was what he calls a "poem" — a really beautiful piece of literature but conceived entirely on generalities. The one concrete criticism which I made to him was that in emphasizing our failure to have a thesis, a program or a firm conviction on any point, he gave the impression that we were entering the Conference without an objective, an admission which I felt would be objectionable to the very groups he was trying to please. Mr. Rogers said that he was none too convinced of the wisdom of his method of approach and was going to let the Secretary decide whether he preferred the more specific lines of approach we had worked out in WE [Division of Western European Affairs] or his vaguer and more general statement. . .[20]

February 11, 12, 13 and 14 [1932].

As far as disarmament is concerned, these have been four quiet days. The opening speeches of the various delegations have continued

[20] Mr. Moffat reported in his diary of January 29, 1932: "The Secretary read over the draft speeches at breakfast this morning and decided that Rogers' draft was more in line with what the President wanted than the others. He, therefore, left it with the President after Cabinet meeting this morning and agreed to go back and talk it over with him at half-past three. The President was in what he described as a 'belligerent mood.' He said that the Rogers' draft was not nearly strong enough and proceeded to interlineate certain strengthening phrases and also to block out in longhand a paragraph concerning the western hemisphere. The Secretary's preoccupation was not to do anything at least until the present crisis is over which might imply a further weakening of our Navy. We took the draft and the somewhat divergent improvements suggested by the President and the Secretary upstairs and tried to weave them into a cohesive whole. The Secretary said that he would have liked to rewrite it

three or four a day. It is interesting to analyze them — not with
a view to picking out the differences of opinion — but to see on what
points all the powers have agreed. Thus, every speaker to date has
come out in favor of abolishing gas and bacteriological warfare and in
favor of devising some means of protecting the civilian populations
against an aerial bombardment. (Parenthetically, I note more and
more reference to bombardment planes as a special category.) Likewise nearly every speaker has favored either the suspension or the
strict limitation of "aggressive armaments". . .[21]

Meanwhile the situation in the Far East goes from bad to worse.
On Friday I went out to "Woodley" for deck tennis and found the
Secretary very tired but feeling that the situation as far as Japan was
concerned was under control.

Saturday Lilla and Peter returned from New York.[22] She is surprisingly well and full of energy, although not allowed to go out at
night for another ten days or two weeks. Peter is an ugly baby
(which augurs well) and has lungs of steel. He is gaining fast and
already shows signs of extreme independence. . .

On March 19 the Conference adjourned for a three weeks' Easter
recess. Little had yet been accomplished in weeding and selecting from the
mass of plans which had been advanced in the plenary sessions. And
Arthur Henderson, the President of the Conference, asked the delegations
to prepare, in the interim between meetings, explanatory and detailed
proposals to supplement their general statements.

Norman Davis of the American delegation was ordered home during
the recess to report and advise the Department of State.

March 28 [1932].

Norman Davis arrived this morning to spend three days in Washington. Unfortunately the Secreary is ill in bed with a feverish grippe

himself in his own language, that such indeed had been his practice at other conferences, but that with the Chinese situation at its most acute phase, he could only devote a few moments time and must rely on our discretion." U.S. Dept. of State,
Foreign Relations, 1932, I, 25-30, contains the text of Gibson's opening speech.

[21] This popular notion that a distinction could be made between "aggressive" and
"defensive" armaments was ridiculed by Winston Churchill in a prophetic speech
made in the House of Commons in May 1932. Winston S. Churchill, *The Second
World War*, vol. I, *The Gathering Storm* (Boston: Houghton Mifflin Co., 1948),
pp. 71-73.

[22] The Moffats' second child, Jay Pierrepont Moffat, called "Peter" in the family,
was born in New York City on January 17, 1932.

and cannot hope to see him before tomorrow. The better part of the day was spent in conference with Rogers, Klots and myself.

It is impossible to boil down a seven hour conversation into one memorandum. The following notes, therefore, will merely touch the high spots of his talk.

Basically he was more optimistic than he had been at any time for the past several years as to the possibility of a political appeasement in Europe. The key to the situation is Tardieu [23] whom he finds distinctly more rational than he has been in the past. Not only is he less nationalistic, but he has apparently reached the conclusion that the days of French dictation to Europe are over; that the depression is reaching such proportions that it is a matter of economic life and death to get Europe thoroughly reorganized and to make some savings on the French military budget. In his view, the disarmament conference will eventually develop into a great European peace conference. He admits that any Franco-German *détente* is impossible until France has reached definite understandings with England and Italy. . .

It was only in the afternoon that we got down to disarmament as such.

He led off by saying that there was unanimity in the Delegation, that we would have to assume an attitude of leadership; that the policy of sitting by and playing the honest broker was not sufficient to get the Conference out of the doldrums; that as we among other things had an interest in speeding up its work toward a hasty conclusion, we must take a more active stand than hitherto. There were a number of points in which he felt that we could take a distinct lead; on two of these we had already more or less outlined our position, namely on the limitation or abolition of aggressive weapons, and on the two computations of personnel into police contingents and defense contingents.[24] There were two other points, however, in which he wished to suggest we adopt a more aggressive attitude. In the first place, he felt that we should agree to a global budgetary cut and in

[23] André Tardieu, chief French delegate to the Disarmament Conference, had become head of the French Government in February 1932, when the Laval ministry fell.

[24] In his opening speech on February 9, 1932, Mr. Gibson had advocated the abolition of aggressive weapons and "the computation of the number of armed forces on the basis of the effectives necessary for the maintenance of internal order plus some suitable contingent for defense." U. S. Dept. of State, *Foreign Relations, 1932*, I, 25.

the second place to the abolition of all military and naval aviation.[25] We discussed these two points for some hours.

The arguments in favor of both points are difficult to meet on the basis of straight logic. None the less, I had the distinct impression, in which I believe the others concurred, that it was going far beyond what public opinion would stand for in this country, and that adopting either of these two positions might well mean the defeat of any treaty in the Senate. Since the Delegation sailed two months or more ago, there has been a noticeable increase in the isolationist sentiment in the country. There are many manifestations of this. You find the Senate despite the nation-wide organized pressure of the various pacifist groups unable or unwilling to agree to the ratification of the World Court Protocols; you find the bankers more and more talking of disassociating American economy from European; you find the trend in Congress not toward reducing tariffs to assist trade but toward actually increasing items; you see the tendency in shipping legislation more and more to isolate us from foreign intercourse; you see the League referred to with less and less respect; and you see in editorial comment from one end of the country to the other a growing sentiment that we are sufficient unto ourselves and that our policy of cooperation has not borne fruit. If to the foregoing, you add the opposition of the War and Navy Departments, which would be inevitable as one or the other unalterably opposes the two concessions under consideration, you reach a situation which would probably foredoom a treaty built along these lines to failure. On the one hand, the country is bitterly opposed to the bombardment of cities by aviation; on the other hand, there is a sentimental attachment to the growth of aviation as an arm in which we especially excel. Mr. Davis maintained that if the President and the Secretary of State should inform War and Navy that certain lines of thought were the American policy, the armed forces would promptly fall into line. . .[26]

March 29 [1932].

Norman Davis went out to "Woodley" to see the Secretary who

[25] The War Department had advised the delegation on March 11, 1932, that of the proposals advanced about military and naval aviation the one which provided for "total abolition of military and naval aviation, rigidly enforced" was most acceptable. *Ibid.*, p. 52.

[26] For another statement of Mr. Davis' views see *ibid.*, pp. 62–67.

summoned Rogers and Klots. The Secretary was in bed and feeling quite poorly. The conversation lasted about two and a half hours and was punctuated by frequent appearances of Mrs. Stimson who made grimaces to Klots to try and break up the interview. Much of the time, I am told, the Secretary lay back on his pillow with his eyes closed. His reaction was as follows: He was not convinced that we should assume too much a position of leadership; he refused to consider any budgetary cut which would affect the Navy on the ground that it would freeze us in our present position of inferiority; this was the more important in that international events might well push us into a position of building up to treaty limits; with regard to aviation he could not agree with Norman Davis' recommendation for the total abolition of military and naval aviation; to his mind we could never afford to give up observation planes either for scouting or for spotting the effect of our naval fire; with regard to aggressive weapons, he was in complete accord with the Delegation's representations; while he thought the plan of computation of strength ingenious, he felt it should be used for purposes of persuasion rather than for purposes of publicity. I had two accounts of this interview, one from Klots and the other, and much more briefly, from Norman Davis. . .

April 2 [1932].

A hectic day. Norman Davis telephoned early in the morning from New York suggesting that we delay no further in sending the Delegation an indication of the Secretary's preference to have the speech on aggressive weapons made the keynote of our activity [27] and to use the formula on the computation of effectives for persuasion in subcommittee. He also asked us to add a paragraph saying that he entirely concurred with Hugh Gibson's recommendations against the President making a speech at this time and would do his best to call it off.[28] I drafted this telegram and took it downstairs to discuss with

[27] Mr. Gibson announced the American proposals in a speech at Geneva on April 11. About aggressive weapons he said: "Fear of invasion is based on the existence of peculiarly aggressive weapons in land warfare, tanks, heavy mobile artillery and the use of gas. The feeling of security will not be restored until we restore to defense the superiority over aggression which it enjoyed in former times. The only way to restore such superiority is to do away with the weapons which I have just mentioned." *Ibid.*, p. 79.

[28] A telegram from Mr. Gibson on April 1 had advised against a speech by the President at that time, because the American proposals needed a fuller and more de-

Mr. Rogers. He was apprehensive of the tendency of the Department to discourage the President on such frequent occasions from making speeches on foreign affairs and felt that we must carefully balance the disadvantages that would be gained by having such a speech made compared to the advantages of letting the President proclaim himself publicly the initiator of our policy, a role which he had laid aside during the Sino-Japanese crisis.[29] While we were talking, Admiral Pratt came in to discuss certain changes he had made in the telegram we had drawn up listing the agreements reached in the meeting on Wednesday. In particular he insisted that the Navy retain torpedo planes. . . By the time we had written up a clean copy of the telegram with the various amendments proposed by General MacArthur and Admiral Pratt, it was nearly twelve o'clock. I went over to General MacArthur's office in order to let him see Admiral Pratt's changes and initial the final draft. He read it through hastily while a look of amazement came over his face; he read it again and the storm burst forth. He said that the introduction by Admiral Pratt of torpedo planes had altered the entire picture; that for years the Army and the Navy had been arguing as to which should have charge of the defense of our coasts; that it had been agreed that it was the function of the Army. Now, in one fell swoop, Admiral Pratt was proposing to cancel this agreement by allowing to the Navy weapons which he wished to take away from the Army. Torpedo planes were a form of bombing plane and if any bombs were allowed either branch of the Service, he must insist upon the right of the Army to have its share. Turning from the interdepartmental question, however, which in the last analysis was only a row between two branches of the Service, he pointed out the jockeying that would ensue if any deviation were made from the general principle. He had modified his own belief in the total

---

tailed statement than the President could make, the President's influence would be even more necessary in the future, and the formula was already scheduled for early consideration by the Conference. *Ibid.*, pp. 69–70.

[29] "The President is anxious," Mr. Moffat wrote in his diary of March 31, 1932, "to make himself the speeches which should be made in Geneva on aggressive weapons and on the computation of strength. Apparently his idea is that it would be a good idea to tie up these ideas with his personal leadership and that he could enthuse the country in the work of the Conference. To the rest of us, it seemed that such a plan would be a great mistake. Foreign nations would regard the plan less as an attempt to convince the Assembly and to reach an agreement than as a political gesture for domestic consumption in this country."

abolition of military and naval aviation, and had accepted a compromise during our conference with Admiral Pratt. Now, however, he considered the situation entirely changed and withdrew his support of the agreement on aviation and on budgetary limitation. He asked me to explain to the Secreary of State that he was not doing this out of pique but on a real question of principle. . .

April 4 [1932].

Norman Davis arrived this morning for the day. I joined him for breakfast at the Metropolitan Club at 8.15, telling him the whole story of the events of the past three or four days. It was clear that we would have to have another meeting between Pratt and Mac-Arthur; the question was (1) whether to see MacArthur first and (2) whether Mr. Davis should see the President before or after the joint meeting. He finally decided to call on General MacArthur first. The latter kept us for nearly three-quarters of an hour developing his theories as to the future of the Army. Briefly he made a few essential points: (1) That aviation was the newest branch of the service and the most expensive. Between 25 and 35 per cent of our Army budget was already devoted to aviation and Trubee Davison [Assistant Secretary of War] was constantly coming back demanding an additional 15 to 20 million dollars each year. (2) Its value as an instrument of war was still undemonstrated. For instance, in the Shanghai fighting where the Japanese had had 100 planes in the air unopposed and were able to bomb constantly a limited area with impunity, they did remarkably little damage to the 19th Chinese Army although they succeeded in destroying four hundred million dollars worth of civilian property and dispossesing over 10,000 noncombatants. (3) That the whole tendency of war, since the idea of the Prussian staff had become generally accepted, was to regard it as a struggle between whole nations rather than between professional organizations. Effectively to arm all nations or to provide the Army and Navy with weapons that could subdue an entire nation was beyond the economic scope of any power and was more than any other factor driving the world into bankruptcy. It cost no more than it would decades ago to keep the same number of men under arms. It was the exorbitant cost of new auxiliary machines of war, such as heavy artillery, tanks, aviation, et cetera, that was making our defense cost so many times its prewar level. Money spent on aviation was money thrown away as when the equipment was used up, there was no salvage value left. If all nations of the world could agree to give up military and naval aviation, the effect upon budgets would be greater than it is possible to calculate. As it is, with the pressure of economy and decreased appropriations, he feared that his Army would be destroyed, as in order to keep up a new and dramatic arm in which the public is interested and on whose retention it insists, the time may come when we will have to reduce other branches below the point of safety. In his idea, our ultimate aim should be to obtain an agreement on the part of all nations that they would give no government support in any form to aviation. In other words, to give up military and naval aviation in their entirety and not to subsidize directly or indirectly civilian aviation. He admitted that this was too radical a solution but felt it should be the ultimate goal. . .

At half-past three came the meeting with General MacArthur and Admiral Pratt. The latter felt himself on the defensive, particularly from a political point of view. Rather more easily than we had anticipated, we were all able to agree on a formula which was modified two or three times in the course of the conference but was eventually subscribed to by everyone present. Sent this off to the Delegation at about half-past six.[30]

April 11 [1932].

Found a telegram from Hugh Gibson which had been in the Department on Sunday and which gave us all great concern. In it he requested authorization for making a short speech on capital ships if the subject should be introduced by any speaker. In this speech he wished to make three points: (1) that the capital ship was a defensive and not an offensive weapon; (2) that if the land powers agree with our point of view we would probably be willing to modify our stand on capital ships; and (3) that we were asking the land powers to give up a possible military superiority much as we had given up our naval superiority at Washington.[31] Before ten o'clock a telegram had gone

---

[30] The agreement stated that the problem of aviation was linked with that of submarines. If submarines were abolished, bombardment aviation could be done away with. U. S. Dept. of State, *Foreign Relations, 1932*, I, 73.

[31] Mr. Gibson thought that the suggestion would be made by some nation at the Conference that capital ships be considered aggressive weapons and be limited even

out that the speech was not to be delivered but that our full views would be telegraphed as soon as possible. The rift in views which I have been fearing for some time now seems complete. Both Bill Castle [William R. Castle, Under Secretary of State] and Mr. Rogers sent for me in the course of the day to talk over the situation. It is clear that the Delegation does not yet appreciate the change of feeling which has swept over the country since last January; the growing concern over the situation in the Far East and its possible repercussions in our policy; the growing feeling that our Navy is improperly equipped to carry out our policies; the visible change in attitude on the part of the Secretary and higher Departmental officials, and finally the diminishing in strength of the pacifist groups. Mr. Rogers, who keeps in close touch along these lines, has made pretty shrewd diagnoses of what the country will stand for. He felt that the brief statement if made might produce a repercussion which would undo all the good that has been accomplished at Geneva to date. He felt that our idea of the self-sufficiency of the arms plan had not been fully grasped in Geneva, and that the Delegation was still too interested in rounding out a finished and logical document. The great thing was for the Delegation to strain every nerve to keep the emphasis on land questions at least until the great land powers had made contributions to the cause of disarmament equivalent to those made by the navy powers. I drafted a telegram setting forth these views, which was strengthened by Mr. Rogers who sent it on to Bill. Bill took it over to the White House and found the President fully as concerned as ourselves. The President took the draft, again strengthened the language and added a last sentence in his own handwriting to the effect that we would be willing to discuss navies as a whole problem but not piecemeal.[32]

May 4 [1932].

. . . I got hold of an advance copy of the speech Bill Castle is planning to make tonight, a speech which reflects the President's in-

---

more strictly than at the Washington Conference. He desired permission to say: "My country would not refuse to deal still more drastically with the subject of capital ships whenever other nations whose primary reliance on armaments is placed on land forces have made the sacrifice of possible superiority over their neighbors which the United States made at the Washington Conference." *Ibid.*, pp. 75–76.

[32] *Ibid.*, p. 76.

most views but which I fear will be none too welcome to the Secretary.[33] He attacks with extreme bitterness the League idea of enforcing peace through the use of force; he definitely rules out the official boycott as a weapon which the administration would in any circumstances countenance; he rejects the idea of joint action of a positive nature; and concludes with a development of what he terms the "Hoover doctrine" of not recognizing the fruits of aggression. I fear that the speech may have unfortunate repercussions.

Lunched with Bill Castle and he told me quite a bit about the genesis of the speech. It seems that the President felt that a speech on these lines should be no longer delayed and that whereas it was his first thought to make it himself, no suitable opportunity arose and he accordingly felt that Bill should do it. The text was personally checked by the President and approved three or four days ago. . .[34]

The second phase of the conference lasted until June, when many of the technical committees reported.[35] The results of their three to four months' study of qualitative disarmament were discouraging. The attempt to solve the technical problems of disarmament on qualitative lines had failed. The experts could agree no more than the politicians.[36]

[33] On May 15, 1932, Mr. Moffat wrote of a conversation which he had with Mr. Castle: "Bill gave me a lift home and asked for my impressions. I think that he had been somewhat apprehensive over the Secretary's reaction to his speech of May 4th. I told him that I had . . . asked Allen Klots. It seems that his [Castle's] speech had been given pretty fully in the Paris 'Herald' of March [May] 5, which he [Stimson] had seen at Lisbon and that while he [Stimson] had seriously deprecated the section on the boycott, he had not in the least resented the 'Hoover doctrine'."

Charles A. Beard, *American Foreign Policy in the Making 1932–1940* (New Haven: Yale University Press, 1946), p. 156, refers to a statement which Mr. Castle made to him in 1946 about Stimson's reaction to the speech of May 4, 1932. Mr. Castle then said that Stimson had told him after returning from Europe that the speech had been "ill-advised" and had cut "the ground from under his [Stimson's] feet in respect of the embargo question."

[34] Mr. Castle in a speech before the American Conference on International Justice said that President Hoover had determined that American foreign policy should be based on the Pact of Paris. The President thought that a deterrent "of the use of force would be to make valueless the results of war. Out of this earnest belief grew that new dictum in international law that territorial gains made by any nation guilty of breaking the terms of the Kellogg pact shall not be recognized." This was the "Hoover doctrine." Mr. Castle also said that the administration rejected the idea of using an embargo or boycott to force another nation to live up to the terms of the Kellogg-Briand Pact, because "an official boycott is an act which would almost surely lead to war." *New York Times,* May 5, 1932, p. 4.

[35] William T. Stone, "The World Disarmament Conference," *Foreign Policy Reports,* VIII (January 18, 1933), 268–271.

[36] The Land and Naval Commissions could not agree on the definition of aggressive and defensive weapons. The Effectives Committee had failed to reach agreement.

While the delegates were making slow and tortuous progress toward an impasse,[37] public opinion in the United States was beating a direct and hasty retreat from support of the conference. And the Department of State, whose policy was "motivated by the state of public opinion at home," had arrived, wrote Pierrepont Moffat, at a "clear-cut difference" of opinion with its delegation. The Department felt that "we must stand on our present position unless and until some affirmative action were taken by the land powers. There is too much feeling in the country that we are ready on all occasions to take the lead in offering to throw away anything and everything." [38]

May 12 [1932].

. . . Rogers . . . told me of a conversation he had had the previous day with Senator Borah, wherein the latter had told him that not only would there be no more money forthcoming from Congress for the continuation of the Conference after the present appropriation was past, but that the temper of both Houses was such that if six determined men set out to do so, they could get through a joint resolution requesting the President to withdraw the Delegation. The second item of interest which Rogers told me was that at a large meeting of lawyers in Washington last week with whom he had spent the better part of two days, not one question or comment had been asked or made concerning the Disarmament Conference, whereas he had been busy answering a steady flow of questions on reparations, World Court, Far East, and other phases of our foreign policies. In other words, he feels that the home front is tending to crumble behind the Delegation. . .

May 17 [1932].

Went out to "Woodley" at half-past five and played deck tennis with the Secretary, Klots, and Herbert Feis [Economic Adviser in the Department of State]. . . The conversation finally swung around to the question of financing the Delegation and keeping it going as long

---

The conclusions of the Air Commission were hedged with so many reservations as to be most discouraging. Only the Chemical and Bacteriological Committee had concurred about how qualitative disarmament should be applied in its field. Toynbee, *Survey, 1932*, pp. 226–233, gives a brief summary of the reports of the commissions.

[37] The many interruptions of the Conference's work also retarded its progress. The League consideration of the Sino-Japanese dispute, the French and German elections, the Easter recess, and the reparations meetings at Lausanne had either halted or slowed the work toward disarmament. *Ibid.*, pp. 212–213.

[38] Moffat diary, April 13, 1932.

as possible. He [Stimson] has convinced himself that if we made an attempt to get any more money we would meet with a flat refusal. He felt that at all costs we must not be put in a position where we might have to withdraw our Delegation while the Conference was actually in session. Therefore, the appropriation should be so strung out that we could count on its lasting until the latest date at which adjournment or recess was possible. This, of course, was just before the Assembly. He asked how we stood and I told him that the Delegation had enough to run on until August 10th at its present rate of speed, but that if the Department did not ask reimbursement of the $10,000 it had already advanced, it would only be necessary for the Delegation to save $15,000, or $5000 a month, in order to carry it until the Assembly. He told me to prepare a telegram the next day warning the delegation to pull in its belt immediately. . .

May 27 [1932].

A telegram in from the Delegation indicating that the peace groups in Geneva are dissatisfied with our stand and are thinking of making a move at the political conventions in Chicago in favor of a more liberal policy.[39] As I see the situation, neither the pacifist groups nor the big army and navy groups are gaining and the great middle mass of opinion is rather indefinite. In the face of the economic crisis, the political turmoil, the conventions, et cetera, the average voter is thinking of other things beside disarmament. His general attitude toward the Conference is that thus far it has done nothing; that it probably will do nothing; and that anything it may accomplish is all to the good and hence deserves a certain amount of friendly support. From what I gather, the President is a protagonist of far more sweeping concessions; that the Secretary is fearful that such concessions will not take into account the realities of our national policies. I know that the two have been discussing the situation back and forth for the better part of a week and have not yet reached a meeting of minds.[40]

[39] The Presidential nominating conventions of the Republican and Democratic Parties were held in Chicago during June and July 1932.

[40] On April 28, 1934, Mr. Moffat made a brief, but interesting, reference in his diary to a conversation which he had with former Secretary of State Stimson: "Saturday afternoon I played golf with Mr. Stimson at the Burning Tree, coming within one shot of my course record. He was full of the Japanese situation and made one remark which struck me quite deeply. He said, 'I make no claim to the verdict of history but I do hope that those of you who are in the Department will realize all

We have roughly ten days or two weeks left. If I diagnose the situation correctly, there will be toward the end of June or the beginning of July another favorable psychological moment, to a certain extent born of despair, for the powers to agree on something real. If that moment passes or negotiations break down, I think the outlook would be somewhat desperate. . .

June 3 [1932].

. . . The Secretary had been planning to spend the afternoon at "Woodley" but he came in unexpectedly at about three-thirty and sent for Rogers, Klots and myself. We told him that we felt our Government had to take a more broadminded attitude on aviation and that even though it meant a sacrifice to us we should advocate the total abolition of bombardment and bombardment planes. He was frankly skeptical and thought that this was taking too revolutionary a step. We told him that General MacArthur was willing to go even further and advocate the total abolition of all military and naval planes. This the Secretary refused to believe although we gave him in some detail General MacArthur's reasoning.[41] Muttering to himself that it was impossible that we quoted him accurately, he seized the telephone receiver and asked the Chief of Staff if he could come around for a few moments. I was a little bit hesitant that General MacArthur might qualify or weaken his statements, but he stuck to his guns firmly and we were treated to the unusual spectacle of the head of the War Department arguing for a decrease in a military arm while the head of the so-called peace department was attempting to prove him wrong. I need not go into the details of his talk as they parallel almost exactly his conversation with Mr. Davis and myself during the former's visit here last April. When he left the Secretary blew up, said that he [MacArthur] was predominantly concerned with his budget and was not thinking of all the occasions when aviation had been use-

---

I was able to accomplish with a pacifist President.' This coincides with my opinion that he would have gone down as one of the great Secretaries of State had he had a President who did not endeavor on every occasion to clip his wings. Mr. Hoover would move forward in jerks, become scared, and retreat. This gave the entire policy of his Administration a jerky, uneven and inconclusive character, but the fault was in the White House and not with Mr. Stimson."

[41] See the conversation of Jay Pierrepont Moffat and Norman Davis with General MacArthur, April 4, 1932.

ful — in Nicaragua, in Honduras,[42] et cetera, in maintaining our rights and protecting our citizens. Allen Klots suggested that he [Stimson] was arguing on the basis of special and relatively unimportant cases, whereupon the Secretary banged his fist on the desk and said, "Good God, Allen, is human life ever relatively unimportant?" The afternoon ended with an invitation to Admiral Pratt to meet the Secretary tomorrow morning when they could again thresh over the aviation question. A few days ago the Secretary was more nearly approaching the viewpoint of the President, but in the last two days he has again veered away and shown on all occasions his intense preoccupation with what may transpire in the Pacific. . .

June 6 [1932].

The Secretary called me this morning at about noon to hand me the final draft of his policy telegram with certain new modifications proposed by Admiral Pratt.[43] He said that he had taken into account certain of my criticisms, notably that based on the aviation problem, but that this telegram was in reply to a specific request from the Delegation to be furnished a general policy of which the different links fitted in one with the other. This was for use in the eventuality mentioned by Mr. Gibson, namely an attempt to solve the whole problem of disarmament by a broad and general scheme. If this should not develop and once again the Conference returned to the idea of limited objectives, then he would consider each problem on its own individual merits. In other words, he had been asked to map out a course for navigation on the high seas and not to furnish charts for the individual harbors in which his ship might eventually decide to seek shelter.

He had an appointment with the President at four o'clock and

[42] The United States had sent marines into both Honduras and Nicaragua in the nineteen-twenties to protect American interests, restore order, and supervise elections.

[43] The Secretary's telegram of June 7, 1932, said in part: "The world today is divided into two hemispheres in respect to the problems of peace and disarmament. One hemisphere contains the pressing disarmament problems of the European nations who are sitting at Geneva, the other the even more burning problem of preventing the spread of war in Asia. America sits between those two hemispheres, and her position at Geneva is in some respects limited by her responsibility on the Pacific. Our fleet today is so far below the London Treaty limits that the greatest care must be taken lest even apparently minor changes disqualify it from continuing to perform the peace duty which it is now performing. Furthermore the armament burdens which trouble Europe are primarily land armaments. . . Thus our naval power really has no influence in preventing European land disarmament." U.S. Dept. of State, *Foreign Relations, 1932*, I, 153–154.

was over there threshing out the problem for nearly an hour. I had anticipated that there might be some divergency of views but the President not only concurred in the Secretary's presentation but went further and strengthened the cautions of the telegram making further naval disarmament dependent on a material cut in land strength. The suggestion of a 33% cut in the defense contingents was the President's addition. The Secretary came to "Woodley" highly elated as he has not only developed a logical whole which he feels might be of real service in the cause of disarmament, but has done so in such a way as to command the support not only of the President but of General MacArthur and Admiral Pratt not to speak of his immediate staff in the Department. . .

From Washington President Hoover had been watching the Disarmament Conference with growing impatience. In June the reports of the technical committees indicated that the conference had reached a deadlock, and the large powers resorted to private conversations to solve their problems. When these informal negotiations seemed to produce no immediate formula, Hoover, motivated by a genuine desire to make a contribution and feeling the moment politically expedient, informed the Department of State of his desire to send his personal proposals on disarmament to Geneva.[44]

The President's hope was that armaments could be reduced by one third, based upon the following principles:

First: The Kellogg-Briand Pact, to which we are all signatories, can only mean that the nations of the world have agreed that they will use their arms solely for defense.

Second: This reduction should be carried out not only by broad general cuts in armaments but by increasing the comparative power of defense through decreases in the power of attack.

Third: The armaments of the world have grown up in general mutual relation to each other. And, speaking generally, such relativity should be preserved in making reductions.

Fourth: The reductions must be real and positive. They must effect economic relief.

Fifth: There are three problems to deal with — land forces, air forces and naval forces. They are all interconnected. No part of the proposals which I make can be disassociated one from the other.[45]

[44] William Starr Myers, *The Foreign Policies of Herbert Hoover 1929–1933* (New York: Charles Scribner's Sons, 1940), pp. 134–152; Hoover, *Cabinet and the Presidency*, pp. 352–357.
[45] The specific proposals in regard to land, air, and naval forces are given in U.S. Dept. of State, *Foreign Relations, 1932*, I, 213–214.

Saturday, June 18 [1932].

The Secretary sent for me as I was leaving for luncheon. He had just returned from the White House, where the President had again brought up his idea of making a sensational speech on disarmament, and announcing to the world the gist of our secret instruction. The idea had been broached before but the Secretary and Norman Davis had persuaded him that it would be better to let negotiations follow their normal course. Now, however, he was faced with a domestic political situation that required a gesture of leadership. Senator Borah was planning an attack, not only on the President's stand on prohibition but accusing him of having "sold out" to the reactionaries. An evidence of "liberal" thought on disarmament would go far toward destroying the effect of Borah's attack. Incidentally, the President is at heart a genuine liberal and one of the tragedies of his administration is that every effort he has made has been to conserve and not to build or reform. Coupled with that domestic situation was the situation arising from the Lausanne Conference. If he could show the world that Europe could save billions in armament, it would make it more difficult for a demand for debt cancellation to be pressed.[46] Accordingly, he wished to make a public statement along these lines indicated within 48 hours. The Secretary told Mr. Rogers, Allen Klots and myself to think it over and come back at three o'clock.

We three lunched together and threshed out the pros and cons. Rogers felt that the Secretary had so often restrained the President, that he should have compelling reasons before again rejecting his plan. But the more we studied the proposal, the greater appeared its dangers. We recognized that all we could do was to list the drawbacks, and if the President, with a broader view of both domestic and foreign angles, still wanted to go ahead no one could gainsay his decision. The Secretary, Klots and I felt that the following risks would be run:

[46] The Lausanne Conference of June 16 to July 9, 1932, had met to consider "intergovernmental debts" and, in particular, German reparations. It was agreed on July 9 by representatives of Great Britain, France, and Germany practically to do away with further payment of reparations by the Germans. On July 13, however, it was revealed that another agreement had been signed by Belgium, Great Britain, France, and Italy that the settlement as it related to German reparations "will not be effected until a satisfactory settlement has been reached between them and their own creditors." Toynbee, *Survey, 1932*, pp. 112–114.

(1) We might be accused of bad faith, or at least disingenuousness, on two counts:

(a) It was American initiative that had persuaded the delegates to abstain from public debate and attempt to settle the underlying political problems in confidential conversation. Now, at last, the very talks which we had been aiming to bring about were starting, and a return to political pronunciamentos might mean their end.

(b) The British had told us in confidence that they were considering sponsoring a broader dramatic plan and had even consulted us as to details.[47] We had discouraged certain phases of their plan and were now about to spring one of our own, claiming credit therefor and without previously consulting them.

(2) We felt that there was a risk that the Conference would be entirely broken up. The French reaction, both as to substance and as to method of presentation, was certain to be unfavorable. Were the advantages sufficiently well defined and concrete to counterbalance these risks?

(3) We would be accused of risking the future of the Conference for purely domestic considerations. This would react to our disadvantage, not only at Geneva, but during the forthcoming economic and monetary Conference.

The Secretary and Mr. Rogers went over to the White House at five. They didn't return till 8. The President overrode their objections. Secretary Hurley was called in. He supported the President largely on the ground that as the Conference was moribund anyway, it would be just as well to kill it once and for all. Rogers tried to argue with him, while the President and the Secretary listened, feeling that he could talk more freely, but even this made no impression. The President was determined to go ahead, irrespective of danger. He knew it might breach the Conference, that it might undo the Secretary's work of conciliation through personal contact, but it might on the other hand "do the trick," and he had accordingly decided to make the speech as planned. He then opened his drawer and pulled out a very rough draft which he asked Rogers to polish off and telegraph to Geneva that very evening. . .

---

[47] On May 13, 1932, Mr. Stanley Baldwin had outlined to Mr. Davis a drastic disarmament plan about which the United States had since been consulted. U.S. Dept. of State, *Foreign Relations, 1932*, I, 121–125, 129–131, 142–144, 157–161, 166–168.

Tuesday [June 21, 1932].

Today was a day full of alarms and excursions. The delegation cabled in the morning that they were all enthusiastic over the President's new draft.[48] At noon, they were less keen. Hugh Gibson telephoned that MacDonald [Ramsay MacDonald, British Prime Minister and chief delegate to the Disarmament Conference] was cooling toward the project; he did not feel he could commit himself on naval clauses without consulting the Cabinet and asked whether it couldn't be postponed while he sent Sir John Simon by airplane to London to obtain a decision. The President at once pointed out that such a journey might result in a British request for changes in the draft, which would mean further negotiations and delay. The French seemed to be starting a backfire of publicity about our presenting an ultimatum to France along the line of "Disarm or no cancellation." All he asked was a general approval in principle from the British.[49]

At a quarter-past two Davis called up again. He said that Hugh Gibson was tired out and that he was talking for him. Sir John Simon had just left them and was terribly upset about the plan. He said that it was counter to the spirit of their negotiations, would upset the private talks that were at last making headway, and bade fair to wreck the Conference. . . Norman Davis urged the President to put off his statement till a later date, and argued word for word as we had done last Saturday. The President however remained adamant, saying that it must be now or never; that he could make it neither during nor after the Democratic convention. . .[50]

Wednesday, June 22 [1932].

At nine the President called in the White House correspondents and gave them the statement for release at 10.30. So busy were they in rushing the news onto the wires that we had peace until nearly 12. Jules Henry [Counselor of the French Embassy at Washington] came down to inquire as to the meaning of some very clear-cut sentences. The French are distinctly uneasy, and despite all denials, view the whole proposal as a shrewd move in the chess game of debts and reparations. The fact that the Secretary was unwilling to tell Claudel

[48] *Ibid.*, pp. 196–197.
[49] *Ibid.*, pp. 197–201.
[50] *Ibid.*, pp. 202–207.

[Paul Claudel, French Ambassador to the United States] anything during his call yesterday and put him off with banalities, has confirmed this still further in Claudel's mind. . .

At four Hugh Gibson called up. The President listened in at the White House, the Secretary at "Woodley," and Rogers, Klots and I in the Secretary's office at the Department. Hugh Gibson was exultant. The plan had gone over better than they had dared hope. Grandi had given it wholehearted support, others approved, the applause showed the temper of the crowd; even the Frenchman (Boncour) went as far in supporting the plan as could be expected of a Minister in the present state of public opinion.[51] If we could now go further and agree on budgetary limitation and on basing our policy on the respect of others of the Kellogg Pact, Hugh Gibson felt we would nearly have reached a meeting of minds. The Geneva crowd were planning to celebrate and would then go to sleep with free and easy minds; we here felt the same; the first round had been won. . .

On July 23 the Geneva Conference adjourned without having taken definite action on the Hoover plan. Instead a resolution was adopted containing such agreements as had been achieved to this time.[52] In voting for the resolution the American delegate expressed regret that the Hoover proposals had not been adopted but said that the present resolution "offered the best hope of eventual attainment of that goal." The next meeting of the Disarmament Commission was set for January 1933.[53]

Thursday, July 14 [1932].

This morning the Secretary told Pierre Boal that he should turn over the Western European Division to me, effective tomorrow, July 15. This is the only official intimation I have had, although it has been common gossip for some weeks and has been discussed with me by nearly everyone in the Department excepting the Secretary and the members of the Personnel Board. . .

[51] Grandi had immediately given complete approval by Italy to the plan. Sir John Simon, although welcoming the "breadth of view" of the Hoover proposal, criticized its details. Paul-Boncour said that "in their attractive simplicity the American proposals were perhaps too simple in view of the complication of certain problems." Germany applauded the principles upon which the plan was based. Russia also signified approval. League of Nations, *Conference for the Reduction and Limitation of Armaments*, pp. 768–769.

[52] The text of the resolution is given in U.S. Dept. of State, *Foreign Relations, 1932*, I, 318–322.

[53] League of Nations, *Conference for the Reduction and Limitation of Armaments*, p. 916.

This entry will end my diary for the year in which I have been working on disarmament in the Department. I have enjoyed it to the full, particularly as I feel the Delegation has done an extremely fine piece of work under circumstances of exceptional difficulty. . .

Thursday, August 18, 1932.

. . . For years the Minister at Berne has been corresponding with the Secretary-General of the League in an informal manner only, starting all notes "My dear Sir Eric" and closing "Sincerely yours, Hugh R. Wilson" without indication of title. Every outgoing routine instruction has directed the Minister to transmit to Sir Eric Drummond "in the usual informal manner" such and such information. For years Hugh Wilson and I have felt that the situation was unnecessary and undignified. We have of late been cooperating so directly with the League on big matters and have addressed the Secretary-General formally on matters vitally affecting our policy that the retention of the personal and informal correspondence seems an anachronism. Hugh Wilson wrote and asked if I could do anything about it, and I persuaded Castle and Rogers that it was time to reform. Henceforth, we will omit the phrase "in the usual informal manner" in our instructions directing the Minister to communicate with the League. As for the Minister, he will gradually slide into the new system without fuss or feathers and without direct instructions from the Department. I wrote a line to Hugh Wilson outlining this arrangement. . .

The 1932 presidential election took place in the middle of the most desperate depression that had ever afflicted the country. In the November election the people demonstrated that they no longer trusted the ability of the Hoover Administration to cope with the crisis and overwhelmingly elected Franklin D. Roosevelt, the Democratic candidate.

Although foreign policy had played a small role in the campaign, two days after the election it became a most pressing problem. On November 10 France and Great Britain, who owed World War I debts to the United States, asked that their payments, due on December 15, be suspended pending a reconsideration of the entire debt question.[54] Shortly afterwards the other debtor nations entered their plea. Hoover wired Roosevelt on November 12 suggesting that they meet to decide jointly what should be done about the debts, since the new Democratic Administration would be responsible for making the best of any policy instituted

[54] U.S. Dept. of State, *Foreign Relations, 1932*, I, 727-728, 754-756.

by the Republicans.[55] The President and the Governor met ten days later.[56]

Wednesday, November 23, 1932.

. . . For the benefit of Joseph C. Grew, I write down the general impressions of the Hoover-Roosevelt talk, as gathered from the Secretary, Klots, Bill Castle . . . Rogers, Ballantine [Arthur A. Ballantine, Under Secretary of the Treasury], etc. Not one, of course, was present, but all are in a position to have gained a fairly accurate picture. The strongest impression all obtained was a desire on Roosevelt's part not to make the President's path harder, and not to play politics with the situation. On the other hand, he did not want to be put in a position of making any definite commitment, until he had full responsibility. What apparently struck Hoover and Mills [Ogden L. Mills, Secretary of the Treasury] was his ignorance of the general problems facing the Administration, particularly in the foreign field. What apparently struck him was that Hoover and Mills, who had been working and struggling with these problems for years, should expect him to have well-defined ideas and policies on them before he and his advisers had a chance to make a careful study based on official information. He seemed to have certain inchoate ideas regarding trade, tariffs, agricultural relief, etc., but not formulated even in his own mind. He virtually said that his Administration was going to proceed slowly and cautiously, and not to commit itself to any radical change of policy for many months.

Analyzing the above, one has the feeling that we shall revert from the policy of the dictatorial executive hammering at Congress and producing a serious deadlock, to a prudent and possibly hesitant Administration which will try to work with the legislative, by methods of leading and not driving. A good many people here expect Roosevelt to recognize Russia, as being something he can do at once and on

---

[55] Myers, pp. 202–206.

[56] Raymond Moley, whom Roosevelt appointed to be Assistant Secretary of State, accompanied the President-elect to his meeting with Hoover. Moley states that Roosevelt had decided before he met Hoover not to get too involved in the debt situation. "He [Roosevelt] had no access to the official records of what had gone before and he would have no control over the negotiations which followed." Roosevelt's major concern was for domestic questions, and he feared that a definite commitment on foreign policy might bring an unfavorable reaction from Congress and jeopardize his recovery program. Raymond Moley, *After Seven Years* (New York: Harper & Bros., 1939), pp. 70–76.

his own, in foreign affairs, and which will have little repercussion or real meaning. Other than that, the general impression is that he will carry on the Stimson policies almost unchanged.

I had a long argument with Klots and Bundy [Harvey H. Bundy, Assistant Secretary of State] as to the wording of the Belgian note [relative to the suspension of payment of war debts], and finally carried my point that it should coincide with the French text. The Secretary arranged to deliver the French and British notes to the Ambassadors at "Woodley" and the Belgian note to Mr. May [Paul May, Belgian Ambassador to the United States] at the Department.[57] When Sir Ronald [Sir Ronald Lindsay, the British Ambassador to the United States] read the British note he became violently agitated, said that British-American relations would not get over it in a decade, that their note to us was draft K,[58] which showed the care with which it had been prepared, that the inference the President read in it of a commitment was utterly unwarranted, etc.[59] He so agitated the Secretary that he withheld the note, rushed down to the White House; the President authorized the excision of large sections. This left the French note stronger than the British, but as it had already been delivered, there was nothing to be done about that. Now it remains to be seen whether the public is satisfied without knowing why the notes were differently drafted, and whether the story of the British note can be kept secret, and if so, for how long . . .

Wednesday, December 21, 1932.

The Secretary sent for Joe Green [assistant in the Division of Western European Affairs] and myself to talk over the message which the President is planning to send to Congress asking for authority to prevent the exportation of arms and munitions to countries at war or threatening to go to war . . .

Meanwhile, the President sent back the message to the Secretary this afternoon, asking that it be redrafted, not as a recommendation

[57] The texts of the American notes in which the United States refused to suspend the December 15 payment are given in U.S. Dept. of State, *Foreign Relations, 1932*, I, 701–703, 732–734, 756–757.

[58] The British note requesting suspension is also in *ibid.*, pp. 754–756.

[59] Premier Pierre Laval of France had visited Hoover in October 1931. It was widely rumored at that time and following that the President had committed the United States to bring about a readjustment of the debt situation. See Myers, pp. 174–201.

from him to Congress, but as a recommendation from the Secretary to the President with a short covering and endorsing message from the President to Congress. He added, rather pathetically, that he thought in this way the chances of its passage would be greater . . .

Friday, December 23, 1932.

. . . I went home to lunch and we had the children's Christmas tree immediately upon getting up from the table.[60] I dressed up as Santa Claus and brought down the children's presents. Edith concentrates intensely. While she is interested in one present, her attention does not wander to the next until she has exhausted its various possibilities.

While I was away from the office, the Secretary buzzed for all of us who had been working on the arms embargo message to say that the President had made up his mind not to send the message, as he was fearful of opposition in Congress. The Secretary had pleaded with him to go ahead irrespective of the fate of the document, pointing out that it would round out his policy. The President still demurred, at which the Secretary then told him that he did not see how he could withhold the message since it had received publicity and since it was known that the arms manufacturers were opposed. Finally, the Secretary just threw up his hands and asked if we saw any way in which the matter might be retrieved. Bill Castle, who never liked the original idea but still felt that the President could not now retreat went over to the White House and had a long talk with Richey [Lawrence Richey, correspondence secretary to the President], pointing out the political dangers of the plan. Richey kept interrupting him by saying that the President had irrevocably decided against the message and then added rather naïvely that the rumors that the Duponts had protested were all wrong; it was not the Duponts who had intervened, but the Colts, Remingtons and Winchesters! [61]

[60] Mr. and Mrs. Moffat celebrated an early Christmas with their children, because the parents spent Christmas day in New York away from them.

[61] Representatives of the Winchester, Colt, and Remington companies appeared later before the Foreign Affairs Committee to oppose passage of the arms embargo resolution, claiming that such a measure would only shift the armaments trade to other countries and would lessen the number of people in the United States trained to produce war materials. U. S. Congress, House, Committee on Foreign Affairs, *Hearings before the Committee of Foreign Affairs on H. J. Resolution 580,* 72 Cong., 2 Sess. (Washington: Government Printing Office, 1933); William T. Stone, "Inter-

Thursday, January 5, 1933.

. . . The Secretary summoned me again in connection with the message, which the President had refused to sign, asking for authority to the Executive to embargo the sale of arms to countries where hostilities were in progress or threatening. Ever since Sir Ronald Lindsay's call, in which he offered collaboration in preventing the sale of arms to the Chaco dispute,[62] the Secretary has been growing more and more restive under the President's refusal to go ahead. He finally had it out with him yesterday and told him that an attack would be forthcoming in a few days if something were not done, as the press was under the impression that he had been intimidated by the munition workers. Finally, without committing himself, the President told him to go ahead and try out something new with emphasis on the ratification of the 1925 Convention [63] rather than on the further grant of powers. The Secretary told me to redraft the message urging (1) ratification of the 1925 Convention, and (2) if the Senate were unwilling to do this, the additional grant of powers. I pointed out the illogicality of this, as it was in effect saying "take a small step in consonance with the rest of the world, but if you are unwilling to do this, take a big step which will penalize our industry alone." The Secretary did not altogether like this, but finally said to go and see what we could do along these lines. The chief problem seemed to be to reduce to commensurate terms two thoughts which were at present incommensurate, namely multilateral action and unilateral action. Finally, we hit on a formula which seemed fairly good. This was . . . to favor multilateral action, the first step of which would be the ratification of the rather anodyne agreement of 1925, and of which the second step would be the formulation of a more satisfactory multilateral agreement in the Disarmament Conference. Meanwhile, the Executive should request authority to cooperate with other arms-producing nations in meeting a given situation by preventing the shipment of

national Traffic in Arms and Ammunition," *Foreign Policy Reports*, IX (August 16, 1933), 137.

[62] Bolivia and Paraguay were at war over the Chaco boundary.

[63] The Convention for the Supervision of the International Trade in Arms and Ammunition and in Implements of War was signed at Geneva on June 17, 1925. The United States was one of the signatories. Although it had been submitted to the Senate, it had not been ratified by 1933. U. S. Department of State, *Papers Relating to the Foreign Relations of the United States, 1925* (Washington: Government Printing Office, 1940), I, 61–93, contains the text of the convention.

arms. Joe Green did the actual drafting, and an excellent piece of work he did. The Secretary took it home with him to "Woodley," saying that time was of essence . . .

Friday, January 6, 1933

The Secretary took the draft Joe Green and I had prepared on forbidding, in cooperation with other producing nations, the shipment of arms and munitions of war to any foreign state when, in the President's judgment, such shipment would promote or encourage the employment of force in the course of a dispute or conflict between nations, over to the Cabinet meeting, and from what I gather, there ensued a knockdown fight in which, at the beginning, the Secretary stood alone against the other nine Cabinet Officers. Their opposition was largely on the ground that we must do nothing that would result in a slowing down of any part of our business organization. At the end, however, the Secretary won the day and the President told him to send over the message. The draft we had prepared was textually accepted and written up in the afternoon and signed by the Secretary about half-past six, the last thing he did before starting up for Mr. Coolidge's funeral . . .[64]

When American companies get into difficulty with foreign countries, the Department of State is very often the peacemaker. Shortly after becoming Chief of the Division of Western European Affairs, Pierrepont Moffat found that he had become a principal intermediary between the Firestone Corporation and Liberia. The quarrel was involved; it related to the concessions granted to the company by the Republic for the development of rubber. These concessions had given Firestone a dominant position in Liberia without appreciably benefiting the treasury or the people of the Republic. In December 1932 the government of Liberia declared a moratorium on the Loan Agreement of 1926, which was connected with the Firestone concessions.[65]

Tuesday, January 17, 1933.

. . . The rest of the day was spent over Liberian matters. The [Harvey S.] Firestones, father and son, not content with having obtained a blanket promise of general support from Bill Castle, insisted

[64] Calvin Coolidge died on January 5, 1933.
[65] Raymond Leslie Buell, "The Reconstruction of Liberia," *Foreign Policy Reports*, VIII (August 3, 1932), 120–134; George W. Brown, *The Economic History of Liberia* (Washington: The Associated Publishers, 1941), pp. 187–203.

on crossing the "t's" and dotting the "i's" with the Secretary himself and stayed over a day on purpose to see him. The Secretary sent for me after Cabinet and asked me to explain the situation to him. It is frightfully involved and I will not enter into it here other than to say that we were faced with two problems: (a) the President, for political reasons, was anxious to do everything that the Firestones wanted and agrees with them that there is a vast British conspiracy to do away with our rubber plantations in Liberia.[66] On the other hand, the Secretary had to bear in mind his past policy, our commitments to the League and Lord Cecil, our unwillingness to bind the new Administration and the necessity not to put ourselves in a position where it could be charged that our policy was inconsistent in Liberia and elsewhere. The Secretary saw them in the afternoon and they took up two hours of his valuable time. Their tactics were deplorable. Knowing that he likes terse, clear-cut statements, and a logically built up case, they wandered all around the field for three-quarters of an hour before coming to the point and even read aloud eight pages of what purported to be purloined minutes of the Liberian Cabinet impeaching Lord Cecil's integrity.[67] The Secretary jumped them on this and asked if they really wanted him as a lawyer to take that as evidence impeaching the integrity of a statesman whom he had known and whose honesty was above suspicion. From that point on, the Firestones began to flounder and the Secretary, pressing his advantage, said that he would fight their fight, but along the lines which seemed to him good. He felt that where we had a good case was in refusing to negotiate further until Liberia repealed its repudiationist legislation; that the League could not help supporting us there and that this was the first line of battle. The Firestones, perfectly content with this but wishing to go further and to pin him down, failed to get anything

[66] After the First World War the British Empire, which produced about 80 per cent of the world's rubber, adopted the Stevenson Restriction Act to control strictly the production and exportation of rubber. This Act was particularly obnoxious to the United States, which used most of the world's rubber. The price of rubber rose from as little as 15 cents a pound in 1922 to about $1.23 in 1925. American users of rubber, such as Firestone, were led to develop new fields where rubber might be grown outside the British Empire. The new plantations were in competition with British growers. Nnamdi Azikiwe, *Liberia in World Politics* (London: Arthur H. Stockwell, Ltd., 1934), pp. 139–141.
[67] The League of Nations had set up an International Committee on Liberia of which Viscount Cecil was president. Concerning Stimson's commitment of cooperation with the League and Cecil's Committee, see Buell, pp. 124–132.

further out of it. They then came upstairs and sat in my office for another hour, frankly unmasking their guns and saying that what they wanted was to profit by the present moment to bind the next Administration to a course of action insofar as possible. We finally agreed that they would write a letter along lines which we might edit in advance, asking us to define the situation as we saw it at Geneva. Thereupon they departed to Akron and we will be busy picking up the pieces . . .

Tuesday, January 24, 1933.

. . . The Liberian situation has grown yet worse. The Liberians have now seized the books, papers and accounts belonging to one of the fiscal agents whom they have dismissed. They have returned unopened our recent note of protest addressed by the Minister to President Barclay. They are about to revoke the Firestone license for his bank, etc. Everett Sanders [Chairman of the Republican National Committee and lawyer for the Firestones] and Walter Howe [lawyer] came in to see me again in the afternoon. We talked over an eventual press release and agreed to let the Firestones have it well in advance of the hour of issue. Just what can be done in the circumstances, nobody seems to know. The Firestones are putting pressure on the White House to send a naval vessel. The Department is bitterly opposed and the Secretary has no wish to see the end of his administration clouded by an act which will be seized upon from one end of the world to the other as directly inconsistent with our entire policy in the Far East and even in Latin America. Rogers even goes so far as to feel that if forced to do so, the Secretary should resign. The suggestion Briggs [Ellis O. Briggs, assistant in the Division of Western European Affairs] and I are working up is to send a man instead of a boat — i.e., a Commissioner of prominence and maturity, who would go over to discuss matters with Barclay, avoiding the reasons why this and that has happened, but endeavoring to work out a satisfactory solution. If a ship becomes absolutely necessary, I am prepared to suggest that it be sent as far as Freetown, 24 hours' steaming distance away, but no further. The whole case is complex enough, but the element of political pressure is what is particularly disheartening . . .

Thursday, January 26, 1933.

. . . While I was with Bill Castle, the Secretary came in and asked me to come into his office, as Everett Sanders was there in connection with Liberia. Lord Cecil had, in reply to the Secretary's letter, sent him one of the strongest documents I have yet read, accusing the company of grave discourtesy to the committee, pointing out that their attitude had made any form of cooperation virtually impossible and implying that while the committee did not approve of Liberia's action, there was a distinct feeling that the company had brought it on itself.[68] The Secretary was very much upset and again went over the dossier, looking into the nature of the company's trafficking with the League. Thus, when Sanders came in again urging the Secretary to send a ship, he unlashed a storm, said that before he would go any further he must be satisfied that the company would play ball with the League if we got them out of this jam; that he had no intention of sending a ship and wished Mr. Sanders to make this extremely plain to his principals, that such action would be highly unfortunate for the Hoover Administration and would be contrary to all that Mr. Hoover had stood for. We had started on cooperation with the League and we must so continue. America was not going to assume exclusive responsibility. It would take its part in joint responsibility. The first step was for Mr. Firestone to make his peace with the League, and he thought that that could best be done by his at once writing us a letter that he would definitely undertake to play ball with them.

Mr. Sanders left rather crestfallen and we are left wondering anew

---

[68] Viscount Cecil's note was transmitted through the American Ambassador in London on January 25, 1933. He said, in part: "I cannot help saying that they [the Firestones] have treated it [the League Committee] with grave discourtesy and have left it entirely in the dark as to what is their real attitude towards the League attempt to come to the assistance of Liberia and prevent the recurrence of the terrible scandals which existed under the administration of ex-President King, who is, I understand, now one of the advisers of the Firestone Corporation. Not once nor twice have hopes been held out to the Committee that the Firestone Corporation would come and assist it with information and advice, and then, when it came to the point, they have declined to be present, even though we were credibly informed that important representatives of the corporation were actually in Paris. I am afraid that several members of the Committee have arrived at the conclusion that the object of the Firestone Corporation was, by insisting on the rigid execution of what was, after all, a very onerous agreement, to drive the Liberian Government into such straits that they would be at the mercy of the corporation." U.S. Department of State, *Foreign Relations of the United States, 1933*, vol. II, *The British Commonwealth, Europe, Near East and Africa* (Washington: Government Printing Office, 1949), pp. 884–885.

why the Firestones should employ the Chairman of the Republican National Committee five weeks before the Democrats came in . . .[69]

Tuesday, February 7, 1933.

. . . The afternoon was largely taken up with the Firestones, who came down to plead their cause for a cruiser at Monrovia, first with the President and then with the Secretary of State. Their tenacity surpasses belief. The interview in the Secretary's room was quite dramatic. A telegram had just come in quoting the telegram which Cecil, yielding to the arguments contained in our messages of Thursday and Saturday last, had dispatched to Liberia.[70] This was a big accomplishment, as it definitely lined up the Committee on our side and enables us to push the matter further internationally. Mr. Firestone brushed it aside, however, as of no consequence and remarked that it would do so little good that it wasn't worth wasting any time over. He was here to ask for a warship, and suggested that the excuse to send a warship would be to convey a Commissioner there to try and straighten out the present misunderstandings. Mr. Firestone concluded by stating that the only way in which Liberia would be convinced that America was prepared to stand up for its rights was to make a show of force and that this would give sufficient aid and comfort to Barclay's enemies, who were basically pro-American, to take matters into their own hands. The Secretary, who did not like having the Firestones appeal over his head to the President and who still less wishes to see the end of this Administration marred by sending a war vessel on a purely commercial case, pointed out that in his opinion there were five serious objections to the course recommended by the Firestones . . .

At this point Mr. Firestone interrupted to say that perhaps the Secretary was giving as much consideration to political difficulties as to the protection of American interests; that he had invested ten million dollars in Liberia and while he might sustain this loss if the Government would not support him, he did not think it was right that American citizens in Liberia should be exposed to danger on the

[69] A memorandum of this conversation between Mr. Stimson and Mr. Sanders appears in *ibid.*, p. 886.

[70] Cecil's telegram pointed out that the Committee considered Liberian action was inconsistent with the League's proposals to assist Liberia, and he urged Liberia to "withdraw recent legislation, orders and action." *Ibid.*, pp. 899–900.

possibility that the new Administration might not endorse the presence of a ship. He said he was prepared to accept the responsibility (at this the Secretary raised his eyebrows) and practically demanded the dispatch of a naval vessel. He grew more and more excited and got up walking around the room waving his arms, etc. The Secretary showed extraordinary restraint in not answering certain gibes and kept the whole conference, which lasted a good 40 minutes, on an outwardly pleasant plane . . .

Tuesday, February 14, 1933.

. . . The two Firestones descended upon us once more for renewed pressure to obtain a cruiser in connection with the Liberian situation. The Secretary flatly refused to receive them so that we had an hour in Mr. Castle's office going over the same old ground. Later on in the day they went over to the White House and repeated the same arguments to the President. The latter, remembering that they were among the largest Republican contributors and also that he personally played a large part in the initiation of their Liberian investment,[71] tries in every way to please them and I rather gather the impression that he encourages them to put pressure on the Secretary while officially upholding the Secretary's hands. In any event, the idea of sending a Commissioner (though not on a warship) has now been approved on all sides and I am scheduled tomorrow to break the sad news to Mr. Carr and see where we can get money to pay him . . .

Monday, February 27, 1933.

. . . The day was almost entirely devoted to Liberia, I hope the last time for some months to come. The Secretary telephoned me early in the morning that Mr. Hull, having consulted Roosevelt by telephone, approved the sending of General Winship to Liberia and authorized me to go ahead with all necessary arrangements. The Firestones, having failed in their desire to obtain a warship from the Hoover Administration, had already been endeavoring to put pressure upon Mr. Hull [appointed to be Roosevelt's Secretary of State], but

[71] Mr. Hoover had been Secretary of Commerce when the British Government had adopted the restrictive Stevenson plan. He had encouraged American businessmen, among them Mr. Firestone, to develop sources of rubber in places outside of the British Empire. Azikiwe, pp. 139–142.

had not impressed him with the force of their contention. We spent some time studying the wording of the communiqué to be issued. It will receive little space in the white press, but as the Negro papers will play it up big, it had to be drafted with meticulous care. As to motive, we so scrambled up the three situations, namely our lack of diplomatic relations with the Barclay régime,[72] the slavery scandal,[73] and the Firestone interests, that it is hard to pick any one out as the controlling cause . . .

We dined at the Spanish Embassy, again a dinner of the Old World as I fear we will never see it again. The flowers which Madame Cardenas who studied flower arrangement in Japan had herself arranged, came from the South. The sole was sent down from New York and the wines were all of rare vintages. The dinner was for the Ogden Mills and the whole table was ablaze with jewels. To realize that outside the banking situation was going from bad to worse, that Ogden Mills was being called to the telephone, that banks were closing all over the country, that confidence was shattered, made the whole episode seem unreal and almost dreamlike. I sat next to Dorothy Mills, who told me that Ogden was desperately worried and feared that the panic might assume nation-wide proportions; that there was banking trouble here in Washington . . . All in all, a depressing situation. When it came to bridge, one of the visiting New Yorkers suggested our old-time stakes. The feeling it gave you was of going to Monte Carlo. However, luck was with me . . .

Friday, March 3, 1933.

I was very much pleased to receive the following . . . this morning from the Secretary.

"My dear Pierrepont:

"This is just a brief message of appreciation and gratitude for the work which you have done in the Western European Division.

"You have had charge of one of the most active fields of the

[72] Mr. Charles Mitchell, the American Minister to Liberia, had had no official relations with the Government of Liberia since his arrival in 1931. Brown, p. 203; U.S. Dept. of State, *Foreign Relations, 1933,* II, 880.

[73] The existence of slave labor in Liberia had been revealed in the mid-twenties. Brown, pp. 148–158, contains an account of the slave practices and their origins in the Republic.

Department and you have handled it with skill, accuracy and good judgment. I have come to rely upon you in all of those respects with the utmost confidence, and you have greatly eased my burdens. The work of your Division has been necessarily of a wide and varied nature, and you have shown great adaptability to the different problems, some of which were of the most important character. I feel confident that you have a fine future in front of you, and you carry my very best wishes for your success, as well as my personal friendship."

III

WASHINGTON

March 1933 – August 1935

"The Germans are trying to break up the solid front"

When Roosevelt took the oath of office in March 1933, the economic crisis had reached its most severe stage. Two thirds of the banks of the country were closed. Millions were unemployed. Suffering was widespread. "The opportunity for Roosevelt is a magnificent one," wrote Pierrepont Moffat, "if he can capture the confidence now in handling this crisis, it may carry him through his entire term of office." [1]

Although domestic problems were the primary concern of the new Administration, certain questions of foreign policy were also hanging fire. [2] Among these was the Disarmament Conference, which had resumed its meetings at Geneva.

Monday, March 6, 1933.

A busy day as may well be imagined. The Secretary [Cordell Hull] did not receive the Department until afternoon as he was . . . at the Capitol. The names of [William] Phillips, as Under Secretary, [Wilbur J.] Carr and [Raymond] Moley as Assistant Secretaries, were sent up to the Senate during the morning and were promptly confirmed. Mr. Stimson came down at half-past three and received the Secretary's flag which we gave him. The entire personnel of the Department then lined up in the corridors, some six hundred strong, and filed by, Mr. Stimson presenting the Chiefs of Division, who in turn stood by and presented members of their staffs [to Mr. Hull] . . .

By way of confidential gossip: Moley held a press conference

[1] Moffat diary, March 4, 1933.
[2] Beard, *American Foreign Policy in the Making 1932–1940*, pp. 117–148, discusses the main problems of foreign relations confronting the Roosevelt Administration in 1933.

today in which he roundly berated the press for referring to him as the President's "Man Friday," and then proceeded to say that he would not be able to receive them frequently as had Mr. Rogers, because he would be running back and forth to the White House. He remarked that he would certainly work to clean out the Department of all Republicans. When the correspondents took our part and said that we had no politics, he remarked that anyone who had served under the Hoover Administration had politics and that there were just as good fish in the sea as ever came out of it. I understand that the pressure for Hugh Gibson's job is very serious, and that there had even been some attempts to undermine Hugh Wilson. Of all the career Chiefs, J.C.G. [Joseph C. Grew, American Ambassador to Japan] seems the safest . . .

Thursday, March 9, 1933.

. . . Outside the day was tense with excitement, as the President sent up his Emergency Banking Bill to Congress.[3] The newspapermen came in to tell me about it. With it he sent an explanatory message of less than 500 words, simple, direct and with a new thrust at the bankers who had betrayed the public trust. The difference between this sort of a message and the average Hoover doctrine, which would have covered two full pages of a newspaper in fine type is startling. Burt Hulen, of the *New York Times*, who is not a Democrat, and who is not given to enthusiasms, came in and said that if we had had this sort of leadership for the past two years, we never would have gotten into this crisis. Congress and Senate passed the legislation in the course of the day and already the President is working on his next two proclamations which will probably deal with public works and veterans' cuts . . .

Thursday, March 16, 1933.

Norman Davis [Chief American Delegate to the Geneva Disarmament Conference] asked me to accompany him on his visits to Secretary Swanson [Claude Swanson, Secretary of the Navy and formerly senator from Virginia] and Admiral Pratt and to General MacArthur

[3] The Emergency Banking Law facilitated the opening of liquid banks and arranged supervision for the banks not able to open, allowed the issuance and purchase of preferred stock by the National Banks, and enabled the Federal Reserve Bank to issue notes more liberally.

. . . Senator Swanson looked longer and seedier than ever. He sat back in his chair puffing away at his long, thin cigar and proceeded to utter pontifical statements about where mistakes had been made at the Conference last Spring. He seemed to feel that we could pick up and go on from the point where he left off last July and was not in the slightest degree interested in anything that Norman Davis told him of changed conditions in Europe. It was like a breath of cool, fresh wind when Admiral Pratt came into the room and it was possible to talk over a problem in concrete terms. He and Norman Davis agreed that the dictates of higher policy made it essential for us to come to a naval understanding with Great Britain before the 1935 [London Naval] Conference; that only in this way could we prevent the Japanese from succeeding in getting the increase of ratio which they desire; [4] that to attain this, some concessions toward the British view must be made, though this could not be accepted in toto. Secretary Swanson kept interrupting, saying that nothing must be done that did not have naval opinion behind it, but Admiral Pratt continued to set forth his point of view with perfect mental precision and calm. Mr. Davis next took up with him the attitude we should assume if, as we foresaw, the British proposed the complete abolition of military and naval aviation. The Admiral replied that we should have to get compensation for giving up our strongest arm and that he could not consider it unless at the same time the submarines were completely abolished. There was a few minutes desultory conversation as we were leaving . . .

From the Navy Department we went to General MacArthur's. He was at his best form. To him it is unthinkable to do away with war. He quoted Aristotle to the effect that only the dead had seen the end of war.[5] To him disarmament had two purposes: (1) to save on appropriations so that the nations' preparations for national defense would not eat too deeply into their budgets; (2) to make war, when it came, less destructive to private property. With the constant increasing of weapons of warfare, the destruction to civil property was

[4] Japan wanted parity in naval armament with the United States and Great Britain. The Washington Treaty of 1922 had set a 5-5-3 naval ratio among the three powers. Joseph C. Grew, *Turbulent Era*, ed. Walter Johnson (Boston: Houghton Mifflin Co., 1952), II, 966; Merze Tate, *The United States and Armaments* (Cambridge: Harvard University Press, 1948), pp. 186–187.

[5] In a speech of July 8, 1952, General MacArthur said: "Our ideal must be eventually the abolition of war." *Chicago Daily Tribune*, July 8, 1952, p. 10.

growing so great that war would soon engulf our entire civilization. For this reason, he favored what could be done to return warfare to the surface of the land and the surface of the sea. Aviation, he repeated, was eating up between 25 and 35 percent of all military budgets and he said that this was only the beginning. More could be done for economy and for civilization by doing away with aviation and secondarily by the abolition of heavy mobile artillery than any other method. However, we must not discard from strength without adequate gain. Our naval aviation was our strongest trump. We should not give it up until we were assured of adequate return.

Norman Davis then left for luncheon at the White House. He told me that the President was really interested in disarmament and that they had talked over what contribution we could most effectively make, both in substance and in procedure. The conversation will be continued at luncheon tomorrow.

In the afternoon the first press reports of the MacDonald plan came through.[6] With the possible exception of the aviation clauses, there does not seem to be anything in it that we could accept. It will prove a bitter blow, however, to the French, particularly the final paragraph that this Convention, together with subsequent ones to be concluded, will replace the provisions of the peace treaties which now limit the armed forces of Germany, Austria, Hungary and Bulgaria. Doubling the number of troops allowed to Germany will be a contributary cause of worry.

Friday, March 17, 1933.

Another long and tiring day, spent for the most part with Norman Davis. The text of the MacDonald plan kept on coming in throughout the day. Much of it is of interest only to Europe. Many of the ideas have been taken from former schemes, but by and large it will

[6] Ramsay MacDonald, the British Prime Minister, introduced a British draft convention to the Disarmament Conference on March 16. This "MacDonald Plan" was in five parts, the first of which proposed that in the event of a violation or threatened violation of the Kellogg-Briand Pact a conference be held to decide what steps should be taken and to determine the responsibility for the breach. The land forces of Europe were reduced to a militia basis, and land, naval, and air matériel was limited with definite figures in number, size, and type in part two of the British plan. The third part concerned exchange of information. Part four prohibited chemical, incendiary, and bacteriological war and the preparation for such warfare in time of peace. The last part set up and described the operation of a Permanent Disarmament Commission. Tate, p. 108.

stand or fall on the last paragraph, which states that this convention and succeeding ones will replace for Germany the military and naval provisions of the peace treaty [Treaty of Versailles]. As for the implications of the political clauses, we have to study them with exceptional care. The Secretary of State is afraid of going beyond the vague provisions for consultation which were to be found in the Democratic platform.[7] Europe is so convinced that the Roosevelt Administration plans to bring us in toward the League of Nations, that the knowledge, when it comes, that our policy will probably be more cautious than under Mr. Stimson will come as a great shock.

Meanwhile, President Roosevelt has grown personally interested in disarmament, but I don't think appreciates the difficulties or the European psychology which he is up against. I am very much afraid that if we are not careful there will be a stubbed toe. Norman Davis and Mr. Hull lunched with the President and saw him again at five o'clock. Mr. Davis took the midnight to New York. He is going over without any plans and with the prospect of using our influence to best advantage that he can . . .

Monday, April 17, 1933.

. . . [To] such a degree our foreign affairs centralize with the President that no one here really knows what is going on. Yesterday, for instance, the President had an hour's talk with the new French Ambassador and no one to date, not even the Secretary or the Under Secretary, knows what it was about. Bill Phillips called me down and said that although our Government's policy is now pretty well determined with regard to the 27 items or sub-items on the agenda for the Economic Conference,[8] there are a whole series of other questions which will undoubtedly be brought up by our visitors on which he ought to have at least some preliminary information. Of course debts are the first item. Apparently the President has some definite idea of

[7] The Democratic Party in its 1932 platform had approved "the Pact of Paris abolishing war as an instrument of national policy, to be made effective by provisions for consultation and conference in case of threatened violation of treaties." *Official Report of the Proceedings of the Democratic National Convention Held at Chicago, Illinois, June 27th to July 2nd, inclusive, 1932* (n.p., n.d.), p. 148.

[8] The World Economic Conference was to assemble in London in June 1933. The agenda for the Conference is given in League of Nations, *The Monthly Summary of the League of Nations*, XIII (January, 1933), 9.

how he is going to handle it, but Bill Phillips does not know what it is . . .[9]

Wednesday, May 3, 1933.

With regard to disarmament, Bill Phillips and I are as much upset over the lack of clear guidance that is being given our Delegation as can be. The President has now taken entire charge, his instructions are very brief and not clear, they are issued without adequate knowledge of what has gone before, and, above all, they are counter to the War and Navy Departments' views. We are not permitted even to send over to War and Navy the texts of the outgoing messages. The President indicated that he wanted to see the Secretary and Bill Phillips on the general situation, but although they stood by all day, a call did not come. Meanwhile, matters in Geneva are going very badly, where the Germans are remaining intransigent in insisting on their professional army in addition to the increased number of troops allowed them . . .

Saturday, May 6, 1933.

The President approved our draft on artillery [10] and authorized us to show it to General MacArthur. Bill Phillips asked me to go around and tell the whole story to the Chief of Staff, but if the storm became too violent, I was to bring him back and let him blow off steam in the Under Secretary's office. As a matter of fact the interview was less painful than I had expected . . . As far as the destruction was concerned, however, he was seriously perturbed. He said that it would mean the entire remapping of our defense and would in effect be throwing away our military impregnability. The effects would not be immediate. For a while at least, we would even be in a relatively better position than we are today. The rub would come later when

[9] According to Raymond Moley the President had a seven-point formula for the settlement of the war-debt problem. This plan was worked out by James Warburg, a New York banker, in consultation with Roosevelt, Mr. Hull, Mr. Moley, and others. The plan is summarized in Moley, pp. 202–203.

[10] The draft stated that any reduction in the maximum caliber of guns down to 105 mm. would be acceptable to the United States. Although opposing the destruction of artillery abolished by agreement, the American delegation was instructed to agree to destruction, if all nations were willing to accept it. U.S. Department of State, *Foreign Relations of the United States, 1933* (Washington: Government Printing Office, 1950), I, 129.

other nations had built up in allowed matériel and we had followed our usual policy of waiting for a war in order to build up our stocks. However, he said that once the President had so ruled, he could do nothing but acquiesce, although he indicated that the Army would have to oppose the idea. He asked if we could soften one sentence, which I agreed to try and do, and eventually succeeded. He said that he was so convinced that neither the French nor the Japanese would sacrifice their reserve of heavy artillery that he was not unduly worried and thought as a diplomatic gesture our attitude was a safe one. He had been aware that the President was giving personal instructions on disarmament and I think appreciated being fully informed of what in fact had transpired.

I was invited to lunch at the White House in honor of Dr. Schacht [Hjalmer Schacht, German Minister of Economics], a men's lunch of twenty. I drove over with the Secretary of State and Mr. Phillips and entered the blue room where we stood around in groups until the arrival of the German guests. About three minutes past one, the President, on the arm of his Military Aide, went out to the front portico to greet Dr. Schacht with as much cordiality as either Mac-Donald or Herriot,[11] and led him into the blue room while the Marine Band struck up "Deutschland, Deutschland, über Alles." The President, with Dr. Schacht and Ambassador Luther [Hans Luther, German Ambassador to the United States] on his right hand, stood just inside the door and we filed by one by one, the Aide announcing us to the President, and he in turn presenting us individually, with just a word or two of explanation, to the Germans. He then walked into the dining room alone, still on the arm of his Aide, and seated himself in the dining room chair, unhitching in some way his braces so as to give him greater comfort. At that point the rest of us filed in and joined him at the table. Toward the end, the President made a very graceful little speech, recalling his early years in school in Germany, paying a compliment or two to Dr. Schacht and Ambassador Luther and asking us to join in drinking the health of the President of the

[11] From April 21 to 26, 1933, Mr. MacDonald had been in Washington at President Roosevelt's invitation to discuss economic and disarmament matters. Édouard Herriot, a member of the Chamber of Deputies, participated in some of the Roosevelt-Mac-Donald conversations and continued his talks after the Prime Minister's departure. Cordell Hull, *The Memoirs of Cordell Hull* (New York: The Macmillan Co., 1948), I, 225; Moley, pp. 201–206; U.S. Dept. of State, *Foreign Relations, 1933*, I, 477–501.

Reich, which we did in cold water.[12] Dr. Schacht replied, proposing the President's health, after which we rose from the table. I watched the President get up. The physical effort was enormous. He turned to one side and raised his weight entirely with his arms, while every vein in his forehead stood out from the strain. The Military Aide promptly took his arm and conducted him to the dining room entrance, where again he shook hands as we all filed by, keeping only Dr. Schacht for a private talk in his upstairs office . . .

Friday, May 12, 1933.

. . . Returned to the Department to hear of the good-bye talk of Schacht with Bill Phillips. The former again proceeded to have one of his tantrums, walking up and down the room until he got red in the face, accusing us of giving aid and encouragement to the French in their exorbitant demands, and of closing our eyes to the national demands of 65,000,000 people, etc. He said that all he asked us was to keep hands off and let France and Germany settle their own trouble, but that if the world proceeded to hold Germany down there would be a smash. Making all allowances for the fact that his visit has been one of exceptional difficulty and that he has been spoken to in no uncertain terms by everybody concerning the policy of disaster which Germany is following, he has shown himself so unbending and domineering that there will be universal relief when he departs . . .[13]

Saturday, June 10, 1933.

. . . The heat wave continues unabated. I went out early Saturday afternoon to take delivery of my next winter's supply of champagne and bring it home. I had gotten it at an exceptionally good price and believe that I know its legitimate origin. However, just as I drove up to the front door of the house, a police car cut in in front of me. I thought for a moment the jig was up, but they were not interested in me and I transported the champagne into the house right in front of their noses . . .

[12] The Twenty-First Amendment, repealing federal prohibition, had been passed by Congress in February 1933, but it had not yet been ratified by the requisite number of states.
[13] For further comments on the visit of Dr. Schacht see Hull, I, 237–238, and Charles Callan Tansill, *Back Door to War* (Chicago: Henry Regnery Co., 1952), pp. 46–48.

Germany's experiment with democracy ended abruptly when Adolf Hitler became Chancellor on January 30, 1933. Within three months the Reichstag had voted dictatorial powers to the new government. In March 1933 steps were also taken to make Germany a centralized state, and the provinces lost their identity as political subdivisions. Local autonomy was strictly limited. In April 1933 the Civil Service was altered to include only loyal Nazis, and the Gestapo was organized. Two months later Goebbels' propaganda ministry was established. In July a law was passed outlawing the existence of any political party except the Nazi Party.

Such policies as these were repugnant to the United States, and during the years of 1933 and 1934 there was much speculation and discussion in the Department of State about what the American attitude should be toward Hitler Germany.

Saturday, August 12, and Sunday, August 20, 1933.

. . . The Ambassador [William E. Dodd, American Ambassador to Germany] thought it would be advisable . . . to make his refusal to go to Nuremberg carry the gist of the message.[14] We rephrased our reply, which had not been sent off to the effect that we did not consider that the Government should take any initiative or act directly in the matter; that it seemed to us a local problem and that we had full confidence in his discretion.

That was not good enough for Mr. Dodd apparently. He sent in a long telegram which arrived on Sunday afternoon saying that he considered it of prime importance for the diplomatic corps not to be dragooned into a demonstration which would be played up as "an endorsement of the present regime" or "a recognition that the German Government and the Nazi Party are the same." He again asked us to urge the French and British not to attend and spoke of the embarrassment in which he would be put were he to take an isolated stand. I took this message out to "Rosedale" where Bill Phillips, Caffery [Jefferson Caffery, Assistant Secretary of State] and myself talked it over. We were more than ever convinced that the Government should not become involved and certainly not approach the British and French, thus giving them an opportunity later to claim that a mistake or unpopular decision was made at our instance or in pursuance of our advice. We repeated to Mr. Dodd that whatever decision he made we would back him up strongly. Caffery, in particular, felt

[14] The Nazi Party Congress was to be held at Nuremberg during the first week of September.

that Mr. Dodd was getting off on the wrong foot and foresaw considerable trouble for us if we did not establish working relations with the Nazis, whatever we might think of them. Bill Phillips and I felt that if the British and French, who have far more at stake than we, could go to Nuremberg, we could do so likewise. If they did not, a common Anglo-French-American stand would defy criticism . . .[15]

Saturday and Sunday, October 7 and 8, 1933.

This morning the news from Geneva took a sudden and marked turn for the worse. The Germans instead of carrying out a conciliatory attitude of the sort indicated by Von Neurath [Constantin von Neurath, German Minister for Foreign Affairs] suddenly assumed an extremely intransigent attitude, rejected the trial period, demanded the right to construct all weapons which would not be totally abolished, though agreeing to negotiate on their numbers, et cetera. They ask for this right at once and emphasize the equality phase of the situation and ignore entirely the security end. Their method seemed as inept as their answer. The German Chargé at London passed on the news to Sir John Simon [British Secretary of State for Foreign Affairs]; the Italians were informed at Geneva, but no information was vouchsafed either to the Americans or to the French. Only when Norman Davis exhibited signs of distinct disturbance did Weizsäcker [Ernst von Weizsäcker, German Minister to Switzerland] come and inform him, while belated instructions were sent to the Embassy in Washington to pass on the same information. The Ambassador was away and so could not see the Secretary before Monday morning at eleven. Meyer, however, the first secretary of the German Embassy, came down to see me at twelve o'clock, to tell us of the German attitude toward the present disarmament discussions as given to the British at London and to the Italians and Americans at Geneva. The information that he gave coincided almost entirely with points (a), (b), and (c) of Mr. Davis' telegram No. 727 of October 6, midnight.[16] Dr.

---

[15] Mr. Dodd decided not to attend the Nazi Party rally. In his diary the Ambassador wrote on August 26, 1933: "I declined it on the grounds of pressure of work, though the main reason was my disapproval of a government invitation to a Party convention." William E. Dodd, *Ambassador Dodd's Diary*, ed. William E. Dodd, Jr., and Martha Dodd (New York: Harcourt, Brace & Co., 1941), p. 28. The correspondence between Dodd and the Department about his attendance at the Party Congress is printed in U.S. Dept. of State, *Foreign Relations, 1933*, II, 255–259.

[16] The position of the German Government, as explained in the Davis telegram,

Meyer then proceeded to talk about the philosophy underlying Germany's position. He said that for fifteen years now Germany had observed in good faith the provisions of the Treaty of Versailles disarming her; that although the Allies had agreed to disarm, nevertheless they had not done so and former German Governments were remiss in not demanding such disarmament with greater vigor. Now there was in Germany a new Government, with whose basic ideas one might or might not be in agreement but which none the less was there to stay and which did represent the aims and aspirations of 60 million Germans. To ask this Government now to accept a "trial period" as if Germany were a naughty schoolboy was not treating it as it had a right to expect. It implied a distrust and negotiations carried on with distrust as a basis were bound to fail . . .

I suggested that I hoped very much that an analysis of the situation would not show that there was a demand for actual rearmament by Germany. He said that he refused to consider that the possession of sample types [17] or even a few examples of individual weapons was "rearmed." In fact he thought that it was only by according Germany these types that disarmament could be hurried along and that it would precipitate a "first step" by the other Powers. He then said that he had merely been instructed to give me the facts of the German *démarche* and that these philosophic explanations were not given under instructions but represented his personal views . . .

I felt that the best thing to do in order not to cross wires with Norman Davis was to prepare the general outline of what the Secretary would say to Luther on Monday, to telegraph this to Norman Davis and ask for his comments. Noel Field [Assistant in the Division of Western European Affairs] prepared the ground for this on Satur-

---

was that Germany regarded the British plan as the basis for a disarmament convention. Upon ratification of an arms treaty, Germany would transform the *Reichswehr* and would go as far as the other nations in scrapping arms forbidden in the treaty. But Germany felt it had the right to unlimited acquisition of weapons upon which the treaty placed no numerical limit. U.S. Dept. of State, *Foreign Relations, 1933*, I, 238–239.

[17] The peace treaties had forbidden the construction of "sample" arms. When the MacDonald plan was introduced, it was interpreted in some quarters as allowing Germany to build samples of guns, tanks, aircraft, and submarines. Herriot wanted an express provision denying the Germans such arms, because "samples once having been constructed could be the means of manufacturing large numbers of these forbidden instruments of war in a very short period of time." The United States was also against permitting sample arms. *Ibid.*, pp. 110, 111–112, 134, 137–138, 140, 225, 228.

day afternoon while I dashed out and played a few holes of golf. I then took his papers home and worked on them after dinner until midnight working out three points which I felt the Secretary could emphasize.

The first of these was an allusion to the fact that the German position was emphasizing equality and ignoring security which went as a by-product. Security is as much as anything else a state of mind induced by confidence in one's neighbors. Given the unstable political conditions in Germany, the fact that her leaders had been prone to provocative speeches before they assumed power, et cetera, it was incumbent on Germany to rewin world confidence. This she could do by proving herself stable and pacific during a few years, while on the other hand a demand for new arms at this juncture would in its very essence create uneasiness and thus render disarmament more difficult. The second point was the fact that eventual equality must be reached by a revision downward of the armaments of the heavy armed states and not a revision upward on the part of any other Power. Should Germany increase her armaments she would be running against the trend of world opinion. Three, the Secretary might possibly allude, though without stressing the point, to the Treaty of 1921 [18] wherein Germany granted us certain rights and privileges, notably in matters of armament. This Treaty was not signed under duress and it followed that any modification must be brought about through peaceful means and mutual consent.

Sunday morning, I threw this into shape at the Department and went up to Jimmy Dunn's [Chief of the Division of Protocol and Conferences] where the Secretary came out to play his week-end game of croquet in the garden. On the whole, the Secretary liked the approach and signed the message asking Norman Davis to get his reply in before 11 o'clock in the morning . . .[19]

Monday, October 9, 1933.

Norman Davis' answer to the suggested basis for a talk with Luther arrived in good time. He suggested omitting any reference to our treaty rights and made a few minor suggestions with respect to the

[18] U.S. Department of State, *Papers relating to the Foreign Relations of the United States, 1921* (Washington: Government Printing Office, 1936), II, 29–31, contains the text of the treaty.

[19] U.S. Dept. of State, *Foreign Relations, 1933*, I, 240–241.

rest of the presentation.[20] Ambassador Luther came in to see the Secretary at eleven. I was not there but from what I gathered the Secretary declined to argue with him but would, after the closing of each Teutonic blast, quietly lift a newspaper off his desk and read to Luther some fresh instance of German provocation or glorification of war.[21] Some three-quarters of an hour later, he came up to my office and said that he wished to tell me of his talk with the Secretary . . . He said that he was completely unable to comprehend the reaction of the world to the latest German disarmament proposals. That they should be badly received in France and certain other countries which were only doing lip service to disarmament, he could readily understand, but that they should receive a bad press in other countries which genuinely desired success in disarmament, notably the United States, was to him a matter surpassing understanding. He wished to say to begin with that if the Disarmament Conference failed, its repercussions on the continent of Europe would be so staggering that their effects would be felt in this country where they would seriously cripple our recovery program. He had no need to go into the details of the German position; the Secretary and myself were both familiar with these details not only from Norman Davis' telegram but also from the talk which Mr. Meyer had had with me Saturday morning.[22] What he wanted to say was that they represented nothing new: they were a restatement of the position which the Germans had been maintaining for years and that they were designed to force the Allies into some definite gesture of disarmament. The French plan for disarmament was a thinly veiled disguise. It endeavored to set up for Germany a "trial period" [23] at the end of which France might consent to disarm. What did this mean when analyzed? It meant that France would succeed in reëstablishing the control over Germany which had been abolished and it did not commit France to do any further disarming than she has agreed to do by the Treaty of Versailles. Germany could never consent to sign a treaty

[20] *Ibid.*, p. 242.
[21] *Ibid.*, pp. 242–243; Hull, I, 230.
[22] See the conversation of Jay Pierrepont Moffat with Ernst Meyer, October 7, 1933.
[23] A four-year transition period had been proposed during which some decrease in European armies would take place and Germany would be permitted to raise her army to 200,000 men. After the transition period the heavily armed European powers would make specific and important reductions along the lines of the British draft convention. U.S. Dept. of State, *Foreign Relations, 1933*, I, 233.

which did not produce actual disarmament. I suggested that the French had gone further and made more definite commitments than ever before, but he brushed these aside as mere words. I then said that frankly we were unable to accept the German thesis of rearmament, in no matter how modified a form. He said he was aware of this philosophic conception and that in theory it would be better to have only disarmament downward on the part of heavily armed Powers. But in practice the others were not coming down and Germany must go up to meet them in order to be able to satisfy its own public opinion. I suggested that it would be extremely difficult for Germany to explain this while the other Powers were actually making a greater effort to go down than ever before. The Ambassador then told me that the Secretary had asked whether the Germans were still guided by the declaration of December 11.[24] At first he was unable to understand the import of the Secretary's question, the answer seemed so clear. Finally it dawned on him that the Secretary felt that the Germans were not paying enough attention to the demand of the other Powers for "security." This to him was as incomprehensible as American reaction as exemplified by the press.[25] He asked how Germany disarmed and living in the midst of heavily armed nations could possibly be a menace to their security. He said that the Secretary had shown him a number of newspaper clippings of alleged provocative German activities. This did not seem fair, he said, as when Polish chauvinists indulged in the same type of activities, it received no adverse comment abroad. The whole history of the past 14 years was one succession of episodes showing that Germany was not a threat to her neighbors. He himself had for years believed in the possibility of a Franco-German rapprochement. He had signed the Locarno Pact,[26] but that Pact had brought with it no results. He believed that Briand was sincere but that his efforts were always checkmated by the French

[24] On December 11, 1932, a Five Power Declaration was signed by representatives of the United States, Italy, Great Britain, France, and Germany, which stated that "one of the principles that should guide the Conference on Disarmament should be the grant to Germany, and to the other Powers disarmed by Treaty, of equality of rights in a system which would provide security for all nations." U.S. Dept. of State, *Foreign Relations, 1932*, I, 527–528.

[25] See, for instance, the *Chicago Daily Tribune*, October 9, 1933, p. 1.

[26] A Treaty of Mutual Guarantee among Germany, Belgium, France, Great Britain, and Italy had been signed at Locarno on October 16, 1925. Luther, who was then Chancellor of the German Empire, signed for Germany. League of Nations, *Treaty Series*, LIV (1926–1927), 290–301.

General Staff. I did not feel it my place to argue the Ambassador's points. I merely said that I agreed with him as to the extremely critical phase of the negotiations mentioned; that our information from Mr. Davis was now some 48 hours overdue, and that the situation was so fluid that it was difficult to know where it was at the moment. It seemed that the critical week had at last arrived and I could only hope with him that an agreement embodying "real disarmament" would ensue.[27]

About the time the Ambassador left the news came through that Norman Davis wished to talk to the President and the Secretary over the long distance at one o'clock, Washington time. The Secretary took me over with him to the White House with a dossier of papers in case any technical questions should arise. The outer office was swarming with people as usual but at two minutes to one we were ushered in to the President's office. The President said to the Secretary, "Now tell me briefly what he probably wants and what is the tenor of our information to date." The Secretary turned to me and said, "You know more about this so I leave the answer to you." I had about a minute and a half and explained that as we saw matters the line for Davis to take was one which would avoid the Scylla of losing our independent position and the Charybdis of allowing a breach in the solid front which had at last been welded between France, England, Italy and the United States. It seemed to us that the Germans were maneuvering in an endeavor to break up this front and to profit by any disagreement that might result. The two points on which they were most insistent were (a) refusal to accept a trial or transition period, and (b) their demand for sample arms. On the latter point, in particular, the President had expressed himself very clearly to Herriot and others last spring. The President answered saying that he was dead against any sample weapons and at that moment the call came through.

Norman Davis said that we were now faced with a situation where we would have to decide whether the Allies would go ahead and negotiate a treaty and then put it up to Germany to accept or reject or whether we should still continue to negotiate a treaty with Germany. He favored the latter. With a view to breaking the deadlock

[27] A memorandum of this conversation between the German Ambassador and Mr. Moffat is printed in U.S. Dept. of State, *Foreign Relations, 1933*, I, 243-245.

he thought it might be possible to work out something along the following line: to tell Germany definitely that we could not allow her any rearmament, in the form of sample types or defensive arms; on the other hand, that we sympathized with her objections to a "trial period" and might accordingly suggest that the double stage theory of a treaty be suppressed, although maintaining enough of its elements to satisfy the French. Thus we might call for a treaty lasting eight years and at the end of two or three years agree to scrap guns over 400 millimeters, at the end of four years over 350 [320] millimeters and at the end of six years over 250 [220], etc. etc. This idea appealed to the President who asked whether the French would accept it.[28] Norman Davis replied with, I thought, a slight hesitation that he believed they would. The President authorized him to go ahead, but added "be sure not to lose the alignment with the others that has been built up. All of our information here leads us to believe that the Germans are trying to break up the solid front." [29] Norman Davis replied that their efforts to that end were unceasing but that they would not be successful. He then asked the Secretary to keep on putting pressure on Luther and rang off.

As we left the President asked if we were satisfied. We both expressed pleasure at the possibilities opened by Norman Davis to which the President replied that he had no objection at all to saving Germany's face. I answered that we must be a little careful not to risk Daladier's position in doing so as it was already shaky and if Daladier would fall, it would mean starting all over again from the beginning.[30] The President said that he was well aware of this and felt that Daladier was due to run into very rough weather before long over his budget. Finally, he turned to the Secretary and said, "Now when Luther comes, be sure that you are firm with him. He is a man that one has to stand up to and speak right out from the shoulder; furthermore," he added, "if the reports in this morning's press are true that

[28] The President asked if the French would agree to eliminate a trial period. To this question Mr. Davis answered: "Yes, they will. We think they will to this effect. We will talk about a . . . treaty, and not talk about a trial period." *Ibid.*, pp. 245-246.
[29] *Ibid.*, pp. 246-247.
[30] In an attempt to ease the financial crisis in France caused by the depression Premier Edouard Daladier had proposed a 6 per cent cut in salaries of officials and other drastic measures. He failed to gain the necessary support for his program, and his government fell later in October 1934. D. W. Brogan, *The Development of Modern France* (London: Hamish Hamilton, 1940), pp. 650-652.

he refused to speak at Philadelphia because of the absence of the swastika flag from the platform, I feel that it shows a rigidity of mind which will not add to his effectiveness here" . . .

Saturday and Sunday, October 14 and 15, 1933.

I had hardly reached the office at nine o'clock this morning when the news associations called up with the news that Germany had left the League, left the Disarmament Conference, dissolved the Reichstag, summoned new elections, et cetera. I promptly got hold of Bill Phillips and together we broke the news to the Secretary. The press, of course, were immediately milling around and anxious for a lead. The Secretary postponed his press conference from half-past ten to half-past twelve, in the meantime hoping that some information would be received from Europe which would help him. None was forthcoming. He finally decided to express regret at the occurrence saying that this was what we had been laboring to prevent and that anything which marked a check to the disarmament movement was a source of great disappointment. We likewise prepared upstairs not for attribution a background statement of our policy during the past week or ten days. This read as follows:

> You may be wondering what has been the attitude of the United States during the recent discussions at Geneva. Briefly stated we have been endeavoring to facilitate an agreement whereby, in the words of the resolution of December 11, 1932, Germany would be "granted equality of rights in a system which would provide security for all nations." It is understood that the practical application of such equality would have to be brought about through stages and through the downward revision in armaments of the heavily armed states; that we were striving to reach a general disarmament convention which would be binding upon all nations as well as Germany; that we were opposed in principle to making the early rearmament of Germany a condition precedent to the signature of a treaty. Thus in substance we were in general agreement with France and Great Britain. As far as tactics were concerned, we were particularly anxious that every way be explored which might lead to a formula that would be satisfactory alike to Germany and to the others, which would meet all susceptibilities

and which would on the one hand avoid rearmament and on the other contain provisions for a specific undertaking of reduction on the part of the armed states at stated periods. That in brief, is a statement of our position during these later stages of the negotiations. Let me repeat my deep disappointment that it did not bear fruit.

As a matter of fact the Secretary embroidered extemporaneously on the first part of the statement characterizing "Germany's action as a break-up of our team play." The correspondents took this, emphasized it out of its context, and some of them, particularly the Hearst press, made a very serious accusation that (a) we had taken sides against Germany, (b) that we were in political alignment with England and France, and (c) that we were committed to sanctions.[31] This essentially dishonest attitude caused a good deal of embarrassment though I doubt if it did much damage as by and large the country discounts what is in the Hearst press anyway . . .

Monday, October 16, 1933.

Again a day busy with disarmament. Found a telegram in the morning from Davis to the effect that he was going to call the President and the Secretary again at one o'clock. The Secretary called in Bill Phillips and myself and once again went over questions of policy. We all of us reached the conclusion that the time had come when we must make it very clear that the unity of front which we have had with France, Great Britain and Italy related to disarmament matters solely and did not involve any political commitments. This was motivated on two grounds: In the first place, the instinctive American reaction to entanglements was again making itself evident, fanned it is true by a series of absolutely dishonest press articles in the Hearst press emanating from Washington. The second reason which was equally important was that French newspapers were beginning to talk

[31] The *Chicago Herald and Examiner*, October 15, 1933, p. 1, reported the Hull statement in these words: "The United States today was plunging headlong into the ominous European imbroglio as the State Department aligned this country behind France and Great Britain in their split with Germany . . .

"Former pretenses that 'Ambassador' Norman H. Davis' presence at the sessions on Europe's private disarmament problems was purely impartial and for the purpose of offering his good offices were flung to the winds . . .

"Despite the administration's protests of Davis' neutrality at Geneva, it developed today he has been supporting the British and French position for some time."

of American support in the event of a preventive war against Germany or any lesser manifestation of direct action . . .[32]

Two methods of procedure are now being discussed. The first is for Mussolini to summon the European leaders either to Rome or Stresa under the Four Power Pact [33] or directly and there try and work out peace. If such conversations were decided on, obviously we should not take part. The second suggestion was to continue to write a treaty without Germany and sign it contingent upon Germany's later acceptance. I deprecate this as the game of bluff would play too prominent a part and it might lead us into political difficulties. If by any chance it were successful I should hate to see European appeasement negativized by Japan's refusal to cooperate. In the circumstances, the only thing to do seemed to be to regard the future as a purely European problem and let Europe in its consultations decide what it was going to do . . .

At a quarter to one the Secretary and Bill Phillips went over to the President who entirely agreed with the conclusions that we had reached. His uncanny political instinct made it clear that an indication of our aloofness from political entanglements must come from Norman Davis himself inasmuch as the opposition had been based on

[32] *The Literary Digest*, October 28, 1933, p. 6, reported that in the period following Germany's withdrawal from the Conference and the League, "as with one voice newspapers throughout the country announced that it should be this nation's fixed resolve to 'keep out of Europe.' " The *Digest* went on to discuss a story in the *New York Herald Tribune*, which stated that the United States must repudiate any political entanglements, not only because newspapers in France were linking their discussions of the German action with what the French termed "Franco-British-American solidarity" but also because the "Administration was under domestic pressure, editorial and telegraphic, to repudiate such assumption."

[33] Envisioning the possible breakdown of the Disarmament Conference, and even of the League of Nations itself, Mussolini proposed in March 1933 that Great Britain, France, Germany, and Italy conclude a pact as the basis for their assumption of dominance over international relations. Mussolini hoped the agreement would facilitate, among other things, revisions of territorial dispensations made in the World War peace treaties and the rearmament of Germany. But the "Great Power" concept underlying Mussolini's project raised an outcry from the lesser powers in the Little Entente, and the British and French could not accept Mussolini's proposals concerning territorial revision and rearmament. Consequently the Four Power Pact as initialled June 7, 1933, was a compromise draft with very little substance. It did, however, contain a statement that if the Disarmament Conference failed, the four signatory parties reserved "the right to reëxamine these questions between themselves under the present agreement with a view to ensuring their solution through the appropriate channels." Arnold J. Toynbee, *Survey of International Affairs, 1933* (London: Oxford University Press, 1934), pp. 208–221.

the theory that Norman Davis was entangling us without our knowledge . . .

Personally, I am coming to the opinion that the Conference holds out little but liabilities and by no means feel that we should take a leading role in fighting for its survival unless Europe itself wishes its continuance . . .

Monday, October 23, 1933.

I met the Secretary in the elevator this morning coming into the building. He asked me to come to his office and talk for a few moments. He thereupon pulled out from his inside pocket a clipping from the Hearst press[34] yesterday indicating that once more he was being relegated to a secondary position in the Government and citing as instances thereof the fact that the President was going to negotiate on Russia himself,[35] that the debt negotiations had been transferred to the Treasury and that his policy on disarmament had been overruled at the White House . . . He could not understand the injustice of these attacks and wondered if they were a part of the deliberate policy of the paper or of the venom of the individual correspondents. I told him that I thought it was undoubtedly the former, but that it was scarcely worth worrying over as the Hearst press was largely discounted in the public eye anyway . . . Apparently the Secretary honeycombs the papers and is far more sensitive to personal press attack than I had anticipated . . .

Wednesday, December 27, 1933.

Subject to the President's approval, the Department has at last decided to register treaties with the League. This is a common sense step which has been blocked by bureaucracy for years.

Our relations with the League of Nations are going to be touched upon by the President in his speech before the Woodrow Wilson Foundation tomorrow night. Bill Phillips sent me up for comment the

[34] This article by Kenneth Clark, entitled "Evidence Seen of Hull's Declining Influence," appeared in the *New York American*, October 22, 1933, p. 14.

[35] On October 10, 1933, Franklin Roosevelt had sent an invitation to President Mikhail Kalinin of the Soviet Union suggesting that conversations be undertaken between the two countries to settle "all questions outstanding." Since the United States had never recognized the Soviet regime, establishment of diplomatic relations was one of the most important matters to be considered. U.S. Dept. of State, *Foreign Relations, 1933*, II, 794.

first draft of the speech as he had received it from the White House, and together we went over it sentence by sentence suggesting a change or modification here and there. On the whole it is an exceedingly adroit piece of work, giving the League encouragement as a necessary prop in the peace structure, pointing out clearly where we work with it and where we do not and bridging the difficult gap between Woodrow Wilson's policies and his own by declaring that the Wilson ideals were the ideals of peoples but that until Governments and statesmen gave up their maneuvering for profit and prestige, the Wilson millennium could not arrive . . .

Thursday, January 18, 1934.

. . . Representative Dickstein came in and spent an hour with Bill Phillips, urging him to support with the President his desire to pass a joint resolution which will enable him to subpoena witnesses and continue his investigation into Nazi propaganda.[36] He left a confidential copy of the hearings of his subcommittee but said that this represented only a small part of the evidences he had found of a determined effort on the part of the Nazis to overthrow our very form of Government. Bill Phillips, much to my surprise, was distinctly impressed and felt that from what he had told him, Mr. Dickstein had serious evidence which should be brought to light. He asked me if I would take home the hearings and read them through. I did so and could find nothing that carried conviction to my mind. The whole proceedings seemed an *opéra bouffe* affair with evidence introduced either by Germans under a concealed name, by Communist editors, or by stewards and waiters on transatlantic ships. The distinction between propaganda and freedom of the press is one which was not brought out and I likewise saw no convincing evidence that the German Government was deliberately behind a widespread plot. Admitting all he said to be true I still feel that if the body politic of America could not withstand such efforts on the part of the Nazis, something must be radically wrong . . .

---

[36] Representative Samuel Dickstein of New York was on the Special Committee on un-American Activities. The hearings of the committee are printed in U.S. Congress, House, *Investigation of Nazi Propaganda . . . and other Propaganda Activities,* Hearings before the Special Committee on un-American Activities, House of Representatives, 73 Cong., 2 Sess. (Washington: Government Printing Office, 1934).

Thursday, March 8, 1934.

. . . The rumblings of German resentment at the mass meeting continued all day. I lunched with Leitner, Counselor of the German Embassy. He could talk of very little else besides the mock trial — Hitlerism versus Civilization — held at the Madison Square Garden March 7.[37] Dr. Leitner said that his Ambassador had been hoping that Mr. Phillips would have a message for him today showing that the Federal Government disapproved of the proceedings. I told him what Mr. Phillips had said at press conference which was to the effect that he had "no comment other than to reëmphasize the private nature of the gathering and that no member of the Administration was present. Anything that was said, therefore, represented the personal views of the individual speakers." Dr. Leitner gave me the impression that he was disappointed that Mr. Phillips had not spoken more openly. He then went on to say that it was "incredible" to him that such an attack on the Chief of State of a friendly nation (he did not use the words "Chief of Government" which would have been more accurate) was permitted, and that apart from its political repercussions in Germany, it was establishing a very dangerous precedent which might come home to plague us some day. There were many people who did not believe in American policies and might so express themselves in ways which gave offense, but our hands would henceforth be tied as the answer to any protests we might make would be met with "you yourselves started it on March 7, 1934." I told Dr. Leitner that I doubted if we would take an unfriendly demonstration quite as much to heart as he seemed to be doing and that we recognized in others our cherished belief in the right of free speech. We talked for

[37] On March 6, 1934, Mr. Moffat wrote in his diary: "The Germans are growing more and more upset over the 'mock trial' scheduled for tomorrow night. They have got their journalists to approach the White House through Early [Stephen Early, press secretary to President Roosevelt]. They have kept coming back to the Department of State and now they are after Mr. Dodd in Berlin. They have handed the latter a memorandum urging that in view of the serious economic situation we let up a little on our insistence on the right of free speech (this seems like a *non sequitur.*) They went on to point out that the press campaign in the United States against Germany was continuing unabated, et cetera. Mr. Dodd held his ground and pointed out that there was still a lot going on in Germany that was shocking to the American public, but then suggested that the Secretary try and moderate the feeling in Germany by statements in the press conference." Tansill, pp. 280–284, discusses the repercussions of the mock trial in the United States and Germany. See also Dodd, pp. 86–87. Mr. Phillips, also, comments upon this incident in William Phillips, *Ventures in Diplomacy* (Boston: The Beacon Press, 1952), p. 164.

a few minutes about what was said, but Dr. Leitner felt that the mere holding of a "mock trial" was so distressing that anything which might have been said or not said was of secondary importance. He concluded by reiterating again and again that while he was quite aware of what had been explained to his Ambassador and himself as to our lack of authority to stop the meeting, none the less it remained an incomprehensible episode to anyone who had a European outlook on problems . . .[38]

Tuesday, April 3, 1934.

   . . . Bill Phillips telephoned me at half-past six with relation to the Hanfstaengl imbroglio. [Ernst] Hanfstaengl was a member of the class of 1909 at Harvard, which is celebrating its 25th anniversary this year. Dr. [Elliott] Cutler as Senior Marshal invited Hanfstaengl to be one of his aides at the commencement. Hanfstaengl accepted promptly and gave the news to the press before Dr. Cutler had received a reply, whereupon the storm burst . . . Finally the pressure grew so great that Dr. Cutler decided that he must withdraw the invitation. He called up Bill Phillips as an Overseer [of Harvard] to see whether the Government would help either directly or indirectly in transmitting his message. Bill Phillips naturally declined, but said he would call back in a half-hour, after talking it over with me to see whether he could offer any suggestions. I told him that he knew well enough my feelings about the Nazi Government, but that in this case if Dr. Cutler should withdraw the invitation, I felt the repercussions would be pretty serious. Hanfstaengl is one of Hitler's Chief Advisers. He was a member of the class of 1909, in good standing, and received and answered an invitation to join his classmates. If this were now rescinded in response to Jewish pressure, the repercussions in Germany would be pretty serious and at this end Harvard would definitely go on record as caring more about the sources of financial revenue than about the bigger principle of intellectual tolerance. Dr. Dodd had given Hitler a little sermon on the freedom of opinion in American universities, but he would be made ridiculous if this should happen. I urged Mr. Phillips to persuade Dr. Cutler to reconsider and to ride

[38] U.S. Department of State, *Foreign Relations of the United States, 1934*, vol. II, *Europe, Near East and Africa* (Washington: Government Printing Office, 1951), pp. 501–521.

out the storm at the cost of embarrassment. If, however, he were to withdraw the invitation, then this Government must keep its hands scrupulously clean of the affair . . .

Tuesday, April 10, 1934.

. . . Dined at the Lothrop Stoddards', and then went on to the Bolshevik Embassy housewarming. Never have I seen anything quite like that. The huge Pullman Palace was brilliantly lighted, attic to cellar. There was a long awning stretching out to the street and a mass of several hundred curious onlookers watching people coming in and going out, a form of sport Washington is not normally given to. About 1000 guests were invited and were checked by name at the door to prevent gatecrashers. We filed up the grand staircase, shook hands with our host and hostess and then wandered loose over the entire house. On every one of the three floors was a huge buffet and every room, literally including bedrooms, was filled with a well-dressed but rubbernecking crowd looking at pictures, photographs, furniture, et cetera. Somebody said that the Embassy represented the marriage of late Louis XVI and early Stalin. Another remarked that it was lucky we had recognized them now as if we had waited a short time they would never have recognized us. Depending on whether one would adopt an economic or political point of view, one's chief interest lay in whether the party set the Five Year Plan back twelve months, or whether they estimated (and probably correctly) that one pound of caviar was equivalent to one convert . . .[39]

Tuesday, June 12, 1934.

. . . Hanfstaengl, in spite of the broadest hints of his classmates of 1909 that they did not want him for the 25th reunion at Harvard, left Berlin by airplane, caught the "Europa," and is now en route. He is now chief of the press section of the National Socialist Party and has been one of the most outstanding and fanatical of the Hitler incense swingers. His presence is going to stir up the whole German-Jewish situation again and is most ill-advised. None the less he is here and the question is what to do to protect him . . . [The secretary of the class of 1909] came down to consult Jimmy Dunn and myself.

[39] The United States had formally recognized the Soviet regime on November 16, 1933.

He said that the reunion would consist of about 1000 members of the class, men, women and children, who would be living in the Yard. He was openly afraid of bombing or some physical attempt. He did not wish to expose the class to danger and wondered if the Government could not protect him. We pointed out the difference of jurisdictions between Federal and State authorities and told him that we were just as anxious as he to prevent any incident. I also told him that he must get in touch with the Mayor of Cambridge, who could of course consult with the Governor of Massachusetts and the latter, if necessary, with the Department of Justice. We stood ready at any time to help out, but it was not our responsibility to protect an individual citizen who was over here on private business . . .[40]

Tuesday, September 11, 1934.

When the Secretary returned this morning, Mr. Phillips laid before him the various protests that we had received from foreign Governments in connection with the munitions investigation.[41] It was refreshing to watch oath after oath pour out of his rather saintlike countenance and then to have him smile and say, "It's not more than once every six months that I use language like that!" Not only did the British protests disturb him but reports were coming in from all over South America that the accusations bandied about of bribery and corruption through Latin America were undoing all the good work accomplished at the Montevideo Conference last autumn.[42] We prepared a series of dossiers for him and a memorandum of what we hoped he could persuade Senator Nye to issue in the way of a disclaimer to European Governments of any intent to give offense. It was a ques-

[40] Hanfstaengl returned to Germany in July after spending about three weeks in the United States. No violent attacks marred his visit, although unfavorable letters about him appeared in newspapers, hostile posters and literature were in evidence at Harvard, and anti-Nazi demonstrations took place. *New York Times*, June 17, 1934, p. 1; June 19, 1934, p. 8; June 22, 1934, p. 1; June 28, 1934, p. 15; and July 9, 1934, p. 5.

[41] A Special Committee had been appointed by the Senate to investigate the private manufacture of arms and traffic in arms. Gerald P. Nye, senator from North Dakota, was the chairman of the committee.

[42] Protests from Great Britain and the Latin American countries against the "insinuations," "accusations," and "allegations" are given in U.S. Dept. of State, *Foreign Relations, 1934*, I, 427–448. The hearings of the Nye Committee are printed in U.S. Congress, Senate, *Munitions Industry*, Hearings before the Special Committee Investigating the Munitions Industry, 73 Cong., 2 Sess., on Senate Res. 206 (Washington: Government Printing Office, 1934).

tion of the Secretary's avoiding two pitfalls. On the one hand, he must not seem to be blocking the inquiry which in general is along the lines the Department desired. On the other hand, he must protect our good name and friendship . . .

Dined with Jeff Coolidge [T. Jefferson Coolidge, Under Secretary of the Treasury], later playing bridge. The whole talk was on the Maine election and the extraordinary swing of the voters in the rock-ribbed State toward the radical standard.[43] It is about time for New Yorkers to see that if Roosevelt fails the popular swing will not be back to the Ogden Mills and the Wadsworths [James Wadsworth, Republican congressman from New York] of this world (at least for 5 or 6 years to come) but in the direction of greater radicalism.

Wednesday, September 12, 1934.

The Secretary sent for me this morning shortly after nine o'clock. I found him with Secretary Roper [Daniel C. Roper, Secretary of Commerce] talking over the question of a personal and confidential report sent in to the Department of Commerce by Douglas Miller, the Commercial Attaché at Berlin, on the German purchases of aeroplanes. The Committee [the Special Committee Investigating the Munitions Industry] wanted very much to put this into the record and approached both State and Commerce in turn trying to play one off against the other. Mr. Hull asked me what I thought. I told him that if it were published, it would be the end of Douglas Miller's usefulness; that he was an intensely valuable man and a particular expert in German finances and economics. To make it necessary for him to leave Germany at this moment would be a very real blow to the United States. Further than that he must realize that our whole system of reporting built up from all over the world was dependent upon our agents being able to obtain confidentially information from personal sources. If now the impression became general that any report an American diplomat or Consul sent in would be published in any Senate Investigating Committee, the efficiency of the Service would be cut in half. We had reached an informal agreement with the Committee that while they could have access to all our files, they could

---

[43] A Democratic governor was reëlected and two out of the three congressmen chosen were Democrats in what the *New York Times*, September 12, 1934, p. 2, called "Maine's endorsement of the New Deal."

not publish any of them without our permission and that as a general rule we did not give that permission for reports coming into us from our own people abroad. Mr. Hull and Mr. Roper said they were in entire agreement and the latter definitely undertook not to give the required permission . . .

Friday, September 14, 1934.

   . . . The Secretary and Mr. Roper again went before the Munitions Commission in Executive Session and flatly declined to authorize the publication of certain reports. They also had an opportunity to talk over some of the dangers. For instance, it appeared that the Committee had unearthed the fact that the son of the President of Argentina had received a 10% commission on certain sales to that country. The Secretary pointed out that publishing this would not help in getting at the main point of how much in the way of munitions we had sent to the Argentine but he added, "for twenty years the Argentine has been the leader of an anti-American bloc. At last we have come to a working arrangement with her and relations are rapidly improving. If you publish that information, it will be another twenty years before we can play ball with her." The Committee was divided about 50–50 as to whether to cooperate with the Secretary . . .

From October 16, 1934, through December 19, preliminary conversations took place at London among the representatives of the United States, Great Britain, and Japan. These talks were to prepare the ground for the London Naval Conference, which was to be held in 1935. While discussions between the Americans and the British raised no insurmountable problems, the Japanese delegates injected into the naval sphere the vexed question of "equality" of armaments. Japan desired that the 5–5–3 naval ratio, which had been set up in the Washington Treaty of 1922, be changed to give Japan naval parity with the two other powers.

October 3, 1934.

   The President opened the conversation by saying that he had run over a memorandum setting forth the views of the State and Navy Departments on possible contingencies with which our conferees might be faced in the forthcoming naval talks in London. He likewise had before him a draft letter for him to address to Mr. Norman Davis setting forth the American position in broad outline, which the latter might eventually read to the Conference or utilize in any other way he saw fit.

The first point he wished to consider was the timing of this statement. He was inclined to think that the best results would be obtained by giving the letter publicity before the British and Japanese had had time to set forth their statements of policy. The President inquired whether or not the Japanese had definitely informed us that they were intending to denounce the Washington Treaty or whether it was merely an impression we had gained from statements of prominent Japanese officials. When he was reminded of the recent conversation between Foreign Minister Hirota and Ambassador Grew,[44] he said that he was more than ever convinced of the urgency of our losing no time the moment the conversations were opened.

This brought up the question as to whether or not we should press for trilateral conversations or should continue a series of bilateral talks.[45] It was the consensus of all present that we must make an immediate effort to persuade the British to formalize the proceedings and prevent their playing the role of broker between the American and Japanese delegations . . .

Admiral Standley [Chief of Naval Operations] asked whether the President would agree to a slight increase of tonnage if thereby we felt we could facilitate an agreement with the British and Japanese. The President said definitely "no" that our policy had consistently been to favor reduction; that it was a policy we had urged time after time not only upon the Naval Powers but upon the Land Powers of Europe; we must continue to maintain a consistent policy in this regard, and he for one was unwilling to sign a treaty or to submit a treaty either to the Senate or to the people which carried with it an increase of one ton over the total figures now appearing in the Washington and London Naval Treaties.

To this end he considered it important that our first statement and his letter to Mr. Davis should be so clear and based on so high a level that the British and Japanese would feel themselves at an immediate disadvantage. Mr. Davis pointed out that the British would endeavor

[44] Koki Hirota had notified the American Ambassador to Japan, Joseph C. Grew, on September 17, 1934, that Japan had decided to give notice before the end of 1934 of the termination of the Washington Naval Treaty. U.S. Department of State, *Papers Relating to the Foreign Relations of the United States, Japan: 1931–1941* (Washington: Government Printing Office, 1943), I, 253–254.

[45] The United States and Great Britain had held preliminary conversations from June 18 to July 19, 1934.

by maneuvering to make it difficult for us to issue such a statement. The President said obviously but that some means or other must be found to emphasize his "letter of guidance" and make it clear that we had laid all our cards on the table . . .

Mr. Davis, however, made it very clear that in his judgment, it was useless to try to argue the Japanese into changing their position, or to obtain results by maneuvering them into an uncomfortable position. As he saw it the one possibility of enabling the Japanese to change their position was for the United States to reach some sort of an understanding with Great Britain. The President tossed out the idea without however pursuing it to a conclusion of indicating to Japan that, while we must insist on a real naval superiority, we would not in time of peace maintain in the Pacific a fleet greater than that of Japan. There were, of course, certain objections — notably a weakening of potential diplomatic pressure. Admiral Standley pointed out that it would definitely take away any possible initiative from the American side but that from a purely defensive point of view it would not have serious consequences.

It was the consensus of opinion that in no circumstances should we indicate any intention either to weaken ourselves in the Orient, to indicate an unwillingness to join issue under certain circumstances or a willingness to allow the Japanese to continue pressing forward without protest on our part. Such a policy we felt would throw England and Japan together to a point where they might join forces in attempting to exclude the United States from the Asiatic market. The President felt that in the case no treaty were agreed to, Japan and Britain would negatively reach an understanding possibly in the form of a bilateral nonaggression pact. With regard to a multilateral pact of nonaggression he would not consider it unless it were to be signed by the Pacific Powers including Russia and China. Objection was raised that even under present circumstances, it would validate Japan's occupation of Manchukuo. The President said "no," that it would not validate the occupation it would merely be a declaration that we would not fight Japan on account of her occupation in Manchukuo.

The President, after this discussion, read aloud the draft letter of guidance to Mr. Davis which had been prepared for him. He remarked that while the points were well taken, it was cast too much in the form of a diplomatic document and not in the form of a living expression which could be understood by the man in the streets . . .[46]

Monday, October 29, 1934.

A quiet day, made the more so by Bill Phillips' absence in Canada, which has meant a postponement of action on a number of dossiers that require his decision. At London the meetings have continued on, one between the Japanese and Americans and another between the British and Americans. The Japanese have shown no signs of modifying their stand in any way. They have endeavored to draw us into technical discussions which we are unwilling to do until the questions of principle have been thrashed out. I detect in the tone of Norman Davis' telegrams a feeling of dismay at the lack of progress he is making not only with Yamamoto [Isoroku Yamamoto, technical adviser to the Japanese delegation], which I think he anticipated, but with Matsudaira [Tsuneo Matsudaira, Japanese Ambassador to Great Britain] with whom he was formerly on the best of terms and who is now as unapproachable as the others. There is no doubt but that the Japanese have been endeavoring to drive a wedge between the British and ourselves and have stressed to the British their fear of our naval establishment. But although when the Japanese came to London, the British were pretty well disposed toward them, there is no doubt but that the British have been shocked with the rigidity of their demands.[47] It has now become clear that in carrying out the Japanese idea of equality, they intend to have the "common upper limit" apply to France and Italy as well, and if this idea were carried further, it would soon include Germany and Russia — a thought which makes even Tory hearts quail . . . All in all the outlook for possible achievement looks as dark as ever. On the smaller front, namely, American popular reaction to our stand, things are moving well as there is a unanimity of opinion all the way over to any but the most pacifist circles that the Japanese are adopting an unreasonable, not to say offensive, position and that she has clearly shown her hand at desiring

[46] The text of this letter dated October 5, 1934, is printed in U.S. Dept. of State, *Foreign Relations, Japan: 1931–41*, I, 282.

[47] See the memorandum of a conversation on October 25 between Mr. Davis and the British representative as given in U.S. Dept. of State, *Foreign Relations, 1934*, I, 312.

only one thing, overlordship in the Far East, which means the expulsion of American rights and the closing of the Open Door . . .[48]

Thursday, November 8, 1934.

Have been trying to crystallize my thoughts on how the London conversations may be terminated. It seems quite clear to me that the Japanese are not going to modify their position and that we have given them every chance in the world to "save face." We have not hurried them, we have listened to everything they have had to say, yet the gratuitous statement makes it clear that only the substance of their demands will satisfy them. How to break up, however, when the psychological moment arrives will at best be a delicate matter. My mind is working somewhat along the following lines: The conversations should be theoretically suspended, not broken off. There should, however, be no definite date for their resumption but a provision written in that if at a later date any one of the three Powers should feel that it had proposals to offer of such nature as to warrant belief in their acceptance, then it should feel free to convoke the other Powers to a further meeting. Jimmy Dunn and Bill Phillips agreed; Stanley Hornbeck was inclined to doubt the wisdom of our making any move at all, considering that it was better to sit in London until Christmas if necessary in order to have any suggestion of adjournment come from the British . . .

Wednesday, November 21, 1934.

No real move as yet in the London talks but a great deal of telegraphing from London looking toward a clarification of the issue. Norman Davis sent in a long telegram in three sections explaining the position he has taken.[49] He reported that, with patience, he believes the issue to be moving toward Anglo-American cooperation. The British idea has clearly been to tie the Japanese up in some form of treaty agreement whereas our idea has been to suspend the conversations, letting the Japanese return home free but emptyhanded and

[48] *The Nation*, CXXXIX (November 7, 1934), 519, stated that if Japanese demands were met, Japan would have not only "full parity" but also "actual superiority" in the Pacific. "The present naval ratios are conditioned on the maintenance of the open door and the territorial integrity of China. Should Japan persist in denying these, it is obvious that the other nations would not dare grant an upward revision of the ratios."

[49] U.S. Dept. of State, *Foreign Relations, 1934*, I, 356–358.

without any agreement in their hands, which they could label as compensation for the treaty or as a victory for their thesis. The intransigent Japanese attitude failure (as reported in the press but not yet indicated to Davis officially) has, however, been playing into the hands of the elements in Great Britain which consider it more important to march in step with us than to reach an agreement with Japan. Furthermore, Japanese diplomacy has not been adroit and the rather clumsy efforts made to drive a wedge between the British and ourselves have widely overshot the mark . . .

Saturday and Sunday, December 8 and 9, 1934.

Late Friday evening a long telegram had arrived from Norman Davis of a very fundamental nature.[50] It dealt with our insistence upon adjournment of the conference following Japanese denunciation of the Washington Treaty rather than a mere recess. He agreed that we should not ease the situation for the Japanese after denunciation and that we should not meet immediately thereafter; on the other hand, he felt it more important that we do nothing to make it appear that we do not want an agreement of any kind and are even unwilling to pave the way for a future settlement. The formula we had suggested, namely, that if at any time one of the Powers felt that it had any proposals to offer it should forthwith convoke the others, Norman Davis rejected on the ground that this would place a responsibility which no one Power would wish to assume and that it ran the risk of resulting in no conference and no future naval agreement. Furthermore, Norman Davis, echoing the British clearly, did not want the meeting to break up with guilt being attached to any one party. He felt that Yamamoto was little by little beginning to see the light and that we should encourage him to go home and persuade the Japanese Government that they were on the wrong track. In the circumstances, he felt that we should accept the British proposal to adjourn before the Japanese denunciation and to meet again in another series of preparatory conversations some time in the future.

I had worked several hours on Friday night on the text of a reply, and Saturday morning the Secretary, Stanley Hornbeck and myself went into joint session. We agreed on certain fundamentals: (1) that any fixed date for a resumption of talks had the disadvantage of ignor-

[50] *Ibid.*, pp. 388–390.

ing future developments and the prospects of success; (2) that an unsuccessful conference was far more of a strain upon international good will than no conference. For instance, during the talks this autumn, Anglo-Japanese relations had deteriorated and even American-British relations had been subjected to a heavy strain; (3) we earnestly advocated British-American cooperation but this implied give and take. We had already acceded to her request to explore compromise proposals with the Japanese in the very face of her announced intention to denounce the treaty, and we had accepted the impression that we were more opposed to granting Japan's parity than Great Britain, whereas on this point we stood as a unit; (4) to accept or give the impression of accepting the Japanese conception that the basis of the Washington Treaty could be altered and then agree to sit down with her at the Council Table as though nothing had happened was we felt scarcely conducive to the ultimate objective of bringing about a change of mind in Japan which alone would make a treaty possible . . .

Once again we came back to what I think is Norman Davis' only weakness as a negotiator, namely, the belief that if he can convince the man with whom he is negotiating, the problem is solved. He tends to overlook the force of circumstances and the power of public opinions. We were working from half-past nine to twelve in the morning on this telegram, so that my desk was piled high with other matters . . .[51]

Wednesday, December 19, 1934.

News came through in the morning of the decision of the Privy Council in Japan to announce the termination of the Washington Treaty. In the afternoon the adjournment of the preliminary conference took place in a tripartite meeting. The connection between the two events is obvious even though the communiqué issued was frankly anodyne.[52] Matsudaira at the last minute tried to set a date for the resumption of negotiations but we promptly vetoed it. He also referred in his closing speech to a resumption of preliminary conversations; we shall see about that. MacDonald stated that there were certain basic considerations which neither pressure nor time could

[51] Ibid., pp. 391–392.
[52] U.S. Dept. of State, Foreign Relations, Japan: 1931–41, I, 272–273.

induce Great Britain to abandon. All in all, I think we have come out of the conversations slightly better than we went in. Our relations with Japan have certainly deteriorated but to compensate for this our working arrangement with England is stronger than it has been for some months past . . .

Saturday, Sunday, Monday and Tuesday, December 22, 23, 24 and 25, 1934.

Saturday morning, December 22, was marked by an attempt to clear my desk before going off for the Christmas holidays. The Secretary sent for me and asked me to rewrite the statement we are going to make when the Japanese denounce the treaty, in pithier terms.[53] He feels that we must put squarely before the Government the question of whether or not henceforth the movement of international cooperation and disarmament must rest on the principle of equality of armament or on the principle of equality of security. I was able to complete a redraft of which I gave copies to the Secretary, Mr. Phillips and Stanley Hornbeck just in time to leave the Department and catch the one o'clock to New York . . .

Monday, the 24th, after a day of shopping, we went over to the family gathering at the old house in Brooklyn and sat down to table four generations strong. Jack Pierrepont, aged 19, who sat next to Edith [Edith Moffat, Mr. Moffat's five-year-old daughter] at table, proceeded to give her a good half-glass of champagne before he was discovered, and if it be true that a slight glow brings out the true nature of man I can only conclude that Edith has the most affectionate of natures for she was expansively charming the rest of the evening. I don't know why this reminds me of a good joke on Lilla who, whatever other virtues she possesses, cannot follow a tune to save her immortal soul. She none the less tried to join in singing some carols and felt amply repaid when the lady next her turned to her at the end and said, "Really my dear to think that you were able to sing alto throughout all the carols!"

Christmas day was stockings, more presents for the children under

---

[53] The Japanese Ambassador to the United States handed the note of denunciation to the Secretary of State on December 29, 1934. It was Japan's right, under Article 23 of the Washington Treaty, to announce thus her intention of permitting the treaty to expire on December 31, 1936. Tate, p. 187.

the Christmas tree, church, et cetera. All in all a good old-fashioned Christmas holiday which children make increasingly strenuous as they add to their number of years.

Returned on the 12.35 A.M. train on December 26 . . .

IV

SYDNEY

September 1935 – March 1937

"We have lost many an opportunity by not treating Australia as a political entity"

In 1935 Pierrepont Moffat completed the fourth year of his assignment in the Department of State. Since it was mandatory at that time that all Foreign Service Officers who had spent four consecutive years in the Department must be transferred to the field, he was sent to Australia as Consul General.[1]

Here he found an opportunity for valuable service. "There is real political work to be done," he wrote. "We have never made any attempt to deal with Australia as a political entity, and anti-American feeling is fairly rife." [2]

[1] This move was also in line with President Roosevelt's wish that all diplomats have at least one consular assignment in order to gain administrative experience and make contacts with the business world. Since Mr. Moffat was one of the first officers of his rank to accept a consular post, the Department of State was interested in his reactions. In response to the request to give his "opinion about the transfer of senior officers from the diplomatic to the consular branch," Mr. Moffat wrote on January 14, 1936: "In all phases of consular work the first emphasis must be placed upon accuracy and timeliness. Each particular field requires a close knowledge of detailed rules and the man handling any one of these problems must make himself letter-perfect. As to the policy of transferring senior diplomatic officers to consular posts, my conclusion is that if they are poor organizers and need experience in administration the training should prove invaluable. If, on the other hand, they do not need this training I am inclined to think that they stand to gain relatively little, as the emphasis in consular work is on perfection in individual problems, rather than in analytical thinking or drawing deductions on broad trends. To these generalities I definitely except Sydney and Calcutta, which I feel should always be manned by a diplomatic officer. In Sydney at least we have lost many an opportunity by not treating Australia as a political entity."

[2] In an undated essay written several months before he left Australia in 1937, Mr. Moffat gave his analysis of the causes of the anti-American feeling in the Commonwealth: "Various explanations are given: our late entry into the war [World War I]; our failure to join the League of Nations; our attitude toward war debts; and our ungenerous tariff policy. To these I would add two which are not generally given:

One of the sources of friction between the United States and Australia was trade. Between 1918 and 1929 from 20 to 25 per cent of the total yearly imports of Australia were from the United States.[3] In the same period the percentage of the total yearly exports of Australia to the United States had dropped from 11 to 4 per cent. During the booming years of the twenties Australia felt it could stand the adverse trade balance. But in the depression decade the Australians turned a jaundiced eye on the statistics of United States–Commonwealth trade.

To ease the burden Australia suggested in June 1934 that a new trade treaty be negotiated between the two countries in line with Secretary Hull's reciprocal trade program.[4] After some prodding by the Australians the United States finally answered negatively in January 1935. The note declined to discuss a trade treaty with Australia at that time, because the major Australian exports, which were wheat, butter, milk, hides, fruit, and wool, were too highly competitive with American products.[5]

This was still where the situation stood when Pierrepont Moffat reached Sydney on September 9, 1935, to take up his post of Consul General, the highest ranking American official in Australia. Two weeks after his arrival he received a telegram from Secretary Hull: "Since the situation with regard to trade agreements with countries whose products are so competitive with ours has not changed since our telegram dated January 15, 1935, we hope that you will find opportunity to drop a hint in the right quarters that an agreement with Australia is not indicated in the near future." [6] Mr. Moffat took the occasion of his first trip to Canberra to convey the "hint."

October 1, 1935 [Sydney].

Stopped by at the office this morning to take my oath of office as

first, a conscious drive on the part of British organs of public opinion to diminish our influence (both commercial and cultural), and second, a form of inferiority complex which makes the Australian resent in others the accomplishments he most craves for himself. But if popular enthusiasm for the United States has died down, it has been replaced by a reasonably healthy though rather critical feeling of comradeship, a tendency to copy many of our ways, and widespread belief that the world would best be served by a British-American alliance, in which America would be expected to limit herself to the role of a brilliant second."

[3] Werner Levi, *American-Australian Relations* (Minneapolis: University of Minnesota Press, 1947), pp. 127–136; Fred Alexander, *Australia and the United States* (Boston: World Peace Foundation, 1941), pp. 44–46.

[4] A summary of the Australian note of June 4, 1934, is given in U.S. Department of State, *Foreign Relations of the United States, 1934* (Washington: Government Printing Office, 1951), I, 841.

[5] U.S. Department of State, *Foreign Relations of the United States, 1935*, vol. II, *The British Commonwealth, Europe* (Washington: Government Printing Office, 1952), pp. 9–10.

[6] *Ibid.*, pp. 15–16.

Foreign Service Officer Class 1 and after a few moments examining the incoming mail proceeded to Canberra for a week's visit.

The journey up was easy, good roads the entire way. Once we left Sydney, however, we entered empty country. For miles and miles there wouldn't be a human habitation visible, just hillsides or valleys dotted with gum trees (half of them ring-barked, the dead trunks standing there silver-colored). Then would come a town of a few hundred inhabitants and once more complete emptiness. As we rose higher the vegetation changed and the wattle trees began to become frequent, green trees with clusters of bright yellow blossoms from top to bottom. Then, over the divide, we came upon country so like portions of our own West that if it were not for the ubiquitous gum tree and the incredibly brilliant-hued wild parrots I should have believed myself in Wyoming or Montana.

Then Canberra. It is a lovely place, only, it is not a city; it is not even a town. The whole impression is that of a nice summer resort, with parliament buildings instead of a Kursaal with the hotel built in a series of pavilions surrounding a central portion reached via open-air colonnades. In the middle distance, a mile or two away are a series of villages with red-roofed bungalows. That is all and that is Canberra. But the setting is lovely, in a lush green plain with blue hills rising on either side which gradually grow higher and higher until in the far south they become true mountains. Everywhere the fruit trees are in blossom, either white or vivid pink. The avenues are lined with exotic trees or shrubs, each one neatly labeled with both scientific and popular names. The weather was warm, a soft inviting warmth that persisted until sundown when it suddenly turned chilly, not to say cold, until the sun returned to warm it.

October 2 [1935. Canberra].

This morning early I set out to pay my calls, starting with Colonel Hodgson, Assistant Secretary to the Prime Minister and permanent functionary in the Department of External Affairs. He said that he had been working for weeks on the Abyssinian question [7] and never

---

[7] On December 5, 1934, fighting had broken out between Abyssinia and Italy over Abyssinian frontierland, and on October 2, 1935, Italian troops invaded the African state. On September 12, 1935, Pierrepont Moffat wrote in his diary: "The Abyssinian crisis is having a direct effect in Australia, partly because any collective action taken against Italy might well result in hostilities, which would threaten the Suez Canal and

had he had a more difficult task than to prepare the papers for the Cabinet, as that body was divided in opinion as to the course Australia should follow. In his own mind, however, there was not the slightest doubt but that Australia's position was to remain solidly behind Great Britain . . . He confided that he was coaching the Cabinet supporters for the coming parliamentary debate on the Abyssinian question, giving each man one or two points to make. Very few knew anything about the subject, either government or opposition, and he feared that the debate would not be on a high level . . .

Luncheon with the Prime Minister [Joseph Aloysius Lyons] turned out to be in his private dining room next door to his office in Parliament Building. Douglas [Ronald I. Douglas, Commonwealth Publicity Officer] and McKenna [Francis Joseph McKenna, private secretary to Mr. Lyons] were the only others present. After the usual interchange of reminiscences . . . the Prime Minister without further ado got down to business . . .

The next subject for discussion was the question of a resident Commissioner at Washington.[8] He told me that the suggestion really came from the President, when they were thinking out loud together about Australian representation . . . At first blush, he saw no insuperable difficulties. He did not want diplomatic representation yet, as it would mean setting up several legations, including one in Tokyo, which he did not feel able to do, either financially or politically . . . I indicated that the President and the Secretary still hoped that some day before so very long Australia could have regular diplomatic representation in Washington.

Speaking of diplomatic representations, Mr. Lyons spoke of Mr. Debuchi's [Katsuji Debuchi, Japanese Vice-Minister of Foreign Affairs and former Japanese Ambassador to the United States] recent visit. He said that he had liked him immensely, and felt that he was a man with whom it was possible to talk freely. I told him in a light vein

---

the Mediterranean and thus dislocate all Australian communication and partly because there is a widespread difference of opinion in the Commonwealth as to the course to be pursued. Labor groups have been exceedingly vocal in their opposition to any form of Australian participation in sanctions . . .

"The general tendency of the present government is to play in strongly with England and to emphasize Imperial unity."

[8] Australian affairs in the United States were handled by the British Embassy at Washington.

of Debuchi's role in Washington during the days of the Manchurian crisis. Well, commented Mr. Lyons, I know how you all feel about Manchukuo and the impossibility of recognizing its present status quo. As a matter of fact I took up with your President my idea of a Pacific Pact, as the most probable guarantee of peace, and then added, "I suppose, however, that you could not see your way to signing an agreement with Japan while she was continuing to violate her Treaties in Manchukuo." The President had replied, "That's going too far; there is a lot we might be able to overlook if we could really help achieve lasting peace. That must always be the first consideration." Mr. Lyons had tried out his idea with Debuchi, who had personally reacted favorably; the idea, at least as I was able to gather it, was rather nebulous, but was based on a recognition of the present status quo in the Pacific as the normal balance of strength which all countries should undertake to respect . . .

As to the Italo-Abyssinian dispute, he said that his government would definitely follow Great Britain. He could never forget that Australia might some day find herself in the plight of Abyssinia. Despite all the telegrams back and forth he did not know the ultimate plans of the British Government, but he did not expect that it would push matters to extremes or run the risk of general hostilities. I asked about the possibility of trying to close the Suez Canal, but he seemed reasonably satisfied that there was no probability of any sanction of such severity. At any rate, he gave me the impression that he hoped there was not such a possibility. "In any event," he added laughingly, "that is something you do not have to worry about. The President told me that never again would the United States be drawn into a European War, regardless of circumstances." He asked about our neutrality legislation and showed a clearer grasp of its purpose and essentials than did Colonel Hodgson. At this point lunch broke up as Mr. Lyons had to leave the house . . .

Thursday, October 3 [1935. Canberra].

I called this morning on Sir George Pearce, the Minister for External Affairs. He is a slow-spoken, kindly-eyed, elderly gentleman, who had the gift of saying some pretty bitter things without giving offense. He had barely completed the usual amenities than he came to what was on his mind. This was that I would find (a) that in matters of politics there was a feeling that America was indifferent to Australia's welfare and could not be counted on to come to her aid in case of need, and (b) that in matters of trade there was a real hostility to the United States.

Discussing first matters political: Sir George started his recital with the visit of the American Fleet to Australia in 1908 [9] when American influence was at its apex. Popular songs were being sung, "We have a big brother in America." From one end of Australia to the other the visit of the Fleet was regarded as a demonstration of white solidarity against the yellow races. This feeling of comradeship and confidence had now almost entirely disappeared. The first shocks were due to our delay in entering the war and refusal to join the League of Nations. The next and greater shock was our insistence on parity in the cruiser class with Great Britain and still more on a proportionate reduction in the number of cruisers,[10] when no Australian could see that we needed so many, having few outlying possessions to defend, whereas the protection of Australia and New Zealand's communications were vital both to the Empire in general and to the Dominions in particular. The third shock was America's increasing indifference to her Pacific obligations, as evidenced by her withdrawal from the Philippines.[11] This had led Australia at large to feel that she could not count on American help in case of Japanese attack, a feeling which personally he did not share, but which none the less existed. This feeling was coloring Australia's policy vis-à-vis Japan. The Government remained suspicious of her ultimate intentions, but with British naval strength reduced below the safety point, and with American aid discounted, there was no policy open to her other than trying to be friendly with Japan, to give her no excuse to

[9] President Theodore Roosevelt had sent the fleet on a round-the-world cruise in 1907. The ships visited Australia among other countries before their return to the United States in 1909.

[10] In the London Naval Treaty of 1936 a six-year holiday had been declared on the building of cruisers in the 10,000-ton class. The United States and Great Britain had signed a separate agreement providing for Anglo-American naval parity. U. S. Department of State, *The London Naval Conference 1935* (Washington: Government Printing Office, 1936), pp. 31–32, 443–444.

[11] The Tydings-McDuffie Act, signed by Roosevelt on March 24, 1934, and accepted by the Philippine legislature May 1, 1934, provided that at the end of a ten-year period the United States would grant complete independence to the islands and withdraw all military bases. Whether the United States should retain naval establishments was left to later discussion.

adopt an aggressive policy vis-à-vis the Commonwealth, and to rejoice (irrespective of the moral aspect) every time Japan advanced more deeply into Manchukuo and North China. He hoped that her energies would be absorbed there for a generation, and so did the Government of the Netherlands East Indies, with which the Australian Government kept in close and constant contact. But the feeling he described existed throughout Australia, and as probably most Australians would be too polite to explain it to me in so many words, he felt that it was his business to tell it to me with all candor.

Developing his second thesis, Sir George said that every man in the street resented not so much America's favorable trade balance, as the fact that it was coupled with arbitrary customs practice, and a high tariff that shut out even noncompetitive products from Australia. For instance, (1) the tariff on the high-grade Australian merino wool did not help American producers; American wool was of a lower caliber and cloth made from American wool did not compete with English or foreign worsteds; (2) with the difference of our seasons there was a time of year when Australian fruits could be admitted to the United States on a noncompetitive basis — as a matter of fact quite a nice trade had started in this a few years ago, when the United States suddenly excluded Australian fruit while a shipment was actually on the water, and resulted in a total loss. This had not been forgotten or forgiven. Something must be done, and done soon to improve our trade balance, or he could tell me frankly that Australia would have to take measures to limit American imports. Nearly every country in Europe with which Australia had a favorable balance was putting pressure on Australia to buy more of *their* goods, and . . . the only place it could give anything was at the expense of the United States.

I told Sir George that he must not hurry us. For the first time since I could remember there was a predisposition in America to do something about tariffs. It was still in an experimental stage watched with suspicion by many interests. It must give proof to the country by results that it was the right policy. For that reason, Mr. Hull was proceeding slowly and scientifically, and was dealing first with noncompetitive products. It would probably be some time yet before we get around to the type of products which Sir George had mentioned. But there was something far broader in Mr. Hull's mind than mere tariff-bargaining. He envisaged his program as definitely designed to help reduce the barriers that were strangling world trade. Every time two nations tried to equalize their trade balance or reduce any inequality against normal trade trends, it turned out to be at the lower, not the higher figure. The ultimate solution lay along the lines of generalization of concessions, and universalizing increases in trade, and only if a country discriminated against us would it fail to get the benefits we gave.[12] I hoped we would never have to retaliate against any other country for an unfriendly policy . . . I had not been long in Australia, but I had been struck by many similarities between our two positions; both of us had active balances, not only absolutely, but with most European countries. If either of us should penalize the trade of the one or two countries with which we had an unfavorable balance, we would be accepting the only principle that in the long run could hurt us most, and reduce our total trade the fastest . . .

Wednesday, April 1 [1936. Sydney].

This afternoon Colonel Hodgson telephoned me from Canberra to the effect that in a surprise motion of adjournment the House had decided to debate the adverse trade balance between America and Australia and the discussion was proceeding at the very moment. He said that while the temper of the House was definitely in favor of restriction, there has been no evidence of anti-American sentiment whatsoever and that one member, whom he had primed, (Sir Donald Cameron of Queensland),[13] had gone out of his way to point out some of the collateral effects of discrimination. He said that Sir Henry Gullett [Minister Directing Negotiations for Trade Treaties] had given a long historical résumé of our case and that he would mail me the *Hansard* of the debate early tomorrow morning in order that I may have it on Friday rather than await the arrival of the corrected text some time next week.[14] Colonel Hodgson did not tell me, how-

[12] On the principles and operation of the reciprocal trade program see Hull, I, 352–377.

[13] Cameron's speech stressed the need for cooperation and good will between the United States and Australia and among all the English-speaking people as a way to insure the future peace of the world. Commonwealth of Australia, *Parliamentary Debates*, CXLIX (1936), 749–750.

[14] Speaking in what he termed "no unfriendly spirit" but compelled by the unfavorable "economic and financial position," Sir Henry Gullett announced that he and a special subcommittee appointed by the Cabinet had already undertaken the study of how Australia could correct the adverse trade balance with the United States.

ever, that the substance of Sir Henry Gullett's speech was distinctly hostile (irrespective of its tone) and that he had definitely announced it as a Cabinet policy that restrictive measures would be taken and announced to the House shortly after Easter . . .

On May 22, 1936, Sir Henry Gullett announced the institution of the trade diversion program which was to reward the good and punish the bad customers of Australian exports. By encouraging the manufacture in Australia of certain imported items and diverting trade from the United States to countries which bought heavily in Australia, the Commonwealth hoped to increase Australian exports of primary products, to expand secondary industry, and to bring about fuller rural and industrial employment.[15] An elaborate licensing system and prohibitive duties were the techniques used to put the trade diversion program into operation.

In analyzing the Gullett statement Pierrepont Moffat decided that 80 per cent of American trade was left untouched:

What he [Gullett] said could be divided into three parts: tariff increases, chiefly on tobacco, lubricating oil, Douglas fir and piece-goods; second, a quota on foreign cars with additional provisions for paying bounties and otherwise encouraging production of a local industry, and third the creation of a list of prohibited items which can henceforth only come in under license. This last list contained about eighty items of interest to us, the principal ones of which are machinery of various sorts. . .[16]

The causes of the Australian action, Mr. Moffat thought, were:

1. British pressure; 2. political gain anticipated by the Lyons Government not only in its fight against Labor, but in bringing back to the fold its representatives from industrial districts who have been on the point of revolting; 3. a psychological wish to join in the game of preferential bargaining, despite the fact that Australia does not know the rules or possess the requisite number of chips.[17]

Monday, June 1 [1936.] At Melbourne.
. . . I told Sir George Pearce that I had come to Melbourne for

Ibid., pp. 744–747. In reporting the appointment of the special subcommittee to the Department Mr. Moffat said: "I think that we must look forward to some formal adverse action (probably discriminatory) if for no other reason than that the Government must try to shift on to other shoulders the blame for a condition of affairs where imports have increased to a point which is causing concern as to the future of Australia's financial credit." Department of State, MS, 611.4731/143.

[15] Sir Henry Gullett's speech of May 22, 1936, announcing the trade diversion policy is given in Commonwealth of Australia, Parliamentary Debates, CL (1936), 2211–2226.
[16] Moffat diary, May 22, 1936.
[17] Ibid., May 23, 24, 1936.

two reasons: (1) in obedience to instructions formally to convey to the Government of Australia certain observations of the American Government on their tariff policy insofar as it was discriminatory to the United States, and was based on the premise of American indifference to Australian welfare, and (2) because I was so concerned at the apparent pulling apart of the two countries that I felt a frank talk, such as we had had last October,[18] might possibly help us find some way of reversing the process and bringing us closer together again.

Sir George read the note through without comment.[19] He then said that he would review the motives which had led to the Government's decision. For a year or more the Government had been seriously perturbed at the state of the London funds and Australia's balance not only of trade, but of payments.[20] Australia was not like other countries; her overseas obligations were such that she must have each year a favorable trade balance of somewhere between twenty-eight and thirty million pounds in order to maintain first her exchange and subsequently her financial solvency. Last year the funds were seriously depleted; this year there was the prospect of a further decline; a drought year or a series of drought years might make it impossible to meet her interest payments. There were three solutions and only three solutions which had been considered by the Cabinet: (a) general restrictions of imports, a practice followed by the Scullin Government,[21] from which the country had not recovered yet; a practice which had penalized good customers and bad customers and had led to retaliation from the former; a practice which had proved unpopular and unworkable and against which the members of the present Government had fought relentlessly while they were in the Opposition. (b) Borrowing again in the London market, a procedure which

[18] See the conversation of Jay Pierrepont Moffat with Sir George Pearce, October 3, 1935.
[19] The American note of May 27, 1936, "deplored" the restraints which Australia had put upon trade, stated that the United States would assume until there was contrary evidence that these restrictions would be applied without discrimination against American commerce, and warned that the United States extended equality of treatment only to those countries which did not discriminate against the United States in trade matters. Department of State, MS, 647.116/135a.
[20] For Australia's situation over a number of years in this period, consult the "Summary Table" in League of Nations Economic Intelligence Service, *Balances of Payments, 1937* (Geneva: League of Nations, 1938), p. 57.
[21] The Labour government of James Henry Scullin was in office from 1929 to 1931.

would increase the public debt, show to all the world the serious condition in which Australia found herself, complicate their present refunding program, and give a jolt to the national credit. (In this connection I was told in confidence by another Australian official that informal soundings had been made on the London money market as to the possibility of a new loan under satisfactory conditions and that the indications had not been favorable.) (c) Discriminatory restriction against the imports of poor customers, of whom the United States was the principal.

This naturally brought up the question of Australia's relations with the United States. These he said had deteriorated sadly during the last ten years: Partly this was due to our attitude with regard to trade, he instanced not only our unwillingness to start negotiations but several "ugly" incidents some four or five years ago, and partly to a growing feeling not only that we were indifferent to Australia, but that we were more and more pursuing an isolationist policy, not only vis-à-vis Europe, but vis-à-vis the Pacific. All these factors taken together had convinced the average Australian that he could not count on our assistance in case of peril. This feeling was constantly growing; he came across it all over Australia and so did his colleagues.

The Australian Government did not therefore consider that regard for American susceptibilities should stand in the way of a policy dictated by vital interests. This was reinforced by Australia's relations with Great Britain. She had two Ministers there at the present time trying to increase the outlet for Australian products. The English naturally had told them, "We must look out for our own producers first," and only by giving British exports a larger share of the Australian market, could the two Ministers hope to win better terms in their negotiations with Great Britain.

Sir George recognized that Australia's new policy was drastic, discriminatory and even dangerous; perhaps it had not been presented to Parliament with due regard to our sensibilities; but he could definitely assure me that the new measure was popular among members of Parliament, perhaps the most popular measure introduced by the present Government, and he felt he should point out that of all people Parliamentarians were the best judges of the way a public was feeling at a given moment. Ten years ago, no Government could have taken similar action which would have injured the United States and survived six months. More clearly than anything else, this statement showed the degree to which closeness and cordiality between the two countries had dropped from warm to lukewarm.

I told Sir George that while I did not admit the accuracy of his diagnosis, yet I could not help agreeing that certain elements in Australia were resentful of our general attitude. But of the policies he complained of, none had been aimed at Australia. Even our tariff, which Australia disliked, was world-wide in its application. Now, Australia was planning to take discriminatory action aimed specifically at us, and admitted as such in public by Commonwealth Ministers. That was a very different and noncomparable thing.

Sir George complained of our refusal to commence trade negotiations. I went over the background in some detail: I explained how for generations we had believed in higher and ever-higher tariffs and in the supreme importance of exports only, how the present Administration, under the leadership of Secretary Hull, had determined to reverse this process, how it had been necessary to change the entire psychology of the American people, how the necessary legislation had only been obtained with the greatest difficulty, how it was still necessary to prove to the country through results that the Administration was on the right track, and how as a result it had been necessary to start off first negotiating with countries whose exports were not competitive with our own. Australia might not agree with Mr. Hull's ideas; in fact, she had rejected them in favor of preferential bargaining; that was water over the dam. But never, even in what was apparently an objective exposé of facts, had the Australian Government made an attempt to explain the American position. Carping references had been made by Cabinet Ministers to "flat refusals to enter negotiations," to "ignoring Australia in favor of countries with which America could drive a harder bargain," etc., but never a word as to what America was endeavoring to accomplish . . .

I asked if he saw any "ray of light," any possibility of bringing us together again. He said that perhaps after the elections we would be willing to negotiate. I said that I had always felt that we would be ready to negotiate with Australia by next winter, but that in the face of drastic discrimination this might prove pretty difficult. I hoped that Australia was not misgauging our psychology and thinking that pressure would facilitate negotiations. I instanced Germany, where we had voluntarily lost a large cotton market rather than compromise with discrimination,[22] and I cited the effect it would have on the forty odd remaining states who were pressing us, just as was Australia.

Sir George said that we did seem to be getting involved. He could not off hand decide who should make the first move or what it should be, but he was convinced in his own mind that nothing useful could be done in any event until after our elections. On the whole he thought it was up to the big nation to hold out the olive branch to the smaller one, not because the latter might have offended, but in spite of it. I said I agreed with this where only two parties were involved, but if it touched the foundations of an entire trade program, with repercussions all around the globe, the problem became much less simple. As I saw it we were caught in a vicious circle: Australia alleges American indifference, discrimination against America, and America, because of discrimination, may be forced onto the paths of indifference.

We then touched lightly on political effects. I said that in Anglo-Saxon countries so much depended, not on written words, but on the reactions of public opinions. And I could assure Sir George of the deep-seated feeling that singling out America for discriminatory treatment could not help provoking. I instanced the editorial in the *New York Times* [23] (which Sir George admitted was friendly to Australia) as a case in point. Should this feeling be given food for development, it might grow to proportions which would be really regrettable.

Sir George Pearce then asked me to talk with Sir Henry Gullett, who shortly thereafter came in to the room, accompanied by Colonel White, Minister for Customs. Summarizing Sir George's attitude, I am bound to admit that while I disagreed with many of the points he raised I could not help admiring his presentation. There was no false

[22] Mr. Hull has discussed the proposed cotton agreement with Germany in Hull, I, 371–375. For a summary of the nature of German commercial and financial discriminations against the United States, see U.S. Dept. of State, *Foreign Relations, 1934*, II, 387–396.

[23] In an editorial entitled "A Ruinous Principle" the *Times* suggested that "the Australians seem to be imitating the Nazi policy" by attempting to obtain a favorable balance of trade with all other countries. The newspaper warned that if this aim should be sought by all nations, it "would be more ruinous to Australia than to most countries," because Australia should recall "that its direct trade with many other countries is just as lopsidedly in its own favor." The editorial, however, urged that the United States adopt a conciliatory attitude and not retaliate against Australia. *New York Times*, May 28, 1936, p. 22.

sentiment, no hypocrisy. He recognized Australia's discriminatory policy for what it was, stated the reasons which had impelled the Government to adopt it, and indicated that Australia was prepared to take the consequences.

Sir Henry Gullett, on the other hand, did not take this detached point of view, but attempted to argue over what seemed to me non-essentials. He tried to make out that Australian policy was not discrimination because it also hit other countries with an unfavorable trade balance: even a sister Dominion was given a quota . . .

Tuesday, June 30 [1936. Sydney].

At long last came through the Department's telegram announcing the suspension of trade concessions to Australian products.[24] I was directed to inform the Australian authorities and was given to understand that there would be no publicity until July 1st. However, before I had even finished dictating my note to Canberra, the newspapers got the news first via a despatch from Montreal and secondly from Washington. Sir Henry Gullett promptly issued a statement that the action would have no effect upon Australian trade, as the items on which lower duties had been granted involved less than £2000 worth of Australian exports.

Naturally the press was hard on my heels. To one and all I made the same comment, that equality of commercial treatment was the basis of American trade policy and that we granted most-favored-nation treatment to every country which extended it to us. In our trade agreement program we freely generalized to all countries which did not discriminate against us the benefit of treaty reductions made under our trade agreements; it naturally followed that we could not do this in the case of countries which discriminated against us. Un-

[24] In a telegram of June 5, 1936, the Department of State requested Mr. Moffat to solicit a reply from the Australian Government to the question whether the "Customs Collector at Sydney is acting under instructions from the Minister of Customs" in applying measures restrictive to United States commerce. Department of State, MS, 647.116/152a. On June 24 Mr. Moffat received a reply from Canberra in which the key phrase was: "Collector of Customs in declining to issue permits for the importation of these commodities are acting under instructions and in accordance with the policy of the Government." Department of State, MS, 647.116/182. A telegram from Washington on June 29, 1936, informed Mr. Moffat that "beginning August 1st next the extension to imports from Australia of the reductions in duties granted by this Government in the trade agreements entered into under the trade agreements act" would be stopped. Department of State, MS, 611.473/22a.

fortunately, Australia's application of her recent licensing system was discriminatory to American commerce; in the circumstances we were left with no choice but to suspend to Australian products the benefit of concessions made to third countries . . .

Friday to Monday, September 25 to 28 [1936].

Four days of delightful rest and recreation. I went up with Dr. Warren Harding . . . to a large sheep station . . .

We did little but eat, sleep and ride. Both Saturday and Sunday we were in the saddle five or six hours each day and not only rode about the different paddocks examining the sheep and cattle, but were lucky enough on four different occasions to find kangaroo and to chase them anywhere from a hundred yards to half a mile. Their ability to bound up a steep hill, however, invariably lost us the chase.

Dr. Harding was most interesting on various phases of his uncle's Presidency and talked entirely without bitterness, excepting when he referred to the efforts of Mr. Coolidge and Mr. Hoover to dodge the dedication of the Harding Memorial at Marion [Ohio]. This, given the fact that but for Mr. Harding, Mr. Coolidge would have remained an obscure ex–Vice President and Mr. Hoover one of the myriads of more or less forgotten Cabinet officers, he found hard to forgive. He told me that even at the time of nomination Mr. Harding's health had worried the family (they were all doctors, his father, his brother, three nephews, etc.). His blood pressure was beginning to go up and his weight was already close to 240 pounds. Already during his time in Washington he had had certain heart symptoms which were causing his medical advisers concern, but which he refused to regard as a cause for letting-up. On the trip to Alaska there was one incident where he climbed 190 steps up a hill to visit an invalid who wanted to see him, but who couldn't come down. From that moment, according to Dr. Harding, the President was never the same man and when he reached Vancouver he was in a serious condition. Brigadier General Sawyer [Harding's physician], however, did not seem to realize that he was threatened with coronary thrombosis and did not keep him absolutely quiet. At San Francisco there was an acute attack of coronary thrombosis and when he sat up in bed, not having been warned to remain motionless, the heart ruptured and he fell back dead. I asked whether, had he recovered, he would have been able to carry on. Dr. Harding said that he would have had to remain a near invalid for at least a year and that he knew as a fact that it was his uncle's intention in that event to resign his office, although fully conscious of the immense sensation which such a step, the first in American history, would have caused . . .

Wednesday, November 4 [1936. Canberra].

. . . [Colonel Hodgson] said that largely as a result of the views I had kept expressing that Australia needed a diplomatic functionary in Washington to explain the background of problems, the decision to appoint an Australian counselor to the British Embassy at Washington had been finalized . . . London had now approved and so had Washington. The chief hitch had been a fear that the Japanese might take umbrage if the same thing weren't done in Tokyo, but it had been decided to introduce the measure as "experimental." I said that while it wasn't quite what I had hoped for, I was none the less delighted, and felt Australia would never regret it . . .[25]

At four I had my appointment with Sir Henry Gullett and went over our note with him.[26] I made an appeal somewhat along the lines I had used to Hodgson, though with some difficulty, as Sir Henry has a habit of interrupting at every little detail. At the end he said with some heat: "If you could show me that our position with regard to our London funds had improved I might feel somewhat differently. Actually, they are not a million pounds better, and that is chiefly due

[25] Although an Australian Counselor was attached to the British embassy in Washington in 1937, it was not until January 1940 that the exchange of ministers between the United States and Australia was announced. The legations in Washington and Canberra were raised to embassies in July 1946.

[26] On October 10, 1936, the Department of State sent to Mr. Moffat the text of a note on trade relations, which it was considering transmitting to Australia. This note pointed out that Australia had stated, when undertaking discriminatory action, that it was "compelled to do so because of conditions which threatened the Australian financial position." The United States called Australia's attention to certain "new" conditions: the satisfactory price of wool and wheat had aided Australia's balance of international payments; the recent Commonwealth budget of September 1936 showed that a healthy financial situation existed in the Commonwealth; and recent policy statements of the United States, France, and, in particular, Great Britain, advocated "that action to be taken without delay to relax progressively the present system of quotas and exchange controls with a view to their abolition." In light of the more favorable financial picture, the United States had "the fullest confidence that the Government of Australia would make its expression of friendship more articulate by more favorable treatment of American commerce." Department of State, MS, 611.4731/188a. This note was not delivered until November 1936 and then included some modifications suggested by Mr. Moffat.

to the in-flight of New Zealand money. The installation of foreign firms does not mean ready money (sic). Our excess of imports over exports the last quarter was greater than last year. We are not out of the woods; we are fighting for national solvency. We have had six good moist years in a row, thank God! But Australia is a country of ups and downs; you have never seen it withered and parched and thirty or forty million sheep dying in a year. But we have. And the vision haunts us. We cannot rest until we have reserves enough to tide us over such a period. That is our first consideration. If not, we might have to default, and nonpayment might gradually weaken the bonds of Empire and then God help us. No, our financial solvency is not only a matter of honor but of self-preservation.

"And now you come along, oblivious of the fact that buying from North America is bankrupting Australia; it is not only you but Canada. That's our next problem. I am not taking exception to the terms of your approach; it is the fact that you should approach us at all that hurts. When we reply it shall be in terms as friendly and courteous as yours, but you and I know each other by now well enough for me to speak freely.

"Your record has been one of unwillingness to help Australia; in years past you had enormous sales for which you never so much as said thanks. You excluded our goods by tariff; you drove out our shipping by subsidies; you threw our fruit overboard; you surrounded yourself by a tariff wall that could not be surmounted. You have reduced this somewhat, but it remains too high to be consistent with your high professions.

"I have tried my best, but I fail to see that a policy which involves discrimination which none the less leaves you a favorable balance of £7,000,000 a year, is more wicked than a nondiscriminatory policy which amounts to virtual exclusion.

"I don't think that either by word or deed we gave any ground for the impression that our trade diversion policy would be short-lived. As a matter of fact, if we had seen any human possibility of our London funds being reëstablished within six months or a year we should never have adopted a licensing system which is so cumbersome that it is wearing me out, as well as my staff. You keep on protesting that we did not need to discriminate, that we might merely have restricted, treating one and all alike. But this would have meant cutting off the last possibility for our good customers — which for the reasons I have explained to you we feel we must keep as our customers — to sell anything at all to us. We must keep our markets diversified and this was our only chance . . .

"Frankly, you seem to me to be placing so much weight on a theoretical principle as to lose sight of the actualities of the situation. Your program is admirable if only all nations were so situated that they could follow it. I don't for an instant doubt the sincerity of your Government's emphasis on nondiscrimination, but frankly I feel just as strongly that you are indifferent to Australia's welfare and unwilling to help by reciprocal trade as you feel that we are indifferent to the implications of discrimination. What I consider unfair is that you should feel that after the way you have treated us we had been unfair to you.

"There," he concluded, "now I have blown off steam. This much I will promise you. I will put your note before the Cabinet and I will set forth both sides of the picture with absolute fairness and reasonableness. The decision will not be mine, but frankly I should be surprised if there could be any modification of our program within a considerable period."

With this I had to be content. As in the past discussion was difficult as he agrees with every point you make theoretically, but claims that it has no application actually. Neither in my talks with Gullett nor with Liesching [Percivale Liesching, Secretary in the Office of the High Commissioner for the United Kingdom] or Hodgson did I get the slightest feeling that the British Government had as yet made any move toward supporting our position . . .[27]

[27] Mr. Moffat felt sure that the Australian trade diversion program had not been undertaken without the Commonwealth consulting Great Britain. In his diary of July 3, 1936, he wrote, for instance: "Incidentally, the cat was let out of the bag with a vengeance when, according to the press, 'a Federal Minister stated that the Government had assurance on the vital features of the new meat agreement early in May, and had taken the precaution of obtaining them [from Great Britain] before any move was made to table the tariff diverting trade from the United States and Japan in Britain's favor.' That should pretty well dispose of the Government's claim that there was no collusion between Australia and Great Britain."

Mr. Moffat had several times advised the Department of State to try to influence Australian trade policies by bringing the position of the United States to the attention of British officials. He had suggested, for instance, in a telegram of August 7, 1936, that an attempt be made "to arouse the concern of Mr. Eden . . . at an Australian policy which can only tend to drive the United States and the British Empire apart

Monday, November 30 [1936. New Zealand].[28]

On Monday, November 30th, a short item appeared in the press
that the Governor-General of New Zealand, who was touring the
South Island, had been recalled to Wellington on urgent business, had
landed at Bruce Bay, and was flying in a small Moth plane to Hokatika
where he would catch the service car to Christchurch and thence sail
for Wellington. The newspapermen questioned the Prime Minister,
who replied that the Government had sent the Governor-General no
despatches, and curiosity died down. It was only four days later that
the crisis over the King's [Edward VIII] intention to marry Mrs.
Simpson became public property, but there can be no doubt that telegraphic word had gone out well in advance for all hands to stand by
for stormy weather.

The consternation in New Zealand was intense, but public opinion
was a unit; if the King married Mrs. Simpson he must abdicate. No
morganatic marriage. Middle-class morality. The Throne was separate
from the occupant, Mrs. Simpson was to blame. The King must do
nothing to weaken the prestige of the monarchy which was the greatest stabilizing force for peace. "When such a thing isn't done, you
know, how could it happen," etc., etc. I looked in vain for one editorial
that might suggest that the King was the best judge of the situation.
I looked in vain for a suggestion that the Anglican Church had been
created to enable a monarch to contract a second marriage with *his*
wife still living. I looked in vain for some more literal interpretation
of the oath of allegiance and loyalty. The colonial public was more
royalist than the King, more legitimist than the dynasty, more British
than the English public.

There can be no doubt but that the loss of prestige to the Throne
hurt British pride frightfully. But now that it is over, the English
public will go on pretending that it never happened, like Babbitt, who
in his adult years committed an indiscretion and being slightly
ashamed never once referred to it, even to himself. With all his faults,
Edward VIII was a man, winsome, stubborn, and knowing his own
mind. But as such he could not fit into the mold which has been cast

_____

at the very moment Britain desires to see a closer understanding in the Pacific."
Department of State, MS, 647.116/235.
    [28] Mr. and Mrs. Moffat took a trip to New Zealand from November 20 to
December 12, 1936.

for British royalty, in which honesty, dignity and conventionality seem the sole attributes. He will be far happier out — and the Duke of York, who is of different clay, will be far happier in . . .

Friday, January 8 [1937. Sydney].

Squire [E. C. Squire, American Trade Commissioner at Sydney] picked up some confirmation of the improved outlook for American trade here which has been appearing in this diary for some months. His information was twofold. The first came from a Canadian friend who quoted Menzies [R. G. Menzies, Australian Attorney General] as saying that many of the Cabinet felt that an error had been made, but that politically it was impossible to rectify it at the present moment, though if an opportunity offered in the next few months, Cabinet would be glad to profit by it. The second was a brief conversation he had had with Abbott [Edwin Abbott, Comptroller General of Customs] at a luncheon. He jocularly remarked that since the Australians had stifled American trade he did not have anything to do but play golf, to which Abbott replied, "Well, it won't be so very long now" . . .

Monday, January 25 [1937. Sydney].

. . . I found a distinct change of atmosphere and a growing recognition that the trade diversion policy as at present drawn up must ultimately be altered. Partly this is due to our increasing purchases, which change the trade balance picture, and partly to be a growing feeling that the United States and the Empire must clean the slate. (I can't help wondering whether Eden, even though refusing Bingham's [Robert Bingham, American Ambassador to Great Britain] request to help him, none the less dropped a few hints to Mr. Bruce [Stanley M. Bruce, High Commissioner for Australia in Great Britain]). On the other hand, although for the first time I feel more cheerful I do not look for any immediate easing of the situation, as I think that Australia wants to finish the Imperial Conference [29] first and to drive as hard a bargain with Great Britain as she can. For the first time since last May I had a feeling, and it is as yet no more than a

[29] The Imperial Conference of 1937, held in London in connection with the May coronation of George VI, was concerned with such imperial problems as trade, defense, and colonial affairs. In attendance were delegations from the United Kingdom, Canada, Australia, New Zealand, South Africa, Southern Rhodesia, India, and Burma.

feeling, that the log jam can with time and patience, and not sending any notes for the present, be broken. It will be easier for Australia to retreat on the basis of Gullett's promise of May 22 to modify the policy as American imports increase from that point forward,[30] than it would be to modify the policy as a result of a formal request or series of observations from ourselves . . .

Wednesday, March 10 [1937. Sydney].

. . . About nine o'clock in the evening a reporter from the *Sydney Morning Herald* rang me up at the house. The following conversation ensued: "We have just had a despatch from Canberra that Sir Henry Gullett has resigned and wonder if you wish to make any comment." "No, I have no comment to offer." "Well, you see, we are putting up a section of tributes and thought you might like to be quoted." "No, I do not consider it would be appropriate for an outsider to express any opinion on what is a development of purely domestic politics." "Ah! Well, that is too bad, but then I don't imagine that anything has happened in the last year or two that would have brought you into particular contact with Sir Henry Gullett." "Good-night." "Good-bye."

The resignation apparently occurred over a discussion of the Canadian treaty developments. Gullett wished to pursue his trade diversion policy to further limit Canadian imports and allocate them to "good customer countries." The rest of the Cabinet apparently pointed out that his trade diversion policy was getting nowhere, that this would cut across inter-Empire trade, etc. Finding himself virtually alone, with only the Prime Minister supporting him, and with his colleagues almost a unit in censuring him, he walked out of Cabinet meeting, resigned then and there and is leaving Canberra today.

This will immeasurably facilitate the ultimate solution of our troubles . . .[31]

March 14 to 31, 1937 [Sydney].

Here I must close this diary of my stay (thus far) in Sydney, as

[30] In announcing the trade diversion program Gullett had said: "The plans outlined are not, of course, of a cast-iron nature, and will be open to reconsideration and re-adjustment as circumstances arise." Commonwealth of Australia, *Parliamentary Debates*, CL (1936), 2218.
[31] Australia was again given most favored nation treatment in December 1937, after it had ended the trade diversion policy. Levi, p. 134.

the tasks involved in closing the house, saying good-bye and "eating our way out" have left less and less time in the office. It has been an interesting assignment, in that the Government's antagonism to the United States, chiefly motivated by trade considerations, reached its climax last May. It required considerable restraint on our part not to retaliate (however justifiably) in a way which would make an eventual easing of the situation more difficult. Many businessmen whose immediate interests were hurt were unsympathetic with our policy of playing a waiting game in the hope and expectation that Australia would retreat from its anti-American trade diversion measures as a domestic decision. For a while no results were visible, but during the last three months there has been a distinct easing of the situation and a growing recognition that Australia acted too hastily and without regard to political considerations. The climax came when Cabinet realized that to carry the trade diversion measures to their logical conclusion it would be necessary to penalize Canada as well as the United States and that this would cut across the entire principle of inter-Empire trade. Gullett, the archpriest of bilateral balancing, left the Cabinet and Mr. Lyons has determined to try and come to an understanding in Washington on his way back from the Imperial Conference. The next moves accordingly will not be in Sydney, but in the United States. It is, therefore, a good moment to go on leave . . .

I sail on Wednesday, March 31st, on the S.S. "Mariposa."

V

WASHINGTON

July 1937 – May 1938

"The dictatorships were speaking in tones of victors"

On July 20, 1937, Secretary Hull signed the order making Pierrepont Moffat the Chief of the Division of European Affairs, which had been newly created by combining the old Divisions of Eastern and Western European Affairs and a part of the Near Eastern Division. Mr. Moffat found that many of the problems that he encountered in the new Division were but continuations of ones which he had handled previously in the Department between 1932 and 1935. German power was steadily increasing, and the Rhineland had recently been reoccupied by Nazi troops. German aspirations had found new friends in Italy and Japan; in 1936 the Rome-Berlin Axis was announced, and the same year the Anti-Comintern Pact was completed with Japan. But between the United States and Germany there had been no improvement in relations. Although there was little likelihood that a change of ambassador at Berlin would alter the situation, within the Department there was a feeling that Ambassador Dodd's antagonism to the Hitler regime was impairing his efficiency as a representative of the United States.[1] When the old question of whether or not the American representative at Berlin should attend the Nazi Party Congress arose again, it created an incident which added to the ill-feeling between the Department and the Ambassador and hastened his replacement in Germany.

Wednesday, August 25, 1937.

. . . Harry McBride [Assistant to the Secretary of State] came up and said that Sumner Welles had telephoned in that he felt the

[1] A recent study of Ambassador Dodd's assignment in Berlin has been made by Franklin L. Ford, "Three Observers in Berlin: Rumbold, Dodd, and François-Poncet," in *The Diplomats 1919–1939*, ed. Gordon A. Craig and Felix Gilbert (Princeton, N. J.: Princeton University Press, 1953), pp. 458–460.

Secretary should review a cable he had signed authorizing Gilbert [Prentiss Gilbert, American Chargé d'Affaires at Berlin] in his discretion to attend the Nazi Congress this year. I told Harry that I thought it would be a good plan for the Secretary to have a small meeting and clear this problem once and for all. . .

I explained that the original instruction had been sent on the theory that once the French and British, who had previously declined to go to the meeting, broke the common front of the representatives of the democratic nations it would be exceedingly difficult for the United States not to follow suit. It was realized that there would be some adverse criticism but it was thought that there would be less criticism (1) if we attended the meeting at the same time as the French and British and (2) if it were a Chargé that went rather than an Ambassador. It seemed to me there were two considerations to be borne in mind: the presence of Mr. Gilbert this year would undoubtedly be criticized but the criticism would be less than would be the case in some future year if an American Ambassador had attended, and the shift in policy were made by us alone and not in company with the British and French. The second consideration arose from the fact that internally the Party and the State are one; if we should decline to join the French and British in this instance would not our position in Berlin be impaired?

Mr. Messersmith [George S. Messersmith, Assistant Secretary of State] said that he always had opposed our going to the Party Congress, and he appreciated how offensive it would be to an American representative to do so this year. However, when he read that the British and French had deserted us, and particularly when he read that they would only be present at a time when no embarrassing speeches would be made, he felt that we could no longer maintain our stand.

Mr. Wilson [Hugh Wilson, Assistant Secretary of State] said that he quite agreed. He said that given the fact that the Party and State were one in Germany and given the fact that we accredited a Minister to Germany, he felt that it would be inconsistent for that Ambassador or representative to continue to boycott the Party Congress.

Judge Moore [R. Walton Moore, Counselor of the Department of State] said that he did not anticipate much adverse criticism from the presence of Mr. Gilbert. He was inclined to think that it was an unpalatable decision which could be taken with less repercussion this year than at some future date. He knew that Mr. Dodd would be disappointed. He wondered whether Mr. Dodd had taken the matter up with the President. The consensus of opinion was that if the President had expressed himself one way or the other, either the President or Mr. Dodd would have informed the State Department.

The conclusion of the meeting was that it would be better to let the instruction stand unless some new development should occur. The Secretary concurred. As a matter of fact, less than an hour later a telegram came through from Prentiss saying that he had already accepted and the matter appeared in the press in the late afternoon. . .

Friday, September 3, 1937.

. . . Just after I left the office the Secretary buzzed for me with relation to a query from the *New York Herald Tribune* that Mr. Dodd was protesting the acceptance by Prentiss Gilbert of Hitler's invitation to attend the Nuremberg Conference.[2] As this could only have been given out by Dodd himself I fear we must check up what amounts to disloyalty to the Secretary among his other shortcomings.[3] The Secretary sent for Hugh Wilson and together they agreed that in no circumstance must Prentiss Gilbert be let down or made to carry more responsibility than was actually the case. . .

Saturday, Sunday and Monday, September 4, 5 and 6 [1937].

As foreseen the press played up to considerable degree Mr. Dodd's difference of opinion with the Department over Prentiss Gilbert's attendance at the Nuremberg Congress. This we decided to spike by deflecting the issue and arranged for a question to be asked in press conference about the recent speeches of Neurath [Constantin

[2] The *New York Herald Tribune* of September 4, 1937, p. 1, carried a story about Ambassador Dodd's protest to the Department of State. Although reference was made to Mr. Dodd's letter, it was not quoted.

[3] Mr. Dodd did not apparently release the letter to the press. In his diary of September 4, 1937, the Ambassador wrote of having seen the article in the *New York Herald Tribune*: "The letter had been sent ten days before I left for Williamstown, for Judge Moore to hand to Secretary Hull without letting anyone else see it. Now it has been published in the press as if I had said it publicly . . ." Dodd, p. 427. See, also, Martha Dodd, *Through Embassy Eyes* (New York: Harcourt, Brace & Co., 1939), pp. 355–358.

Von Neurath, German Minister for Foreign Affairs], Bohle [E. Wilhelm Bohle, leader of the Foreign Department of the Political Organization of the Nazi Party] and others on Nazi activities abroad which would enable the Secretary to point out that Americans even of German birth could only have one loyalty which was to our Constitution, our laws and our flag. He could then go on quite casually to say that the Gilbert attendance had been decided upon with the French and British; that attendance at a meeting did not mean that one agreed with what was said and that as we maintained normal relations with Germany it was normal to accept an invitation from the Chief of State. So successful was this that after running the Secretary's statement in all papers on Sunday [4] the question faded from actuality and there was no publicity whatsoever on either Monday or today (Tuesday the day of dictating). I saw the Secretary for a moment on Sunday and he expressed himself as delighted over the way the situation had worked out. . .

Tuesday, September 7, 1937.

At eleven o'clock this morning Dr. Thomsen, the German Chargé d'Affaires called. I quote the memorandum I made of his visit. He said that he had been highly perturbed to read the press accounts of Doctor Dodd's attitude concerning the acceptance by Mr. Gilbert of Hitler's invitation to attend the Nuremberg Congress. He explained that he had as yet received no instructions on the matter from his Government but felt that he would have to make some sort of report and hoped that he might be able to prevent what he feared would be an embarrassing situation. Of course if Dr. Dodd had decided that he was not returning to Berlin it would be perfectly normal for him to speak freely, but Dr. Dodd had said that he was returning which put a different complexion on the matter. I said that as far as I knew he was returning to Berlin. Dr. Thomsen went on that speaking personally it was hard to see how he could usefully go on with his mission, that this was not the first occasion on which he had expressed himself to the embarrassment of the Government to which he was accredited: for instance, his letter of last Spring to the Senators was a case in point [5] and some interviews he had given. Dr. Thomsen

[4] A report of the Secretary's comments to the press is given in *New York Herald Tribune*, September 5, 1937, p. 5, and *Washington Post*, September 5, 1937, p. 3.

[5] Ambassador Dodd wrote a letter to several senators concerning the reorganiza-

could not help wondering what would be our attitude if the roles were reversed and a German Ambassador accredited here refused an invitation, or even counseled the refusal of an invitation from the President, on the ground that he did not like his political views.[6]

I replied that we had greatly regretted any publicity given in the matter of our authorization to Gilbert to attend the Nuremberg Congress; that we always worked on the theory that everyone was free to give what advice he pleased on the understanding that this was confidential and that the final decision reached represented the American stand. This was the same principle followed in the British Cabinet and in many other organizations. Mr. Gilbert's acceptance of the invitation had been authorized and the basis on which the decision was reached had no outside interest. Hence the less said the sooner mended. . .

Following the signing of the T'ang-ku Truce in 1933 a period of uneasy peace began between China and Japan: the Japanese sought to establish themselves firmly in Manchuria and North China and to profit from their penetration there, while the Chinese, faced with acute internal problems, were able to achieve a degree of solidarity before the next thrust of the Nipponese invader. This came after fighting broke out on July 7, 1937, at the Marco Polo bridge at Lukouchiao between Chinese and Japanese troops. The conflict spread widely in the north, and in August the Japanese attacked Shanghai. After the Chinese Government on September 12, 1937, called the attention of the Secretary-General of the League of Nations to the Japanese invasion of China, the League Council summoned the Far-East Advisory Committee to consider the situation. The United States was asked to sit with the League Committee.

Friday, September 17, 1937.
. . . Spent several hours with Hugh Wilson and Stanley Hornbeck [Adviser on Political Relations in the Department of State] working on our reply to the League invitation to sit with the Ad-

---

tion of the Supreme Court in which were the sentences: "There are individuals of great wealth who wish a dictatorship and are ready to help a Huey Long. There are politicians who think they may gain powers like those exercised in Europe." *New York Times*, May 12, 1937, p. 4.

[6] When Mr. Dodd returned to the United States on August 4, 1937, he gave an interview in which he said that some European powers wanted "to frighten and even destroy Democracies everywhere." The German Ambassador immediately protested this statement. *Ibid.*, August 5, 1937, p. 3; U.S. Department of State, *Documents on German Foreign Policy 1918–1945*, vol. I, *From Neurath to Ribbentrop* (Series D; Washington: Government Printing Office, 1949), pp. 627–628.

visory Committee. It is a case of damned if we do and damned if we don't. If we don't we will be accused of abandoning Japan and of dealing entirely into the isolationist sphere. If we do we are to a certain extent the victims of League strategy. Instead of sticking to their normal procedure the League is trying to dump the whole Far Eastern mess onto the Advisory Committee which was set up under different terms of reference.[7] We all agreed that we must make it patent that sitting with the Committee did not imply that we assumed any of the responsibilities of the Members of the League which devolved upon them from the fact of their membership. We would not be willing to discuss courses of action which might have been suggested but not acted upon and we would not give our opinions on hypothetical questions. Finally we had to point out that there were on our statute books certain laws which under given contingencies controlled the actions of the Government. On substance there was no disagreement but in drafting there was a lot; Stanley wanted to lecture the League on what it should do; Hugh Wilson and I maintained that it was sufficient to maintain our position but that we must not tell the League its own business. By four o'clock we thought we had a satisfactory draft, but when we got into the Secretary's office Stanley reverted to his original position and the long and short of it was that the matter went over until tomorrow. . .

Saturday and Sunday, September 18 and 19, 1937.

   . . . At this point the Secretary buzzed for me and we went into a long conference on our note to the League safeguarding our position in rejoining the Advisory Committee.[8] Stanley had taken the draft Hugh and I had worked over and recast it in complicated language. However, with two exceptions we had no objection to the substance and after considerable argument Hugh and I won our points. Hugh Wilson then went over with the Secretary to the President to

   [7] The Far East Advisory Committee was set up by the League of Nations in 1933 to "follow" the Sino-Japanese situation and "to aid the Members of the League in concerting their action and their attitude among themselves and with the non-member States." The United States had been invited to participate. Westel W. Willoughby, *The Sino-Japanese Controversy and the League of Nations* (Baltimore: The Johns Hopkins Press, 1935), pp. 520–521.
   [8] Statements of policy by the Secretary of State about joining the Advisory Committee are contained in two telegrams to the American Minister to Switzerland on September 24, 1937, and September 28, 1937. U.S. Dept. of State, *Foreign Relations, Japan: 1931–41*, I, 373–377.

clear this and three or four other points before the latter departed for the West. As far as the Advisory Committee was concerned the President approved the proposed action and left the safeguarding phraseology entirely to the Department without even reading the draft. Hugh Wilson then brought up the subject of Mr. Dodd and the hint given me by Thomsen some ten days ago that the German Government felt that his usefulness might be impaired by his attitude toward Gilbert's presence at the Nuremberg Conference. The President asked whether if a term were set to Mr. Dodd's mission any embarrassments might be avoided; Hugh Wilson replied that he thought they would. The President thereupon authorized him to call in Thomsen and tell him that Mr. Dodd was returning now but would be relinquishing his mission around the end of the year. . .[9]

Friday, October 1, 1937.

Mallet [Victor A. L. Mallet, Counselor of the British Embassy at Washington] stopped in at my office for ten or fifteen minutes while awaiting the time for his appointment with the Secretary. He commented on how rapidly the temper of public opinion was rising against Japan throughout England and said that he thought there was more bitterness and greater demand for action in England than in the United States. I said that whereas possibly the thermometer did not register as highly here none the less the base of resentment was broadening rapidly and public opinion as judged by editorial comment was becoming increasingly concerned even in the Mississippi Valley over Japanese aggression.[10]

He then went down to the Secretary and presented a memorandum

[9] According to Ambassador Dodd President Roosevelt asked him on August 11, 1937, to return to Berlin "for two or three months." Dodd, *Ambassador Dodd's Diary*, pp. 426, 430. Hugh Wilson informed Mr. Thomsen of the President's decision on September 20, and Sumner Welles repeated the information to the German Ambassador, Hans Dieckhoff, on October 1, 1937. U.S. Dept. of State, *Documents on German Foreign Policy*, I, 632.

[10] The following results had been obtained in a poll which questioned where the public's sympathies lay in the Sino-Japanese conflict:

September 1937		October 1937	
With neither	55%	With neither	40%
With China	43%	With China	59%
With Japan	2%	With Japan	1%

George Gallup and Claude Robinson, "American Institute of Public Opinion — Surveys, 1935–38," *The Public Opinion Quarterly*, July, 1938, p. 389.

which in effect inquired whether we would be prepared to consider measures amounting to a boycott against Japan. Obviously such a measure on the part of one country alone would be valueless.

As usual we had a long meeting in the Secretary's office to talk this thing over. If we say no flatfootedly to the British they can accuse us of blocking action, much as we feel that Sir John Simon blocked us in 1932.[11] If we accept we are going (a) beyond any existing legislation; (b) in contravention of the spirit of the Neutrality Act; (c) we would be naming an aggressor and taking sides in the struggle; (d) we would in effect be aligning ourselves with Great Britain; and (e) if it led to hostilities we alone would bear the brunt as we alone would possess a fleet that could be sent into Far Eastern waters. It is very curious that England should be prepared to propose to us a stand she is unwilling to assume with the League Powers in Geneva. . .

Tuesday, October 5, 1937.

Two more meetings in the Secretary's office today. We were polishing off the last draft of our reply to the British *aide-mémoire* regarding a boycott when the ticker service brought in the text of the President's Chicago speech. We had known that he was to make a speech along these general lines and in fact many notes had been prepared for him by Norman Davis and the Department, but he dramatized them in a way we had little expected, and the sentence regarding the quarantine of nations was a surprise.[12] The Secretary was delighted at the speech and the majority thought it would be strongly approved by the public.[13] It will make easier our subsequent moves

[11] In February 1932 Secretary of State Stimson had requested Simon, the British Foreign Minister, to make a joint statement with the United States about Japanese action in Manchuria. Simon was not willing to join in such a *démarche*. Stimson, *The Far Eastern Crisis*, pp. 162–164.

[12] This sentence was: "When an epidemic of physical disease starts to spread, the community approves and joins in a quarantine of the patients in order to protect the health of the community against the spread of the disease." Franklin D. Roosevelt, *The Public Papers and Addresses of Franklin D. Roosevelt*, 1937 vol., *The Constitution Prevails* (New York: The Macmillan Co., 1941), pp. 406–411.

[13] The Secretary's "delight" was short-lived. He has written: "The reaction against the quarantine idea was quick and violent. As I saw it, this had the effect of setting back for at least six months our constant educational campaign intended to create and strengthen public opinion toward international cooperation." Hull, I, 545; William L. Langer and S. Everett Gleason in *The Challenge to Isolation 1937–1940* (New York: Harper & Bros., 1952), p. 19, have said that "Mr. Hull and Mr. Davis were shocked beyond words" by the quarantine idea.

but I am not at all sure that it will not ultimately drive us much farther than we would wish to go.

Jimmy Dunn [Adviser on Political Relations in the Department of State] at once got Bucknell [Howard Bucknell, American Consul at Geneva] on the telephone, who in turn informed the League authorities that the President's speech would be received in an hour over the short-wave radio. Its effect in Geneva was instantaneous and put an end to considerable shilly-shally that was going on. We can now regard a nine-power conference as almost inevitable. Three technical steps remain to be done: the first is to prepare a statement agreeing with the conclusions found by the League that Japan had in fact violated the Nine-Power Treaty and the Kellogg Pact; [14] the second is to prepare an answer to the invitation to join the other signatories of the Nine-Power Treaty and to incorporate a suitable reservation that if this conference should report to the Assembly we would not join in that report, even though we would take full part in the discussions; the third was to formulate in our minds what might be done in the way of constructive action at such a conference. . .

Wednesday, October 6, 1937.

A few of us feel that in the development of the situation we have almost passed the danger line and feel that we should take stock of what can be done further without running the risk of retaliation and complications. It seems to me that we have deliberately put ourselves in the position occupied by England two years ago in the Ethiopian matter. At that time all the countries were willing to apply sanctions against Italy, secure in the knowledge that if it led to trouble it would be Britain that would have to bear the brunt. Today, if the same thing happens in the Orient, it would be the United States and the United States alone that will bear the brunt. Once again Great Britain would have somebody to fight her battles for her. However these are minority views. . .

Thursday, October 7, 1937.

Norman Davis turned up today preparatory to the President's

[14] The report of the League Advisory Committee, which concluded that Japan's actions in China were not in accord with the principles of the Nine-Power Treaty and the Pact of Paris, is printed in U.S. Dept. of State, *Foreign Relations, Japan: 1931–41*, I, 384–394. The statement issued by the Department of State concurring with the League's conclusion is in *ibid.*, pp. 396–397.

return to Washington tomorrow. According to Norman the latter will make no further move until he "hears from the country." Norman and I differ considerably as to what we hope the country will say, and Sumner, Hugh Wilson and I have been talking the problem out with him whenever we could.

The Conference in the Secretary's room dealt largely with procedural questions. The British approached us to ask if we would not father the Nine-Power Conference and hold it in Washington. This we were able to reject without further ado and reached the conclusion that it should be held in some small European capital. Norman Davis, sniffing a conference from afar like a battle horse, was inclined to favor London but gave in when the majority pointed out that (a) the Japanese hostility to England would make London a useless city, and (b) the delegates would be too much at the mercy of a perfectly controlled British press. Someone suggested Brussels, to which Norman took exception on the ground of the climate. We finally agreed to reply that it should not be America and that we doubted the advisability of holding the conference in any large capital. . .

Sunday, October 10, 1937.

. . . Sunday morning we had a most interesting conference at the Department: the Secretary, Bill Bullitt [American Ambassador to France], Bill Phillips [American Ambassador to Italy], Hugh Wilson, Jimmy Dunn and myself. The President is making a radio talk on Tuesday and seems to feel that he must elaborate a little on his Chicago speech particularly as with the waning of the first burst of applause public opinion is again crystallizing against any involvement.[15] For instance, the poll of the institute of public opinion, which has been astoundingly accurate reports nearly seven to three in favor of passing stricter neutrality laws, rather than leaving the job of keeping us out of war up to the President.[16] Hearst likewise is alleged to

[15] This "fireside chat" of October 12, 1937, did not explicate to any appreciable extent the meaning of the Quarantine Speech. Arthur Krock characterized the chat as "a mere restatement, in far softer terms" of the Chicago speech. Roosevelt, pp. 429–438; Beard, pp. 192–194.

[16] In October 1937 the question was asked: "Which plan for keeping out of war do you have more faith in — having Congress pass stricter neutrality laws, or leaving the job up to the President?" Sixty-nine per cent were in favor of stricter neutrality laws, and 31 per cent wanted to leave the job to the President. Gallup and Robinson, p. 388.

be about to start a campaign against the idea of "quarantine" or "positive concerted action." Those of us who had lived abroad were a unit in pointing out that we could not go on to take sanctions, no matter what their form, without risking retaliation; that even though there might be equality of sacrifice on the part of the sanctionist Powers there could never be equality of risk, that if effective and Japan were completely downed China would merely fall a prey to Russian anarchy and we would have the whole job to do over again and a worse one. . .

Often the low tide in human life and history is equally interesting and compelling and more significant than the triumphs. Such a moment was the Conference of Brussels. Here nineteen of the states of the world met from November 3 to 24, 1937, to consider action which might be taken to end the conflict in the Far East between China and Japan. The opinions varied from those who were willing to risk war to end war to those who balked at supporting a statement upholding principles of international law in relation to the incident. From the compromise of such extremes little could be hoped and little resulted. When the conference closed it had hardly contributed more than pious good wishes toward the solution of the conflict. But the conference had presented a revealing study in the bankruptcy of policy.

Brussels, October 28, 1937.

On Saturday, October 16, the orders came through appointing the Delegation to the Nine-Power Treaty Conference with Norman Davis as sole delegate, Stanley Hornbeck and myself as advisers, Robert Pell as press officer, and Chip Bohlen as secretary. In order to reach Brussels on time, it was necessary to sail on October 20, which meant a hectic three days getting ready both officially and personally.

The genesis of the Conference was really the Roosevelt speech of October 8.[17] Up to that moment, there had been few indications that the matter would not remain in the hands of the League. However, with its strong tone and ambiguous phrasing it caused an immediate change of plans in Europe, and Great Britain promptly informed us that it considered a Nine-Power Conference essential. We in turn had always maintained that, if invited, acceptance was a foregone conclusion even though it was not clear just how the Conference would work out.

[17] Mr. Moffat is referring to the Quarantine Speech of October 5, 1937.

All during the days of Saturday, Monday, and Tuesday our group met in the Secretary's office. There were as many different opinions expressed as there were individuals present, but roughly the meeting lined up into two groups: one which felt that we must go very slowly, on the ground that if Japan should retaliate we alone would bear the burden; the other, which felt that if we did not stop Japan at present we should eventually be confronted by a yet stronger Japan. The final upshot of these talks was rather inconclusive, for the primary reason that the President was in Hyde Park and could not be consulted. We did, however, work out certain ideas as to what might ultimately be the basis of the solution which involved concessions from Japan, China and the Powers, and yet would not seem in any way to be a Hoare-Laval plan.[18] The day before we left, Norman Davis motored up to Hyde Park and had two hours with the President. I have seen the memorandum and reluctantly reached the conclusion that he did not see his way out of the situation any more than did we. He emphasized that the word "quarantine" which he used in his Chicago speech had a friendly sound, and was far less minatory than ostracism or similar synonyms. He wished Norman Davis to avoid any commitments that might tie our hand from "exerting pressure" (the word sanctions is to be rigorously avoided), but in the early stages of the Conference at least our tone was to be one of high-minded cooperation. The note which kept running through the President's talk was the development of public opinion in the United States and his indications that our policy would eventually be governed by the reactions of the citizens at large.[19]

Meanwhile, at Washington, the British kept bombarding us with

[18] In December 1935 Sir Samuel Hoare and Pierre Laval had formulated proposals upon which to base a settlement of the Italo-Ethiopian conflict. The Hoare-Laval Plan, which called for the cession of Ethiopian territory to Italy, had so aroused British public opinion that it led to Hoare's resignation. Arnold J. Toynbee, *Survey of International Affairs, 1935* (London: Oxford University Press, 1936), II, 291–311.

[19] Secretary Hull's summary of the Davis memorandum is given in Hull, I, 552. A memorandum from the file of President Roosevelt's secretary apparently gives Roosevelt's views as expressed to Davis: "The point to be made clear is that the United States proposes in general as the basis of discussion, the same policy which has proved so successful among the twenty-one American Republics — no one nation going out to take the lead — no one nation, therefore, in a position to have a finger of fear or scorn pointed at it.

"In the present Far Eastern situation it is visualized that whatever proposals are advanced at Brussels and whatever action comes out of Brussels, the proposals and the action should represent, first, the substantial unanimous opinion of the nations meet-

questions and memoranda. They even went so far as to inquire whether we knew quite what were the implications of the President's speech and when we said we did they came through with a long treatise on the effect of sanctions in the Far East, the burden of which was that a necessary preliminary would be a joint guaranty to France and the Netherlands of their Far Eastern territories. They kept indicating that "Britain could be counted on to go as far as America" but made it clear that in the event of trouble they were so preoccupied with the Spanish and German situations that they could do little east of Singapore. They also considered it essential that Russia and Germany, particularly Russia, should be invited to attend the Conference and finally by sheer persistence had their way.

It is not necessary to discuss at length the voyage. The "Washington" was a comfortable ship, we had a remarkably smooth voyage for late October, with only one rough day, and we did some work on Norman Davis' opening speech, Stanley Hornbeck writing the Far Eastern section, I writing the section dealing with general principles, and Norman Davis attempting to marry the two styles. His habit of work consists in revision after revision, weighing the use of a word here and a clause there. The danger is that by super-refining a speech it loses some of its original punch.

We reached Paris about noon on October 20 [20] and after unpacking went straight to the Embassy for lunch with Bill Bullitt. After luncheon, he read us his recent telegrams to the Department and elaborated on the French attitude toward the Far East. Briefly, this is that France is so worried, not to say afraid, of the situation in Europe that the situation in the Far East is a matter of relative indifference to her. She considers that French Indochina is hopelessly exposed to Japan's aggression and that therefore she will do nothing to anger Japan unless England and America specifically guarantee the integrity of Indochina. . .

We talked a little about Russia's attitude at the forthcoming Conference. Litvinov [Maxim Litvinov, Soviet Minister for Foreign Affairs] has apparently been talking in diametrically opposite senses to different people. To the English he has been saying that Russia would

ing at Brussels, and later the substantial unanimous opinion of the overwhelming majority of all nations, whether in or out of the League of Nations." Department of State, MS, 793.94 Conference / 73d.

[20] The delegation arrived in Paris on October 27.

attack and defeat Japan if England could guarantee that Germany would not attack Russia during the process. To France he has been saying that the longer the war lasts the more Japan will exhaust herself, which will enable Russia to play a more preponderant part in Europe. The general belief was that Russia's role at Brussels would be to embarrass all the great powers in turn and if possible to prevent an agreement, at least until Japan had come to the end of her resources. . .

Brussels, October 29, 1937.

. . . At a quarter to twelve, Norman Davis and Hugh Gibson [American Ambassador to Belgium] went over to pay a courtesy call on Mr. Spaak [Paul-Henri Spaak, Belgium Minister for Foreign Affairs]. The latter told them that he had just received word that Germany had declined to attend the Conference on the ground that it was too closely linked with the League of Nations,[21] while Russia, in accepting, had scolded the Belgian Government because it had not specifically indicated that the Conference was a child of Geneva.[22] They talked for a moment about procedure and agreed that after the opening speeches the Conference should again address an invitation to Japan, so phrased as to induce and facilitate her acceptance. Beyond that Mr. Spaak's ideas were as vague as anyone else's. . .

Brussels, October 30–31, 1937.

. . . We are going to have trouble with the press. Hearst has sent . . . a young man fresh from California who apparently has orders to destroy our work if possible. He tried twice to make Pell lose his temper and say things he shouldn't. Whether he will accuse us of concocting a Hoare-Laval plan or whether he will accuse us of allowing the Conference to drift aimlessly, or both alternately, it is too early to say. The main difficulty is that he is out to make trouble.

[21] The German *note verbale* indicated that the German Government would not attend the Brussels Conference, because it was called on the basis of and in application of the Nine-Power Treaty of which Germany was not a signatory. The full text is in U.S. Department of State, *The Conference of Brussels* (Washington: Government Printing Office, 1938), p. 22.

[22] Delegations from the following countries attended the Conference: Union of South Africa, United States of America, Australia, Belgium, Bolivia, Canada, China, Denmark, France, United Kingdom, India, Italy, Mexico, Norway, New Zealand, The Netherlands, Portugal, Sweden, and the Union of Socialist Soviet Republics.

Sunday morning, in addition to the long telegram on the text,[23] there were two other interesting messages from the Department which gave us food for thought.

The first was from Joe Grew indicating that he, Craigie [Sir Robert Craigie, British Ambassador to Japan], and Henry [Charles Arsène-Henry, French Ambassador to Japan] had sent a joint estimate of the situation to Washington, London and Paris.[24] This was to the effect that the Japanese would definitely reject mediation by the Conference and would still more decisively reject a joint Anglo-American mediation. On the other hand, they might eventually accept mediation by one power, preferably the United States or Great Britain, and Joe urged that we do not close the door to the possibility of such an eventual solution. Norman Davis saw in this some of Craigie's poison and sent a private wire to the Secretary saying that he had worked closely with Craigie for many years and knew not only his pro-Japanese bias but also the way his mind was working. He felt we should be careful not to fall into the trap as he knew we could not afford to mediate alone and that it would be very much against our interests to let the British mediate alone. The latter, however, was obviously what Craigie was working toward.

The other telegram was a suggested resolution which the Department asked us to consider and use after the Japanese had returned their expected refusal to a further invitation from the Conference to attend. It would be presented by one of the smaller powers and would, after a lot of whereas's, appoint a committee of the United States, Great Britain, and Germany to keep in touch with Japan and China, see what could be done, and meanwhile adjourn the Conference for a more or less prolonged period. They asked Norman Davis' advice on this. His answer was, obviously, to the effect that he could not give a definite recommendation at this point as too much depended on future developments. He deprecated, however, an adjournment before it was seen what the Conference could do in the way of galvanizing moral forces throughout the world. The real thing that disturbed him, however, was that the Department's mind was obviously running along different lines from that of the President. Either the

---

[23] The Department had sent a telegram commenting on and revising the text prepared in Brussels of Mr. Davis' opening speech.

[24] Mr. Grew's telegram of October 30, 1937, is summarized in Grew, II, 1185–1186.

latter had changed his mind, which seemed unlikely, or else the Department and the President were working at cross purposes and this should be cleared up.

The only two suggestions I had as to the reason for this change of front were: one, that there was a political disadvantage in having the Conference wrangling while Congress was in session; and, two, that Lord Cranborne's inept speech [25] had had repercussions at home more widespread than we anticipated. . .

Brussels, November 1, 1937.

. . . I have never known a conference where even before we meet people are discussing ways to end it. The Belgians quite frankly would like to see us finish and go home, and several other powers feel the same way.

All the publicity emanating from England is to the effect that this is our conference, and that the Far East is our problem. Anthony Eden was heckled in Parliament yesterday and made the statement that the United States had taken the initiative in selecting Brussels once it was decided that the conference was to be held.[26] He went on to say that this conference was the only way in which America could be brought in with equal representation and equal responsibility, and that to bring this about he would gladly walk not only from Geneva to Brussels but from Melbourne to Alaska. The press became intensely excited and we had telephone call after telephone call from correspondents in London. Most of them misread Eden's speech and

[25] Viscount Cranborne, Under-Secretary of State for Foreign Affairs, in a speech in the House of Commons on October 28, 1937, about the League of Nations had said: "His Majesty's Government should go as far as the United States and as fast as the United States, but no faster. That is the view of His Majesty's Government." He went on to point out that at the meetings of the Advisory Committee at Geneva the United States was "there only in the position of observer, and that they took no part in the discussions or in the voting. But they are actually a signatory to the Nine-Power Treaty, and that puts them in a very different position." Hansard, *Parliamentary Debates* (Fifth Series), CCCXXVIII (1937), 299.

[26] Mr. Eden, the British Foreign Secretary, had said that "in order to get the full cooperation on an equal basis of the United States Government in an international conference, I would travel, not only from Geneva to Brussels, but from Melbourne to Alaska, more particularly in the present state of the international situation." In commenting on the implication given by another member of the House of Commons "that as a result of pressure from us the Conference was being held at Brussels," Mr. Eden stated: "I feel I ought to make it clear that the initiative for the holding of the Conference in Brussels never came from us at all, but from the United States Government itself." *Ibid.*, p. 583.

thought he was claiming that America had taken the initiative in call-ing the conference, not merely in selecting its place. But even without this slight inaccuracy, the American newspapers are going to react very badly to Eden's speech,[27] the more so as it comes on top of Cranborne's unfortunate utterance of October 29 [28].

We had a discussion in the delegation as to whether Eden had been very clever or the reverse. If England did not want anything to transpire at the conference and wished to hide behind America's skirts, I do not think that he could have chosen a more effective way to consolidate American opinion against "pulling the British chestnuts out of the fire." Norman Davis, on the other hand, thought that the speech was merely an instance of British desire to have us cooperate on a full basis and that Eden with his insularity had either misjudged or paid no attention to our psychology.

A telegram in from Mr. Bingham [Robert Bingham, American Ambassador to Great Britain] reporting a conversation he had had with Eden [on October 28] in which, under instruction from the President, he told him a number of truths about British policy which Norman Davis had been planning to do himself. In particular, he had urged the British, on behalf of the President, not to take the lead in this conference and still less to push the United States out in front. The best policy would be to let the smaller powers hold the center of the stage. Eden had agreed, and a few hours later had publicly announced that England would go as far as the United States and in general model her policy on America's. So much for "not pushing America out in front" . . .

Brussels, November 2, 1937.

Today was a busy day — the first day of good old-fashioned Con-ference rush.

In the morning Anthony Eden, Malcolm MacDonald [British Secretary of State for Dominion Affairs] and Sir Alexander Cadogan [British Under-Secretary of State for Foreign Affairs] called on Mr.

[27] Eden's speech did not occasion much unfavorable comment, but the *Chicago Tribune*, November 2, 1937, p. 1, said: "Diplomatic observers considered Eden's statement was tantamount to laying the baby on the doorstep of the United States . . . Tangled up somewhere in these [Eden's] words is perhaps a hint of an explanation as to how British diplomacy succeeded in getting Mr. Roosevelt to take the lead in calling the Brussels conference when every one from the Japanese to the Italians had been preparing to get angry at the British for assembling the powers at Brussels."

Davis, who asked Stanley and myself to join him. The conversation lasted till lunch time and was resumed at lunch, where we were all Eden's guests. It was entirely disjointed, but the following notes which I dictated for Norman Davis (subject to his later revision) give a fairly exact picture of the general tenor of the conversation.

Mr. Eden explained that Great Britain was seriously disturbed over developments in the Far East. At the same time, she felt herself threatened in Europe and did not see any lifting of the clouds in the near future. The more she examined the question of lawlessness in the world, the more she reached the conclusion that only by Great Britain and America standing shoulder to shoulder could the present threats be dispelled. He had no doubt that eventually the democracies would wake up, but whether or not it would be in time was a question that was worrying him. In the circumstances, he wished to give Mr. Davis a categorical assurance that Great Britain would be willing to go just as far in the way of direct action in the Far East as the United States, but no further. For obvious reasons, the British Government has been playing down its willingness to take so strong a stand, particularly as it could not judge how far America would be willing to go; but the assurance he had given was not given lightly, and represented the considered views of the British Government.

Mr. Davis pointed out that we were engaged on a constructive effort to bring about peace by agreement; and that until this had conclusively failed we would not even consider what we might do from that point on. Mr. Eden agreed, although he implied that we should not waste too long over the early phases of the Conference. Mr. Davis then went on to explain that there was a large body of public opinion in the United States which felt that American interests in the Far East were infinitesimal as compared with Great Britain's and that the latter being unable to protect her own interests was trying to maneuver us into "pulling her chestnuts out of the fire for her." Mr. Eden said that he knew this feeling existed, even though he greatly deplored it. He [Mr. Davis] then went on to say that if by any chance the two powers should pursue policies which provoked retaliation the United States would have to bear the brunt. Mr. Eden indignantly denied this and said that although the bulk of the fleet had to remain in Europe none the less Britain could and would send some ships to Far Eastern waters and assume her share. Furthermore, he added, the British Admiralty felt that the power and effectiveness of the Japanese navy was greatly exaggerated by the general public, both in Great Britain and the United States.

Mr. Davis told him that it would be impossible, from a political point of view, to take joint action with Great Britain; that, however, this did not preclude our taking independent action which paralleled that of Great Britain.[28] This was a distinction which we must be careful to observe. It was a distinction of form and not of substance. It was, however, an important one in the eyes of public opinion, which insisted on our pursuing an independent course.

Mr. Eden then referred to some of his own difficulties. He said that he, too, must take into account public opinion and that he had been fairly hard pressed in the House of Commons yesterday. He said the Japanese press had been singling Great Britain out for some time with more vituperation than the United States and that every step taken thus far had appeared to be a British move. He therefore decided that he must bring the United States into the picture and had told the story of our selection of Brussels as the site of the Nine-Power Conference. When Mr. Davis told him that it was not his speech, but Lord Cranborne's speech of October 29 [28] that had given us concern, Mr. Eden shrugged his shoulders and did not pursue the subject. . .

All present agreed that the Japanese position was serious but by no means desperate, and that a cooperative attitude from Japan was not to be expected, at least until the situation became far worse. They referred to Mr. Yoshida's assurances that the military were getting "fed up" and that the moderate elements in Japan were on the increase.[29] Both Mr. Eden and Mr. Davis agreed that it was not possible to attach any importance to the assurances of Mr. Yoshida. They

[28] Secretary Hull had noted several times in policy statements that he preferred "parallel" action. In his telegram of September 28, 1937, for instance, he said: "In general, it is felt that spontaneous separate action on parallel lines, should two or more governments feel moved thereto anywhere, indicates more strongly serious feeling regarding matters under consideration and is more likely effectively to serve to attain the objectives sought than would inspired joint action." U.S. Dept. of State, *Foreign Relations, Japan: 1931–41*, I, 376.

[29] Shigeru Yoshida, who was the Japanese Ambassador to Great Britain, had seen Anthony Eden on October 29 and Mr. Bingham on the following day and told them that the Japanese people and the Government wished to end the fighting in China. For an account of these conversations and the reaction of Ambassador Grew to Yoshida's statements, consult Grew, II, 1187–1189.

deprecated the lack of influence exercised by Yoshida, Matsudaira [Tsuneo Matsudaira, Japanese Minister of Imperial Household], and others upon the course of events, despite the high positions they occupied in the government.

As to Russia, Mr. Eden said that the British had no deeper motive in wanting her present than the fact that no permanent settlement could be reached in the Far East without her participation. . .

Mr. Davis summed up the American position by saying that we were going to make a genuine effort at the Conference of producing some constructive result; that in the process public opinion would be crystallized; that we did not view the problem as merely a Far Eastern one but as a world problem where the forces of order had a direct interest in preventing lawlessness and aggression; that President Roosevelt's Chicago speech had been an effort to show public opinion that America's interests had been directly affected by international anarchy; and that if our attempts at a constructive solution failed we would have to be guided in any next step by public opinion in the United States.

Mr. Eden summed up the British position by saying that they would neither attempt to take a lead nor to push America out into the front; that if constructive efforts failed he would be willing to join in direct pressure on Japan, although he would not embarrass us by advocating it if the idea was unwelcome; and that he could make us a promise that he would not only second any initiative of the United States during the Conference but that he could and would base British policy upon American policy during the present crisis. . .

At 5 o'clock I accompanied Norman Davis to the Belgian Foreign Office where Spaak held a meeting of three leading delegates, Davis, Eden, and Delbos [Yvon Delbos, French Minister for Foreign Affairs], to discuss procedure tomorrow. I did Mr. Davis' interpreting. It is not worth entering the various points discussed. The only impression worth recording is that both Spaak and Delbos were clearly of the opinion that the best thing we could do was to adjourn the conference at the slightest excuse. Mr. Davis' ideas of gradually educating public opinion were quite alien to their concepts and even Eden was constantly trying to hurry matters as he wants to return to London. Mr. Davis even had quite a fight to get one public session as both Spaak and Delbos felt that a series of keynote speeches would bring out the differences between the delegations rather than the similarities of view. . .

Brussels, Wednesday, November 3, 1937.

The session opened this morning at the Palais des Académies. The room was a long, dignified, but rather dreary hall with the press at one end and the long green-baize horseshoe table at the other, with three or four boxes occupied by the diplomatic corps, the Belgian Ministers of State, et cetera. The atmosphere was depressed, there was a notable lack of enthusiasm, and I was perfectly well aware that eight persons out of ten had uppermost in their minds how to close the Conference.

Spaak gave the opening address,[30] clear and to the point; and immediately following him came Norman's statement.[31] It was well received, but without enthusiasm. The British, who had hoped that he would go further, concealed their disappointment and at the end Eden came up with a smile and told Norman Davis that it was one of the great speeches of our time! He also said that he had had a speech prepared (last night at 10 o'clock he told us that he hadn't) but that Norman Davis had expressed so much more eloquently the points he wanted to bring out that he had thrown it away and would content himself with about three minutes of seconding the Davis speech! [32] Delbos did much the same, a useful support but quite colorless.[33] The fireworks began when the Italian delegate made a rather caustic speech telling us that he was not going to be applauded for what he said but that he felt it a duty to utter some homely truths.[34] The most this

[30] Mr. Spaak welcomed the delegates to Brussels, described the way in which the conference had come to be called, noted the refusal of Japan and Germany to attend, and emphasized that the purpose of the conference was to conciliate, to mediate, and to arbitrate. U.S. Dept. of State, *The Conference of Brussels*, pp. 21–23.

[31] The full text of the Davis address is given in *ibid.*, pp. 24–27. Mr. Davis referred to the formulation and purpose of the Nine-Power Treaty, deprecated the use of armed force to settle disputes, mentioned the changes in Japan and China and the hostilities between them, and concluded by saying: "We have come not with the expectation of working miracles, but with the intention of appealing to reason. We expect to join with other nations in urging upon Japan and China that they resort to peaceful processes. We believe that cooperation between Japan and China is essential to the best interests of those two countries and to peace throughout the world."

[32] Mr. Eden's speech, which was brief and "in full agreement with every word" that the American delegate had said, is printed in *ibid.*, pp. 27–29.

[33] *Ibid.*, pp. 29–31.

[34] Count Luigi Aldrovandi-Marescotti of Italy said that the main object of the conference should be "to lead the two parties towards a peace — and a lasting peace —

Conference could accomplish would be to make it possible for Japan and China to get into direct touch with one another, and even this would not be possible unless there were complete impartiality vis-à-vis the two powers. We had seen instances of international attempts to solve international difficulties. He recalled the Lytton Commission during the Manchurian crisis of 1932, which had had to bring in a compromise report, and even this had done nothing more than to force Japan out of the League of Nations. We had had the Chaco Committee, which had frankly not attempted to do anything because if it did anything positive either Paraguay or Bolivia, or both, would have left the League of Nations.

So much for the morning. In the afternoon session Litvinov took the floor and made one of his really clever speeches. He said that he came to give just one word of warning, that he has seen many conferences, and that there was always a danger that a conference would regard its own success as more important than the successful solution of the difficulty it had been called to meet. After a conference had gone on for some time, there was an almost irresistible tendency to say to the aggressor, "If you will make peace and give us credit, you can have most of your terms," [35] and to say to the victim, "Make peace with the aggressor, and God bless you." [36] Thereupon the conference would adjourn, consciences fully satisfied, the individual delegates saying to themselves, "We have been the peace-makers." [37]

The Portuguese delegate then made a speech of one minute and a half, for the brevity of which he was roundly cheered.[38]

The final speaker was Dr. Wellington Koo, who presented China's case.[39] His delivery was probably the most distinguished of any dele-

---

by bringing them together and by persuading them to look straight ahead and eliminate the hidden and deep-rooted causes of their dissensions." *Ibid.*, pp. 31–32.

[35] The verbatim record of the conference gives Litvinov's words as: "Take your plunder, take what you have seized by force, and peace be with you." *Ibid.*, p. 34.

[36] The victim of aggression was often told, Litvinov said: "Love your aggressor, resist not evil." *Ibid.*

[37] This part of Litvinov's address read: "But while that may constitute a superficial success for the Conference, it does not represent the victory of peace or the victory of the peace-loving countries." *Ibid.*

[38] The speech of Mr. Augusto de Castro of Portugal is given in *ibid.*, p. 45.

[39] Dr. Koo, the Chinese Ambassador to France, in the course of a lengthy address called attention to the ways in which Japan had contravened her obligations under the Nine-Power Treaty, attempted to refute Japanese statements of justification for action toward China, welcomed the participation of other powers in the settlement of the dispute, and said that the Chinese Government "has been fighting only to resist

gate's. In eloquent language, and with restrained yet convincing tones, he brought out the history of the attack and China's position; but the speech was too long, people's interest flagged, and when it was all over the general impression was, "Well, he made some very telling points, but after all we are not sure just what he was after."

This brought us up to about a quarter of 7 and we were all pretty weary when we got up to the hotel. However, the day was not done as at half-past 9 Delbos came to call on Mr. Davis. He was accompanied by De Tessan [François De Tessan, French Under Secretary of Foreign Affairs]. Eden was to have been present but excused himself as he was dead tired and went to bed early; but Malcolm Mac-Donald and Cadogan came in his place. I was present to make the memorandum and made very careful mental notes of a conversation which showed up, even more clearly than I had anticipated, what the French were trying to draw us into at this Conference. . .

Mr. Norman Davis opened the conversation by asking Mr. Delbos what he envisaged in the way of practical results from the Conference.

Mr. Delbos replied that while he felt we should make every effort to bring about a peace by agreement he was frankly skeptical of any successful issue. The only chance which he foresaw for getting Japan to agree to mediation and the conclusion of peace in the Far East was in the event that her military situation became a cause of concern to her, and even in this case he was not sure whether the Conference could be of any help. He felt, accordingly, that France, England, and the United States should discuss together what they might do in the event of failure. He was not in favor of punitive sanctions against Japan, but he was in favor of aid to China. Even this, however, involved certain risks and he thought that we should be discussing certain possibilities. The first was that Japan would undoubtedly tighten the blockade of the Chinese coast and interfere further with foreign shipping. We might now be discussing some

the Japanese invasion. We desire peace but we know that we cannot obtain it in the presence of Japanese aggression. So long as that aggression persists, so long we are determined to continue our resistance . . . It is only by accepting a peace based upon the principles of article I of the Nine-power Treaty of Washington, under which we are sitting, that China, by her tremendous sacrifices during the past few months, will be contributing to the cause of law and order in the relations between nations." *Ibid.*, pp. 35–45.

system of convoy or mutual protection of our ships in Chinese waters, so that supplies could reach China by sea. We might also be considering the situation of Indochina, which was one of the principal means of entry to China. Already Japan had politely warned France that if supplies were sent to China by this means Japan might have to take steps, and, although Mr. Delbos did not go so far as to suggest a guaranty by Britain and America for Indochina, he did suggest that we consider steps to assure that there might be free entry to and egress from Indochina.

Mr. Norman Davis replied that we were here for the primary purpose of seeking a solution by peaceful means. He did not see how we could hope successfully to mediate on the one hand and consider forms of pressure on the other. He felt that we should certainly try and unite all powers, big and small, into exerting moral pressure to put an end to the conflict. If that failed, then we will reach a point where we must decide whether to drop matters or to decide what to do next, but that bridge shouldn't be crossed till we came to it. . .

Mr. Davis suggested that Mr. Delbos was limiting the conversation too much to the Far East. He must remember that in democracies it was impossible to give advance commitments. Big decisions were made by public opinion, and public opinion depended upon developments. There was a large section of public opinion in America which felt that there was nothing in the Far East worth fighting about, that we were getting out of the Philippines, and that anyway our interests were far less there than those of France and England. As a matter of fact, we felt that the troubles in the Far East were only one part of a much larger problem, namely, the protection of the world against law-breakers. Mr. Davis did not conceive the problem as a struggle between the haves and the have-nots, but between the law-abiders and law-breakers. He said there were many small countries which did not have all they coveted but were nevertheless not pursuing a policy of trying to get what they want by lawless means.

Mr. Delbos said that what Mr. Davis had just said was exactly what the French believed. We must align the democracies against the dictators. Civilization had been retreating. There were wars without declaration, there were bombardments of open towns, there was piracy; in short, international anarchy. The free nations were richer, were stronger, were more numerous; and yet were the vanquished.

The dictatorships were speaking in tones of victors. Only an organized front of the free nations could put a stop to this retreat, and there was only one leader in the world who could organize such a "peace front." This was President Roosevelt, and he might call a world conference, after adequate preparation, to settle the troubles in the world. Meanwhile, however, we should have to concert our action in the Far East and consider what we should have to do. We should have to do it, just the three of us. It was useless to expect eighteen nations to decide what should be done to protect civilization from Japanese aggression.

Mr. Davis replied that he thought the President would have no appetite for calling such a conference. He would feel that it was useless to try to settle all problems if we weren't meanwhile able to settle one. As he saw it, France and England were faced with two simultaneous crises, one in Europe, one in the Far East. France must choose which could most readily be settled. In the European one, our public opinion would not permit us to help; in the Far Eastern one we might be able to help somewhat as we were members of the Nine Power Treaty and had certain obligations. . .

Brussels, Thursday, November 4, 1937.

Today our troubles began. Most of the Continental powers made it exceedingly clear that they had no wish to stay in Brussels and that the Conference should resolve itself into a small subcommittee which would have the task of making contact with the Japanese and possibly working out the basis of mediation between Japan and China. On this all parties were agreed but when they came to working out the composition of the committee we broke down completely. At first the French agreed that if they were invited they would decline, leaving the way for England, America, and a small power; later, however, Delbos said that he had talked by telephone with Paris, which refused to agree to this solution, alleging that France, by virtue of being a great power and possessing Indochina, must sit on any subcommittee. Litvinov, who took Mr. Davis to lunch, told him that the committee to be effective should be made up of Great Britain, the United States, and Soviet Russia. Italy insisted that she must be a member as otherwise, "The jury would be packed." A number of the more objective powers favored a committee composed of two big and two small nations, namely, Great Britain, the United States, Belgium, and Holland. The British did not want Russia on the committee; on the ground (a) that it would prevent Germany's joining, (b) that it would make it harder for Japan to talk matters over with the committee, and (c) that Russia had made trouble on whatever body she was sitting. Mr. Davis rather favored the inclusion of Russia on the ground that it would show Japan we meant business. He suggested that the thing might be done in two stages, namely, to have a first sub-committee of nine, which in turn would appoint a sub-sub-committee of three. The whole question became so involved that Eden, Mac Donald, and Cadogan had a further talk with Mr. Davis, Hornbeck, and myself from 6 to 7. Eden favored as first choice a committee of three, namely, the United States, United Kingdom, and Belgium; as second choice a committee of six, adding thereto France, Italy, and the Netherlands; as third choice, a committee of nine, adding thereto Soviet Russia, Germany, and one Dominion. The matter became so involved that in the evening the principal delegates left the room at the official reception and went on with the debate for another two hours, finally reaching the conclusion that the question must be side-tracked and that for the moment the whole conference would agree on a draft approaching Japan. If this were accepted we would then come back and fight out the composition of the committee. To one who is not versed in conference procedure this seems a pretty to-do about nothing, but the question of prestige is still so great in the world that few countries were willing to subordinate themselves to assisting an effective piece of work. . .

Brussels, Friday, November 5, 1937.

Session of the Conference at 10.30 to consider the draft reply to Japan prepared by Mr. Spaak. The discussion waxed fairly warm, when suddenly it was announced that through an oversight the draft, which was a secret document to be considered in secret session, had been given to the press and already telegraphed around the world. The result was that everyone realized the amendments must be reduced to a minimum or the Japanese would realize the divergence of views within the Conference and draw comfort therefrom. It was arranged that any delegation might submit amendments in the course of the afternoon and that these would be considered in Mr. Spaak's office at 5 o'clock. The session broke up at about a quarter-past one.

Anthony Eden, who was coming to luncheon with us, decided to fly back to London by a Royal Air Force plane which had been sent over for him. If he did not get away by 2 o'clock, he could not make the journey by air as at this season of the year the low-lying fog settles down in England at about half-past 4 and makes landing dangerous. However, before going he told Mr. Davis that he had been immensely encouraged that the smaller powers were beginning to speak up and felt the day was one of real encouragement. I analyzed to the best of my ability what the change had been but could not see that this statement was in any way warranted. In fact I think Malcolm MacDonald let the cat out of the bag later when he said that the press reaction in England to the first two days of the Conference had been pretty bad and that Eden had taken a strongly optimistic tone with the British newspapermen to counteract this publicity. . .

Spent the afternoon drafting memoranda and telegrams. One message I prepared giving an analysis of the picture as I saw it upset Mr. Davis to a point where I think he would have liked to send me home for pessimism. I summarized the attitude of the different powers: Italy openly playing Japan's game, even if not effectively; France only interested if she can get out of the Conference a guaranty of Indochina or if she can use it as a means of building up a political front of the great democracies; Belgium openly anxious to close the Conference, or at least to divest herself of the responsibility; the Netherlands remaining in the background as much as possible; China, instead of voluntarily withdrawing, merely offering to withdraw in case the Conference asked her to, which, of course, was not done; Russia arguing in favor of a close lineup between Britain, the United States, and Russia; the smaller powers playing an inactive role. All of this he eventually agreed to but definitely cut out the paragraph I had prepared on the British attitude. Unfortunately, on the role of Britain I fail to see eye to eye with Norman Davis, as to me Britain is in this Conference to tie us up to direct action with them against Japan, in which their "proportionate share" would be a very small proportion indeed. . .

Brussels, Saturday and Sunday, November 6 and 7, 1937.

Saturday morning's session succeeded in passing the draft text inquiring whether the Japanese would be willing to meet a small subcommittee of the Conference, and what is unusual the text of the note at the end was better than at the beginning.[40] This was due in large measure to the extraordinary presiding ability of Mr. Spaak, who is impressing us all more and more with each day that passes. When one considers that he is spending his nights trying to form a new Cabinet,[41] it is more astounding that he is able to put his whole mind on his task of presiding. The moment the text was passed, a number of delegates wanted to adjourn the Conference until the Japanese reply had been received but Norman Davis blocked this on the ground that we must at all costs prevent the impression that we cannot continue our work without a favorable reply and that we must give the impression that we have other strings to our bow. Our chief opponent in this thesis was the French, who have done more to block our work than even the Italians.

In fact the French showed such signs of annoyance that Norman Davis thought it would be a good plan to call on De Tessan and reestablish friendly relations. The French have been tipping off their press in Paris that we have opposed the inclusion of France on the negotiating committee and favored the inclusion of Germany. We have never taken this stand in Brussels, but the idea was outlined in a telegram from the Department sent in our best code. The conclusion is inevitable that the French cracked it on the way through. The talk with De Tessan was not very satisfactory. He would not listen to the end of any of Norman's sentences and would interrupt with a short formula and repeat it *ad nauseam*. However, it gradually transpired that France felt that we attached more value to Great Britain than to herself and that this had wounded her deeply. No matter what the circumstances, France must be included on a footing of

[40] In making a final effort to get Japan to come to Brussels, the states met in conference pointed out that the situation in the Far East was just the kind which the Nine-Power Treaty had envisaged might require such "full and frank communication" as was taking place in Brussels. To allay Japanese misgivings that it would be ill-advised to try to solve an Asian problem at a conference where so many powers with only negligible interests in Asia were present, the powers requested a Japanese reply to the proposal that Japan send representatives to meet with a small number of powers. U.S. Dept. of State, *The Conference of Brussels*, pp. 51–52.

[41] The Belgian Prime Minister had resigned on October 24, 1937, after attacks on him because of the maladministration of the National Bank of Belgium of which he had been a vice-governor. A new government was not formed until November 24. Arnold Toynbee, *Survey of International Affairs, 1937* (London: Oxford University Press, 1938), I, 367.

equality in any body in which Great Britain and America took part. . .

Brussels, Monday, November 8, 1937.

. . . Mr. Davis had Litvinov to lunch and the latter for the first time let it be seen that he was in a difficult situation. He said that if the powers did not intend to treat Russia on a basis of complete equality and put her on essential committees they should never have invited her. He said that Russia, once she had espoused the policy of working with the Western powers, had done so wholeheartedly and had taken some terrible beatings in consequence. He had been in two minds as to whether or not he should accept the invitation to come to Brussels, and said that it would be exceedingly difficult for him to return with completely empty hands. This conversation bears out the theory we have been getting from our people in Moscow, that Litvinov's position is not as strong as it once was; that the younger men who are now surrounding Stalin have no knowledge of Europe, despise all foreigners, and want to withdraw Russia into its own shell and concentrate on their own development rather than on foreign politics. For the first time Litvinov has been accompanied to a big international conference by another high-ranking Russian, this time Potemkin [Vladimir P. Potemkin, Russian Commissioner for Foreign Affairs]. Usually he just has a few young men with him. He remarked once that while he was given a pretty free hand in formulating Russian foreign policies he must personally take the rap for any failures. . .

Brussels, Wednesday, November 10, 1937.

From 9 to 12 this morning we were busy working on a telegram for the President and the Secretary pointing out that it would not be possible to prolong the Conference for an extended period, as the President had hoped, as only the British could see the objectives of such a plan, whereas the other delegates almost to a man were anxious to adjourn. It was even questionable how much longer the British and ourselves could hold them in line. The question therefore arose as to how to close the Conference, which in turn called for a greater knowledge than we possessed of what was running through the President's mind. We put up several alternative suggestions. It was a pretty important telegram and we have all been working on it off and on for the past three or four days. . .[42]

Mr. Delbos returned from Paris last night and came to see Mr. Davis by appointment at 12 o'clock today. Mr. Eden joined the conversation. . .

Mr. Davis suggested that we ask China whether she would be prepared to accept the good offices of the Conference and publish her affirmative reply, thus emphasizing Japan's refusal (for everyone assumed the reply would be negative). Both Mr. Delbos and Mr. Eden questioned the wisdom of this move, saying that if, after Japan's refusal to deal with the Conference, China agreed to do so it might be interpreted in the Orient as an evidence of weakening of the Chinese position. Mr. Davis said that he perhaps had not expressed his thought very well, but that what he had in mind was obtaining a declaration from China that she would not deal directly with Japan or with any other mediator than the representatives of the Nine-Power Treaty Conference. This would forestall any offer of mediation by Hitler.

Mr. Delbos then said that we should already begin to consider how far we would be willing ultimately to go. Mr. Eden agreed, saying that while he had every sympathy with our idea of educating public opinion we could not remain in Brussels indefinitely and that the sooner we got down to brass tacks the less delay there would be ultimately.

Mr. Delbos said that he wished to reiterate what he had said previously, that France was prepared to go as far as the United States proposed, provided there was complete solidarity. He said that Japan was deeply involved in China; that China was not resisting as well

---

[42] The delegation suggested three possible courses of action if Japan persisted in her refusal to attend the Conference. One possibility was for the Conference to declare that it had failed to induce Japan to join in the peace effort and to adjourn while the delegates went home to discuss future steps with their governments. Or, a second course would be for the Conference to try to agree on some form of pressure against Japan in trade or shipping. The third suggestion was for the Conference to agree to a resolution embodying the following points: no discrimination against the Chinese military effort; no effort to persuade China "to enter into an agreement involving unwilling concessions"; no recognition of "changes" in China inconsistent with the Nine-Power Treaty; no countenance of loans and credits to Japan in connection with the hostilities; and no military assistance to Japan, if she became involved with any other Conference power before ending the conflict by agreement with China. Department of State, MS, 793.94 Conference /219.

as we had hoped, but none the less they were continuing to hold up the Japanese; that Japan had little stomach for risking hostilities with the Western powers if she knew that they were definitely united. Perhaps none of them would do very much, but if all of them made a small contribution the sum total of their contributions would be pretty large. He then went on to explain France's position with regard to traffic in munitions through Indochina to China and reverted to the idea of a guaranty of Indochina. He said that France would be glad to guarantee anyone else's possessions in the Far East, but that she in turn must receive a guaranty of her possessions. This was what he meant by solidarity.

Mr. Eden then explained that England was willing to go as far as the United States. He assumed that we might have given consideration to stopping all sales to and purchases from Japan. This would be none too popular in Great Britain on account of the Ethiopian precedent, but the Government could none the less carry it through and he thought that if England and the United States should take a positive stand the smaller powers would follow suit, even if reluctantly. If this idea were not practicable, we might send ships to the Orient, making a display of force.

Mr. Davis said he agreed that we could not much longer delay discussing the substance of our problem. Our situation was somewhat difficult in that the hands of the Administration were tied by our neutrality legislation, which he sincerely hoped might be altered by Congress when it met. Congress would meet next week and we should undoubtedly have some indication of what the Administration could or could not do. In the last anlysis, public opinion would have to guide any decisions of the American Government. It was still too early to know what we could do and he was not sure whether the best place to discuss it was at Brussels during the Conference or by direct negotiations with the individual Foreign Offices.

Mr. Delbos, Mr. Eden, and Mr. Davis all agreed that meanwhile they could take a useful step at Saturday's meeting if one after the other made a substantially similar declaration that the problem in the Far East, in its broader aspects, involved the question of whether the relationships between nations should be determined by conflicts of ideology or by the undertakings solemnly entered into by treaty. It was felt that the small nations which had heretofore kept rather in the background would support such a declaration and that a rather impressive demonstration of solidarity would result. . .

At 6, went back with Mr. Davis to a further meeting of the Delbos-Eden-Davis trio, in Eden's room. It was agreed (one) that on Saturday the morning session would be devoted to detailed remarks on the Japanese reply; (two) that the afternoon session, which would be public, would be consecrated to a series of declarations along the line worked out at lunch today; and (three) that the evening session would act as a drafting committee to approve the text of a further communication to Japan. This further communication would be much firmer in tone and would announce that the Chinese delegation had informed the Conference that it would not enter into direct negotiations with Japan nor accept mediation from other sources than the Nine-Power Conference. After this was despatched there would be a delay of about a week pending the receipt of a reply. During this time the Belgian delegation would be in London for the King's visit.[43] Mr. Eden would be back and forth, et cetera.

The final resolution of this phase of the Conference would be prepared. But there was considerable doubt as to just what this would contain. Everyone agreed that it should contain a long enumeration of the efforts made and the proposal submitted. Mr. Davis suggested that there be added to this a series of undertakings extending the principles of nonrecognition, including a refusal to extend loans and credits to enable the aggressor to profit by the fruits of his aggression. He pointed out that this was a personal suggestion and that he could not speak on behalf of his Government. As a matter of fact, Congress was meeting early next week and he thought that the indications then received would help the President to gauge the extent to which he could take a strong stand.

Mr. Delbos replied that if it were not for the necessity of awaiting the meeting of Congress he would be strongly opposed to proceeding at as slow a pace as we have been pursuing.

He then said that he was still greatly preoccupied over the question of transit of materials through Indochina. It was not a pressing problem because France had agreed to let the war materials already en route pass and that they probably would always let airplanes

[43] King Leopold of Belgium visited the King of England from November 16 to 19, 1937.

through. However, the Government of Indochina was already asking for more ships and more troops. France does not wish to have to back water in the affair. If she is not supported it would be necessary for her either to send more ships and men, which she cannot do as a result of conditions in Europe, or else she will have to close the railroad. He thought that the final resolution of the Conference might consider this phase of the problem and that all the powers could agree that France should keep the railroad open, and assume some sort of joint responsibility. France would help keep Hong Kong open and he hoped that the British would help keep Indochina open. Mr. Davis indicated he would have to give this pretty careful thought.

Mr. Delbos then went on to say that President Roosevelt . . . had said that he hoped France would keep the railroad open and that if Indochina were attacked it would create a community of interest and might even constitute a threat to the Philippines. On the basis of this . . . Mr. Delbos felt certain that Mr. Davis would agree to what he wanted. . .

The Japanese replied on November 12 to the *note verbale* sent five days earlier from Brussels. The Imperial Government said that the China Incident did "not come within the scope of the Nine-power Treaty and that there is no justification for discussing the applicability of the latter." Japan also restated the conviction that the "intervention of a collective organ such as the present Conference would merely excite national feeling in the two countries and would make it more difficult to reach a solution satisfactory to all." [44]

Brussels, Friday, November 12, 1937.

All morning we were at work on various documents, Stanley on the draft to Japan, I on the speech for tomorrow. Everyone's mind is now running to ways and means of closing the Conference, and even those who are most anxious ultimately to do something to Japan have pretty well come around to the feeling that the Conference is not the place to do it. The British, French, and Americans have tended a little too much to think that what they decided would automatically be accepted by all the other powers except perhaps Italy. However, the first shock came when Canada flatfootedly said, "Condemnation if

[44] U.S. Dept. of State, *The Conference of Brussels*, pp. 53–54.

you will, but no sanctions." The second shock was received when I reported to Mr. Davis and Mr. Eden (who was with him) a conversation I had with Aubert, the Norwegian delegate.

I had called on him at Mr. Davis' request. We discussed the Japanese reply, which he said had been no surprise to him. He asked what steps, if any, we were envisioning for the future. I told him that various steps were under consideration, but that only one matter had been decided as yet; that was, that Messrs. Davis, Eden, Delbos would take the occasion tomorrow, apart from any discussion that they might choose to have on the Far East, to speak in general terms in support of international law and the sanctity of treaties as the basis for international relationships. I said that we felt it would be far more impressive if we were supported in this by some of the smaller powers, and that, if he saw his way clear to make a speech along the general lines of the three delegates mentioned, even if he did not choose to point it up specifically toward the Far East, we felt it would give a useful impression.

Mr. Aubert replied that while he could say that every word of the philosophy referred to was accepted by his Government nevertheless it might be a very difficult matter for him to make any utterances along these lines in this Conference. He said that the instructions which he, and for that matter his Swedish and Danish colleagues, had received was to take no action whatsoever without referring it back to their Governments, or even to associate themselves in anything that might be construed as in the least degree critical of Japan. He said that the circumstances under which the three powers had adhered to the Nine-Power Treaty were not very clear, but that he was convinced that if the decision were put before them today they would not even consider adherence. It was all very well for the big powers to pursue a policy which they could maintain if necessary by force of arms, but since the experience of the Scandinavian countries with sanctions, which had cost them dearly and brought in no corresponding gain, either material or spiritual, he felt that the whole national point of view was against being involved any further in anybody else's quarrel, irrespective of whether right was strongly on one side or not. This policy, which might be called the policy of self-preservation, might seem at variance with Norway's obligations under the League, but even the League ideal had lost immeasurably since the

Ethiopian fiasco and the virtual withdrawal from the League of Italy, Germany, et cetera.

Mr. Aubert had been giving a good deal of thought these past few days to what might eventually be done. The conclusion he had reached was that the sooner the Conference adjourned the better, for the simple reason that it had nothing further to do. If anything further were to be done, it had better be done by the powers who would do it, and not by the Conference. He knew that Mr. Davis was averse to cutting short the sessions of the Conference, and I explained to him once again the reasons why. He doubted, however, whether the premises on which they were based were right; namely, that the Conference would educate public opinion.

Going back to the suggestion I had made, he said that he would discuss the matter in confidence with his Swedish and Danish colleagues, but that, frankly, he felt that it would be a departure from instructions which, even if they should put it up to their Governments, would not be authorized.

Eden's immediate reaction was, "They will need further education, and besides they haven't got their first-string men here." Further reflection, however, made him reach the conclusion that we must adjourn anyway most of next week, that he would go back and have a further talk with London and then come back with definite proposals to put up to us. Norman Davis told him that as far as he could make out public opinion had not moved one iota as a result of this Conference. . .

Brussels, Saturday, November 13, 1937.

Today as we all foresaw was probably the turning point of the Conference. Sessions were held morning and afternoon, and for the first time the delegates approached a discussion of realities.

In the morning, Wellington Koo opened up with a speech in which he flatly asked for sanctions against Japan.[45] In view of the uncompromising nature of the Japanese reply, he felt that the Conference would be stultifying itself if it did not withhold aid from Japan. This speech went further than he had hinted to the three prin-

[45] Koo's speech in which he asked that war materials and credit be withheld from Japan and aid be given to China is in U.S. Dept. of State, *The Conference of Brussels*, pp. 55–58.

cipal delegates. When their turn came to speak, they paid no attention whatsoever to Koo's remarks and went on with their three set speeches calling attention to the generality that international relations must be governed not by violence but by the law and not by the conflicts of national dogmas but by the respect of treaties.[46] The newspapermen, who by nature want action, were upset by these speeches which they felt at best were marking time. The Soviet representative then got up and said that Russia would join fully in any concrete measures proposed by the Conference;[47] but the bombshell was thrown by the Italian delegate, who in a speech of not over a minute said that we were already getting outside the terms of reference of the Conference, ending with one question which he wanted answered: "What more does the Conference think it can do?"[48]

At this point the session closed and the President announced that he was circulating a draft declaration, jointly submitted by the British, French, and American delegations. This would not be a communication addressed to Japan — for after the nature of her reply no one felt that another plea was in order — but would serve to put the Conference on record as refusing to accept the Japanese arguments as valid. The discussion of this draft would take place during the afternoon session.

True enough, from half-past 4 till 8 the delegates wrangled over the text, and once again the document came out from the mill better than it went into it. The genius of Mr. Spaak in presiding was largely responsible.

The Italian announced that he could not accept the draft in whole or in part and the three Scandinavian countries indicated that they must have permission from their Foreign Offices to accept the text. Adjournment was therefore taken until Monday afternoon, and an exodus of delegates started; Delbos back to France, Eden to London, Bruce [Stanley M. Bruce, High Commissioner for Australia in Great Britain] back to London, et cetera, et cetera.

Meanwhile the delegation had received a number of telegrams

[46] The address of Mr. Davis was in support of international law as a means to settle disputes. The speeches of Mr. Eden and Mr. Delbos were also of a general character. *Ibid.,* pp. 58–63.

[47] *Ibid.,* pp. 63–64.

[48] *Ibid.,* p. 64. The last sentence of Count Aldrovandi-Marescotti's address read: "What is there now that remains for this Conference to do?"

from the Department, all of them indicating that it did not wish this Conference at least to take any positive steps.[49] Whether or not the Department wished to keep in being a body which had neither condemned Japan nor advocated any steps against her, in the hope that perhaps at some future day its existence might be of use, was not made clear. In any event Mr. Davis was cautioned to initiate nothing more than platitudes and was given a number of suggestions for a resolution to be passed by the Conference before its recess, almost all of which had already been included in the declaration discussed today.

Mr. Davis' first reaction was one of pretty bitter disappointment and a feeling that he had been left out on a limb. On second thoughts he decided that he could still persuade the Department to permit the passage of a resolution restating the nonrecognition principle and extending it by advocating a prohibition of Government loans and credits to Japan and discouraging private loans and credits.

There have been further talks with Eden. He is still courting us assiduously. I am still convinced that ultimately he would like to see us embroiled side by side in the Far East, on the theory that in such a contingency Germany and Italy would be immobilized, as an extension of the conflict would involve them in hostilities with the United States; if, on the other hand, they should move, then England could count on us as a cobelligerent. This is a tall order, however, and I suspect that in his heart of hearts Eden does not think we will fall into the trap. Meanwhile, however, when he sees that we cannot advance up one alley he suggests we proceed together up another alley. I admire his technique even though I have no sympathy with his objectives.

As a matter of fact, our delegation is well balanced. The three of us approach the problem before us with three separate preoccupations. Mr. Davis starts on the premise that the existence of the British Empire is essential for the national security of the United States and that while we should not follow Great Britain nevertheless we should not allow the Empire to be endangered. Stanley Hornbeck reacts to everything that comes up in specific relation to the Far Eastern situa-

[49] In reply to the important delegation telegram of November 10, 1937, for instance, the Department wired: "In our opinion none of the measures envisaged therein should be proposed by the United States." Department of State, MS, 793.94 Conference / 219.

tion and the Far Eastern situation alone. My personal preoccupation is to prevent at any costs the involvement of the United States in hostilities anywhere, and to that end to discourage any formation of a common front of the democratic powers.[50]

These three points of view represent three phases of American public opinion and I think any course we can all three agree upon should prove pretty satisfactory at home. . .

The draft declaration of November 15 was described by the correspondent of the *Manchester Guardian* as "a severe admonition to Japan and an impressive and excellent proclamation of the principles of law and justice which should govern the Far Eastern conflict as well as all other international affairs." [51]

Stressing that the Sino-Japanese conflict was of concern to the whole world and not just to the principals involved, pointing out that there was no warrant for Japan to use armed force to intervene in Chinese internal affairs, and reiterating the hope that Japan would not persist in her refusal to confer with the powers at Brussels, the delegates mustered courage to hint that they might take some concerted action.

Though hoping that Japan will not adhere to her refusal the above-mentioned states represented at Brussels must consider what is to be their common attitude in a situation where one party to an international treaty maintains against the views of all the other parties that the action which it has taken does not come within the scope of that treaty and sets aside provisions of the treaty which the other parties hold to be operative in the circumstances.[52]

This veiled threat lost all potency almost as soon as it was made, because, as the *New York Times* expressed it, the conference was "bathetic" and would soon become "pathetic." [53] The delegates were anxious to complete the funeral arrangements, bury the conference, and depart.

In Washington Secretary Hull, convinced that the conference was "fruitless" and irritated because "the burden for its fruitlessness was

[50] Such statements as this have led some to classify Mr. Moffat within the "isolationist" wing of the Department of State. A fairer interpretation of his views, as expressed in his diary and supported by the testimony of his friends, is that he agreed in many points with his father-in-law, Joseph C. Grew. Both men saw the danger that war against the fascist dictatorships might destroy their menace but augment the power of the communist dictatorship. Thus one adversary would be replaced by an even more powerful one. It might also be said that Mr. Moffat's thought during the period underwent changes, as the condition of international affairs changed. Certainly by the time he reached Canada he seems to have been in favor of any support which the United States could give to the democracies.

[51] Toynbee, *Survey, 1937,* I, 289–290.

[52] U.S. Dept. of State, *The Conference of Brussels,* p. 67.

[53] *New York Times,* November 21, 1937, part IV, p. 3.

constantly being cast upon the United States," cabled curtly to Mr. Davis on November 16. Mr. Hull asked the American delegates to do what they could to counteract the publicity placing the onus of responsibility for inaction upon the United States. He further invited Mr. Davis' attention to the fact "that questions of methods of pressure against Japan are outside the scope of the present conference." [54] The following day this telegram reached the delegation at Brussels.

Brussels, Thursday, November 18, 1937.

. . . Telegram after telegram poured in today from the Department. The tenor was a clearer expression of what we have been gathering for the past few days, namely, that the temper of the country was definitely against any form whatsoever of pressure against Japan. Personally, I am delighted, though in view of the personal instructions given to Norman Davis by the President at Hyde Park he is going to have a somewhat difficult time in retreating quite the length that the Department wants him to. Up to three days ago the press comments from here had been pretty satisfactory; during the last three days they have all gone haywire.

The Department had one excellent idea, however, namely, that in winding up instead of adopting a second resolution the Conference should draw up a report to the participating Governments, which will enable them to make a far fuller presentation of the case than would otherwise be possible. So much said, I have less admiration for the idea of the Department drafting a report and then sending it textually in double code (it took nine hours to decipher) and then telling us that while this is what they want we must neither propose it nor make it seem our own.

The other telegrams were definitely critical of Mr. Davis' handling of the publicity, notably in his allowing the impression to prevail that this was *our* Conference. Our constant surprise has been not that such publicity occurred but that there was so little of it. Every delegation here, for purposes of its own, has been trying to make its action dependent upon ours. First they tried to make us take the lead, which we refused; then they tried to make us agree to direct pressure, which again we refused; then they tried to make us recess, which under orders from Washington, we blocked (I think this has been our biggest mistake); now they are trying to throw the blame

[54] Hull, I, 554–555.

on us, some because the Conference has done nothing, and others because they think Mr. Davis would have liked to go beyond what they consider the narrow terms of reference of the Conference though stopping far short of pressure. I must have spent six hours trying to persuade him not to scold the Department in return, and above all not to enter into a telegraphic controversy on perfectly subsidiary remarks in the Department's telegrams, even though they contained incorrect statements. I did succeed in materially reducing the volume of argumentative material though he still felt that he must, as a matter of self-respect, refuse to accept all that was said. Personally I felt that at this point the least said the soonest mended. For better or worse, Washington has made a decision of policy. To my mind the only legitimate grievance he has is that Washington was so slow in telling it to him. . .

Brussels, Saturday, November 20, 1937.

MacDonald and Lord Cranborne accompanied by Cadogan came to Mr. Davis' room at a quarter-past 11, to discuss what to do when the Conference met next week. Mr. Davis pointed out that he thought instead of having a new resolution or declaration we might make the closing document in the form of a report to governments. MacDonald replied that he did not think this would do as everybody knew that Eden had gone back to London to make a report and that a Cabinet had been called to consider action. From the British point of view it was essential to have the Conference adjourn in such a way that the Chinese would not be justified in asking that the problem be returned to Geneva. The only way to prevent that was to introduce some new element and the only new element that he could see was the possibility that the United States and Great Britain should meanwhile jointly offer mediation to Japan or at least announce their readiness to do so. On the basis of this announcement the Conference could adjourn and any appearance of failure might be avoided. Mr. Davis did not think that this would offer many possibilities. He feared it would be resented by the Conference, he did not think the time was ripe for it, and he did not really think that it would ease an adjournment. He offered a compromise suggestion, namely, that the Conference should, in addition to a report which would be primarily for the record but which might be sent on to other nonparticipating governments, pass a resolution calling on the Japanese and Chinese for a suspension of hostilities coupled with a standing offer of good offices in facilitating an armistice. This was a step which had not been taken and which if we wanted to build up a perfect case against Japan should not be omitted. A second resolution might contain directions to the parties to the Conference to keep in touch with one another and continue to discuss the attitudes of governments toward the Far Eastern situation. Both MacDonald and Lord Cranborne kept pressing Mr. Davis very hard. He left them in no doubt, however, that he did not regard their suggestion as practical. They all agreed that it would be a good plan for Mr. Davis and MacDonald to call on Spaak late this afternoon and discuss matters with him. Meanwhile both the British and ourselves would put on paper what we had in mind in connection with possible resolutions and reports and that eventually we might be able to form a small joint drafting committee (to which others might be invited) to marry the two drafts. . .

Brussels, November 21, 1937, Sunday.

This morning another telegram came in from the Department — none too closely reasoned — the burden of which was that press despatches were still coming in from Brussels indicating that the failure of the Conference was ours and ours alone, and that while the Department had thus far not made any answer on such comment, none the less they felt that they had a good case to present if need be. Stanley Hornbeck was so upset by what he called this "stinkbomb" that he interrupted what he was doing and proceeded to draft a four-page telegram setting the Department aright. Bob Pell meanwhile had prepared a careful summary of the problems he had been faced with at various stages of the Conference with the American journalists. Most of these, despite the policies of their newspapers, were in favor of a strong American policy against the dictator countries.[55] They had arrived here convinced that the President's speech

[55] The *Chicago Sunday Tribune*, November 21, 1937, part I, p. 9, reported: "The European hope of pinning the responsibility for the fiasco of the Brussels nine-power treaty conference on the United States brightened tonight when it was learned that the American government has cabled imperative orders to the American delegation to catch the first boat home. . .

"The Europeans contend that the real fiasco of the conference — the reason why it has damaged the prestige of the western democracies grievously — is not that it failed to do anything, but that it talked so much about doing something and then

sounded the clarion call to renewed activity on the part of America on behalf of the democracies, that the State Department's endorsement of the League condemnation of Japan gave weight to this view, and, finally, there was the selection of Norman Davis as the delegate. From the very beginning they were subject to a barrage of pressure from the other delegations, all of it to the effect that whereas their countries would be willing to go as far as the United States they would not take any action unless the United States would join them; in other words our decision depended upon theirs. About the middle of the Conference, first Kurusu, the Japanese Ambassador, and later one or two of the other delegates, told the press that they had received word from their Washington representatives that the American Government would do nothing; that as they expressed it we would "curl up." From that point on many of the stories were friendly enough to the delegation but unfriendly to Washington's policy, and although Pell had them in one at a time and would periodically set them straight they would none the less continue to absorb and pass on the poison fed out to them by the British, French, and Japanese. . .

Brussels, November 22, 1937.

Having reached a meeting of minds with the British at 2.35 in the morning, we were back again on the job at 9 o'clock. I accompanied Mr. Davis when he and the British called on Mr. Spaak. The latter agreed to circularize the text saying that it had been prepared at his request by the British and American delegations in consultation with other delegations as a basis for discussion. Shortly thereafter the French, to our considerable pleasure, arrived from Paris and asked to be associated with us among the sponsors. I don't think they had ten minutes in which to read the document, and certainly it was not what they had been advocating, but they were so afraid of being left out of the *combinazione* that they swallowed it whole. The British and ourselves divided up the other delegations to show them advance copies. The British took on the Dominions, Italy, and Portugal; we took on Russia, Holland, the Scandinavians, Mexico, and Bolivia. Mr. Davis himself saw Potemkin, who was dissatisfied but obviously not in a position to stand out on his own; and then sent me

---

backed down at the crucial moment. This, they say, definitly [*sic*] is the fault of the United States, which insisted on a strong moral stand against Japan."

driving around the town rounding up the others. I had pretty good luck with the Swedes, Danes, Dutch, and Bolivians; more difficulty with the Norwegians, who have left a new man here who seems to have on the one hand an ambition to speak on all occasions and on the other to justify Norway's policy of independence; and most difficulty of all with the Mexican, who just didn't know what it was all about and kept reverting to the League of Nations when no one else wanted to speak of it.

In the early afternoon the Paris papers arrived indicating the hostility at home to the Conference . . . Senator Lewis' demand on the President to recall the delegation in order to avoid the onus of responsibility of failure (what a *non sequitur!*).[56] Mr. Davis telephoned to Mr. Hull, really for no other reason than that he felt the need of hearing a friendly voice at the other end of the wire, and shortly thereafter he held a press Conference in which he at least straightened out our newspapermen here. . .

Brussels, Wednesday, November 24, 1937.

An active morning as we were getting the Dutchmen, the Bolivian, and other delegates, who had some personal ideas, into line. The result was that the ground was thoroughly prepared and the afternoon session, which we had feared would go on for six or seven hours, was completed in two and a half. The declaration passed with virtually no amendments, there were a series of speeches indicating that our adjournment did not mean the termination of our efforts, there were the usual compliments and felicitations, and recess was taken.[57]

This ends one more chapter, and now back to Washington!

After the murder of Dollfuss in 1934 by agents of the Austrian Nazi Party, the influence of Germany within Austria grew increasingly stronger. In 1938 Hitler determined to gain control of the Austrian Government by insisting that Austrian Nazi leaders be placed in the

[56] Senator J. Hamilton Lewis of Illinois said it seemed that an effort was being made to blame the United States for the Sino-Japanese incident and asserted: "I think that the President should investigate and if he finds our representatives are innocently or otherwise being put in the position of being blamed they should be withdrawn to America." *New York Times*, November 20, 1937, p. 6.

[57] The final declaration reindorsed the principles of the Nine-Power Treaty, reaffirmed the interest of all the signatory nations in the Far Eastern conflict, and urged suspension of hostilities. The final speeches, the declaration, and the report are printed in U.S. Dept. of State, *The Conference of Brussels*, pp. 69–80.

Cabinet. On February 12, 1938, Kurt von Schuschnigg, the Austrian Chancellor, and Guido Schmidt, the Austrian Foreign Minister, met Hitler at Berchtesgaden.[58]

Tuesday, February 15, 1938.

. . . The Austrian situation . . . is even worse than I had anticipated, and I was generally considered a pessimist at that. As further details have come in it becomes clear that Schuschnigg was faced by Hitler who throughout the interview had three generals, including the notorious Reichenau [General Walther von Reichenau], standing motionless behind him. Apparently Schuschnigg was confronted with the choice of the Germans taking over Austria at once or his admitting Nazis into the Cabinet which means the same thing at a later date. Wiley's [John Wiley, Counselor of the American Legation at Vienna] reports which were at first somewhat confused have gradually been able to fit in the missing pieces in the mozaic. Wiley himself made the blunder of telling Guido Schmidt that we urged Austria against any action which might be assumed to threaten her independence. . . We certainly can't be thought, whatever our sympathies may be, to assume any responsibility legal or moral, in Europe at the moment. . .

Friday, February 18, 1938.

. . . In the afternoon the Secretary sent for me to talk over the direction in which Europe was headed. Personally I can see no cheer, though I expect that Germany will now mark time as far as other nations are concerned while continuing to burrow into Austria. Schuschnigg told Messersmith that no matter how bad things looked he would remain as Chancellor if he saw any hope in the situation, conversely, if ever he resigned it would be because he had given up all hope. The only real optimism in Europe is Mr. Carr [Wilbur Carr, American Minister to Czechoslovakia] who has taken the position that Czechoslovakia is in no way threatened and is sticking to his story. . .

Saturday and Sunday, February 19 and 20, 1938.

. . . The drama of Anthony Eden's resignation to some extent is concealing its more unfortunate implications.

[58] For an account of this incident and the Austrian crisis of 1938, see Kurt von Schuschnigg, *Ein Requiem in Rot-Weiss-Rot* (Zurich: Amstutz, Herdeg & Co., 1946).

For two years Anthony Eden has been subordinating his own convictions to Cabinet decisions. He believes in the right of Cabinet as a body to determine policy and has accepted on several occasions an overruling which would have forced another man to resign long ago. Chamberlain [Neville Chamberlain, British Prime Minister] has for many months been out of sympathy with Eden's ideas, we saw clear proof of that in Brussels, but being an astute politician knew that Eden's strength in the country was so great as to make it inadvisable to drop him. For Eden to have considered that the time had come when he could no longer stay, and for Chamberlain to have decided that the time had come when he must risk the threat to his government by letting him go, leads one to the inescapable conclusion that the decision of Chamberlain to "play ball with Hitler and Mussolini" has reached a concrete stage and is no longer a mere abstraction.

This is the first occasion I can think of in recent British political history when a Minister has been allowed to go while being the target of attacks from abroad. Hitler and Mussolini have made no secret of their distrust of Eden and all that he stood for. It is also the first time I can think of when Britain has proposed to yield to a country which that very day attacked her and publicly threatened the Empire. To me the most interesting aspect of Hitler's speech was that he took his dominance over Central and Eastern Europe as an accomplished fact and intimated that the British Empire was the long range target of his policy.[59]

The most serious effect of Eden's going will be felt on the continent of Europe. There will undoubtedly be a strong reaction in France, because the French Government has been following British foreign policy consistently and at times almost slavishly, only to have Britain apparently desert her. Italy will take renewed courage. The smaller states will feel that the chief democracy has ceased fighting, and that the juggernaut of totalitarianism can proceed forward unchecked. The belief will grow that Britain's interest in principles and in democracy was skin deep, something to be played up when it coin-

[59] On February 20, 1938, Hitler spoke before the Reichstag and attacked Mr. Eden severely. Of England, Hitler said: "Nor has Germany any quarrel with England unless perhaps it may be our wish for colonies." Adolf Hitler, *The Speeches of Adolf Hitler*, ed. Norman H. Baynes (London: Oxford University Press, 1942), II, 1376–1409.

cided with Britain's material interests and to be discarded as soon as it no longer served a useful purpose. . .

Monday and Tuesday, February 21 and 22, 1938.

The Eden resignation and its probable effects on world developments occupied most of our time today. Its future effects will certainly make the Secretary's policy more difficult of accomplishment. The public at large feels that Britain has deserted her cause and that we should more and more withdraw into our own hemisphere. The Secretary called a few of us to his office to discuss the Hitler speech and whether or not it called for some statement on our part. Every one present advised that he say nothing whatsoever for the moment. I told him that the public mind was focused not on Hitler's speech but on the Eden-Chamberlain duel and that anything he had to say in reply to Hitler would be construed as a rebuke to Chamberlain.

Telegrams from France indicated complete bewilderment and utter bankruptcy of policy. As far as Austria is concerned France has just thrown up her hands and there are increasing indications that she will not take a strong stand anywhere in Central Europe. France is still trying to pay for the last war, is still trying to prepare for the next war, and at the same time through extreme social legislation is lowering national income. . . Pretty soon she will have to make a choice; either to give up her advanced labor legislation in order to be strong enough to pursue an active policy beyond the Rhine or else to withdraw behind the Rhine and let Central Europe go. I suspect she will make the latter choice. . .

On March 11, 1938, the German army pushed over its frontiers into Austria. It was one of those days, Pierrepont Moffat wrote, "which used to happen every generation or so but which are now happening with alarming frequency, when the whole structure of Europe is shattered." The news of Schuschnigg's resignation, the massing and movement of troops, the formation of the new Austrian Government were reported in quick succession that afternoon. Mr. Moffat summed up his reaction to the events of the day by writing that Hitler had mounted "one more step on the ladder to complete European domination." [60]

Saturday, March 12, 1938.

All through Saturday and Sunday the news regarding Austria be-

[60] Moffat diary, March 11, 1938.

came worse and worse until by Sunday night Hitler and the Austrians announced the annexation of Austria subject only to a *pro forma* plebiscite next month. Saturday Prochnik [Edgar L. G. Prochnik, Austrian Minister to the United States] received orders to hoist the swastika flag over his Legation and as much as anything else the sight of that flag floating conspicuously in the spring breeze brought home to Washingtonians that Austria was no more.

The Secretary sent for me four or five times on Saturday. In the first place he, Herbert Feis and myself are about the only three in the building who believe that the Rome-Berlin axis will survive. In the second place Dieckhoff came in to see him for no apparent reason other than to tell him the German thesis of events. The Secretary confined himself to two questions, whether Dieckhoff thought this would prove a contribution to European peace and whether Dieckhoff thought that it would impair German-Italian relations. In reply Dieckhoff made it clear that he thought it would facilitate peace in Europe by removing an anomaly, and that most emphatically it would not affect Germany's relations with Italy. . .

Tuesday, March 22, 1938.

Norman Davis arrived much refreshed by his stay in South Carolina. He will be here two or three days. We talked over world conditions and found ourselves far more nearly in agreement than we have been for some months past. British reaction to what has been going on is, of course, the key to the whole situation and with each day that passes it becomes clearer that England is willing to surrender Eastern Europe to German ambitions. When Germany has consolidated these gains the accretion of strength will make her a far more dangerous foe to Britain throughout the world. . .

‏ VI ‎

WASHINGTON

July 1938 – June 1939

"The eternal question mark of American foreign policy"

When Mr. Moffat returned to Washington on July 28, after spending a month's vacation in New Hampshire,[1] he found that the Department of State had been "relatively quiet" in his absence. There had been four problems on which work had concentrated: the British trade agreements; the refugees at Evian and London; the Spanish Civil War; and the Czech situation.[2] During the weeks which followed his return the last problem developed into a world crisis.

Since June 1937 the German General Staff had been working on a plan for the invasion of Czechoslovakia, and as early as February 20, 1938, Hitler had ominously pointed to the ten million Germans who lived in two adjacent states. The ease with which the Austrian Germans were brought within the borders of the Reich encouraged Hitler to intensify his efforts in regard to Czechoslovakia.

The situation deteriorated rapidly in the summer of 1938. The Czechoslovak Sudeten leader, Konrad Henlein, and his Sudeten German Party were valuable pawns of the Reich Chancellor in enunciating, pressing, and aggravating the claims of the German minority within the Czech State. Hitler encouraged "incidents" and outbreaks of violence within Czechoslovakia and then took military measures in Germany in response to these "atrocities."

Friday, August 12, 1938.

. . . The Czech Chargé d'Affaires called in the morning to say that he was increasingly worried over the situation in Europe. Everything that is happening seems to make the outlook worse. The recent

---

[1] Moffat diary, July 28, 1938.
[2] *Ibid.*

reports from Germany of the commandeering of automobiles, postal busses, et cetera, in the Bavarian area, the transfer of German troops, all indicated a heightening of tension. In many ways he felt the situation was worse than during the crisis of May 21st,[3] because at that time an agreement with the Sudeten Party seemed possible, whereas now, with these increasing evidences of German force, he thought the outlook for agreement was almost hopeless. He could not say whether he considered the most dangerous moment would be next week or at the time of the Nuremberg Conference in early September, but he did feel that the danger to Czechoslovakia was no longer theoretic, but was very real and very imminent. He implied that if the Secretary of State were planning to issue another statement similar to the one he gave out on May 28th he hoped he would do so fairly soon.[4] I answered cautiously that the Secretary was following every move, and attempting to appraise its significance. . .

The President returned and held a Cabinet meeting that very afternoon. One of the first results was a request to Berle [Adolf A. Berle, Jr., Assistant Secretary of State] to prepare two speeches for the President to make in Canada, to be ready by Tuesday. Berle sent for me to talk over the one which he wished to dedicate to European affairs. At first blush we saw nothing more than to embroider on the theme of the eternal question mark of American foreign policy, namely, that our best contribution would be to create a doubt in the minds of Germany and company that we would under all circumstances stay out and at the same time to create a doubt in the mind of England and company that they could count on us for direct assistance no matter what transpired. At this moment the Secretary rang for me and took me along to the croquet field where he had an hour and a half's game.

[3] On May 20, 1938, information had reached Prague that the German army was being mobilized along the frontiers of Saxony, from which it would launch an attack upon Czechoslovakia. The Czech Government immediately assembled an army of a million men to fight for the Republic, and England and France made strong diplomatic representations in Berlin. For twenty-four hours Europe seemed on the verge of war, but the crisis passed.
[4] Hull's message called attention to the Kellogg Pact, in which war had been renounced as an instrument of national policy. He stated that the United States was watching the European situation "with close and anxious attention," and he expressed his country's "desire that peace be maintained no matter where or in what circumstances there may be controversies between nations." S. Shepard Jones and Denys P. Myers (eds.), *Documents on American Foreign Relations, July 1939–June 1940* (Boston: World Peace Foundation, 1940), II, 286.

Dined with Truelle [Jacques Truelle, French Chargé d'Affaires] on the terrace of the French Embassy. The heat wave had broken and it was almost too cold, but it was a clear night, and people felt after fifteen days of a Turkish bath that life was worth living again. . .

Friday, September 2, 1938.

. . . The French Chargé called in the afternoon to read me the text of the confidential instructions sent the French Ambassador at London on August 31. These were to the following effect:

The French Government was very pleased with the recent speech of Sir John Simon [British Chancellor of the Exchequer] and thought that the British Government was quite right to be preoccupied about not hurting Hitler's pride.[5] On the other hand, the French Government hopes that the British won't believe that Simon's speech or instructions based upon it will effectively stop Hitler if he and his advisers really plan to go ahead. Only a belief that it would be impossible to localize a German-Czech conflict would stop Hitler.

The French Government hopes that the British will give further thought to the position of Italy. Trouble in Central Europe would be the great opportunity for Mussolini to profit by the Rome-Berlin axis which thus far has brought him in no dividends except the *Anschluss*. Leaving aside the question of a possible move in North Africa, it is not improbable that the moment trouble should break out in Bohemia, Italy would intervene more actively in Spain, to the great discomfort of England and France. In order to minimize any temptation to Germany in this respect the French Government agrees for the present not to make any change in its Spanish policy despite the unfortunate answer of General Franco on the nonintervention plan.[6]

The French Government congratulates Lord Runciman [7] and

[5] This speech is printed in part in the *Times* (London), August 29, 1938, p. 7. Viscount Simon summarized the main point of the speech in his book, *Retrospect* (London: Hutchinson & Co., 1952), p. 245: "The substance of what I said amounted to a warning that if Hitler used force against Czechoslovakia, it might well be impossible to localise the resulting war, and we might ourselves be involved."

[6] The twenty-seven nations of the Non-Intervention Committee had proposed that Franco and the Loyalists allow foreign volunteers to "withdraw" from Spain. Although the Loyalists were willing to agree, Franco rejected the idea and almost all other parts of the plan. The text of Franco's statement is in the *New York Times*, August 22, 1938, p. 4.

[7] The British Government had sent Walter Runciman to Czechoslovakia to in-

has noticed recent signs of Czech conciliation. The great problem is now to force the Sudetens to be more reasonable. One fortunate factor not to be overlooked is the following: as Hitler allegedly is only interested in backing up the Sudetens, any time these declare themselves satisfied Hitler can claim a great diplomatic victory, and he can achieve this result at any time by instructing the Sudetens to declare themselves satisfied.

As the Reich has, in effect, mobilized, France has had to take certain precautionary measures but has made these public judging it more advantageous to spread the news.[8]

The French Government's final plea was that the British should recall that the smaller countries in Europe plus Poland will in the last analyses be guided by the British decision and that the more strongly Britain speaks at present the more firmly they can be held in line.

The Chargé d'Affaires hoped that this information would be of interest to the Secretary and the President. I thanked him for his courtesy in communicating it to us.

The Chargé then went on to say that he had been a little worried by the Press reports that Great Britain was pressing us for a definition of what we would do and what our attitude would be in the event that Britain went to war. I told Mr. Truelle that the press reports were scarcely accurate. He was glad to hear that, but even so he felt that any attempt, direct or indirect, "to put pressure" on American public opinion was psychologically wrong; that American public opinion, which was already almost unanimous,[9] would gradually move in the right direction under wise leadership but that it would move in the other direction if the impression arose that foreign interests were attempting to influence it.

Bill Bullitt telephoned the Secretary and asked permission to reinstate one of the phrases from his speech which we had asked him to

---

vestigate and mediate in the crisis. Viscount Runciman described his mission as being set "adrift in a small boat in mid-Atlantic." R. W. Seton-Watson, *From Munich to Danzig* (London: Methuen & Co., 1939), pp. 47–53.

[8] French army maneuvers took place at Besançon near the French-German-Swiss borders. More than 20,000 men participated in the war games. *New York Times*, August 28, 1938, p. 28; August 29, 1938, p. 5.

[9] A survey of public opinion reported on July 27, 1938, that 65 per cent of the people questioned stated their sympathies would be with England and France in case these two countries became involved in war with Italy and Germany. Three per cent answered that their sympathies would be with Italy and Germany, while 32 per cent were undecided where their sympathies lay. *Ibid.*, July 27, 1938, p. 7.

delete. He said that he was willing to modify it slightly but said that if he did not hint that we might eventually be drawn into a war the speech might seem a step backward from his earlier speeches. Rather than do this he thought that he should feign illness and not appear at all. The Secretary did not like the sentence but Bill Bullitt kept at him so hard that he finally transferred the call to the President; the latter worked out some sort of a compromise sentence meeting Bill Bullitt's position at least two-thirds of the way.[10] The real truth of the matter is that the Secretary will always refer Bullitt, Kennedy [Joseph Kennedy, American Ambassador to Great Britain], and Daniels [Josephus Daniels, American Ambassador to Mexico] to the White House as he considers these the President's personal selections. . .

Wednesday, September 7, 1938.

. . . About noon Mallet came in to deliver to me for transmission to the Secretary of State a further *aide-mémoire* from the British Government bringing the information regarding the Runciman mission up-to-date.[11] A cursory reading showed that the British Government were conveying to the Czechoslovaks their belief that the Czechs should make concessions at least as far as the Carlsbad points [12] demanded by the Sudetens.

While I was reading the *aide-mémoire* I let Mr. Mallet read the United Press flash quoting an editorial in the London *Times* making the suggestion that if all other solutions failed, Czechoslovakia should permit its Sudeten area to secede and join the German Reich.[13] I

[10] William C. Bullitt, the American Ambassador to France, delivered a speech at Bordeaux on September 4, 1938, at a ceremony dedicating a monument commemorating American participation in the First World War. In his speech he said that if "war should break out again in Europe no human being could undertake to state or prophesy whether or not the United States would become involved." *Ibid.*, September 5, 1938, p. 9.

[11] This telegram is printed in Great Britain, Foreign Office, *Documents on British Foreign Policy 1919-1939*, ed. E. L. Woodward, Rohan Butler, and Margaret Lambert (Third Series; London: H. M. Stationery Office, 1949–), II, 252-253. It indicated that the British representative in Prague had advised Czechoslovakia to "go forthwith and unreservedly to the limit of concession and added that this limit should not fall short of the Karlsbad points, if settlement could not be obtained otherwise."

[12] For a statement of the Carlsbad Points and an analysis of the Czechoslovak attitude toward them in September 1938, see the *Times* (London), September 7, 1938, p. 12.

[13] *Ibid.*, p. 13. Winston Churchill in *The Gathering Storm*, p. 296, wrote about this article: "Although the British Government stated at once that this *Times* article did not represent their views, public opinion abroad, particularly in France, was far from reassured."

ventured the opinion that such an editorial might complicate the situation and Mr. Mallet expressed some surprise that it should be published at this juncture. However, he made it clear that if England should have to fight it would be not out of friendship for the Czechs but out of hatred for the Germans. He said that the British were on the horns of a cruel dilemma in as much as if they stayed out of war Germany would have an immense accretion of strength, while if they entered a war, brought about by Czechoslovakia's resistance to Germany, they would in any peace settlement have to avoid the original mistake of putting the Sudetens under the Czechs. Furthermore it was becoming clearer that the Dominions were isolationist, and there would be no sense in fighting a war which would break the British Empire while trying to assure the safety of the United Kingdom. . .

Friday, September 9, 1938.

The papers have been most alarmist. Shrieking headlines, "Today Gravest Since 1914," appear in the largest type to be found in the compositor's box. But none of the information reaching us justifies the alarming headlines in this afternoon's press that the Czech situation is at the breaking point. . .

In France Bullitt has reported two long conversations, the first with Daladier, who was militantly firm; the second with Bonnet, who seemed to be looking for a line of retreat which would not involve a loss of prestige by France.[14] Daladier told the German Chargé that if one German soldier crossed the Czechoslovak border France would move.[15] To him the issue was whether Germany should be allowed to dominate through war or threat of war. On the other hand, he admitted that Beneš' [Eduard Beneš, President of the Czechoslovak Re-

[14] Georges Bonnet, the French Foreign Minister, had suggested that conversations be held to develop the positions set forth in the speeches of Mr. Hull and President Roosevelt in August 1938. He also recommended that the President issue a statement, if the crisis in Czechoslovakia was settled by negotiation, in which Roosevelt expressed the hope that this settlement might be the basis for real peace in Europe. Hull, I, 590.

[15] Edouard Daladier, the French Prime Minister, told the German Chargé that "the occasion of any armed intervention by Germany in Czechoslovakia would mean the application of the *casus foederis*, and with that a general armed conflict." This conversation of September 7, 1938, is given in Germany, Auswärtiges Amt, *Documents on German Foreign Policy 1918–1945*, vol. II, *Germany and Czechoslovakia 1937–1938* (Series D [1937–1945]; Washington: Government Printing Office, 1949), pp. 712–714.

public] proposals were extremely confused and probably not ultra-satisfactory. The French, however, made it clear to Bullitt that they did not know what their position would be if a plebiscite were demanded. To us here it looks more and more as though ultimately a plebiscite would be agreed upon as the best way out. Probably Germany, which stands to gain from it, would rather see the idea proposed by Lord Runciman than propose it herself.

Wilson [Hugh Wilson, American Ambassador to Germany] has returned from Nuremberg [16] and reported considerable criticism by the rank and file over the Government's running a risk of war on the Czechoslovak issue. On the other hand, most of the leaders were more pessimistic than a fortnight back. The main conclusion Wilson drew was that, to an unbelievable degree, the fate of Germany depended upon Hitler's personal decision.

The Secretary was much put out by the indications appearing . . . that there was a London-Paris-Washington peace axis. He attributes this entirely to the three Ambassadors: Kennedy, Bullitt, and Wilson pursuing personal policies. Being tired this worries him more than it need, but it is becoming a leitmotif with him. Had several talks on the matter with the Secretary and with McDermott [Michael McDermott, Chief of the Division of Current Information] today. For instance, Bill Bullitt indignantly denies that he said at Bordeaux that the "United States and France were indefectively united in war as well as in peace." [17] He made the Associated Press print a retraction which it did together with the correspondent's comments that although the Ambassador denied having said the words he had personally heard them. But I notice that in big things when there is little to do one spends a disproportionate amount of time on small details, particularly if they have a personal tinge. . .

Saturday and Sunday, September 10 and 11, 1938.

Saturday morning the news from Europe grew definitely worse.

[16] Mr. Wilson had attended the Nazi Party Congress at Nuremberg, September 6–12, 1938.

[17] The *New York Times*, September 4, 1938, p. 12, quoted the Bullitt speech. Five days later the newspaper printed a correction by Bullitt with the correspondent's statement that he had, in fact, heard the Ambassador speak in this way. On September 12, 1938, the same correspondent was quoted in the *New York Times*, p. 2, as saying "that there had been a misinterpretation of the words that the Ambassador actually pronounced."

There is a telegram in from Kennedy reporting various talks with English leaders in which for the first time there was a slightly hysterical tone. . .

About half-past twelve the French Chargé d'Affaires turned up. He was obviously much perturbed over the President's press conference at Hyde Park yesterday in which the latter made it clear that this Government was in no way committed to any foreign powers as to the course it would follow in the event of war.[18] He said that he had been receiving telephone messages from New York and elsewhere during the morning indicating "shocked surprise" on the part of both the President's friends and opponents, and telegrams were coming in from France, though none from the Foreign Office, seeking an explanation. He said that he had studied the reports with some care; he found a wide variation in different papers depending upon the accuracy of the reporting officer. But the sum total of his impressions was that the misleading, and above all, the abbreviated accounts might convey an erroneous picture to the Germans. He said that at Paris everything was so tense and the need of playing cards carefully was so vital that any appearance of vacillation or retreat even if not borne out by the facts, would cause a doubly painful impression.

I told the Chargé that I did not think he would find that the President's position had varied in any degree from that set forth in the Kingston speech which in turn bore a close relation to the Secretary's speech of August 16 and his declaration on the anniversary of the signing of the Kellogg-Briand Pact.[19] He admitted this. I also told him that I thought that accuracy had a way of prevailing in the long run and that the false interpretation that he feared could not in the nature of things persist. . .

At Sunday's meeting we went over the technical steps that would

[18] The President was reported to have "let it be known by implication that this government was in no way committed to any foreign powers as to the course it would follow in the event of war." *Ibid.*, September 9, 1938, p. 1.

[19] The speech was delivered by President Roosevelt at Queens University, Kingston, Ontario, Canada, on August 18, 1938. S. Shepard Jones and Denys P. Myers (eds.), *Documents on American Foreign Relations, January 1938–June 1939* (Boston: World Peace Foundation, 1939), I, 23–26. The Hull speech of August 16, 1938, restated the principles of his "Eight Pillars of Peace." *Ibid.*, pp. 19–23. On August 28, 1938, the *New York Times*, p. 1, reported the Secretary's statement on the anniversary of the signing of the Pact of Paris. Hull said, in part, that "on the observance or nonobservance of the solemn pledges made ten years ago depends the preservation of all that is valuable and worth while in the life of each and every nation."

be necessary to put into effect the Neutrality Act. I urged strongly that if and when this became necessary, the President issue a short statement to the effect that he had proclaimed the embargo to carry out terms of legislation which were mandatory. No one could foresee at this time whether in its practical application the Neutrality Act would justify itself or whether it would create a new series of problems to supplant those it was designed to remedy. It would be for the Congress when it meets to consider on the basis of actual experience whether the present legislation is in the best interests of the United States, or whether and to what degree it should be altered. . .

The Czech situation if trouble comes is the worst of all as it would be completely isolated and the only possible egress through Poland or Hungary. There are 2000 known Americans in the country with about 5000 more borderline cases. Poor old Mr. Carr who was supposed to be having a quiet post in which to pass his declining years certainly seems to have been forced into the thick of it. . .

Tuesday, September 13, 1938.

The French Ambassador called this morning on his return from leave. He outlined developments up to the time he had left Paris, which coincided in almost all essentials with the reports received from Ambassador Bullitt and which I shall therefore not elaborate on.

He referred with appreciation to the speeches of the President and the Secretary of State and asked whether we had supplemented them by having our Ambassador make a confidential *démarche* to the German Government. I replied, no, that we had chosen to make our position clear by means of public statement.

He asked if we did not think a further *démarche* to Germany would be of value at this time. I told him that we had very carefully estimated our position on the basis of being as helpful as we could without provoking a reaction in public opinion here.[20]

The Ambassador said that he was aware of the first draft of Mr. Bullitt's speech and the changes that had been made; he felt that the

[20] On August 29, 1938, the French Chargé d'Affaires had asked Mr. Moffat "in a purely personal manner" if he "did not feel that perhaps a confidential warning to the German Government through our Ambassador was called for." Mr. Moffat had answered that he thought "that anyone who carefully read the Secretary's speech of the 16th, the President's speech at Kingston, and Secretary's statement on the 10th anniversary of the Kellogg-Pact would appreciate that we had given a clear indication of American reaction to developments." Moffat diary, August 29, 1938.

President undoubtedly had good reason for suggesting its modification. I said the second consideration we always had in mind was whether or not any position we took would be helpful vis-à-vis Germany. The Ambassador replied that he thought a *démarche* at Berlin, if kept confidential, would be helpful, but agreed that any public warning would be a mistake. I left the Ambassador with the impression that we felt we had made our position very clear and that we had been as helpful as possible in our general policy of trying to preserve peace. . .

"Ich bin von Himmel gefallen," is the way Hitler is supposed to have described his feelings, when he learned that the British Prime Minister proposed to fly to Germany to discuss the Czech situation.[21] Chamberlain, disturbed by the increasing gravity of events had determined to take action "when things looked blackest."[22] The violent tone of Hitler's speech on the twelfth, the rejection two days later by Henlein of Czech proposals to settle the Sudeten problem, and his demand for foreign intervention, the occurrence of "incidents," the outbreak of fighting in the Sudeten area — all led Chamberlain to believe that the most dangerous moment had arrived on September 14, when he sent his proposal to the German Chancellor.

Wednesday, September 14, 1938.

This was a day of ups and downs. Early in the morning came through the news of the fighting in the Sudeten area, 2000 Sudetens pitched against the police with heavy casualties. Then came the break in sterling and in British Government loans, with repercussions on our own market. Then came the indication of a change in French sentiments, a reluctance to envisage war which was in dramatic contradistinction with their attitude to date. Finally at about four o'clock the news of Chamberlain's flying visit to see Hitler, news of which Kennedy had had only two or three hours' advance notice, and the French even less. Immediately the outlook changed, markets and prices turned upward, sterling regained two cents, and an optimism which was as out of place as the earlier pessimism reigned. As usual the British asked the President to issue a public approval of Mr. Chamberlain's move. After talking it over, the Secretary, Messersmith, and I

[21] L. B. Namier, *Diplomatic Prelude 1938–1939* (London: Macmillan & Co., 1948), p. 35.
[22] Keith Feiling, *The Life of Neville Chamberlain* (London: Macmillan & Co., 1946), p. 363.

unanimously agreed that this would be a tragic mistake. We did not know what Mr. Chamberlain was going to do, whether it was to sell out the Czechs or not. In any event we should not be put in the position of writing him a blank check. Ever since the beginning of the crisis the British have been maneuvering to get us to give advice or to express ourselves, in particular as opposed to general terms, with the sole view of throwing responsibility on us in case their ultimate decision is an unpopular one.[23] When the President did, on Sumner's [Sumner Welles] advice, give a general blessing to the Chamberlain-Mussolini agreement, the British promptly used it in Parliament for their internal political advantage. Even the President's Kingston speech was made use of for British purposes in Sir John Simon's Lanark speech. . .[24]

Thursday, September 15, 1938.

Today was the day of the Chamberlain meeting with Hitler. All day long reports would come in culminating with the sudden decision of Chamberlain to fly back to London after one brief talk with Hitler. There is no use speculating, we will know in good time, and meanwhile the respite will probably continue for 36 to 48 hours more. I doubt, however, if as much was accomplished as Chamberlain had hoped.[25]

[23] On September 1, 1938, Mr. Moffat wrote in his diary: "Few developments in the Czech crisis other than that the British seems to be maneuvering to obtain some sort of an expression of advice or opinion from us by which they could throw responsibility on us. This is an old game but Joe Kennedy seems to have fallen for it. He keeps asking on behalf of Chamberlain and Halifax what would be our reaction in every sort of contingency. Finally a fairly curt message went out to the effect that the Secretary's and the President's speeches which had been prepared with great care clearly set forth our viewpoint and we saw nothing to be gained by committing ourselves as to hypothetical circumstances." Joseph Alsop and Robert Kintner, *American White Paper* (New York: Simon & Schuster, 1940), p. 7, report that one man summed up the Department's attitude toward British and French suggestions for consultation by stating: "If we start 'continuous consultation' now, we'll find ourselves being treated as an 'associate power' before we know it."

[24] At Lanark Simon had referred to the "striking speech" by Cordell Hull, in which, Simon said, the Secretary had stressed "the widespread reactions of war" and "the necessity for substituting the method of friendly cooperation. What he said, and what President Roosevelt said a few days later in Canada, must waken a responsive echo in many British hearts." The *Times* (London), August 29, 1938, p. 7.

[25] Mr. Chamberlain met Hitler at Berchtesgaden where the two held a lengthy conversation. Hitler said that if Great Britain agreed to the separation of the Sudeten area from Czechoslovakia and changes in the constitution of the Czech state, the problem could be solved. Mr. Chamberlain replied that he personally was agreeable

It became perfectly clear that the Secretary could not avoid all mention of the interview at his press conference. He wished, however, to say the minimum. He therefore evolved a brief sentence pointing out with what interest the meeting was being watched by all nations which are concerned in the preservation of peace, but he committed himself in no way as to the possible substance of the conversations.[26]

At twelve o'clock the French Ambassador came to see me to find out what our reaction was to the visit of Chamberlain to Hitler. He said that the liberal elements in New York were fearful of what this might bring forth, but he had told them that he thought it a good move which should be tried. In any event, no one had suggested anything better. Several newspapermen had asked him for off-the-record conferences and he had taken this point of view.

He asked whether we had any confirmation of reports that the Germans had put as a condition to Mr. Chamberlain's trip the holding of a plebiscite under international control. I told him that we had no information to that effect. He asked what we thought about it. I told him that no matter what transpired, the visit would give us thirty-six to forty-eight hours of respite and that that definitely was to the good; for instance, I had seen no reports of rioting in Sudetenland this morning. The Secretary would undoubtedly be questioned at the press conference, and, if so, was planning to say that the historical meeting between the Prime Minister of Great Britain and the Chancellor of Germany was being observed with the greatest interest by all nations which are concerned in the preservation of peace. The Ambassador said he thought that would be useful and that it would not set off any unfavorable reactions.

As a matter of fact, the Secretary in his talk yesterday had informed the Ambassador that there had been a new flare-up of isolationist sentiment. He had not appreciated it at the time, but in the last twenty-four hours he had been studying editorials from all over the country and appreciated that there had been this small flare-up.[27] On the other

---

to the separation, but he would have to consult his Cabinet before stating the attitude of his Government. Great Britain, Foreign Office, *Documents on British Foreign Policy*, 3rd Series, II, 338–351; Feiling, pp. 366–368.

[26] Secretary Hull said: "The historic conference today between the Prime Minister of Great Britain and the Chancellor of Germany is naturally being observed with the greatest interest by all nations which are deeply concerned in the preservation of peace." Hull, I, 589.

[27] The *Chicago Tribune*, September 13, 1918, p. 14, for instance, reproduced an

hand, the tone of the great New York papers struck his as most helpful and as seeing the picture in its major proportions. . .

Friday, September 16, 1938.
    . . . Secretary buzzed for me and asked me to prepare a draft for
him to submit to the President in case the latter should wish to make
some statement on the European situation. It was understood and approved by everybody that the Secretary would urge the President
against any statement at the present time on the ground that if we
emphasized peace as the essential we might be accused of endorsing
Chamberlain's policy of "selling Czechoslovakia down the river." On
the other hand, if we should emphasize the importance of a just settlement and England went to war, she might later say that we had given
advice in that otherwise she would have sold the Czechs down the
river and hence that we had assumed a moral responsibility. However,
to be on the safe side Norman Davis, Messersmith and myself prepared
a short draft which we felt avoided the Scylla and Charybdis as well
as possible. Fortunately it was never used as the President agreed with
the Secretary's recommendation for nonaction. . .

Saturday, September 17, 1938.
    . . . We then had a small conference, just six of us, the Secretary,
Norman Davis, Messersmith, Berle, Jimmy Dunn, and myself, to talk
over what should be done. One and all agreed that nothing could be
done until we knew the extent of the sell-out which the British and
presumably the French were about to approve. Our general impression
was that despite the sell-out, Czechoslovakia would fight. We would
be faced with a German-Czech war and wondered whether despite
all their resolutions England and France could stay out. This was the
period when, if any, a United States contribution might be made, but
as to what such a contribution could be there were no clear-cut

---

editorial from the Peoria, Illinois, *Journal-Transcript* about Bullitt's speech assuring France that the United States and France were united in peace and war. The
Peoria paper said: "Americans have not yet forgotten the futility of the last war to
save democracy, or the iniquitous peace treaty that fomented new trouble. Ambassador Bullitt goes far beyond his authority in pledging the peace loving American
people to a war at the side of France." The Galesburg, Illinois, *Daily Register-Mail*,
September 10, 1938, p. 4, stated that Americans sympathized with the democracies of
Europe against dictatorships "but that sympathy is not now, nor do we believe it
ever again will be, sufficiently strong to entangle us in another European war. One
disillusioning experience in 'saving the world for democracy' is enough."

opinions. Berle views the present troubles as the birth pains of a new eastern empire, a German succession to the old Austro-Hungarian Empire. Others see it merely as strengthening the domination of the Fascists over the democracies. Both British and French are trying their hardest to bring us into the picture now so that we share responsibility for the "sell-out," but on this score I believe their hopes are vain. . .

Tuesday, September 20, 1938.

. . . The French Ambassador called in the morning. He said that the decision France had made had been a very painful one, but was due to the fact that France was not prepared to fight. Her inferiority in the air made this out of the question, and he only wished that the Government might be able to explain this to the people as the underlying reason, but doubted whether, as a practical measure, it could do so.

The Ambassador said he had been quite shocked at the tenor of some of the editorial comment in this country during the last forty-eight hours. He had little complaint to make of the *New York Times* or the *Washington Post*, but there were many editorials that were wounding him as well as a large number of letters, more or less insulting, that were being addressed to his Embassy and to the various French Consulates. He had reported briefly on these attacks to his Government in Paris, but urged them, under no account, to enter into polemics.

The Ambassador went on to say that while he had a high regard for Mr. Blum, he felt that his recent appeal to the President had been ill-advised.[28]

As a matter of fact Mr. Jouhaux [Léon Jouhaux, French labor leader] had seen the President a day or two ago. The President had referred to this message of Mr. Blum's, but pointed out that he did not feel the situation warranted any initiative from him. Such an initiative, if not accepted, might make the situation even worse than it was. Mr. Jouhaux then asked the President if he could not summon a conference. The President had replied that the same considerations would militate against this, but that if England and France should

[28] Former Premier Léon Blum, leader of the French Socialist Party, asked in an editorial in *Populaire* on September 18: "Is it not time that he [President Roosevelt] address himself to Europe with all the prestige of his person and with all the authority of the State whose moral or material support would be finally decisive in any general war?" *New York Times*, September 19, 1938, p. 6.

summon a conference and invite the United States, he was prepared to accept. Mr. Jouhaux had then asked whether he might make use of this information. The President replied that it should not be given publicity, but that he might discuss it with his friends.

Mr. Jouhaux had naturally reported this to the French Ambassador, but upon being interrogated frankly admitted that he did not know what the President had in mind, whether it was a political conference, a disarmament conference, a conference for the humanization of war, et cetera. He did not know whether the President was thinking in terms of an immediate conference or at a later date, though the Ambassador added that if it were put off too long Germany would have had what she wanted. As Mr. Jouhaux was undoubtedly going to influence both the French and British in the direction of initiating such a conference, the Ambassador thought that it was very important to get the President's ideas a little more clearly before his Government, and to that effect asked me to present this matter to the Secretary of State in order that the latter might be able to give him more specific information when he came to call, probably on Thursday. . .

The Czech Chargé called at noon. He made an impassioned plea for some statement to Czechoslovakia in her hour of need by either the President or the Secretary of State. I told him that the difficulty lay in saying anything that would not be construed at this moment as advice to some nation either to fight or not to fight and that we were unwilling to assume the responsibility of giving any advice either directly or inferentially. I felt that advice which was not to be implemented should not be given. The Chargé said that he was still convinced that Czechoslovakia would fight and that any government which advocated surrender would probably not be able to stand up. . .

Upon returning from Berchtesgaden Mr. Chamberlain in consultation with Daladier and Bonnet produced a plan which asked Czechoslovakia to transfer to Germany without plebiscite all districts in which over 50 per cent of the inhabitants were German.[29] When the Czech Government rejected this proposal, the British and French pressed the Czechs to accede, warning that they would "disinterest" themselves in the situation if Czechoslovakia persisted in this attitude.[30] On September 21 the

[29] Great Britain, Foreign Office, *Documents on British Foreign Policy*, 3rd Series, II, 404–405, has the complete text of the Anglo-French plan.
[30] *Ibid.*, pp. 437–438; Seton-Watson, pp. 65–71.

Hodža Cabinet "exposed," as they said, "to pressure for which there was no precedent in history" submitted to the Anglo-French plan and resigned.[31]

Early on the morning of the twenty-second Mr. Chamberlain flew to Godesberg to inform the German Chancellor of the Czech surrender and to reach what he thought would be the final settlement of the matter. Here Hitler confronted him with additional demands, which were later described by the Czechs as such to "deprive us of every safeguard for our national existence." [32]

On the other borders of Czechoslovakia Polish troops were closing in on Teschen, and Hungary cast covetous eyes on Slovakia. The Czech State was beleaguered from all sides.

Thursday, September 22, 1938.

A day of ups and downs. Chamberlain and Hitler met at Godesberg but agreed to continue conversation tomorrow. The Czechoslovak Cabinet fell and was replaced by a military Premier. Polish troops were reported moving. Fighting broke out on the Sudeten borders. Three French Cabinet Ministers tried to resign. A crowd in Whitehall demonstrated against Chamberlain. No, the crisis is not over and I am still fearful that the German troops may march into the Sudeten areas tomorrow only to be met with armed resistance.

Keith Officer [Australian Counselor of the British Embassy] called on two minor matters . . . We then got to talking about Australia's position in this crisis. He was quite clear in his own mind that the

[31] Seton-Watson, p. 71. The Hodža Cabinet was replaced by a government led by General Jan Sirovy, who had been Inspector General of the Czech Armed Forces.

[32] Hitler demanded the evacuation of areas within the Czech State within a week, the discharge from the Czech Army of Germans, the release of German political prisoners, a plebiscite in certain other, still undefined, areas before November 25, and the transfer to the Germans, undamaged, of all goods and material within the evacuated territory. Germany, Auswärtiges Amt, *Documents on German Foreign Policy*, Series D, II, 870–879; Great Britain, Foreign Office, *Documents on British Foreign Policy*, 3rd Series, II, 463–473, 495–496. The Czechoslovak Minister to Great Britain, Jan Masaryk, in communicating the Czech answer to the Godesberg demands described them as "a *de facto* ultimatum of the sort usually presented to a vanquished nation and not a proposition to a sovereign state which has shown the greatest possible readiness to make sacrifices for the appeasement of Europe . . . We are to yield up large proportions of our carefully prepared defences and admit the German armies deep into our country before we have been able to organize it on the new basis or make any preparations for its defence. Our national and economic independence would automatically disappear with the acceptance of Herr Hitler's plan. The whole process of moving the population is to be reduced to panic flight on the part of those who will not accept the German Nazi regime. They have to leave their homes without even the right to take their personal belongings or even, in the case of peasants, their cow." *Ibid.*, III, pp. 518–519.

Australian advice to Britain had been not to be maneuvered into going to war for Czechoslovakia; the Rhineland was the furthest frontier that Australian public opinion could allow Great Britain. On the other hand, should war break out Australia would immediately follow. He thought the shipping shortage would prevent the sending of anything more than a symbolic expeditionary force but believed that Australian troops might be sent to Singapore, India, or other places to replace British troops which were called home.

Dr. Brejška, the Czech Chargé d'Affaires, called quite bewildered and unable to understand what is going on in Czechoslovakia. He was convinced that Chamberlain would yield Teschen to the Poles and southern Slovakia to the Hungarians but he added, "I shall live to see the Poles humiliated as we have been and forced to surrender to Germany the very territory they are taking today". . .

Friday, September 23, 1938.

The situation today grew worse and worse. The Chamberlain-Hitler conversations instead of being resumed were carried on by means of letters sent from one hotel on one bank of the Rhine to the other hotel on the other bank of the Rhine.[33] The Czech Army mobilized. France partially mobilized. All communications between Praha and the outside world were cut. Then at the last minute, just as we expected to hear the troops had begun moving, Chamberlain and Hitler went into a three hour conversation ending at 1 A.M. and again a pale glimmer of hope arose.

The Polish Chargé called in the morning to tell me that the Polish Government had in fact asked for the cession of Teschen and Polish Silesia. He emphasized that Poland had not taken this action until after Czechoslovakia had agreed to cede the Sudeten regions. Poland had not wished to assume the responsibility of influencing in any way Czechoslovakia's decision, but once she had agreed to yield a foreign minority to its mother state, Poland must demand equality of treatment. The Chargé told me that the Polish demands had had a very

---

[33] The letters which passed between Mr. Chamberlain and Herr Hitler are printed in *ibid.*, pp. 482–483, 485–487. The unsatisfactory nature of the talks at Godesberg and the events occurring along the Czech-German border led the British and French Governments to cancel previous advice to the Czech Government against mobilization. The Czechs ordered mobilization immediately. *Ibid.*, pp. 483, 492.

bad reception in London.[34] He then went on to say that the man in the street in Poland had turned against the French in an extraordinary way, arguing that if France put pressure on one of her allies to cede territory not to another ally but to an hereditary enemy, an alliance with France ceased to have any value; Poland would, therefore, do better to stand on its own feet . . .

Just before going over to Cabinet the Secretary asked me to prepare a one page analysis of the situation to guide him in his presentation of the foreign situation and make certain that he did not omit any of the important factors. I quote the short analysis I prepared for him:

"Many people assumed that when the Czechs yielded to the British and French the crisis was over; instead I fear that it is entering its most dangerous stage today.

"In the first place, when the Czechs agreed to yield to Franco-British pressure and give up the Sudeten areas, they thought they were only giving up territory to a stronger neighbor. They have not yet agreed to give up territory to Poland or Hungary, both of whom they look down on. The better evidence that we get points to the fact that the Czechs if attacked will definitely fight, probably on the theory that even though the French and British have deserted them there is a 20 to 30% chance that if they can resist for three weeks or a month the French will ultimately enter the war. If fighting breaks out Germany is in a fairly good position: (1) Poland would be with her, and the interesting thing is not that the Polish Government may have made a deal with the German Government, but that the Polish people, which heretofore has been pro-French, seems to have turned against the British and French. (2) Russia has given no signs of doing more than sending some airplanes to help the Czechs. Stalin stands to profit by other people fighting, but not by fighting himself. The only thing he has to fear is a successful war which might build up a new Napoleon, or an unsuccessful war that might create a new chaos that would destroy him. (3) The reports from our Legation at Bucharest indicate that Rumania is virtually impotent for attack or defense. (4) Yugo-

---

[34] The British Government in a communication to Warsaw on September 22, 1938, protested the Polish military measures "which appear to have no other object than to intimidate the Czechoslovak Government." The telegram stated that there was "no justification whatsoever for attempting to compel an immediate settlement of their claims by direct action instead of through the processes of normal negotiation." *Ibid.*, pp. 459–460.

slavia is afraid that if she helped Czechoslovakia her own minorities might be snatched from her and also that she might be involved with Italy. In addition, while the Yugoslav people are still pro-French and pro-Czech the Stoyadinovitch Government is against Beneš who, according to rumors, has been encouraging to the opposition.

"All of these factors coupled with the known inferiority in the air of France and Great Britain create a situation which may well encourage Hitler to cross the Rubicon; on the other hand if he waits, he stands to gain what he wants without risk, thus winning an unprecedented diplomatic victory". . .

Saturday and Sunday, September 24 and 25, 1938.

. . . At one o'clock the Secretary sent for Messersmith, Berle, Jimmy [Dunn] and myself to talk over the situation which from all accounts was going from bad to worse. The consensus of opinion was that the time was not yet ripe for any statement by the President. The meeting was adjourned until three when Sumner Welles, just back from Europe, joined us. There seemed three courses possible: (1) an appeal to pallid principle; (2) a call for an international conference to write a treaty on peace (presumably implying revision) before the war, not after. The third was to give some definite threat, expressed or implied, that we could not be indifferent if the Germans provoked hostilities. Point three was obviously out of the question. Point two involved a host of practical difficulties. Point one appealed to no one.

Sunday morning we resumed with the same group. The President telephoned over and asked how our minds were running and suggested that we have a draft message ready for his consideration when he returned from a day on the water at half-past six. He apparently had not formulated his ideas but felt that if we must act it would probably have to be done with only an hour or two delay.

Berle and I therefore returned after lunch and drew up a draft "appeal to the American people" based on a modification of point two, the modification being that instead of a conference we suggested that the President tender his good offices if invited by all the countries. There was a definite hint of treaty revision in the note, designed like bait to induce Germany to request the President's good offices. It pointed out that good offices could only be effective if it was understood by all parties that there were no commitments on the part of the person tendering them; that no involvements had been assumed, nor would any be assumed. After working till nearly five we took the draft out to the Secretary who was playing croquet. He liked it fairly well but Norman Davis took violent exception to any suggestion of treaty revision, claiming that it was not the Treaty of Versailles that was the root of all evils but our betrayal in not ratifying it . . .

Got home for a late dinner and had just gotten to bed and tuned in on the Ford Concert when the telephone rang and the Secretary asked me to come right down to the Department. He said that the President had received such bad telephonic reports from both Kennedy and Bullitt that he felt he could no longer keep silent.[35] That he wanted to send a direct appeal to Hitler, Beneš, Chamberlain, and Daladier urging them to keep the negotiations going and adding as a further step, but subsidiary thereto, an offer of his good offices. Sumner Welles took the draft Berle and I had prepared, kept the first half and then drafted the second section along the lines laid down by the President. We went over this with some care and were all in agreement by eleven except on one point. The Secretary and Norman Davis both jibed at the tender of good offices fearing that the public would confuse good offices with mediation. Those of us who were looking at the problem from a purely European angle favored its inclusion, arguing that without this point the appeal became a mere exhortation. At midnight it was decided to put the point up to the President who finally agreed to omit the tender of good offices on the ground that it was implicit in the exhortation. From half-past twelve to half-past one I was busy seeing that the messages got off properly. The ones to Hitler and Beneš being sent directly by the President, the ones to Daladier and Chamberlain being sent through the Secretary of State, and the ones to Warsaw and Budapest being sent through our Legations for transmission to the respective Foreign Offices.[36]

Home at about half-past one in the morning only to be wakened

[35] Mr. Bullitt had asked that an offer by the President to arbitrate be included in the message. Hull, I, 591–592.
[36] The President's statement called attention to the fact that peace was being endangered and that dire consequences would follow in the wake of war. It pointed out that means existed by which disputes could be settled pacifically. The message urged that negotiations be continued until a peaceful settlement had been achieved. Jones and Myers, Documents, Jan. 1938–June 1939, I, 286–287.

by the telephone jingling at 5.15. It was Bill Bullitt who asked whether the text of the President's appeal had been sent to the Paris Embassy. I told him that it had been sent off this morning.

He then said that when the Secretary had telephoned him last night there was talk of including a "further step" [37] in the note. This was now missing. Mr. Bullitt asked if I could tell him whether the idea had been discarded or was merely held in abeyance.

I replied that I understood that the "further step" had not been included for two reasons: (1) that it was considered implicit in the appeal and (2) that it was feared it might have some untoward domestic effects.

Mr. Bullitt said that point one seemed to him to lack validity. As to point two he understood our reluctance but felt that we must make up our mind to take this step very shortly if we would save the situation. The appeal might hold things for a day, possibly two, but it would not be enough and he hoped that we would be considering the next step already.

He said that he had just talked to Hugh Wilson on the telephone. The latter did not think that Hitler would announce in his speech tonight that troops were marching. He believed he would confine himself to justifying and explaining his demands. . .

The Czechs, having refused the Godesberg demands, were able to get Great Britain and France to support this decision. France renewed the pledge to come to the aid of Czechoslovakia if that country were attacked. A British communiqué announced the intention of the British to stand by France.[38] Two categories of French reserves were called up, and the British fleet mobilized. The evacuation of Paris began. The school-children were moved from London. War seemed only as far away as 2 P.M. on September 28, the time when Hitler had threatened German mobilization would begin.[39]

Monday, September 26, 1938.

Meeting in the Secretary's office at 9.20 this morning. The Secre-

[37] The "further step" to which Bullitt referred was an offer by the President to arbitrate.

[38] The British Cabinet had decided on September 25 to refuse the demands made by Hitler, and on the same day and the day following at meetings at which Chamberlain and Halifax met Daladier and Bonnet, France agreed to march in case of an attack on the Czechs. Great Britain, Foreign Office, *Documents on British Foreign Policy*, 3rd Series, II, 520–535, 536–541.

[39] Hitler had stated that he must have an affirmative answer from the Czechs by 2 P.M. on Wednesday, September 28. Field Marshal Goering said that "mobilization will

tary was perturbed and annoyed because he found that some quarters close to the White House had been circulating the whisper that he was opposed to all action and that the President had not only decided on the appeal to Hitler and Beneš but had drafted it himself.[40] As a matter of fact, this small group does this on all occasions, forgetful that an Administration is judged on the sum total of all its accomplishments rather than on individual brilliancy anywhere.

While we were in the Secretary's room Kennedy called up to report on developments in England. The tide is running strongly against Chamberlain's peace policy both in the Cabinet and out and there is little doubt but that England would cast her lot with France. Parliament will be called on Wednesday, but apparently to ratify decisions made rather than to consult. In fact through all this crisis what has surprised me is that the governments of the democracies have not taken their people or their Parliaments into their confidence and that there has been more accurate news in the Berlin papers than in the British. . .

At half-past ten I received a call from Mr. Eastwood, head of the Communications Division in the British Foreign Office, who dictated to me over the telephone Mr. Chamberlain's reply to the President's message.[41] As Sumner Welles was leaving for the White House we had it in the President's hands seven minutes after receipt. . .

After luncheon we all congregated and listened to Hitler's speech over the radio waiting for a clue to the future. There was some division of opinion, but to me the speech was uncompromising to a degree, both in tone and substance. In fact, the only out that I could see Hitler left himself was in the event that Beneš should retire, in which case Hitler could readily make the necessary concessions. But knowing Beneš this is improbable. There are many reports that he feels Czechoslovakia would do better to fight now than later, but a

---

be ordered at that hour and occupation of Sudeten areas will begin immediately." *Ibid.*, pp. 556–557, 561–562.

[40] The Secretary of State wrote that he did not oppose the appeals, but he was not certain the "results would justify them." He thought nothing short of force would stop Hitler and feared that an appeal by the President might lead some to class Mr. Roosevelt as an "appeaser." The Secretary has written: "Welles kept pushing the President on, while I kept advising him to go slow." Hull, I, 591.

[41] Chamberlain's note of approval expressed gratitude to the President for his message of September 26 and assured him that Great Britain was doing everything possible to obtain a peaceful settlement through negotiation. Jones and Myers, *Documents, Jan. 1938–June 1939*, I, 288. The French reply is given in *ibid.*, pp. 287–288.

fight now would mean the end of all social structures as we know them. . .[42]

Tuesday, September 27, 1938.

Still no ray of light in the crisis. Chamberlain's speech this afternoon, which was primarily designed to influence the Dominions, revealed a tone of such hopelessness that when he had finished the impression was prevalent that nothing could now stop the holocaust.[43]

We spent the better part of the morning in the Secretary's office. We all agreed that no stone must be left unturned. One suggestion was to circularize all other countries asking if they would send appeals to Hitler and Beneš comparable to that sent by the President urging the continuance of negotiations.[44] This was motivated on the possible cumulative effect of an expression of world opinion. Another suggestion was the possibility of a personal and confidential appeal to Mussolini to help in such ways as he could. A third suggestion was given by Bullitt, namely, for the President to reply to Hitler [45] that we agree that many injustices had flown from the Treaty

[42] Speaking at the Sports Palace in Berlin Hitler gave a long account of the Sudeten problem and German attempts to solve it peacefully. He attacked President Beneš and his policy toward the Germans in Czechoslovakia, ending with the warning: "Sudeten Germany my patience is now at an end! I have made Mr. Beneš an offer which is nothing but the carrying into effect of what he himself has promised. The decision now lies in his hands: Peace or War!" Hitler, II, 1508–1527. Beneš' views at the time of Munich are discussed in Edward B. Hitchcock, "I Built a Temple for Peace," The Life of Eduard Beneš (New York: Harper & Bros., 1940), pp. 264ff.

[43] In his broadcast Chamberlain stated that the quarrel between Germany and Czechoslovakia had been settled in principle, and Hitler's demand for immediate effecting of the terms of the settlement was "unreasonable." "I see nothing further that I can usefully do in the way of mediation," Chamberlain added. The Times (London), September 28, 1938, p. 10.

[44] Secretary of State Hull sent telegrams on the afternoon of September 27, 1938, to all American diplomatic missions accredited to governments which had not already taken action. He instructed that the appropriate official of each such government be approached with the suggestion that its chief of state send to Germany and to Czechoslovakia a reminder of the importance of foregoing the use of force in the current dispute. The American official was to make it clear that the United States government implied no opinion on points of the dispute at issue. James W. Gantenbein (ed.), Documentary Background of World War II (New York: Columbia University Press, 1948), pp. 149–150.

[45] Hitler's reply of September 26 to the Roosevelt appeal of the same date opened with a lengthy statement of the problem of the Sudeten Germans in Czechoslovakia, by which Hitler attempted to show that Germany had been a guiltless, patient, reasonable, and sincere participant in the negotiations to settle the Sudeten question. The Chancellor closed by saying that an immediate solution must be found. The Germans had proposed a settlement which exhausted the possibilities of keeping peace. It was

of Versailles, that these did not justify a war but a conference, and that a conference should be held at The Hague within two days to which if bidden we would send an observer without power to bind but empowered to use his good offices in the negotiations. I was instructed to prepare a draft of the circular, Jimmy of the message to Mussolini, and Sumner and Berle would prepare a draft along the lines of Bill Bullitt's suggestion.

Fortunately the Secretary scented the dangers in Bullitt's plan and by the time it got through its third or fourth draft there was little left but a vague suggestion that a conference might be one solution.

The Italian Chargé d'Affaires called this afternoon. The primary purpose of his call was to tell me that although he could not understand why, nonetheless it was quite clear that there was an undertone of resentment in Rome that a copy of the President's appeal for peace had not been sent to Mussolini. I replied that the appeal had been sent only to the parties directly negotiating in the Czechoslovak dispute, and that it had not been felt that this included the Italians. It was not a question of addressing the parties to a wider problem. On this score I could reassure him, and felt that if any resentment had been felt it would be dissipated by a knowledge of the facts.

We then got to discussing the outlook for peace in Europe. Mr. Cosmelli told me that since this morning he had become markedly more pessimistic. He felt from his personal reading of Mussolini's speeches as though the combinations were lined up and the die pretty nearly cast.[46] He felt that England and France would fight. He did not know whether Italy would mobilize, would remain on the defensive, or would attack, and if so where. He assumed that the Embassy here would be cut off from all mail communication with Italy. . .

In a personal message to Hitler on the morning of September 28 Chamberlain suggested a meeting of representatives from Great Britain, Germany, and Czechoslovakia, as well as France and Italy, if desired.[47] To Germany's Axis partner the British Prime Minister sent another mes-

---

now up to Czechoslovakia to determine whether there should be war. Jones and Myers, *Documents, Jan. 1938–June 1939*, I, 289–292.

[46] Mussolini had begun on September 17 a tour of the Venetias, during which he spoke at many places, always emphasizing his hope for a peaceful solution, although making it clear that in case of war, Italy would stand by the Axis. Elizabeth Wiskemann, *The Rome-Berlin Axis* (New York: Oxford University Press, 1949), p. 126.

[47] Great Britain, Foreign Office, *Documents on British Foreign Policy*, 3rd Series, II, 587.

sage asking Mussolini to communicate to Hitler the willingness of Italy to participate in such a conference.[48] Mussolini contacted his Ambassador in Berlin by telephone, and about noon on the twenty-eighth Hitler agreed to a Four Power Conference.

The next day at Munich Chamberlain, Daladier, Mussolini, Hitler, and their subordinates met to decide the fate of the Czechoslovak State without the presence of the Czechs.[49] The fortuitous absence of the victim made agreement easier to achieve: the occupation and evacuation of the Sudeten areas were to take place between October 1 and 10; an international commission was to determine areas where plebiscites should be held and to fix the final delimitation of frontiers; the right of option into and out of the transferred territory was to be allowed for six months; the Czechs were to release Sudeten Germans serving in the Czech army and imprisoned for political offenses. When these terms were presented to the Czech Government, there was little left for them to do but accede.

Mr. Chamberlain had made his "peace with honour," but Winston Churchill called the Munich agreement "a total and unmitigated defeat."

Wednesday, September 28, 1938.

What a day of contrasts! It opened in the deepest gloom. Sterling broke twelve cents. The security markets were disorganized. German ships were called home from the high seas and everything seemed set for war. Then suddenly came the announcement that Hitler had accepted a Four Power Conference and immediately public opinion changed over the entire world. Sterling recovered. Stocks surged forward, and everyone whom you met said, "Well, it's all over now." I wish I had the nature to swing to such extremes. I do think the chances of preserving peace have immeasurably improved but it likewise is difficult for me to see how this can be done except at the expense of Czechoslovakia.

The President's second plea sent out last night has received a very good press and papers here are prone to give it credit for saving the situation.[50] That it was a contributory cause I have no doubt, but equally it would seem as though Mussolini's intervention were the principal one.[51] Whether he got cold feet or whether he saw a chance to gain something from England and France by blackmail time alone

[48] *Ibid.*, pp. 587–588.

[49] *Ibid.*, pp. 627–629, 630–635.

[50] President Roosevelt's second appeal to Hitler stressed that "continued negotiations remain the only way by which the immediate problem can be disposed of upon any lasting basis." Jones and Myers, *Documents, Jan. 1938–June 1939*, I, 293–294.

[51] The story of Mussolini's intervention is given in Wiskemann, pp. 127–128.

can tell. At any rate there things stand and we shall wait what the next forty-eight hours bring forth.

The Czechoslovak Minister called in the morning. He said he knew he could speak for his Government in saying that they had been deeply moved by the President's recent appeals. The fact that Hitler had accepted a Four Power Conference he felt was due, in large degree, to the President's messages.

However, he was deeply fearful that the new conference would result in further pressure being exerted on Czechoslovaks by the British and French. He had been in Praha all during the painful earlier days of the crisis. The country, in agreeing to the Berchtesgaden demands, had come to the very verge of suicide. It could not stand for more. (The Minister spoke with such emotion that at one point I feared that he was going to break down completely.)

His request was as follows: that inasmuch as we had a share in inducing Hitler to call the Four Power Conference, we should now try to influence the British and French not to agree to anything in that conference which would result in further requests for Czechoslovak concessions . . .

Thursday, September 29, 1938.

The entire day was spent waiting for the result of the Four Power Conference at Munich. The answer came through late in the afternoon and as foreseen was a virtually complete victory for Hitler. The paradox of the situation is that when Mr. Chamberlain sold out Czechoslovakia the first time he was greeted by hisses everywhere; today, a fortnight later, he sells it out even more completely and is welcomed as a hero in those same circles.[52] Now it is up to the Czechs. The pill will be a difficult one to swallow but it is a choice between dismemberment and suicide. . .

Friday, September 30, 1938.

The clouds continued to lift all day. Sterling recovered twenty-two cents from its low. The stock market boomed. Steamship companies resumed their normal sailings. War insurance dropped from

[52] Chamberlain received over 40,000 letters approving his action at Munich. The reasons for the favorable reception of the Munich agreement are discussed by Feiling, pp. 378–382.

five dollars to twenty-five cents, et cetera. On the other hand the liberals began to raise their hands in holy horror and it is already possible to foresee the time when the public will forget its fright, overlook the fact that war was only two hours away, and once again blame England for having sold Czechoslovakia out.[53] And sell that country out they did. An analysis of the terms shows more and more clearly that Hitler got the substance of everything he wanted. He probably could have taken over without plebiscite even more territory, but was clever enough not to ask for more. As it is he will poll a comfortable majority in the plebiscite areas whereas if he had taken more now he would have had a smaller proportion of votes in the remaining districts.

We had a long session in the Secretary's office as to how he should comment. Three points were agreed upon: (1) that the preservation of peace had provoked a universal sigh of relief and pleasure; (2) that we were not concerned with the merits of the dispute at issue but in seeing it was solved by reason, not force; and (3) that the work for peace should not be relaxed but redoubled, and that an opportunity for real appeasement resting on sound economic foundations was at hand. . .[54]

Mr. Moffat's final comment on the Munich crisis was in the form of a poem which he had found circulating in Washington and which he included in his diary, because it appealed to his sense of humor:

> Meine Herren and Signori,
> Clients of the British Tory,
> Kindly note that No. 10
> Requests your patronage again.
> Opening as from today,
> As Chamberlain et Daladier.
> Messrs. Hoare, Laval, successors
> For doing business with aggressors.
>
> Frontiers promptly liquidated;
> Coups d'état consolidated;

[53] The Gallup poll asked the following question: "Do you believe that England and France did the best thing in giving in to Germany instead of going to war?" The results revealed that 60 per cent of the people queried thought that the democracies had been correct in agreeing to Hitler's demands. Forty per cent answered in the negative. *New York Times*, October 12, 1938, p. 20.

[54] The statement of Secretary Hull as given in his press conference on September 30, 1938, is printed in Jones and Myers, *Documents, Jan. 1938–June 1939*, I, 297.

Pledges taken and exchanged;
Acquisitions re-arranged.
Loans on Fascist risks advanced;
Nazi enterprise financed.
European intervention
Given personal attention.
Have you problems of partition?
Let us send a British Mission.

Breaking with Geneva's firms
We offer Nazis favored terms.
Let us lend, to back your name,
England's honorable fame.
For dirty deals both great and small
Our representatives will call.
Orders carried out with speed;
Satisfaction guaranteed.
We obsequiously remain,
Daladier and Chamberlain.

In the wake of Munich came no tide of friendliness between the democracies and Germany. Space had been traded for time, and nothing more. No permanent territorial settlement had been effected, no era of good feelings launched. The foreign and domestic policies of the Nazi state were still often repugnant to the American people, and pressure increased upon the Department of State to act in regard to Germany. Hints of rapprochement, such as that given by Ambassador Kennedy in a speech in Great Britain, met with quick protest.

Friday, October 21, 1938.

The Secretary is very upset over the effect of Kennedy's recent speech.[55] He loses his amiability and wishes that all Ambassadors would forego all speeches. He says that every time our foreign policy has run off the rocks it has been because of a speech made by one of our Ambassadors abroad. He thinks we should have definitely called Kennedy off in advance, despite his claim that he was advancing a "pet theory of his own."

[55] On October 19, 1938, Ambassador Joseph P. Kennedy delivered a speech at the Trafalgar day dinner of the British Navy League. In this speech Kennedy advanced a theory of his own that "instead of hammering away at what are regarded as irreconcilables, they [the democracies and the dictatorships] could advantageously bend their energies toward solving their common problems by an attempt to re-establish good relations on a world basis." This led to speculation in the press about whether or not Kennedy's speech presaged a new attitude of the United States toward the dictatorships. *New York Times*, October 23, 1938, part IV, p. 3.

The Secretary asked Sumner why he did not see the danger of the speech. Sumner replied that he had been thinking of Mexico and had assumed that the Secretary himself had given attention to the matter and had initialed blind. The Secretary then said that I had not appeared unduly perturbed when I discussed the matter with him. This is not strictly accurate as I told him there would undoubtedly be repercussions, but that I thought the phrase "a pet theory of my own" would keep the Department and the Secretary out of the range of editorial attack. The truth of the matter is that the Secretary dislikes calling down Kennedy and Bullitt as they have a way of appealing to the White House over his head. The speech also came at a time when the trade agreement negotiations were in a most critical state and Kennedy was taking the ball and not inspiring the Secretary with the greatest confidence in the way he was carrying it. However, a "goat" is needed and I shall have to be the goat. In the long run, however, no one is going to be hurt unless it be Mr. Kennedy himself. . .

Arthur Krock [of the *New York Times*] dropped in to discuss the Kennedy speech. He wondered how and why it had ever been passed and pointed out the complete confusion it created in the public mind.[56] He wondered whether Kennedy was advocating burying differences of foreign policy between the democracies and the autocracies, or whether he merely advocated a cessation of the name-calling game. At any rate I assured him that the speech marked no change in policy, that if and when policy changed it would be announced by the President and the Secretary and developed in their speeches, and that the idea we would sound off through an Ambassador could be rejected off-hand as a tenable theory. . .

Monday, November 14, 1938.

. . . The German situation was uppermost in our minds. The wholesale confiscations, the atrocities, and the increasing attacks not

---

[56] Mr. Moffat wrote in his diary on October 22–23, 1938: "The columnists are still writing about the Kennedy speech. Dorothy Thompson calls names, Walter Lippmann says that however unsatisfactory career Ambassadors may be in certain lines, they are perhaps less of an evil than political Ambassadors who try and play individual roles instead of merely as members of the team. Arthur Krock says that at the very least the speech has caused confusion in the minds of the public as to what our policy is. I think the Secretary will speak next week before the Foreign Trade Council and show conclusively that our policy has not, will not, and can not change."

only on Jews [57] but on Catholics [58] have aroused opinion here to a point where if something is not done there will be combustion. The difficulty was to find ways and means of making a gesture that would not either inherently hurt us or provoke counter-retaliation that would hurt us. The final decision was to order Hugh Wilson home for "report and consultation." We had several conferences with the Secretary during the course of the day as we had to determine: (a) how to phrase the instruction; (b) how to give it publicity and (c) how it could best be followed up by the President at Press Conference tomorrow. Hugh Wilson happened to be planning to come home on leave next week, we therefore had to telegraph him without delay to sail on the next non-German ship. As a matter of fact, the papers played it up even more than we anticipated.[59] The supposition was fairly general that it was either a breach of relations or might develop into a breach of relations. The French Ambassador telephoned me about ten minutes after McDermott had given the news to the press and I tried to put the thing in proper perspective for him. It is more than a struggle between Christian and Jews, it is as much a struggle between two factions of the Nazi Party for dominance. Unfortunately, all the information we get is that the wild men are winning . . .

Thursday, December 22, 1938.

Sumner Welles sent for me this morning and opened the conversation by saying that it was a black day indeed. The two things he

[57] A seventeen-year-old Jewish boy, incensed by the fact that his parents had been driven from Germany into Poland, entered the German Embassy in Paris and killed the German Counselor. When the death was announced on November 9, 1938, it touched off a vicious attack upon Jews in Germany. Synagogues, homes, and stores were wrecked. Thirty thousand Jews were arrested, and many were driven from Germany. The Jewish people in the Reich were fined one thousand million marks as damages for the Counselor's death. A description of the November pogrom is given in G. Warburg, *Six Years of Hitler* (London: George Allen & Unwin, 1939), pp. 253–265.
[58] There seemed to be indications in November that the same type of campaign which had been directed against the Jews might be begun against the Catholics. For instance, a Catholic religious gathering was broken up in Munich on November 13. Windows in the home of the Catholic Archbishop of Munich were broken. *New York Times*, November 15, 1938, p. 3.
[59] The Department of State's action in calling Mr. Wilson home aroused speculation in the press as to whether or not this presaged a break in relations. *Ibid.*, November 15, 1938, p. 1; *New York Herald Tribune*, November 15, 1938, p. 1; *Washington Post*, November 15, 1938, p. 1.

had on his mind were (a) the difficulties in Lima where the Argentines are succeeding in blocking the resolution of solidarity; [60] and (b) a press report from Berlin that the Germans had protested against "the coarse and insulting manner of Secretary Ickes." [61] While I was there the President rang up and after discussing with Sumner Welles the Lima situation they together discussed the German announcement. They agreed that inasmuch as Sumner Welles had previously told Thomsen that he would hold the German protest and our rejection thereof in confidence provided the Germans did the same, none the less if the Germans gave it publicity he would give our reply publicity. The President and Sumner Welles recognized that this might have serious consequences but decided that the Germans only responded to strong action and that any appearance of weakening now would be totally misconstrued. I suggested that while I did not believe it would result in a break of relations, none the less I thought that if we "played up the incident" it would mean that many of our citizens and their interests would be seriously prejudiced. That was admitted. Sumner then asked me to look up certain references for him so that he would know that he was on safe ground. We collected all of Hitler's speeches since last March. We got Dietrich's [Otto Dietrich, State Secretary in the Reich Ministry of Propaganda] statement that the German press was under complete discipline and responsible to the government. We got out reams of inspired editorials that were offensive. I brought this down to Sumner Welles and suggested that he confine his statement to the one salient paragraph without going through the whole conversation. He rejected my recommendation and

---

[60] The Declaration of Lima, affirming the solidarity of the American Republics, was unanimously adopted on December 24, 1938, although the Argentine Government had held up the formulation of the declaration. Secretary Hull, who was the chief American delegate, has described in detail the difficulties with Argentina. Hull, I, 601–609.

[61] In an address in Cleveland, Ohio, before a Zionist Society, Secretary of the Interior, Harold L. Ickes, although not mentioning Hitler by name, had deplored the acceptance of decorations by Americans from "a brutal dictator who, with that same hand, is robbing and torturing thousands of fellow human beings." On December 21, 1938, the German Chargé d'Affaires, Hans Thomsen, had called on Under Secretary Welles to protest the remarks made by Ickes. Mr. Welles informed Mr. Thomsen that he was not willing to accept the protest. The memorandum of the Welles-Thomsen conversation is in the *New York Times*, December 23, 1938, p. 12. Mr. Thomsen's memorandum is given in Germany, Auswärtiges Amt, *Documents on German Foreign Policy 1918–1945*, vol. IV, *The Aftermath of Munich* (Series D [1937–1945]; Washington: Government Printing Office, 1951), pp. 662–663.

said that he planned to give it all out for attribution. Now there was nothing to do but to wait and see. . .

The rejection of the German protest was received ominously in Berlin, newspapers there noting that the relations between the two countries had "reached their lowest point." [62] Uneasy over the response, Mr. Moffat discussed with Mr. Messersmith and Mr. Dunn possible courses of action in case of a break in relations.

The prospects did not seem dismal enough, however, to prevent the Moffats from going to New York City to keep Christmas in the traditional way. On Christmas Eve they went to No. 1 Pierrepont Place in Brooklyn where the family had gathered to have dinner together, exchange gifts, and talk. Other days away from Washington were spent on things for which there was scarcely time or opportunity in the capital — an evening at the Metropolitan for "Tristan and Isolde," consulting a lawyer about personal business matters, taking the children to Radio City Music Hall and then to the top of Rockefeller Center to watch the city begin to light up for the night.[63]

When the four-day holiday in New York was over and the Moffats returned to Washington on December 26, the threatened rupture of relations with Germany had dropped from sight and other problems taken its place. The Spanish Civil War, the fratricidal struggle which had been bloodying the soil of Spain since 1936, was nearing a final decision. Since the war had engendered intense loyalties and bitter quarrels within and without Spain, as the end seemed near the Department of State was subjected to increasing pressure from the partisans of the Loyalists or Franco to reconsider, on the one hand, or to retain, on the other, its policy of nonintervention toward the strife.

Monday, January 9, 1939.

The morning was given over almost entirely to Spain. This is the first day of "Lift the Embargo Week" with enthusiasts pouring into Washington from all over the country. The Catholics and others opposed have organized a counter "Keep the Embargo Week" and they are vying with each other in meetings, pressure on Congressmen and the like.

First of all I sat in with Sumner Welles while he received a group which favored raising the embargo. The text of my memorandum follows:

"At the request of the White House the Acting Secretary of State

[62] The Berlin paper, *Zwoelf-Uhr Blatt*, was quoted to this effect in the *New York Times*, December 25, 1938, p. 1.
[63] The Moffat diary, December 23, 24, 25, 26, 1938.

today received a delegation of eight, headed by Mr. Paul Todd of the League for Peace and Freedom, Mr. Rockwell Kent, Mr. Louis Bromfield, et cetera. The delegation stated their point of view that it was to the interest of the United States, and it would certainly be responsive to the wishes of the American public, to have the embargo against Spain lifted. The chief arguments advanced were:

"(a) That the recent Gallup poll had shown the Americans were over 75% in favor of the Loyalist cause; [64]

"(b) That the embargo was penalizing a democratic government and assisting the Fascist powers;

"(c) That a Franco victory would result in an early spread of Fascism through South America; and

"(d) That conditions had so changed during the two years since the embargo was applied that its effects were the opposite of those desired by the Congressmen and Senators who had voted for it.

"Mr. Welles replied that there was so much confusion concerning the legal status of the Spanish embargo that he wished to make an explanation of fact. The Embargo existed by virtue of two pieces of legislation: the Joint Resolution of January 8, 1937,[65] and the so-called Neutrality Act of May 1, 1937.[66] The first of these Acts referred specifically to Spain and could only be revoked by the Executive if and when the President found that a state of civil strife no longer

[64] In a poll reported in December, 1938, 76 per cent of those asked were found to favor the Loyalists, and the other 24 per cent sympathized with Franco. *New York Times*, December 30, 1938, p. 6.

[65] This resolution said in part that "during the existence of the state of civil strife now obtaining in Spain it shall, from and after the approval of this resolution, be unlawful to export arms, ammunition, or implements of war from any place in the United States, or possessions of the United States, to Spain or to any other foreign country for transshipment to Spain or for use of either of the opposing forces in Spain." U.S. Congress, *Congressional Record*, 75 Cong., 1 Sess., vol. LXXXI, part I (Washington: Government Printing Office, 1937), p. 90.

[66] Section 1 of the Neutrality Act provided that whenever "the President shall find that a state of civil strife exists in a foreign state and that such a civil strife is of a magnitude or is being conducted under such conditions that the export of arms, ammunition, or implements of war from the United States to such foreign state would threaten or endanger the peace of the United States, the President shall proclaim such fact, and it shall thereafter be unlawful to export, or attempt to export, or cause to be exported, arms, ammunition, or implements of war from any place in the United States to such foreign state, or to any neutral state for transshipment to, or for the use of, such foreign state." U.S. Congress, Senate, *Neutrality*, Document No. 40 (Washington: Government Printing Office, 1937). A discussion of the Resolution of January 1937 and the Act of May 1937 is given by Norman J. Padelford, *International Law and Diplomacy in the Spanish Civil Strife* (New York: The Macmillan Co., 1939), pp. 175–184.

existed. The second was more flexible in its provisions, but even if under this Act the President withdrew his proclamation with reference to Spain, the mandatory provisions of the January 8th Joint Resolution would still apply. Mr. Welles recognized that many eminent lawyers felt that the so-called Neutrality Act had repealed the January Joint Resolution. The Department of State had studied the matter at length, making use of its best legal talent. The decision was that repeal by implication was not favored; that an extension of this doctrine would work havoc with regard to the interpretation of legislation by the Executive, and could not be accepted. The question of raising the Spanish embargo therefore was no longer in the hands of the Executive, but was in the hands of Congress. Last week the President had discussed the question of our neutrality legislation in his message,[67] and had made certain very clear-cut recommendations which it was now up to Congress to implement or not in its judgment. He suggested that the members of the group, either as individuals or as representatives of their separate organizations, could very well call on the Chairman of the Foreign Relations Committee of the Senate or the Acting Chairman of the Foreign Affairs Committee of the House and set forth their point of view. . .

Thursday, January 19, 1939.

. . . I was called away in the middle of this conference to the Secretary's office where the question of our attitude toward the Spanish embargo was under discussion. A distinguished Conservative Republican [Henry L. Stimson] had written the Secretary making a strong appeal for the Government to take the lead in reversing our unfortunate neutrality policy by a dynamic step which would not only lessen the danger of a Franco victory but would electrify and energize French and British democracies.[68] Judge Moore, Mr. Hackworth [Green H. Hackworth, Legal Adviser to the Department of

[67] In regard to neutrality legislation President Roosevelt had said in his annual message of January 4, 1939, that when we "legislate neutrality, our neutrality laws may operate unevenly and unfairly — may actually give aid to an aggressor and deny it to the victim. The instinct of self-preservation should warn us that we ought not to let that happen any more." Franklin D. Roosevelt, *The Public Papers and Addresses of Franklin D. Roosevelt*, 1939 vol., *War — and Neutrality* (New York: The Macmillan Co., 1941), pp. 3–4.

[68] Former Secretary of State Stimson had written to Mr. Hull urging that the embargo on arms, ammunition, and implements of war be lifted in regard to Spain. The text of this letter is given in *New York Times*, January 24, 1939, p. 6.

State], Jimmy Dunn and myself ran over all the pros and cons of the situation. Bill Bullitt then came in. He said that if we should take this action France and England would immediately follow suit. He felt, however, that before we made a decision we should have to be prepared to answer three questions. The first: Would it really save the Loyalists? The second: Would we be prepared in case it led to serious trouble or hostilities between Germany and Italy on the one hand and France and England on the other to "go through with things," or would we merely start a movement and then duck and run before its consequences? The third was: Whether or not Congress would definitely support the President, as it would be a capital blunder to urge a course of action only to have it defeated? At this point the Secretary called up Senator Pittman who said that the Committee unanimously voted to drop any consideration of the neutrality or Spanish embargo legislation for the present. He said the conflicting avalanche of telegrams from both sides had convinced individual senators that they were on too hot a spot to sit with ease and that the sooner they could get off it by avoiding the issue the happier they would be. Incidentally, Joe Alsop told me last night that Senator Taft had received 15,000 telegrams over the weekend urging him "to keep the embargo". . .

Monday, January 23, 1939.

Long sessions in the Secretary's office regarding the reply to the Stimson letter. There is wide divergence of opinion as to how it should be handled. Judge Moore and Hackworth think that a friendly answer to the effect that we were giving careful consideration to the suggestions he advanced would be sufficient. Sumner Welles thinks that we should at least indicate the lines along which we should ultimately urge a revision of the Neutrality Act. Norman Davis wants to take this occasion to make a frontal attack upon the basis of existing neutrality legislation entirely, subordinating the Spanish embargo feature. The Secretary's main preoccupation is not to transfer to the ultimate debates on neutrality legislation the bitter clash of opinion which now exists on the Spanish embargo. As a matter of fact, no course of action that we pursue is entirely free from embarrassment; if we send a noncommittal reply the press will allege that we are pussyfooting; if we argue with Mr. Stimson and call attention to certain inaccuracies of statement in his letter we shall be offending a man who has supported our foreign policy, and we shall, incidentally, not be giving a true picture of our feelings; if, on the other hand, we agree with everything that he says we are admitting that our course during the last two years has been wrong and that the opinions of our Legal Advisers are not valid. However, any way you look at it we are in for some trouble. Just how the letter leaked to the press will probably never be known. Mr. Stimson telephoned to say that he had shown the text to nobody; there were very few people here who knew of its existence. . .

Wednesday, January 25, 1939.

. . . Another long session in the Secretary's office while he is trying to formulate his ideas not only in relation to the Stimson letter and the Spanish embargo, but to the broader policy of our role as a neutral in the event of a European war. All of us agree that Section 1 of the Neutrality Act should be repealed and that the United States should revert more nearly to its time-honored neutrality policy.[69] This should be tied up, however, with a cash and carry provision. The main reason for wanting to see this change is that the British and French would then know in advance whether or not they could obtain supplies from the United States in time of war instead of having the question mark. Conversely, the Germans would know that France and England could obtain unlimited supplies instead of perhaps making a wrong assumption that the United States would retain the embargo. A clear-cut clarification of our position in advance might prevent trouble. But while all of us agreed on this there was considerable discussion as to the tactics, at least half of us maintaining that while people's thoughts were entirely centered on Spain and the Spanish embargo any discussion of the Neutrality Act would be considered by both the Congress and the public in relation to that particular struggle and not in relation to the broad European field. . .[70]

[69] The United States had in the past allowed friendly, established governments to obtain arms in the United States to suppress revolts. Padelford, pp. 178–179.
[70] The Department of State had been formulating its views on the Neutrality Act for a long time. On October 18, 1938, for instance, Mr. Moffat wrote in his diary: "A long session in Judge Moore's office, some ten of us, with regard to the Department's policy on amending the Neutrality Act. The views naturally covered a wide range and it was not always clear whether we were discussing what was theoretically the ideal or what was practical politics. My own point of view was that the simplest

Monday, February 13, 1939.

. . . Just as I was going home Sumner Welles sent for me. He has been so busy of late with the Aranha visit [71] that he has had little time for other problems. He told me, however, that he had spent an hour with the President this morning on a variety of subjects. The President was still in bed and according to Sumner Welles looked very badly. They had talked over at some length whether or not Hugh Wilson should return to his post. Sumner felt that we were at the parting of the ways, that we could either renew relations now or run the risk of their deteriorating to the point of a full break. On the pro side was the fact that Germany had, at least in principle, recognized our treaty rights and had offered a plan for the orderly emigration of Jews which was better than was hoped for. On the con side were considerations of domestic politics plus the fact that the return might be misconstrued in Germany to mean a weakening of the President's desire to assist the democracies. At best it was a question of balancing up the disadvantages and seeing which way our interests lay. The President has not yet made up his mind and probably will not for two or three days. He asked Sumner, however, to talk it over a little more and bring it up again before he sails. Hugh Wilson is very anxious to return, Messersmith is very anxious for him not to return, the rest of us are more or less indifferent. Sumner Welles asked if I could draft a brief statement which could be given to the press should the decision be to return Mr. Wilson. We could always discuss matters better if we saw such a statement in black and white. This I did in the course of the evening. . .

---

move was to repeal Section 1, which placed an embargo on the export of arms and ammunition, but strengthen the provisions that arms bought by belligerents should be paid for in cash, that title should pass at the water front, and that in no circumstances might they be carried on American ships. Those who thought of our policy in terms of Europe concurred in this view, those whose minds were on the Far East disagreed. The only things we all agreed on was the impossibility of working out any formula that would meet our needs in all circumstances." And again on November 19, 1938, Mr. Moffat recorded: "From eleven until twelve we had a long meeting in the Secretary's office with regard to the possibility of announcement by the President that he would ask Congress to repeal the Spanish embargo measure in January. The President is clearly anxious to do so. We talked over the pros and cons. Judge Moore and Hackworth were opposed to taking such action, with Jimmy Dunn inclining to favor them. Personally, I favor doing so . . ."

[71] Brazilian Foreign Secretary Oswaldo Aranha arrived in Washington on February 9, 1939, to confer with officials about United States–Brazilian relations. *New York Times*, February 10, 1939, p. 8.

In the early morning hours of March 15, 1939, Hitler did what he termed his "last good turn" for the Czech people. Having summoned the elderly Czech President, Emil Hácha, to Berlin, the German Chancellor gave him the choice between the annihilation of Czechoslovakia and the incorporation of the country into the Reich. Hácha decided to place "the fate of the Czech people and country in the hands of the Führer of the German Reich." [72] At 6 A.M. the German army entered the Czech state, and later on the fifteenth Hitler proclaimed that "Czecho-Slovakia has ceased to exist." [73] The next day Bohemia and Moravia were annexed to the Reich, and Slovakia was taken under protection. At the same time Hungarian troops were invading and occupying Ruthenia.

Tuesday, March 14, 1939.

Today the Czechoslovak crisis was in full swing. . .

Dr. Brejška said that the Minister and he had spent considerable time trying to envisage the future. He said that Slovakia was so poor a territory that it had always had to be financed from Praha. If Germany took it over, or even insisted on its independence, the logical thing would be to expect Germany to finance its deficits, but Hitler had already declared that he would not let Slovakia "cost Germany a farthing." If Hitler's designs were not to occupy further Czech territory they were probably to render Praha completely impotent while the Czech and Slovak elements in her Army and Administration were being unscrambled. Later on there might be renewed demands for a customs or monetary union.

The attitude of Dr. Brejška, whom I saw nearly every day during the crisis last summer, has completely changed. He seems apathetic and defeatist. Formerly he had always emphasized the innate power of resistance of the Czechs; today he shrugged his shoulders as though he felt that no resistance was left.

Almost synchronously with Dr. Brejška's call came through the expected news that the Slovakian Parliament had declared independence and that there would be no objection from Prague. Next, in quick succession, came reports of the fall of the Government, of German mobilization, of the German threat first of all to occupy the two German speaking islands, and then the whole of Bohemia; next

---

[72] Germany, Auswärtiges Amt, *Documents on German Foreign Policy*, Series D, IV, 267, 270.

[73] Martin Wight, "Eastern Europe," *The World in March 1939*, ed. Arnold Toynbee and Frank T. Ashton-Gwatkin (London: Oxford University Press, 1952), pp. 286–293.

in order the Hungarian twelve-hour ultimatum for Czech troops to leave Ruthenia, then reports of Polish and even Rumanian troop movements, and finally the departure of the President and Foreign Minister of Czechoslovakia to Berlin. One more State is on the way to extinction.

Unfortunately Mr. Carr was caught napping. As late as five o'clock yesterday afternoon the purport of his message was that despite the alarmist reports the situation held out no probability of serious trouble.

We have two theses to consider: the first that Germany's action against Czechoslovakia is to liberate her back door in case she should decide to move West. At the same time, by letting the Hungarians join with the Poles, they are temporarily holding in abeyance their Ukrainian move in the hopes that they can come to terms, first commercially and then politically, with Soviet Russia instead. The other thesis is that Germany had obtained her Western push and is continuing toward the East. The evidence is still not clear-cut. I incline to favor the former, Sumner Welles the latter. . .[74]

Wednesday, March 15, 1939.

The crisis continued in intensity throughout the day. The German troops overran the whole of Bohemia and Moravia before nightfall. The Hungarian troops reached the Polish frontier. Henlein (cruelest cut of all) was appointed Administrator of Bohemia; Ritter was made Liaison Officer with foreign legations and consulates in Praha, et cetera.

Certain factors became self-evident: (1) That Germany had once again violated Hitler's solemn pledges that he was through with European conquests and that he did not wish to absorb any non-Germans;[75] (2) that what has been done is a destruction of the Munich Settlement which, even if the guarantee was never implemented, was based on the continued independence of the remnants of Czechoslovakia; (3) what Hitler has done is counter to the principle of self-

[74] Mr. Moffat's appraisal was correct. On March 25, 1939, Hitler stated that he had given up his plans for the immediate establishment of a Ukrainian state. *Ibid.*, p. 289.

[75] Speaking in Berlin on September 26, 1938, Hitler had said that after the Sudeten problem was settled there was for Germany "no further territorial problem in Europe." He also affirmed: "We want no Czechs." Hitler, II, 1508–1527.

determination on which he justified his earlier move into Czechoslovakia to regain the Germanic-Sudeten people. More and more the comparison with what is going on now and what went on in the Napoleonic era is becoming apt, only it looks as though Hitler were more successful even than Napoleon.

What to do is the question. Bill Bullitt telephoned the President late last night and was almost hysterical. He wanted the President to make a ringing denunciation, to go to Congress and urge the repeal of the Neutrality Act, et cetera. The President was none too keen to follow these recommendations. I suspect that his mind may be running on the idea of complete severance of relations with Germany. In any event, the idea of Hugh Wilson returning to Berlin, which had virtually been decided upon Monday, has been completely abandoned. We had a round-table discussion as to what would be the significance should relations be severed. Leaving aside the fact that our citizens and interests would be left without any protection whatsoever, I feared that it would be like pushing off a toboggan which would lead down a long slope towards eventual war. Norman Davis urged in favor of the emotional relief of quarantining nations whose word no man can trust. George Messersmith, his eyes aglow, favored any move directed against the Nazis. Berle, Dunn, Hackworth, and myself saw the drawbacks and obstacles more clearly than we could see the advantages.

The Czech Minister came in late this afternoon after seeing Sumner Welles. It was an emotional talk. I had earlier in the day been able to do him a small favor by sending off a telegram on behalf of Miss Alice Masaryk [daughter of Thomas Masaryk, the first President of the Czech Republic]. What is perplexing him now is what he shall do if he receives orders from the Germans to close up his Legation. This raises the question: Will we or will we not recognize the de facto extinction of Czechoslovakia? [76] The Germans are alleging that they went into Praha on the invitation of the Czech President. Sumner Welles obviously told him that with a situation chang-

---

[76] On March 20 Acting Secretary Welles gave the German Chargé d'Affaires a statement which said, in part: "The Government of the United States has observed that the provinces referred to are now under the de facto administration of the German authorities. The Government of the United States does not recognize that any legal basis exists for the status so indicated." Jones and Myers, Documents, Jan. 1938–June 1939, I, 303.

ing hourly we could not express any opinion. In the meantime Hurban is going to consult Beneš and Jan Masaryk. . .

Friday, March 17, 1939.

The President approved the course of action we had worked out with Sumner Welles last night, both as to the timing of the three steps — the Welles statement, the withdrawal of Czech concession rates through the occupied areas, and the imposition of countervailing [increased] duties, as well as the text of the Welles statement itself.[77] In addition he felt that we must take the lead in withdrawing Mr. Carr before the Germans asked for his withdrawal, and to that end suggested that we send a telegram directing Mr. Carr to wire that as he was unable to maintain contact or transact business with any Czechoslovak officials he desired to know what disposition this Government wished to make of him. In reply we would tell him to close the Legation and to turn over the files and archives to the Consul General. The two telegrams would be drafted in such form that they could be given publicity. . .[78]

Thursday, March 23, 1939.

The crisis passed through two or three more phases today with the completion of the occupation of Memel,[79] with the signing of the German-Rumanian Trade Agreement, and with strenuous efforts on the part of France and Poland to ease the Hungarian-Rumanian tension.[80] However, until we know what Italy wants and how far she is prepared to push her claims the crisis will not be past.

[77] The statement issued on March 17, 1938, by Mr. Welles expressed "this country's condemnation of the acts which have resulted in the temporary extinguishment of the liberties of a free and independent people" and stated that "acts of wanton lawlessness and of arbitrary force are threatening world peace and the very structure of modern civilization." *New York Times*, March 18, 1939, p. 3.

[78] The text of Mr. Carr's telegram to Mr. Welles, dated March 17, and the response of the Acting Secretary are printed in U.S. Department of State, *Press Releases*, March 25, 1939, p. 222. In Washington the German annexation of Czechoslovakia was not recognized, and the Czech Minister continued to be received by the Department of State.

[79] After a German ultimatum had been sent, Lithuania ceded Memel to Germany on March 22.

[80] Since World War I Hungary and Rumania had quarreled over the boundary between them set by the Treaty of Trianon in 1920. Hungary's seizure, with Hitler's blessing, of Ruthenia in mid-March, 1939, and subsequent Hungarian troop movements apparently menacing Rumania had led Rumania to begin mobilization at the frontiers. The crisis seemed to ease, temporarily at least, when Rumania and Germany con-

England has made two separate moves: One, she has asked France, Russia and Poland to join in a declaration of consultation in the event that Germany makes a further move in the East.[81] The second and quite independent *démarche* was an inquiry of France, Poland, Russia, Turkey, Greece and Yugoslavia as to what they would do in the event Germany invaded Rumania.[82] The newspapermen are mixing up these two separate *démarches*. The whole thing seems curiously inept. For Britain to try and make the border states lie down with Russia when they hate Russia slightly more than Germany is almost inviting Eastern Europe to be less alarmed at German aggression. In any event the results are none too pleasing. In reply to the first inquiry Russia has, of course, accepted, glad to be back in the respectability of the Western family, while Poland declines to commit herself.[83] In reply to the second inquiry about Rumania, nearly all of the Eastern countries have replied with varying degrees of politeness, "How can we tell what we will do unless we know what you (England) are prepared to do yourself?" [84] A pertinent query. . .

Friday, March 24, 1939.

The flood of alarming telegrams from Europe died down today but it became apparent that the British diplomatic offensive had come to a complete halt. Poland declined to lie in the same bed with Russia, Holland and Switzerland expressed displeasure at rumors that France and England planned to guarantee their integrity, et cetera. As some one remarked, Hitler has had three victories in a week —

---

cluded on March 23, 1939, a trade agreement making Rumania an economic vassal of Germany. The Second Vienna Award of August 30, 1940, declared by Germany and Italy, restored about half of Transylvania to Hungary.

[81] On March 20, 1939, the British Government requested France, Poland, and Soviet Russia to sign and publish the following declaration: "We the undersigned, duly authorized to that effect, hereby declare that, inasmuch as peace and security in Europe are matters of common interest and concern, and since European peace and security may be affected by an action which constitutes a threat to the political independence of any European State, our respective Governments hereby undertake immediately to consult together as to what steps should be taken to offer joint resistance to any such action." Great Britain, Foreign Office, *Documents on British Foreign Policy*, 3rd Series, IV, 400.

[82] This query was sent on March 17, 1939. *Ibid.*, pp. 360–361.

[83] *Ibid.*, pp. 463–464, 467.

[84] Mr. Moffat's information was probably based in large measure upon two despatches of March 21 and 22 from the British Government to the British Ambassador in Washington for communication to the Department of State. *Ibid.*, pp. 420, 465–466.

the first in Czechoslovakia, the second in Memel, the third in London. I am rapidly lowering my estimate of the cleverness of British diplomacy. . .

Oumansky [Constantine Oumansky, Soviet Russian Ambassador to the United States] also took occasion to say that he had had a telegram from Moscow giving the Soviet estimate of the European situation. According to Russian reports the spine shown by Chamberlain in his Birmingham speech [85] was not being followed by acts, and the outlook for a positive British policy was as questionable as it was a couple of months ago. Oumansky then added with considerable emphasis, "Although the outlook presages war some time in the future, I am convinced that as far as my government is concerned nothing will occur that will disarrange certain plans it now has for this Spring and Summer."

Sunday, March 26, 1939.

. . . Sunday morning I spent an hour with the Secretary. Although he looks much better after his rest he is still coughing. Above all he has been deeply wounded by the press reports that it was a curious coincidence that every time we take a strong stand in foreign policies he is absent.[86] The implications given by several columnists went further and indicated that he was not in sympathy therewith. His mind tells him that it is part and parcel of a political campaign trying to discredit him before the 1940 Convention,[87] but his feelings have been bruised and he believes that this attack on him would never have happened had some of his friends told the press at every point that the President, he and Welles were at one in each step taken. . .

Tuesday, March 28, 1939.

. . . Today the big news was the fall of Madrid. Not a shot was fired and the war may now be considered as finished in fact. Jimmy [Dunn] and I went down to see Sumner Welles to find out what

[85] Chamberlain had warned that "no greater mistake could be made than to suppose that, because it believes war to be a senseless and cruel thing, this nation has so lost its fiber that it will not take part to the utmost of its power in resisting such a challenge if it ever were made." Feiling, p. 400.

[86] Mr. Hull had been vacationing in Florida during the time of the German absorption of Czechoslovakia.

[87] Mr. Hull had been mentioned as a possible candidate for the Democratic presidential nomination in 1940.

was in the authorities' minds with regard to recognition of Franco. We were not advocating any immediate move but with the President leaving tomorrow we felt that the Secretary and he should reach a meeting of minds as to when and in what circumstances recognition was probable. We talked a little bit about Mr. Bowers [Claude G. Bowers, American Ambassador to Spain], who, according to the President, has given no indication that he wants to leave the Diplomatic Service but who is believed to be seeking a domestic post. Sumner further said that the President had definitely selected his new Ambassador to Madrid but he did not tell us who he was. Yesterday the Spanish Ambassador came down to the Department to say that Besteiro [Julián Besteiro, Spanish Councillor of State] was urging him to return to Madrid to assist in negotiations for surrender. This he was planning to do, so an appointment was made for him to say good-bye to the President, of course today's news alters the situation completely. Sumner Welles rather hopes that De los Ríos will voluntarily vacate the Embassy even before a decision is reached on the recognition of Franco. He therefore asked me to call down Meana [Don Juan Antonio Meana, Second Secretary of the Spanish Embassy in Washington] and throw him out a hint to this effect in any way I saw fit. The task was neither easy nor particularly agreeable. . .

Wednesday, March, 29, 1939.

. . . We had a session in the Secretary's office in the late afternoon. Nearly everyone present, in varying degrees, thought that we should recognize the Franco regime in two or three days, partly because it is the only government, partly because our business interests demand it,[88] partly because it is vital to us to maintain American control over all communications between Europe and Latin America which center in Spain; partly because we and Soviet Russia alone have not recognized the inevitable, an embarrassing partnership. The President, however, is in no hurry at all and wants to see if there are large scale persecutions and massacres. The only fallacy of this way of thinking is that if we are to have any influence at all with the

[88] On March 4, 1939, for instance, Mr. Moffat wrote in his diary: "Concurrently, we are getting daily messages not only from the International Telephone and Telegraph but from other commercial sources telling us that each day's delay is costing American business untold sums."

Franco regime in avoiding these massacres it will be if we get on speaking terms with him. . .[89]

Friday, March 31, 1939.

. . . Joe Kennedy telephoned Sumner about a quarter of ten to tell him that Chamberlain would make a speech in the House of Commons agreeing under a series of well-defined conditions to fight for Poland's independence.[90] The British were inclined to expect that Hitler's reaction would be violent, but felt that if the crisis was coming it had better come now.

A short while later Senator Pittman called up Sumner and asked him for some comments. He in turn gave me twenty minutes to dictate a short statement which he could use. I am not particularly proud of the effort but there was no time to sit down and prepare a more thoughtful statement. Here it is:

"The Chamberlain statement to the House of Commons today seems to have had a double purpose: (1) to call a halt to possible German aggressive designs in the East by making it plain that under certain conditions (to be discussed below) Great Britain would fight; (2) to satisfy those elements in Great Britain which felt that a constant policy of retreat was actually encouraging the Germans to increase their demands.

"Many students have always claimed that had Sir Edward Grey [former British Foreign Minister] before the War set forth clearly that Great Britain would fight in certain circumstances, the War would never have occurred. Apparently Chamberlain has made up his mind that this will not occur a second time.

"The most significant part of the speech is that, despite its limitations, it does commit England to positive action in Eastern Europe, which she has never before been willing to consider. Throughout history she has successfully stopped all powers who had obtained or threatened to obtain mastery over the Continent of Europe. Her present decision is predicated upon the belief that Germany is within

[89] Secretary Hull announced in his press conference of April 1, 1939, that he had sent a telegram to Franco's Foreign Minister in which he indicated that the United States was favorably disposed to establishing diplomatic relations with Spain. The recognition of Franco was completed on April 3. U.S. Department of State, *Press Releases*, April 1, 1939, p. 245.

[90] Mr. Chamberlain's statement is printed in Hansard, *Parliamentary Debates*, CCCVL (1939), 2415.

striking range of achieving such a position. Consequently if she is to be stopped ultimately, it is necessary for Britain to keep in being potential allies, such as Poland and Rumania.

"There is little doubt but that at present the Chamberlain statement will be very popular in England. Despite press reports, there is no cleavage whatsoever within the Cabinet. There are certain clear-cut limitations in the statement. In the first place, it would seem to involve only the independence of Poland. This is a broad phrase, and probably would exclude Danzig and certain other types of arrangements that could be reached between Poland and Germany. In the second place it only holds good for the duration of the present crisis. Public opinion in Great Britain is definitely behind Chamberlain at the moment, but whether the British public would wish to keep in existence a commitment to Poland in normal times, irrespective of the attitude of the Polish Government is open to question.

"The important development to watch is the attitude of Hitler to this move. It is generally expected that he will be thoroughly indignant, if not enraged. It should be remembered, however, that in the past (for instance at the time of the Czech mobilization in May last year), he was able to contain his rage, but to continue making more effective preparations for ultimately assuaging it. . ."

Monday, April 10, 1939.
. . . In the afternoon the Finnish Minister came to see me. He told me in great confidence that the Soviet Government had invited the Finnish Government to cede three islands off Leningrad to the U.S.S.R. Finland had declined but had made a counterproposition to the Russians whereby Finland would guarantee to maintain her neutrality in the event of a European war, but should she be attacked to defend herself to the last man; conversely, Russia was to promise that she had no territorial designs on Finland. No reply has as yet been received to this proposal. It is entirely secret as the exchange occurred during some trade talks.

The Minister asked that the American Government do its best to persuade the Soviet Government to soft-pedal in its dealings with Finland. I evaded the request by saying that I doubted whether the United States had much influence with the Soviet Government. The Minister said that on the contrary we were the only government the

Soviet authorities would listen to. He said that he did not wish to be importunate, but he felt that the matter was urgent and he hoped that we would act without delay.

The Minister then said that he hoped we had no doubt as to the sincerity of the neutrality of the four northern countries. I replied that I thought their record was clear and beyond suspicion.

The Minister said he was greatly disturbed over the situation in Europe and felt that it would be of intense value to everyone to see that the four northern countries were able to keep out of the struggle.

As to Soviet Russia the Minister said he had been impressed by the failure of the Russians to protest recent German aggression. His information on Russia was not very detailed, but he thought this new attitude was due in part to Russian weakness, in part to a desire to stay out of a European war until the very end when she could come in and claim her reward.

The time is rapidly approaching when the President will want to make some sort of a personal move in the situation. His ideas are running along the line of a message to Hitler and Mussolini asking them if they will guarantee him that their troops will not invade a whole series of neighboring countries. On thinking it over the answer is too easy, namely that they will give such guarantees provided their security is not menaced, the same phrase we use for ourselves. The Secretary sent for me to come to his apartment at six o'clock and he, Norman Davis, Berle and I sat until nine blocking out a somewhat different type of approach which Berle will draft. He is really a lord of language and can make words sing. . .

Saturday and Sunday, April 15 and 16, 1939.

Saturday the President announced the despatch of his message to Hitler and Mussolini on which we had been working the better part of the week.[91] The idea was essentially the President's and the first draft entirely his. This Berle redrafted with a view to giving more of a "sing" to the note. Much of this redraft was retained, though

[91] The message of April 14, 1939, to Chancellor Hitler and Premier Mussolini called upon the two nations to give assurances that their armed forces would not attack the thirty-one countries which President Roosevelt listed. If such assurance were given, the President agreed to undertake to obtain like assurances from the thirty-one nations in regard to Italy and Germany. Discussions would then be held to solve problems of armament and international trade. No direct reply was ever received by the President to this message. Roosevelt, *Papers and Addresses, 1939*, pp. 201-205.

the President took this and personally pointed it up. Some of the arguments in the President's second draft worried the Secretary of State who urged the President to omit them.[92] The final draft was prepared by Sumner Welles and very cleverly was halfway between the President's and the Secretary's thesis. Such is the history of the preparation of the message. The last draft Sumner, Jimmy and I spent two hours on Friday going over each sentence with a microscope.

A half-hour after the President had announced the despatch of his message, the Navy Department ordered the fleet back to the Pacific. . .

Sunday morning we all met in the Secretary's office and read over the telegrams coming in from all over the world on the President's message. South America is a unit in praise. Western Europe is delighted. . .

Monday, April 24, 1939.

. . . News came through today that the British Government had decided in principle on conscription. To me this is the biggest news throughout 1938 or 1939 and it will either produce war within a year or materially diminish its ultimate risk. Personally, I fear that more than any one measure it may be the straw that breaks the camel's back and goads Hitler into desperation. . .

Friday, April 28, 1939.

Today began at 6 A.M. listening over the radio to Hitler's speech.[93] It lasted for two and one-half hours and was most adroit. When all was said and done, however, I found it rather hard to determine to my own satisfaction just where it left us. I had several impressions: one, although Hitler enjoyed his sarcasm against President Roosevelt and was skillful in dialectic, yet the real hate, the real jealousy, the real antagonism of Germany was toward England. The second impression I had was that Germany, by cancelling the Anglo-German Naval Pact and the Polish-Nonaggression Pact of 1934,[94] completely

---

[92] Hull, I, 620.

[93] In speaking before the Reichstag on April 28, 1939, Hitler replied at length to Mr. Roosevelt's message of fourteen days earlier. This part of his speech is given in Hitler, II, 1633–1656.

[94] In the pact of January 26, 1934, Poland and Germany renounced for ten years the use of force in settlement of disagreements between them. The Anglo-German

freed her hands so that she could move in any direction. Three, the conception of Germany as merely reuniting scattered Germans under one flag has given way to the idea of empire, power, living room, colonies and wealth.

We had a long session, in fact over two hours, in the Secretary's office discussing what leads, if any, should be given to the press. We found ourselves handicapped by lacking an official text as well as by the fact that the Secretary called the meeting before we had had time really to digest what we had. The conclusion was not to take any drastic stand until we were clear in our own minds whether Hitler meant to leave the door an inch ajar or whether he meant to slam it shut and turn the key. The only thing that we felt could be given as guidance to the press right away was that Hitler did not answer in the same spirit as the President had asked; in other words, Hitler had gone on the assumption that the President's message was a trick or a trap and not bona fide.

The Latvian Minister called this morning. He felt that on the whole the Hitler speech was encouraging. He felt that his offer to give guarantees to his neighbors, even under conditions, should be carefully studied. What had struck him most clearly was that no mention whatsoever was made of Russia.

To the Latvian Minister, Russia is the key to the picture. He believes that Russia will join up with England and France only if it does so on its own terms, which would amount to their writing it a blank check for a period of years. Failing such a blank check he thinks that Russia will continue a discreet and somewhat disguised friendliness toward Germany which bodes ill for Poland.

As to the Baltic States he says that policy can be gauged on the basis of their danger. From Germany it is as follows: Poland 100%, Lithuania 75%, Latvia 50%, Estonia and Finland 25%. From Russia: Poland and Finland 100%, Estonia 75%, Latvia 50% and Lithuania 25%.

The Minister said that a few years ago the Russian Military Attaché here had told him that in event of a Russian-German war Russia

---

naval agreement of June 18, 1935, limited German naval strength to 35 per cent of the British except for submarines. These two pacts Hitler denounced in his speech of April 28, 1939. This denunciation constituted Hitler's answer to the mutual defense agreement just concluded between England and Poland.

would immediately attack and overrun Finland in order to guarantee the safety of the Murmansk Railroad. . .

Thursday, June 8, 1939.

Today virtually all work stopped. The visit of the King and Queen [King George VI and Queen Elizabeth of England] was made the occasion of an unofficial but nevertheless complete holiday for the entire city. Temperature was 94 in the shade and over 100 in the streets. The weatherman had promised "Fair" in the morning with thundershowers in the afternoon. Actually, the thundershower did not come until eight o'clock that night.

The morning ceremonies were watched by Lilla from a large corner room at the Hotel Willard which the Blisses [Robert Woods Bliss, retired diplomat] had rented for the occasion. She saw the great crowds on Pennsylvania Avenue, the parade, the one hundred and fifty women who fainted and were carried into the First Aid tent which was right under their window, the tank which caught fire, et cetera.

I was detailed for duty at the White House to help marshal the Chiefs of Mission for the Royal circle and to accompany the six members of the Royal Suite who followed Their Majesties, without, however, being presented. The White House was air-cooled but fortunately not to an unpleasant degree. Chiefs of Mission came in by the East entrance, were announced in a loud voice by an Aide, and were given their exact place to stand. They were requested to be there before 11.45 but the traffic congestion was so great that some of them just got in under the deadline.

As the Albanian Minister passed me going into the East Room he stopped for a moment and said, "My presence here reminds me of a case cited in Schopenhauer, where the actor continued with his part after the curtain had fallen". . .[95]

The Suite, all dressed up in their glittering gold uniforms, came up the staircase, while the King and Queen and the Lindsays [Sir Ronald Lindsay, British Ambassador to the United States] came up by the elevator. The King, Sir Ronald and Summerlin [George T. Summerlin, Chief of Protocol in the Department of State] first made the circle, some ten or twelve feet behind them the Queen, Lady Lind-

---

[95] Italian troops had entered and occupied Albania beginning on April 7, 1939.

say and Spruks [H. Charles Spruks, Ceremonial Officer in the Department of State] made the second circle, some twelve feet behind them our third group followed after.

It was the Queen, not the King, who "stole the show." The King looked like his pictures, was courteous, correct and well-groomed, but lacked that indefinable something known as "personality." The Queen, on the other hand, was short, verging on plumpness, and not, according to classical standards, beautiful, nevertheless every eye in the room instinctively watched her and ignored everything else.

In the afternoon took place the far-famed Garden Party at the British Embassy, the Garden Party that has caused more heartburns, more adverse press comment, more of a tempest in a teapot than any social event I can recall in this country.[96] However, it went off beautifully. To our great surprise Lady Lindsay had written us asking us if we would not come to the Embassy early, ask for Colonel Read [R. V. Read, Military Attaché of the British Embassy at Washington] who would escort us to the main drawing room, and then conduct us to the portico where we would be presented before the King and Queen made their *tournée* through the gardens. We found ourselves in a group with the Vice-President, the Speaker, Secretary of State, Judge Moore, the Governors of Virginia and Maryland, the Norman Davises, et cetera, and at a given moment were led out and placed on the portico steps, with the entire fourteen hundred in the garden faced our way. At the given moment "God Save the King" was played and the King and Queen stood with the Lindsays on the steps to acknowledge the greetings. The Royal Party came down the steps and we were all in turn presented. The political wives, per-

---

[96] On March 20, 1939, Mr. Moffat wrote in his diary: "I learned on the side that the British Embassy and the Irish Legation are having fun over the King's visit. The Ambassador wanted the Minister to meet the King at the station, to attend a dinner with other Dominion representatives, and to go to the Garden Party. The Irish Minister put the matter up to Dublin, which replied that as the Minister would be in Los Angeles . . . the problem did not arise. The Ambassador then came back and asked that the Secretary be at the station and attend the Garden Party; the dinner was obviously out. The matter was again referred to Dublin, which ruled against the Secretary going to the station, but allowed the Garden Party. The Ambassador, undeterred, asked reconsideration about the station as the Secretary of the Irish Legation in Paris had been at the station when King George arrived last year. The Irish Minister said that this was a new element, and he would again ask for instructions, but to his friends he added that he thought it was more likely that his telegram would result in cashiering the Irish Secretary in Paris than it would in obtaining instructions for the Irish Secretary in Washington to be at the station to greet the King."

haps thinking of votes at home, failed to curtsy but Lilla, on the theory that we were on British soil, did curtsy which was duly picked up in the Washington press and emphasized in both the *Post* and *Herald*. As a matter of fact, she was dead right and received many compliments for recalling we were on British, not American, soil. The King and Ambassador preceded by two Aides went off on one tour of the garden while the Queen and Lady Lindsay preceded by two Aides went off on another. They stopped frequently for the Ambassador or Ambassadress to make presentations and at length, after a hot half-hour's work, returned to the portico where they sipped a glass of cool lemonade and made their adieus. . .

◆ VII ◆

WASHINGTON

July 1939 – May 1940

"The issues involved are so terrible"

"Everything is still very quiet," Mr. Moffat wrote of Washington on August 1, 1939. Secretary Hull had left for a three-weeks' vacation, and James Dunn was gone for the month. The President was at Hyde Park.

The departure of government officials from the hot and humid capital was in part both cause and effect of the lag in work. During the week since Pierrepont Moffat had returned from his vacation at Hancock, his schedule at the Department had been filled with "routine" and "miscellanies." He had worked with Sumner Welles on the Intergovernmental Committee concerning refugees, considered with Mr. Berle the effects of extending cotton credits to Spain, and discussed in conference the reverberations of the renunciation of the Treaty of 1911 with Japan. But "despite the era of greater optimism," he wrote to a friend, "through which we seem to be passing, I still think that in all probability there will be some sort of crisis in August or September." [1]

Many of the reports coming into the Department indicated that the Danzig dispute would reach a critical point within the latter part of August. Hitler had openly called for a "settlement" with Poland of the Danzig and Corridor issues. In October 1938, January of the next year, and, again, in March 1939 he pressed his case in Warsaw. On March 26 the Polish Government rejected his proposals. Rebuffed in what he termed his "generous and modest" offer, Hitler ordered on April 3 that plans be prepared for an attack upon Poland to take place sometime after September 1, 1939. When the Polish Chargé d'Affaires called on Mr. Moffat on July 25, he said that the Polish people were convinced that "war was inevitable." [2]

Working in the uneasy calm of the Department of State in late July

[1] Jay Pierrepont Moffat to Mrs. Learned Hand, July 24, 1939.
[2] In a report of the French Ambassador to Poland on July 9, 1939, this attitude of the Polish people was confirmed in almost the same words. France, Ministère des affaires étrangères, *The French Yellow Book* (New York: Reynal & Hitchcock, 1940), p. 204.

and early August, Pierrepont Moffat wrote: "People here have heard the cry 'wolf, wolf' so often that they do not appreciate the dangers involved." But the proportions of the impending crisis soon began to be evident.

Thursday, August 3, 1939.

Today the news from Germany for the first time showed signs that military preparations were being begun on a large scale. Nearly three times as many reservists are being called up as last year, troops are being sent by sea to East Prussia, and other forces are moving toward strategic positions on the Polish border. In spite of which optimism is prevalent here, the market continues its course upward, and most of the guidance given the press in England is definitely optimistic.

Sumner and I talked the situation over. I told him that I was more inclined to think the showdown would occur between Germany and Poland than to the southeast as he was inclined to believe. My reasons were:

Hitler has in the past always gone after what he announced and this year he has made no secret of his desire to get Danzig; [3] if, instead, he should move toward Yugoslavia he would be tackling the one problem where the interests of Germany and Italy were diametrically opposed. If he merely changed the Government in Hungary he would stir up a lot of sentiment in the western countries without fundamentally changing the situation; if he should move on Rumania before Poland he would worry the Russians and Turks more than an advance on Poland. It seemed to me that the unknown factor today was whether or not the British and French having placed the pistol in the hands of Poland could prevail upon the latter not to fire. . . I question whether in the state of tension now existing Beck [Colonel Josef Beck, Polish Foreign Minister] could make a *volteface* even if he wanted to without being overthrown or assassinated. Sumner said, however, that such a move on his part would give England and France an out if they were looking for one.

All in all, I think the next ten days should begin to show premonitory signs of crisis. . .

[3] In his speech of April 28, 1939, for instance, Hitler had said: "Danzig is a German city and wishes to belong to Germany." As part of a settlement of German-Polish issues he had proposed to Poland that "Danzig returns as a Free State into the framework of the German Reich." Hitler, II, 1629, 1631.

Wednesday, August 16, 1939.

All day long the temperature in Europe was rising. Reports kept coming through that concentration is proceeding; that Prague had been ordered to prepare food for the passage of a large army; that German reservists had been called home; that Italian troops in Albania had been concentrated in the south on the Greek frontier; et cetera. Even Kirk [Alexander Kirk, Counselor of the American Embassy at Berlin] who is by no means given to hysteria feels that the situation has never been so grave and that in a very few days the irreparable decision will have been made unless something is done.

Messersmith, Berle and I had a session with Sumner Welles this morning to discuss whether any possible moves were open to us. Various ideas were discussed and dismissed though one or two drafts were made to be used in case of need. We also decided that it was time to hold a technical conference with the other Departments, notably Treasury and Justice, to discuss practical questions in the event of a sudden emergency. Two long telegrams were sent off to the President whose ship is now off Cape Edward Island.[4]

The Polish Ambassador and the Rumanian Minister were both in the Department today; in both cases their previous optimism had completely evaporated and they are now fearful of the worst.

Frank Page [vice-president of International Telephone and Telegraph Corporation] telephoned from New York getting me out of the dining room in the Metropolitan Club to say that they had received telephonic advices from their German subsidiary to "batten down the hatches," a warning they had not even received in 1914. . .

Thursday, August 17, 1939.

Frank Page telephoned from New York to give me the estimate of the situation as seen by the I. T. & T. The head of the German subsidiary had been allowed out to see Colonel Behn [Sosthenes Behn, president of International Telephone and Telegraph Corporation] but had been instructed to be back within four days; he returned this morning. Probabilities, as the I. T. & T. see them, are that Danzig will be declared part of the Reich within ten days. . . If Poland objects to Danzig, Germany will move against Poland. Germany does

[4] President Roosevelt, who was vacationing, had left Hyde Park to cruise in the waters off Nova Scotia.

not believe that France and England will enter the war quickly. (All the information reaching the I. T. &. T. is that they will.) Italy definitely did not want to go in the war but cannot help herself; she recognizes that she is peculiarly vulnerable. Spain definitely will not go into the war. On the other hand, Spain has become a pure Fascist State and the Royalist move may be considered as dead. Being a Fascist State her sympathies will be with the Axis but not her sword.

Summing all its information the I. T. & T. believes the chances in favor of war breaking out are roughly 6 to 4.

From our own Departmental point of view all day long the news went from bad to worse and with a rare unanimity from all our Ambassadors foreseeing trouble. The reason I am so pessimistic is that: (a) I am convinced Germany still believes she can localize a Polish-German war;[5] (b) because the two theses have been set out in such terms that a compromise is no longer possible, only a backdown. I excluded a backdown by Germany. I excluded a backdown by England or France. That leaves only Poland and here the possibility of a backdown is lessened by Germany's increasing further demands to cover not only Danzig but the Corridor and other grounds taken from Germany during the war.

In the afternoon we held a long conference in Sumner Welles' office. Present: Welles, Messersmith, Berle, Feis [Herbert Feis, Adviser on International Economic Affairs], and myself for State, Louis Johnson and General Marshall for War, Thurman Arnold for Justice, Mr. Charles Edison and Admiral Stark for the Navy, and John Hanes and Dan Bell for the Treasury. We went over in review all the steps that it would be necessary to take should war break out. Proclamations, supervision of neutrality, communications, prohibitions of loans and credits, cancellation of licenses, et cetera, and divided up among the various Departments the necessary work. Everything is reasonably well organized in advance but, of course, if war should come there would be hundreds of new situations which have not been foreseen. . .

---

[5] In a conference on August 22, 1939, with his commanders-in-chief Hitler is supposed to have said that the "chances still are that the West will not interfere." Grand Admiral Erich Raeder, Commander-in-Chief of the German Navy, wrote on September 3, 1939: "To-day, the war against England and France broke out, the war which, according to the Fuehrer's previous assertions, we had not need to expect before about 1944. The Fuehrer believed up to the last minute that it could be avoided."

Friday, August 18, 1939.

. . . The Polish Ambassador called. He had little to offer other than to reiterate the belief of his Government that German strength was overrated. I remarked that the situation worried me as the points of view of Germany and Poland were so clear-cut that no compromise seemed possible, and that it was difficult to see either side backing down. The Ambassador said that of course Poland would never back down, but that he did not exclude the possibility of Hitler's weakening.

He said that the German army was not the army of 1914. The officers had insufficient training and had not been allowed to remain long enough with the same units of troops. The best generals had been liquidated, and the remaining generals were merely "Party hacks." ! ! The German people did not want to fight, and it would be suicidal to start a war when conditions were already so bad that people were being rationed as to foodstuffs. Furthermore, Germany was burdened with an ally which was scared and whose soldiers would "run like rabbits."

The whole conversation represented a point of view of unreasoning optimism and still more unreasoning underrating of one's opponent, that, if typical of Polish mentality in general, causes me to feel considerable foreboding. . .

Monday, August 21, 1939.

Today turned out to be one full of drama. When we came to the Department in the morning the situation seemed if anything slightly eased. There were two phases that gave us a limited degree of comfort; the first, the fact that the British and Italians seemed willing to talk and to make some sort of a joint study of the situation; the second was an invitation given by Goering to Lipski, the Polish Ambassador to Berlin. This optimism, however, was not of long duration. All through the day reports kept coming in of moving German troops; of the departure of mechanized units from Berlin and Bremen; of the flight of vast numbers of airplanes to the East, et cetera. . .

A long telegram came in from Tony Biddle [American Ambassador to Poland] asking for authority to commence evacuating the

---

Namier, p. 301; Anthony Martienssen, *Hitler and His Admirals* (New York: E. P. Dutton & Co., 1949), p. 19.

families of the Staff to Scandinavia at Government expense. We had a long session as to whether or not we could authorize such action which would probably start a panic among Americans and a commencement of the backward rush. I stood out very strongly for giving the authorization on three grounds: (1) that Warsaw was of all places the most exposed and had no facilities such as subways as a protection against air raids; (2) that Biddle's recommendations were entirely along the line of the general circular we had sent out telling Chiefs of Mission that we relied on their best judgment as to when a situation became critical; (3) that between the criticism of spending some money needlessly and the criticism of having waited too long and lost some human lives there was little to choose. The telegram accordingly went out, and I suspect the news will break tomorrow. In the middle of the crisis Arthur Schoenfeld chose to start on leave from his post in Finland. This made us all extremely angry and resulted in a circular which I drafted at Sumner Welles' orders cancelling all further departures on leave without specific and renewed authorization that had been granted to Chiefs of Mission or Foreign Service Officers.

At about half-past five the bombshell came through of the German-Soviet Nonaggression Pact and the impending voyage of Ribbentrop to Moscow.[6] There is no doubt that Germany has pulled off one of the greatest diplomatic coups for many years and what its effect will be upon Poland only the next few days can tell. It looks to me as though Germany had promised Russia no objection to the latter taking over Estonia and Latvia and, in effect, agreeing to some form of new partition of Poland.[7] Sumner Welles, Adolf Berle, and I discussed its effect back and forth, but we differed on the way it might affect the events of the next few days. At this moment Bill Bullitt called up from Paris and told Sumner Welles that from two or three sources he obtained the information that Thursday the 25th was to be

[6] Ribbentrop's meeting with Stalin took place on August 23, 1939.

[7] The text of the Nazi-Soviet Treaty of Nonaggression and documents on the initiation and progress of the discussions between Germany and the Soviet Union prior to the signing of the Treaty on August 23 are printed in Raymond James Sontag and James Stuart Beddie (eds.), *Nazi-Soviet Relations 1939–1941* (Washington: Government Printing Office, 1948), pp. 1–110. A Secret Protocol added to the Treaty limited the spheres of influence of the Soviet Union and Germany: in the Baltic, the dividing line was the northern boundary of Lithuania: in Poland, the rivers Narew, Vistula, and San were chosen. Both countries stated that only further developments could determine whether it was desirable to maintain an independent Poland.

der Tag and suggested that the President cut short his vacation and return to Washington.[8]

Tuesday, August 22, 1939.

All day long the news went from bad to worse.

In Warsaw Beck sent for the British and French Ambassadors and told them that the Russian-German pact had not surprised him, that he had never believed the Soviet Government was sincere, but that in any event what had happened did not affect Poland's position in any way.[9] He was chiefly afraid of the effect of the agreement on public opinion abroad. Paris was stunned. It felt that it left France in a tragic situation as Turkey could not help Rumania unless Russia were bound to England and France, and without Rumania there was no way to get arms to Poland. The British gave way to less signs of worry, and proceeded to reaffirm their commitments to Poland. Whereas early this summer I thought the chances of war were 50–50, and recently raised the odds to 60–40, I now feel that they are about 75–25 in favor of hostilities. . .

I have been feeling for some time that we could not much longer delay an announcement discouraging further travel by Americans to Europe. I drafted such a statement for Sumner Welles. Biddle is urging Americans to leave Poland; Bullitt is privately advising all who do not need to remain in Europe to return. He asked whether we planned to issue a general warning to Americans in Europe. We replied that for those who were abroad we left the matter of cautionary advice, both as to timing and as to substance, in the hands of the man on the spot. From this end we would only give advice to travelers still in America.

[8] Mr. Bullitt had been informed by Alexander Kirk from Berlin that Hitler had given orders for the attack on Poland to begin on August 24 or 25, 1939. The French Foreign Office had also told Bullitt that the 25th was the day set.

Although the morning of August 26 had been chosen by Hitler to start his invasion, a German Admiralty record reveals: "The *'Incident Weiss'* [the attack on Poland] *already started will be stopped at 20.30* (8.30 P.M.) because of changed political conditions." This is followed in brackets by the explanation: "Mutual Assistance Pact between Great Britain and Poland of August 25th noon, and information from the Duce that he would be true to his word but has to ask for large supplies of raw materials." Hull, I, 655, and Namier, p. 329.

[9] After hearing from the Havas representative in Warsaw that Ribbentrop was on his way to Moscow to sign a nonaggression treaty with the Soviet Union, Léon Noël, the French Ambassador to Poland, went to see Colonel Beck. His version of the conversation with the Foreign Minister is given in Léon Noël, *L'agression allemande contre la Pologne* (Paris: Flammarion, 1946), p. 424.

In the afternoon we had a two-hour meeting of the full committee of representatives of State, Treasury, War, Navy, and Justice. As most of the chief figures in the executive departments were present the Press was in a dither of excitement and stood twenty or thirty strong outside Sumner Welles' door hoping for crumbs of news. As a matter of fact, while we covered a great deal of ground the meeting was utterly devoid of drama. We went over the texts of countless executive orders drafted to meet different emergencies. We solved various questions of overlapping jurisdiction, and agreed to meet again Thursday for final approval of all the documents before the President returned on Friday. Nothing was to be said to the Press, however, which, having to draw its own conclusions, emphasized the very minor portion of our discussions, namely, the facilities for getting Americans home.[10]

At the conclusion of the meeting I found the French Ambassador waiting for me upstairs. He had very little to say and wanted to know if we had any late news from Europe. As a matter of fact there was at that time almost none. Official circles in every country were so stunned that they had not even straightened out their thoughts, much less determined on any action. . .

Wednesday, August 23, 1939.

. . . Sumner Welles at last issued the warning to Americans to postpone any travel to Europe unless there were compelling reasons for them to undertake the trip. At the same time various Chiefs of Mission started giving advice in Europe, the result was that before the day was over Bullitt telegraphed us that every ship from Europe to America was full to overflowing and that he must know at once what plans had been made for the evacuation of Americans. All we were able to telegraph in reply was that we arranged with the U.S. Lines to turn their vessels around in France rather than to waste a week going on to Germany; that we authorize American ships to take more passengers than their safety complement allowed; that we were diverting two Dollar Line ships which had passenger accommodations but were proceeding through the Mediterranean as freighters. The rest the Maritime Commission will have to work out for itself. . .

[10] See, for instance, *New York Times*, August 23, 1939, p. 1.

In the midst of all this the President announced his return a day earlier. Everyone was speculating whether or not he is planning some dramatic gesture, other than the telegram we all know about,[11] and whether he is planning to summon Congress before war breaks out. . .

Thursday, August 24, 1939.

. . . About five o'clock Sumner Welles sent for me to tell me of the President's plan to send messages to Hitler and the President of Poland. I don't think that anyone felt there was more than one chance in a thousand that such messages would affect events, but it seemed that that chance should be taken and above all that the record should be abundantly clear. Sumner prepared the first draft of the message to Hitler and Berle of the message to the President of Poland. I offered a few suggestions of phraseology which were accepted, the three of us went in to the Secretary's room. He approved them forthwith and took them across to the White House.

Meanwhile, Joe Kennedy had called up Sumner Welles to say that he thought the President's message to King Victor Emmanuel was "lousy" and pleased nobody in England. He said that the British wanted one thing of us and one thing only, namely that we put pressure on the Poles. They felt that they could not, given their obligations, do anything of this sort but that we could. As we saw it here, it merely meant that they wanted us to assume the responsibility of a new Munich and to do their dirty work for them. This idea received short shrift from the President, the Secretary, and Sumner Welles down.[12]

At 7.30 the President had approved the texts of the two messages. I dictated the telegrams to the four or five interested Missions, includ-

[11] On August 23, 1939, a message from President Roosevelt was sent to King Victor Emmanuel of Italy in which the President expressed his "belief and that of the American people that Your Majesty and Your Majesty's Government can greatly influence the averting of an outbreak of war." Roosevelt suggested that the Italian Government formulate proposals to settle the crisis based upon "an understanding that no armed forces should attack or invade the territory of any other independent nation, and that this being assured, discussions be undertaken to seek progressive relief from the burden of armaments and to open avenues of international trade including sources of raw materials necessary to the peaceful economic life of each nation." S. Shepard Jones and Denys P. Myers (eds.), *Documents on American Foreign Relations*, II (Boston: World Peace Foundation, 1940), 324–325.

[12] See Hull, I, 662.

THE MOFFAT PAPERS

ing one to Phillips directing him to submit the text to the Italian Government under instructions of the President who regarded the messages as supplementary to that he had earlier sent the King of Italy. . .[13]

Friday, August 25, 1939.

. . . Representative Bloom called on another matter but told me that the crisis was not serious, furthermore, that he had doped out why Hitler came to terms with Russia. This was to give Hitler an asylum when he was ultimately thrown out by the Germans. No other country would accept him. Such is the deep political thinking of our Chairman of the Foreign Affairs Committee. . .

Meanwhile news went from bad to worse; mobilization nearly everywhere; Poland cut off from communications across Germany, then all telephone and telegraphic wires in Germany were silenced; next the Tannenberg speech [14] was cancelled and the only mystery that remained was what proposition did Hitler put up to Sir Nevile Henderson at their noonday conference. Henderson jumped on a plane for London, and London acted mysteriously about the whole matter.[15] Negotiations of appeasement began to appear in the British press for the first time. . .

[13] These two messages were based on the suggestions set forth in Roosevelt's message of April 14, 1939. The President also urged "that the Governments of Germany and of Poland agree by common accord to refrain from any positive act of hostility for a reasonable and stipulated period, and that they agree likewise by common accord to solve the controversies which have arisen between them by one of the three following methods: first, by direct negotiation; second, by submission of these controversies to an impartial arbitration in which they can both have confidence; or, third, that they agree to the solution of these controversies through the procedure of conciliation. Roosevelt, *Papers and Addresses, 1939*, pp. 444-445, 447-448.

[14] The Germans had planned to celebrate on Sunday, August 27, the twenty-fifth anniversary of Field Marshal Paul von Hindenburg's World War I triumph at Tannenberg over Russia. Included in the ambitious plans for the celebration was a speech by Hitler, which rumor promised would contain an important announcement. It had been hoped that the speech would offer some hope for peace, or that at least Hitler would not attack Poland until after the Tannenberg festivities. The sudden cancellation of the celebration, accompanied by intimations that Germany would be too busy with more important matters, seemed to portend an immediate outbreak of hostilities. *Chicago Tribune*, August 23, 1939, p. 2; August 26, 1939, p. 1.

[15] Ambassador Nevile Henderson has described his meeting with Hitler on August 25 in his book, *Failure of a Mission* (New York: G. P. Putnam's Sons, 1940), p. 272. "Briefly put, Hitler's proposals therein dealt with two groups of questions: (a) the immediate necessity of a settlement of the dispute between Germany and Poland, and (b) an eventual offer of friendship or alliance between Germany and Great Britain." The full text in translation of the verbal communication given by Hitler to Henderson

Saturday and Sunday, August 26 and 27, 1939.

These last two days have given me the feeling of sitting in a house where somebody is dying upstairs. There is relatively little to do and yet the suspense continues unabated.

At the request of the Secretary we have set up a radio listening group. Pell [Robert Pell, Assistant Chief of the Division of European Affairs] and Reber [Samuel Reber, Assistant in the Division of European Affairs] taking turns are at the radio steadily from 6.30 in the morning until 8.30 at night, sending down bulletins every hour or hour and a half as to the tenor of the news being disseminated; in this way we have gotten in information some times an hour or more ahead of its arrival from any other source. Copies of the hourly bulletin are sent to the President, the Secretary and the Under Secretary, and even the President has expressed his great pleasure with the system.

Saturday morning I had no callers other than newspapermen who came in for guidance. The telegrams showed at least a pause in the downward path of the crisis and all attention was centered on Great Britain; there the Cabinet met, and adjourned until the next day, and rumors that "appeasement" was again in the air began coming over the radio in increasing volume. I don't think that the British have been entirely frank either with the French or with us. Although they purport to tell us the facts they are being couched in vague generalities; my conviction is that while they are telling us the truth they are not telling us all the truth. Incidentally, they make no secret of the fact that they are not communicating Hitler's message to the French until they have made up their own mind about it. This breach of joint action has certainly not escaped the Germans.[16]

Saturday afternoon when I came back Victor Mallet asked if he could come down. He had an urgent telegram from his Government

---

is in Great Britain, Foreign Office, *The British War Blue Book* (New York: Farrar & Rinehart, 1939), pp. 155–158, and the German version of the talk can be found in Germany, Auswärtiges Amt, *Documents on the Events Preceding the Outbreak of the War* (New York: German Library of Information, 1940), pp. 468–470. For a discussion of these two versions and the relation of the meeting of Hitler and Henderson to other events of August 25, see Namier, pp. 320–326.

[16] The account of his interview with Hitler which Ambassador Henderson gave to M. Coulondre, the French Ambassador in Berlin, appears in *The French Yellow Book*, pp. 306–307. The outline of the British reply was given to the French Ambassador in London by Viscount Halifax on August 26, and the final text was communicated on August 28. *Ibid.*, pp. 328–331, and Namier, p. 343.

to the effect that it was on the point of arming certain of its merchant ships defensively. The British Government assumed that there would be no objections on the part of the United States to such defensively armed vessels entering or leaving American ports. Mr. Mallet thought that the first of such armed ships might be expected in about six days. . .

I took this up with Sumner Welles when he came in about half-past five, and he in turn discussed matters with the President. At eight o'clock he telephoned me at the Club to inform Mallet that the understanding of the British Government that there would be no objection to the entry or egress of defensively armed merchant ships was correct. This I did by telephone, and the whole matter was thus settled in approximately four hours.

Sunday was again a day of waiting. The British Cabinet meeting was twice postponed but finally took place in the afternoon, London time. Kennedy in a guarded conversation over the phone indicated that "the jig was up" and that he had sent a long telegram which was the most serious one he had ever sent in his life. On the strength of this cryptic talk the Secretary sent for us all again in the afternoon and we sat around for two or three hours. The Kennedy telegram when it came did not bear out the sensational forecast. It recounted the British Cabinet decision which struck all of us as a mere play for time and completely unrealistic in relation to German psychology.[17] The most charitable explanation was that Britain and Germany were planning to throw the blame for an actual breach on the other. The less charitable explanation was that the British were not above a dicker leaving Poland to pay the price.

At five o'clock the Secretary and I dressed in tail coats, top hats, et cetera, left for the station to greet the Prince of Luxemburg. The troop of cavalry was out, marines lining the walk, and all the trappings of visiting royalty. "A small Court rates a big hat," as the old German saying goes.

The President asked us all in to tea at the White House, and we sat around informally for some fifteen or twenty minutes. The President looked well but serious. He kept conversation on a light vein

[17] Ambassador Henderson flew back to Berlin with the British reply on August 28, 1939. Great Britain suggested that Germany enter into direct relations with Poland and that both Poland and Germany work toward relieving the tension in regard to minorities. The reply is printed in *British Blue Book*, pp. 162–165.

with the Prince, talking over the origins of the Delano family, the racial background of the early New England and Canadian settlers, et cetera.

By this time we all of us felt that we had at least twenty-four and probably thirty-six hours before the final crisis so work was suspended for the day. . .

Monday, August 28, 1939.

Today was a day where optimism and pessimism seesawed back and forth. On the whole it was a day of encouragement. Hitler did not automatically reject the British note; the Soviets postponed ratification of their German agreement;[18] Franco renewed his pledges of neutrality, et cetera.[19] But for commentators to assume, as they have been, that Germany has lost the war of nerves and that the danger point in the crisis is over is an error of judgment. England, I feel, is still playing for time; Germany is playing for position. Of course she would prefer to get her way without war and to the very last minute she will try to split the British and French, to encourage the opposition in England, to break down morale in Poland, et cetera, but I have seen no signs of a faltering in German resolution.

We had the customary meeting in the Secretary's office. There really is not much for us to do other than wait. What trumps we had were long since played. There was considerable indignation over Hitler's answer to Daladier due in part to its plausibility.[20] There was a good deal of talk on the importance of educating the American pub-

[18] Max Beloff, *The Foreign Policy of Soviet Russia 1929–1941* (London: Oxford University Press, 1949), II, 273–274.

[19] An editorial in the August 28 issue of the Falange newspaper *Arriba* to the effect that the Spaniards wanted no political war, and comments in the Madrid newspaper *ABC* that Spain would move against no one if no one moved against Spain were taken as assurances of official Spanish neutrality. *Chicago Tribune*, August 29, 1939, p. 7. The conditions which kept Spain neutral during World War II, despite Franco's pro-Axis bent, have been treated in Herbert Feis, *The Spanish Story, Franco and the Nations at War* (New York: Alfred A. Knopf, 1948), a study of the diplomacy that focused on Spain during the years 1939–1944. For the Spanish position up to the outbreak of the war and the formal announcement of neutrality on September 4, see *ibid.*, pp. 17–20.

[20] On August 26 Daladier sent Hitler a message in which he reaffirmed the desire of France for peace, pointed out the willingness of Poland to settle disputes by conciliation, and confidently predicted that there "is nothing to-day which need prevent any longer the pacific solution of the international crisis with honour and dignity for all peoples." Hitler's reply expanded upon the "insanity of the solution of 1919" and "formulated a precise demand; Danzig and the Corridor must return to Germany. . .

lic, but no indication as to what they were to be educated toward. I was instructed to have prepared a memorandum indicating the various occasions when Hitler had gone back on his pledged word. This was done by Pell and was ready by evening. . .

Wednesday, August 30, 1939.

The crisis dragged along. During the day I feel it grew distinctly worse. The exchange of notes between Britain and Germany continues. Each side is trying to build up a case for eventual use, and apparently each side is seeking delay, Germany to complete her military measures, England in the hopes that "something might happen." When all is said and done, however, Germany has not modified her position; Hitler still insists on the immediate return of Danzig and the Corridor after which he will negotiate other difficulties. England declines, outwardly at least, to put pressure on Poland, but we see signs of a willingness to compromise from several factors: (a) British pressure on Poland to defer general mobilization; [21] (b) lack of adequate consultation with the French; (c) phraseology of notes which leaves the impression in Berlin that the final draft was a compromise between two clashing factions. Paris has stood on its position without weakening, Poland declines to send Colonel Beck to Berlin as Hitler demanded (incidentally Sir Nevile Henderson supported this request but his government did not support him).[22] Thus the picture goes with ups and downs, but unquestionably further down at the end of the day than it was twenty-four hours ago. . .

I do not see the possibility of bringing to a pacific solution a Poland who now feels herself inviolable under the protection of her guarantees." *French Yellow Book*, pp. 311–312, 321–324.

[21] See Poland, Ministry for Foreign Affairs, *Official Documents concerning Polish-German and Polish-Soviet Relations 1933–1939* (London: Hutchinson & Co., n. d.), p. 108, and Noël, pp. 462–467.

[22] In agreeing on August 29, 1939, to enter into direct negotiations with Poland, Hitler had told Ambassador Henderson that the Polish representative must come with full powers within twenty-four hours. Commenting on this proposal Viscount Halifax in a telegram to Henderson said: "We cannot advise Polish Government to comply with this procedure, which is wholly unreasonable." The Polish Government did not meet Hitler's time limit in regard to the arrival of the plenipotentiary. On August 31, 1939, at 6.30 P.M. Ambassador Lipski brought Ribbentrop the Polish reply, which said that the Polish Government was "favorably considering the British proposals" about the negotiations. *British Blue Book*, pp. 175–178, 183–187, and Namier, pp. 355–359, 373–375.

Thursday, August 31, 1939.

A day of curious developments in Europe. During the morning a report came through from Kirk that he understood the German terms to Poland consisted of a 16-point program including the immediate cession of Danzig, a road across the Corridor and a Plebiscite in the District of Pomorze based upon the inhabitants of 1918.[23]

Next came the news of British general mobilization, followed by the cutting of the telephonic communication and the censorship of cable and wireless messages. Then came reports of talks between the Polish Ambassador in Berlin and the Foreign Office, between Kennard [Sir Howard Kennard, British Ambassador to Poland] and Beck indicating that there seemed a possibility of negotiation.[24] Finally, in the evening came rumors out of Germany that Hitler was to call the Reichstag, that he wasn't to call the Reichstag, that there were border incidents, et cetera. Throughout the day the telephone bell was ringing constantly and I found it almost impossible to do any connected work. . .

By evening I was tired out and went up to dine with Jimmy Dunn and Hugh Wilson.[25] After dinner we sat in the garden and listened to the entire "Mass in B Minor" by Bach. It was a pleasant relief to get one's mind off war for a space of two short hours.

Friday, September 1, 1939.

I was sound asleep this morning when my telephone bell rang at 3.35. I took off the receiver. "This is Hull speaking," the voice said, "the President has just had a call from Bill Bullitt that the Germans are bombarding four Polish cities and their troops are pouring across the frontier. I sent for Sumner, and we are going to issue a Presidential Appeal against bombing from the air. I think you will want to come down to the Department." [26]

[23] These proposals are printed in *British Blue Book*, pp. 192–197, and Germany, Auswärtiges Amt, *Documents on the Events Preceding War*, pp. 485–488.
[24] Reports of these conversations can be found in Poland, Ministry for Foreign Affairs, *Documents concerning Polish-German Relations*, pp. 118–120, and *British Blue Book*, pp. 189–192.
[25] Hugh R. Wilson, who had been recalled from his post as Ambassador to Germany, was assigned on September 6, 1939, to the Department of State as Special Assistant in the Special Division.
[26] For Cordell Hull's account of the activities of this day in the Department of State, see his *Memoirs*, I, 671–675.

I jumped into my clothes and reached the Department in approximately ten minutes. The Secretary was again on the phone with Bill Bullitt who said that the news he had given the President was now amply confirmed. The Polish Ambassador in Paris had been talking with his Foreign Office in Warsaw which told him that while conversation was going on bombs were falling on Warsaw.

A few minutes later Sumner arrived, and the message which had been prepared and held in Sumner's safe was put on the wires at once.[27] In about half an hour to an hour various people who had been working on the European problem began to straggle in, we kept up a desultory conversation punctuated by radio bulletins, the ticker account of Hitler's speech,[28] et cetera, until after six o'clock.

Two problems were brought up: (1) should we join with the neutrals in trying to get a clear definition that each state is sovereign of all the air above its territory, and that flights by belligerents across neutral territory are breaches of neutrality. (2) The other is should we immediately join with the Belgians and Dutch in working to keep a shipping lane open to Antwerp and Amsterdam. Undoubtedly this would require rationing, and if so how far should we go in urging the British to work this out at once.

Two or three calls came through from Kennedy indicating that the British information was far less complete than ours and that while he thought Britain would declare war before the end of the day, nonetheless they could only act upon official advices from their own Embassies and Consulates, which had not yet been received.

At six o'clock I went back and had an hour's rest, returning to the Department about eight.

The rest of the day I was on the run. Buzzed first by the Secretary, then by Mr. Welles, then by Mr. Messersmith, et cetera. Most of it was frankly small matters: telegrams to draft authorizing Bill Phillips to take over French interests in Italy; sending on to Berlin some requests from Lothian [British Ambassador to the United States] regarding the protection of British interests; a telephone talk to Murphy [Robert Murphy, Counselor of the American Embassy at Paris] in

---

[27] This appeal, addressed to Great Britain, France, Italy, Germany, and Poland, called upon them to refrain from the bombing from the air of civilians or unfortified cities. Roosevelt, *Papers and Addresses, 1939*, p. 454.

[28] This speech is printed in Germany, Auswärtiges Amt, *Documents on the Events Preceding War*, pp. 498–504.

the Embassy in Paris in which he gave me a graphic description of the pressure of Americans desiring to get home; talks with Norman Davis and Ernest Swift of the Red Cross; with Hugh Wilson who presented his resignation this morning as Ambassador to Germany; with Messersmith on shifting the setup of the new Special Division,[29] et cetera; with McDermott [Michael J. McDermott, Chief of the Division of Current Information] regarding press releases; with officers of O.N.I. and M.I.D.; with one or two applicants for jobs, et cetera. . .

On rereading the foregoing it seems that I was so busy with little things that there was scant opportunity to think of bigger matters. The issues involved are so terrible, the outlook so cloudy, the probability of ultimate Bolshevism so great, and the chances of a better peace next time are so remote that if one stopped to think one would give way to gloom.

Tired out after a day from 3.30 A.M. to 7.00 P.M. so went home and promptly to sleep.

Saturday and Sunday, September 2 and 3, 1939.

Saturday morning we had a long meeting in Judge Moore's office to determine whether in the proclamation of neutrality we should list the Dominions as belligerents before they had taken affirmative action by declaring war themselves. . .

While our discussion was adjourned without final decision, events caught up with us, as by Sunday night Australia, New Zealand, and Canada had come out with specific enunciations of the automatic war. The decision, therefore, was to include as belligerents "The United Kingdom, the British Dominions Beyond the Seas, and the Empire of India." Ireland is left out partly because of her declaration of neutrality, partly because of the ambiguity of her position, and partly because of political considerations at home.

Later in the morning we had a meeting in the Secretary's Office, but as news was scarce it did not amount to much. We knew that Britain and France had sent ultimata without time limits to Germany; [30] we knew that there was some difference of opinion, par-

[29] A Special Division was established to handle some particular problems arising from the outbreak of war in Europe, such as liaison with the Red Cross, repatriation of American citizens, and representation of the interests of other governments.
[30] These communications are printed in the *British Blue Book*, pp. 216–217, and

ticularly in France, as to the length of time limit to be allowed; we knew that the Poles were pressing both countries to act subjectively under the terms of their commitments. We also knew that the Italians were making a last-minute attempt to bring about an international conference [31] and that the Germans were not pushing their attack in Poland with its maximum intensity.

There was evident a feeling that throughout the day we were watching "a shadow war." Before we left late Saturday afternoon, however, news came through that a time limit would be set, and shortly before 5 o'clock Sunday morning my telephone bell rang to announce that Chamberlain had declared that, as Germany had not answered England's ultimatum, England was now at war.[32]

The Secretary called the group together for an 8.30 conference. We ran over many things. We canvassed the state of armaments orders and got a report that there were very few airplanes on the verge of completion, ready for shipment abroad. We discussed the date when we felt that the President's embargo proclamation should be issued, most of us feeling that if he delayed unduly the feeling would grow up that he was not carrying out the mandate of Congress, which in turn might affect his desire to obtain the repeal of the embargo provisions. We discussed the location of German shipping and found that whereas in 1914 we had a vast amount of German tonnage, this time there were at best one or two German ships. . .[33]

At 9.00 we listened to the President's broadcast, in which he pledged himself unequivocally to try to keep this country out of war. It was a much needed speech. . .[34]

Tuesday, September 5, 1939.

. . . The President summoned the Secretary, Welles, and Berle to go over the Neutrality Proclamations one last time before sign-

French Yellow Book, pp. 377–378. The British and French did not consider these messages as "ultimata" but as "warnings." Henderson, p. 293.

[31] See Namier, pp. 384–389.

[32] *British Blue Book*, pp. 224–225, 228–230.

[33] This meeting is described by Secretary Hull in his *Memoirs*, I, 675–676.

[34] In his Fireside Chat the President said: "I hope the United States will keep out of this war. I believe that it will. And I give you assurance and reassurance that every effort of your Government will be directed toward that end." Roosevelt, *Papers and Addresses, 1939*, pp. 460–464.

ing them. He took the ground that if we could possibly do so we should not consider Canada a belligerent. In fact, despite all the arguments of Berle and others, a telephone call was put through to Mackenzie King who, of course, urged that Canada not be mentioned as presumably he was anxious to get delivery of three or four Douglas planes which are near completion. Accordingly the stencils had to be recut omitting Canada and South Africa (a half hour later South Africa took affirmative action which will necessitate a special Proclamation applying the Acts to her). I regret the decision as I think it is bad law as well as bad policy. . .[35]

About quarter-past twelve the Polish Ambassador came in with Mr. Wankowicz [Witold Wankowicz, Counselor of the Polish Embassy] after having seen Mr. Messersmith.

The point they wished to make was the following:

They had reason to believe that in the draft neutrality proclamation as presented to the President Poland was listed as a belligerent. They urged that Poland should not be included on the theory that there was no declared war between Germany and Poland (even though there was declared war between Germany on one side and France and England on the other), and hence that the analogy of the Chinese-Japanese conflict, where the embargo was not applied, should govern.

They asked that I send a message over to Mr. Berle at the White House. This I declined to do until I had an opportunity to talk with Mr. Hackworth [Green H. Hackworth, Legal Adviser to the Department of State].

We all went down to Mr. Hackworth's office, who held that, legally speaking, you could not differentiate between parts of a war in which Poland, France and England were fighting as allies (the agreement between England and Poland, which Poland invoked, prevents there even being concluded a separate armistice or peace).

Quite apart from the legal aspect, I raised the question of the political effect should the President appear not to be carrying out the law fairly impartially and as intended by the Congress. I thought that any ultralegalistic interpretation might create the nucleus of

[35] Secretary Hull also opposed the inclusion of Canada in the proclamation. On September 10 the proclamation was extended to cover Canada. Hull, I, 678–679.

an opposition which would make it harder to effect the repeal of an embargo as soon as Congress meets. The Ambassador asked if I were certain that such was the intention of the Administration. I told him that I thought the President's radio speech on Sunday, as well as the attitude of the Secretary of State throughout these past months, made it clear. . .

After they departed I did send over a memorandum containing an account of the interview to Berle who was at the White House. He subsequently told me that he read it to the President but the latter agreed that the Polish Ambassador's point had no validity as a practical proposition. . .

Friday, September 8, 1939.

The chief problem before us is that of getting the Americans home, and the burden of this is carried by Breck Long [Special Assistant in Charge of the Special Division] and his Division. What the public does not realize is that American vessels which were to have left early this week have not yet sailed as the crews have been striking for higher wages, war bonuses, and assurances that non-American members would not be impressed into military service. Kennedy and Bullitt are on the phone several times a day. They offer the helpful suggestion that the President "cancel the first papers of any seaman who will not sail," as if the President had a legal power to do any such thing. Breck Long asked Bullitt to obtain assurances from the Foreign Office in Paris that they would not seize any French-born member of the crew, and Bullitt flatly refused to carry out "any such insulting instructions". . .

The war news looks none too good. The Germans are rapidly approaching Warsaw, and I don't see how the city can be saved. In the meantime the continuous headlines of allied victories in the west seem to have no substance, and I am very much afraid the public will soon disbelieve what it hears from London.

We had a session in Judge Moore's office to discuss what should be done about limiting the use of the Trans-Atlantic Clipper to the point where any war risks would be minimized.

Later we had a most interesting session in the Secretary's Office — Hornbeck, Ballantine [Joseph Ballantine, Assistant Chief of the Division of Far Eastern Affairs], Henderson [Loy Henderson, Assistant Chief of the Division of European Affairs] and myself — to discuss the possibility of a Russian-Japanese non-aggression pact which has been haunting us. We all agreed that on the general subject there was no "news" to be obtained, and that we would have to rely on our powers of deduction. . .

What had seemed "a shadow war" in its first days soon took the solid form of disastrous defeat. By the second week of September the Polish army was no longer an organized force. Inferior numbers and equipment gave way before the Blitzkrieg tactics of the Germans. When on September 17 the Soviet Union invaded Poland on the eastern front, the complete and imminent collapse of Polish resistance could not be doubted.

President Roosevelt, upset by the quick rout of Poland, pressed his efforts to obtain the revision of the Neutrality Act. On the day when war broke out he and Secretary Hull agreed that a special session of Congress should be called to consider such revision. And on September 12 Mr. Messersmith sent for Pierrepont Moffat to inform him that the President would issue a call for a special session "very shortly, that Senator Byrnes would lead the fight for the repeal of the embargo and that Savage [Carlton Savage, Assistant to the Counselor], Dunn, and myself were charged with preparing all necessary and available material." [36]

Monday, September 18, 1939.

Today was a dark day ushered in by news of the sinking of the British aircraft carrier "Courageous" and continuing with reports of added Bolshevik gains in Polish territory.

The Polish Government having now fled to Rumania the question arises as to what to do with Biddle. Presumably the Polish Government will move to France and set itself up there as a government in exile, somewhat as did the Belgian Government during the last war. Our theory is that Biddle should for the present follow the government to France. Whether we will keep an Ambassador residing near a government which is established in a third state is a matter for future consideration and Biddle has been told not to commit himself as to the permanence of any plans he may make. . .

We had a discussion in the Secretary's office as to whether or not we should apply the embargo against Soviet Russia because of her invasion of Poland. The consensus of opinion was that we could well wait a day or two. The main difficulty confronting us is that Russia's action in occupying Polish territory is so similar to Japan's

[36] Moffat diary, September 12, 1939.

action in occupying Chinese territory that it will be hard to explain why we consider one a belligerent and not the other. . .[37]

The main business of the day, however, was a consideration of what should be contained in the President's message to Congress on the repeal of the embargo.[38] The President outlined what he had in mind and asked Berle to prepare a draft. This draft did not prove satisfactory to the Secretary who feels that a single false step might lose the whole battle. The Secretary then prepared a counterdraft which to my mind was too defensive in that the greater portion of it repelled possible arguments against the repeal of the Act instead of advancing arguments in favor of its repeal. Furthermore, neither draft to my way of thinking offered a substitute program designed to keep us out of war which the Administration could emphasize as a safeguard. The Secretary asked several of us to prepare drafts which we could consider tomorrow morning. Inasmuch as we only have until three o'clock tomorrow afternoon this did not seem a very orderly procedure; however, along with several others I ran off a very rough draft which I then took down to Berle, suggesting that in a revision of his draft he might include the points I mentioned and take out certain paragraphs which might be construed either as "I told you so," or as advising the Senators how to carry on their debate. . .

Tuesday, September 19, 1939.

It is quite clear that the President and the Secretary do not see eye to eye as regards the tactics to be used in urging the repeal of the embargo. The President favors a mere presentation case; the Secretary feels that the essential arguments should be uttered by the President as only in this way can they get the widest publicity. If the vote were to be held today the Administration would win hands down, but the opposition by labeling itself the "Peace Party" is rolling up considerable strength. The battle can be won unless false tactics are used. We had one more meeting shortly before lunch, and Berle agreed to prepare some form of a composite draft. As a

[37] Cordell Hull has written in his *Memoirs*, I, 685, that he and the President decided not to apply the Neutrality Act to Russia, because they "did not wish to place her on the same belligerent footing as Germany, since to do so might thrust her further into Hitler's arms."

[38] For a discussion of the problem of the revision of the Neutrality Act consult Langer and Gleason, pp. 218–235.

matter of fact, this is waste motion as Berle's draft of yesterday was
sent to the White House at midnight, and the President has been
writing his own speech most of the day. . .

Wednesday, September 20, 1939.

. . . The German Government has apparently served an ultimatum on Rumania that in addition to interning Marshal Smigly-
Rydz it should intern the entire Polish Government. If this demand
is not complied with Germany threatens to invade Rumania. The
French and British who want to see the Polish Government established in France have protested violently at what they consider a
"breach of international law." Rumania's apparent willingness to
agree they characterize as a "despicable betrayal." Bill Bullitt has been
so excited that he has been telephoning the White House. He virtually persuaded the President to protest to the Rumanian Government.

The Secretary sent for several of us, who had already gone home,
to discuss the situation. I urged against any protest on the following
grounds:

Let us assume that we protest; let us assume that as a result of
our protest Rumania allowed the Polish Cabinet to depart; let us then
assume that as a result Germany invaded Rumania. What would be
our obligations to Rumania? Would we not have injected ourselves
into the European fight, would not the immediate effect be to endanger the embargo repeal and the ultimate effect to involve us in
war? In any event, these considerations prevailed and the upshot after
a telephone talk between the President and the Secretary was to ask
Gunther [Franklin Mott Gunther, American Minister to Rumania]
informally to inquire what was the attitude of the Rumanian Government toward this reported German demand.[39]

---

[39] On September 28, 1939, Secretary Hull asked Mr. Gunther to inform the
Rumanian Government "that the Rumanian treatment of President Mościcki of
Poland and other members of his Government who had sought refuge in Rumania
was being anxiously watched." President Roosevelt on October 19 sent the Secretary
of State a memorandum asking him to have Mr. Gunther contact King Carol and indicate that the United States would gladly receive Mościcki. Mr. Gunther replied
that the King had been sympathetic, although Minister Cretzianu had earlier told him
that "Rumania could not afford to provide Germany or Russia or both an excuse to
invade Rumania or otherwise make it difficult for her." President Mościcki was
released on Christmas Day. For a more complete discussion of the attitude of the
President and the Department in this matter, see Hull, I, 686–687.

Thursday, September 21, 1939.

The President today went before Congress and made his speech in support of the repeal of the embargo. The speech followed in general the lines of the drafts we had been working on, but had been completely rewritten by the President in person with considerable change in order and in emphasis.[40] To my mind the speech was not the President's best effort. There was too much "I told you so" in it and some of his arguments were a trifle thin. However its weaknesses were amply covered by the excellence of his delivery which was fully as impressive as ever in the past.

To me the interesting thing was not the speech but the points at which Congress applauded. Apart from the obvious places like the President's determination to keep the country out of war Congress applauded every time the President referred to keeping ships out of danger zones. Although he did not use the phrase he made it amply clear that he was prepared to support cash and carry, and there was no doubt but that cash and carry was immensely popular with the Congressmen who had just returned from their districts. There was one minor incident when the President said that he did not feel he must ask for additional powers, a statement at which there was audible laughter throughout the House. . .

Monday, October 2, 1939.

At the Secretary's request I drafted the statement for him to use at press conference to the effect that mere occupation of territory did not destroy a state and that the United States continued to regard the Government of Poland as in existence despite the seizure of its territory. There is a provision in the constitution of Poland (it turned out to be a very wise one) that in time of war the President of Poland could designate his successor. The Polish Ambassador has informed us that the former President of Poland designated Raczkiewicz [Wladyslau Raczkiewicz, former President of the Polish Senate] as his eventual successor while he was still on Polish soil. This keeps the

[40] For the text of the speech, see Roosevelt, *Papers and Addresses, 1939*, pp. 512–522. A discussion of the preparation of the drafts of the President's message in the Department of State can be found in Hull, I, 682–684. The policy of the Department as described by Secretary Hull was that the embargo should be repealed, that American citizens should not be allowed to travel on ships of belligerents, that American-owned ships should not go into the combat zone, and that there should be a cash-and-carry provision regarding arms and other materials of war.

legal continuity intact. The statement did not contain the phrase "we do not and never will recognize the fruits of aggression"; for the present it accomplishes quite the same purpose but does not bind our hands for the future.[41]

By the time I had, at the Secretary's request, obtained the approval of Hackworth, Judge Moore, Berle, Breck Long, and Stanley Hornbeck it was noon. The Secretary obtained the President's approval by telephone and gave it out at press conference.

At eleven o'clock we had a meeting in Breck Long's office with the Navy and the Maritime Commission concerning the note given us Saturday by the German Chargé d'Affaires asking that American shipping avoid certain suspicious acts in dangerous waters.[42] Every member of the Navy and Maritime Commission voiced the opinion that the note was proper and the requests reasonable. Nevertheless, the press played it up with banner headlines, "Germany Warns American Shipping." [43] One cannot help wondering what forces are at work trying to push us nearer and nearer to war. . .

During the latter part of September and early October the Soviet Union attempted to effect a settlement with the Baltic States and Finland, which would insure the security of the northwestern Soviet borders. Estonia, Latvia, and Lithuania were forced to accept mutual assistance pacts, and Finland was invited on October 5 to send representatives to Moscow "to discuss concrete political questions." The Helsinki Government, however, did not intend to accede to Soviet demands. On October 11 the Finnish delegates reached Moscow with instructions, which permitted little compromise with the Soviet proposals.

In Washington the Ministers of the Scandinavian countries tried to obtain the aid of President Roosevelt and the Department of State in averting the crisis. On October 10 the Swedish Minister, Mr. W. Boström, called on Secretary Hull, and the following day he talked with Pierrepont Moffat.

Wednesday, October 11, 1939.
    . . . The Swedish Minister called.

[41] The statement which the Secretary issued said, in part, that Poland "is now the victim of force used as an instrument of national policy. Its territory has been taken over and its Government has had to seek refuge abroad. Mere seizure of territory, however, does not extinguish the legal existence of a Government." U.S. Department of State, *The Department of State Bulletin*, October 7, 1939, p. 342.
[42] The Chargé d'Affaires had protested that neutral vessels were trying to avoid stopping for search by the German navy.
[43] This is part of a headline from *New York Times*, October 3, 1939, p. 1.

He said that he had seen the Secretary of State just before the latter left for New York yesterday noon and had spoken to him confidentially as follows:

"The Swedish Minister has, upon instructions from his Government, on October 10th 1939 drawn the attention of the United States Government to the difficult situation which will arise in case, in connection with the Russian Government's invitation to negotiations with Finland, demands will be presented which seriously threaten the integrity and independence of Finland."

The Secretary had replied that he feared American intervention at Moscow might do more harm than good.[44]

In the course of the afternoon the Minister had called on the President and had left him a note from the Crown Prince of Sweden, in which the latter urged the President to use his influence in Moscow to counteract any possible attempts of an aggressive nature toward Finland. The President had replied that his influence in Moscow was just about zero. To this Mr. Boström had answered that his influence could not be zero anywhere in the world and again urged that he send a message to Stalin.

The President apparently replied that he might be willing, after consulting with the Secretary of State, to send a message to Mr. Steinhardt [Laurence Steinhardt, American Ambassador to the Union of Soviet Socialist Republics] directing him to tell Molotov that it was the President's hope that Russia would not make war upon Finland.

Mr. Boström apologized for making any observation, but he thought Molotov would reply that the U.S.S.R. had not made war on Estonia or Latvia and had no intention of doing so on Finland. The Minister asked if he could not phrase his message to the effect that the United States hoped that the U.S.S.R. would not make any demands upon Finland which would seriously threaten the integrity and independence of that country.

The President agreed in principle, and said he would talk it over with the Secretary just as soon as the latter returned to Washington.

Later in the day the Finnish Minister made a similar appeal to the

---

[44] Secretary Hull felt that intervention by the United States might alienate the Soviet Union, which he hoped would pull away from Germany at some time in the future. Secondly, he thought an American message might aggravate the Soviet Union still further against Finland. Hull, I, 702.

President from the President of Finland, and, according to Mr. Bos-tröm, the President was even more prepared to send such a message.

Mr. Boström asked me to bring this to the Secretary's attention immediately upon his return and to let him know if and when a message were sent.

No sooner had the Swedish Minister left than Judge Moore sent for me to say that he had been at the White House and that the President had dictated in the rough the text of a message to Kalinin [Mikhail Kalinin, President of the Praesidium of the Supreme Council of the Soviet Union] which he did not want sent out before the Sec-retary's return. The Judge and I cleaned up the language a little and awaited the Secretary's return about two o'clock. It was obvious that the Secretary did not like the idea at all, fearing that for the President to intervene in one case would create a precedent that would come home to plague us. However, in view of the President's commitments the utmost he could do was to suggest certain drafting changes. The way it worked out was that we sent over two alterna-tive paragraphs for the President's choice. He got the Secretary on the telephone and together they agreed on some wording. The Secre-tary felt very strongly that we should not tell the Swedes and Finns what we had done even though they were calling up every fifteen minutes to inquire whether the telegram had been sent. The press was after them and the Norwegian Foreign Minister added fuel to the flames by saying that he could not deny that plans were afoot for the United States, Norway, and Sweden to intervene at Moscow. When, therefore, the Swede and the Finn caught up with me in the evening at my house I said that I could not answer their question but that I could tell them a parable: namely, that if a message had in fact been sent along the lines that they hoped for, its effect would be in inverse proportion to the number of people who knew it at home, or even among our friends abroad. The Swedish Minister asked if I had any objection to his telegraphing home that he had reason to believe that a message had been sent. I said he could telegraph home what he wanted provided: (a) he emphasized that we hoped the whole sub-ject would be treated with strict secrecy, and (b) that he was tele-graphing his own conclusions and deductions. . .[45]

[45] The President's message was sent on the evening of October 11. Roosevelt ex-pressed the hope "that the Soviet Union will make no demands on Finland which

In a speech on October 6 Hitler made vague statements which seemed to indicate that he would consider making peace.[46] He had given his "outstretched hand." A day later Alexander Kirk, Chargé d'Affaires in Berlin, relayed to Secretary Hull "the thought" which one of the Chancellor's intimates had expressed that President Roosevelt might respond to Hitler's speech by sending a message encouraging him in his peace offer and trying to draw him out on specific bases for the peace settlement.

Other cables were received in the Department of State urging the President to mediate.[47] On October 7 Pierrepont Moffat had a long talk with Mr. Berle "over whether there existed any possibilities of the President's offering mediation. The conclusion we reached in our own minds was that the time was not ripe for mediation but that it might be ripe for setting forth certain broad principles on which ultimate peaceful relationships would have to be built which would at least focus the direction of people's thinking."[48] Two days later the Secretary sent for Mr. Moffat "to run over one or two points in the European situation, particularly in relation to the rumors from abroad that the President will be encouraged to mediate. Mr. Hull is very fearful that at the present stage an offer on the President's part to mediate would (a) not be successful; (b) would prove embarrassing to England and France, and (c) would tend to embroil us in Europe."[49]

The sentiment in the Department of State was already forming against the idea of making a positive move toward peace, when on October 12, 1939, William Rhodes Davis came to the Department to talk to Mr. Berle and Mr. Moffat. Davis had just returned from a trip to Germany and Italy. His business, with which a continuation of the war would seriously interfere, was selling Mexican oil to Germany.[50] Through his business connections he was in touch with leading figures in Germany, particularly Dr. Joachim Hertslet, who had banking and industrial connections. Dr. Hertslet had contacted Goering and this led to an invitation to Davis to visit Germany. On September 15, 1939, Davis had discussed his plans with President Roosevelt. Later Davis was granted a passport to make the trip. Twice he talked to Goering, who suggested that President Roosevelt assume the role of mediator and arrange a world conference, where a "new order" could be established, which would be the basis for

---

are inconsistent with the maintenance and development of amicable and peaceful relations between the two countries, and the independence of each." Roosevelt, *Papers and Addresses, 1939*, pp. 538–539.

[46] Adolf Hitler, *My New Order*, ed. Raoul de Roussy de Sales (New York: Reynal & Hitchcock, 1941), pp. 721–757.

[47] These are discussed in Hull, I, 710–711.

[48] Moffat diary, October 7, 1939.

[49] *Ibid.*, October 9, 1939.

[50] See Josephus Daniels, *Shirt-Sleeve Diplomat* (Chapel Hill: The University of North Carolina Press, 1947), pp. 251–253, for further information about Mr. Davis.

lasting peace. Although Goering said that this new order would mean "the complete liquidation of the Versailles system," he promised that Germany would allow a new Polish and a new Czechoslovak government to be set up.[51]

When Mr. Davis came to the Department to report on October 12, Mr. Moffat met with him. In his diary he wrote: "From three to half-past four I was attending an interesting session in Berle's office for the purpose of having two independent *aide-mémoire* written up for the record."

October 12, 1939.

At your [Adolf A. Berle] request I submit the following account of the meeting this afternoon between Mr. W. R. Davis, Mr. [Walter A.] Jones, you, and myself.

Mr. Davis opened the conversation by saying that the trip he had just made to Italy and Germany, while a hard one, had been worthwhile. He had spent the last day and a half in preparing two full reports for the President, one setting forth an account of his talks, the other setting forth his conclusions and prophecies. The first report was ready and was read over hastily by Mr. Berle and Mr. Moffat; the second report was brought into the room by Mr. Davis' secretary during the conversation but was not examined.

After reading the report Mr. Berle said that he had a few preliminary observations to make. He made these for the purpose of keeping the record straight. They were based on a hasty reading only and it might be that the impressions he had gained would not be borne out by a more careful study of the document. Nevertheless, said Mr. Berle, he had gained the impression that Mr. Davis had stated in Germany that the President had asked him to undertake the trip to Italy for the purpose of ascertaining the views of certain Germans, whereas in reality Mr. Davis' trip had been planned before he had even seen the President. Mr. Davis agreed that Mr. Berle's point was well taken. In the second place Mr. Berle pointed out that Mr. Davis apparently quoted the President as judging the motives which impelled England and France to enter the war whereas in reality he had impugned the motives of no nation. Mr. Davis replied that he thought that a careful reading of the transcript would show that he had not quoted the President but had given his own impres-

[51] Charles Callan Tansill, *Back Door to War* (Chicago: Henry Regnery Co., 1952), pp. 559–560.

sion of what he believed the President to think. In the third place, continued Mr. Berle, he gained the impression that Mr. Davis quoted the President as being willing to offer himself as a mediator if he could satisfy himself as to certain facts whereas in reality the President had made it clear in his talk with Mr. Davis that at most he would consider the possibility of mediation should he be asked officially by interested governments. Mr. Davis replied that his observations to the second point held true here also and that his plan throughout his talks had been to give impressions about the President's views only when he felt that it would elicit further information from the Germans with whom he was talking.

Mr. Davis then gave the story of his trip. On arriving in Italy he was met by representatives of the German army, navy, secret police, and import-export organization. He was not satisfied that they had sufficient authority to commit themselves or their government. After some delay arrangements were made through Mussolini and Ciano for Mr. Davis to proceed to Germany. There was not time for him to get his passport amended valid for Germany, but he felt the importance of the trip justified him in overlooking this technicality. He started by train with H [Dr. Hertslet] but left the train at Munich, where he was met by some German officers who took him to a plane. The plane, instead of proceeding to Berlin, took him to the first airfield east of Saarbrucken. He remained twenty-four hours on the front, slept underground in the Siegfried Line, witnessed some desultory artillery firing between the Germans and French and considerable fraternizing between the troops, et cetera. From the west front he was flown to Danzig, then to Warsaw, where he said the damage had been greatly exaggerated, then over the part of Poland held by the Russians and back to Berlin. He stayed with Hertslet at his house.

During the course of the next three or four days he had three talks with Goering, the details of which were set forth in his report to the President.

Mr. Berle remarked that when Mr. Davis had seen the President, he indicated that he had information that Goering might be planning to take over the government in Germany and that there might even be a *coup d'état* engineered by the army. Mr. Davis remarked that while one heard an occasional rumor that Goering might take over the government and Hitler revert to the position of Party Leader, this did not seem probable. The General Staffs of both army and navy were working closely together and were united in their opposition to Ribbentrop and his policies. Goering too hates and detests Ribbentrop, largely because Hitler relies on him to such an extent, but will do nothing to force Ribbentrop completely out of the picture unless absolutely necessary. Goering appreciates that Hitler so much incarnates the German will and that he is so much the core around which the German national effort is built that his removal would spell disaster for Germany during a war. Despite all this Goering is the strongest man in Germany and in the last analysis what he really wants goes. Goering, according to Mr. Davis, is determined to have peace if peace can be had. He feared that a situation had now arisen which might be described as a deadlock between Hitler and the Allies. Neither can publicly back down. If peace is not arranged then war will occur that will devastate and exhaust Europe and destroy international capitalism. Only America can prevent this, and now that the President knows what the Germans would or would not accept, "the United States can write the ticket." Mr. Berle remarked that it was a bit unusual for a neutral to "write a ticket" but Mr. Davis brushed this aside with the remark that the President could, if he would, force peace on Europe.

The talk then reverted to Mr. Davis' return via Italy. He said that Germany wanted him to send large quantities of oil to Germany via Italy. He said that he would not consider this partly because in a short time it might be illegal, partly because England, knowing Italy's normal consumption, would not allow greater quantities to enter Italy during the duration of the blockade. He is, however, considering setting up a refinery in Italy to cover Italian, Swiss, and Yugoslav needs. The Italians are not helping the Germans to obtain oil because they are anxious to sell as much as possible to England and obtain strong currency for their own purpose. Germany, Mr. Davis said, is now building pipe lines from the Rumanian oil fields to the navigable part of the Danube River which will do away with a great deal of lighterage and transportation by tank cars. These pipe lines should be completed in about four months. Mr. Davis' friend Hertslet is trying to prevail on the Italians to give the Germans greater economic collaboration and is remaining in Rome.

At the conclusion of the talk Mr. Berle reverted to the three points in Mr. Davis' report which were discussed at the beginning of the conversation, and Mr. Davis reiterated the same replies he had previously made.[52]

When the Arms Embargo was repealed in the House of Representatives on November 2, 1939, Mr. Moffat wrote: "I cannot help feeling that the British may draw false conclusions from the size of the vote and think they have us in their pocket. As it is, we are getting more frequent indications of the cavalier way in which they are treating us in the blockade. They are trying to blacklist American shipping companies which carry cargo for firms they have blacklisted in South America. They are holding up cables to American businessmen just long enough to see that a British company gets the contract, et cetera."

The problem of neutral rights in wartime, which had caused so much bad feeling between the United States and Great Britain during the First World War, again assumed serious proportions in 1939. Contraband lists, blacklists, and stoppage on the high seas complicated the daily work of the Department. Although there was no intention of allowing British-American relations to reach the point of bitterness achieved under Wilson, Pierrepont Moffat reported the slogan of some in the Department had become: "No help to Germany but no Dominion status for ourselves."

Monday, November 6, 1939.

The better part of the day was spent in a series of conferences in the Secretary's office.

The first one, which took up over two hours, dealt with the pros and cons of allowing the British to set up a navicert system in the United States. A navicert is a form of commercial passport which is issued by the British to a shipment destined for a neutral when the British have satisfied themselves that the consignee will not reship to Germany. As the system grows, shippers will only take navicerted cargo in order thereby to shorten the delays at Kirkwall [Scotland] and other blockade stations. As a result, it is open to considerable abuse on the part of the British. For instance, they can, while apparently granting or refusing navicerts on the basis of bona fides of the consignee, actually refuse it because they do not like the American vendor and thus work a form of concealed black list. At the meeting

[52] Mr. Berle's account of this meeting coincides with Mr. Moffat's. On October 13, 1939, Mr. Berle sent his report of the Davis conversation to President Roosevelt. Berle diary, October 13, 1939.

the Legal Adviser's office protested strongly that we should oppose the system, arguing (1) that it enabled the British to control American exports — something which even the Federal Government only did in time of emergency, (2) that it was an infringement of our sovereignty, (3) that it would discourage other neutral powers from making satisfactory terms with regard to rationing with Great Britain, et cetera. The rest of us felt that there was no violation of sovereignty involved, that it was not the system but the abuse of the system which we should fight, and that there was nothing we could do about it anyway. We accordingly recommended that we tell the British that we had no comments to offer, that the matter was one between themselves and American shippers, but that we reserved all our rights should any abuse develop. The upshot was that a memorandum was to be prepared representing the majority view which would be passed at a further meeting tomorrow. . .

Wednesday, November 8, 1939.

Derek Hoyer Millar [Frederick Hoyer Millar, First Secretary] and Foster [J. G. Foster, First Secretary] came down from the British Embassy on a series of matters:

(1) The British Embassy had received a telegram from London pointing out that Kirkwall was now in the combat area and that American ships under our law could no longer put in there voluntarily for examination. They wished to remind us that our law could not estop them from carrying on the war, and that their rights as belligerents under international law took precedence of other considerations. They therefore reserved the right to take American ships bound for Bergen into Kirkwall for examination. They wondered if we could not write in our regulations a provision exempting from penalty American ships which were taken into Kirkwall as a result of legal compulsion. Mr. Hickerson [John Hickerson, Assistant Chief of the Division of European Affairs] and I laughed gently at the use of the word "legal," but seriously speaking said that we were not impressed by the suggestion. . . Mr. Hickerson and I said that we hoped very much that they would be as careful as possible about taking American ships into Kirkwall (1) for the legal reason that if they did so and the ship was subsequently sunk in the combat area, there would be a valid legal claim against Great Britain

for the entire loss; and (2) more important, that it would probably raise an amount of public resentment here out of all proportion to the cargo involved. . .

After Hoyer Millar and Foster left, we had a meeting in the Secretary's office with regard to the black list. One idea was to try and obtain now a pledge from the British that there would be no indirect black list in the Western Hemisphere. In other words, that while there was no objection to stopping British firms from dealing directly with black-listed firms, there would be no extension of the black list to American or Latin American firms whose only crime would be trading with other American or Latin American firms which had been black-listed. We have already had one disagreeable case where an official of the British Legation in Uruguay succeeded in taking away quite a lot of business from an American shipping concern merely because it carried from Uruguay to another American port cargo of a firm which they had black-listed. After some talk it was decided to go at the thing piecemeal; to call in Lothian, tell him the whole Uruguayan story, and say that if this sort of thing continued he would have all the Western Hemisphere on his ears, and see if the British could not be persuaded to volunteer a hemispheric exemption from indirect black-listing rather than to ask for it in so many words. . .

Wednesday, November 22, 1939.

. . . [We] had a long conference in Sumner Welles' office — Berle, Hackworth, Hickerson, and myself — to discuss what attitude we should take toward the new British plan to seize goods of German origin wherever found on the high seas. To extend the doctrine of continuous voyage to exports is without justification under international law. Furthermore, it harms the neutral nations who are carriers of such goods far more than it harms either Germany or ourselves. We all agreed that there was nothing we could do to stop it as the war, from Britain's point of view, had become a war to block every avenue of foreign exchange. On the other hand, we all felt that having preached the doctrine of respect for international law, to allow continued British infringements to go by default without protest would be very ill-advised. Probably, without getting into an argument, we shall base our protest on the needs of belligerents to allow the smaller neutrals to live. . .[53]

Wednesday, November 29, 1939.

The Finnish crisis moved rapidly toward a head today. The continued torrent of abuse that the Soviet press was pouring upon Finland passed the bounds of mere pressure tactics. We finally decided that some form of action was called for. Of all the possibilities suggested the one that appealed to us most was a public statement in which we offered our good offices. I had prepared a short draft which was accepted with one or two minor drafting changes. The Secretary felt that he must speak to the President, who was on his way by train from Warm Springs to Asheville. Connection was finally made, the President approved, and the statement was given to the press at three o'clock.[54] About 4.30 news came through that Russia had broken off diplomatic relations with Finland. At 5.30 came through the fiery Molotov speech,[55] and, to get ahead of my story, before the night was out the telephone rang and I was told that Russian troops were attacking Finland by land, sea, and air.

During the afternoon the Swedish, Norwegian, and Danish Ministers came down in a body to tell me of the solidarity of their Governments with that of Finland. By solidarity they apparently meant only deep sympathy. I read them the Secretary's statement, which had been released to the press some two minutes before. They were immensely pleased and could hardly wait to get back to their respective Legations to send off their telegrams. They asked me to tell the Secretary and Under Secretary that they had called and beat a hasty retreat. . .

[53] The protest which was delivered to the British Foreign Office on December 8, 1939, is printed in Jones and Myers, *Documents, 1940*, II, 707–708.

[54] This short statement said: "This Government is following with serious concern the intensification of the Finnish-Soviet dispute. It would view with extreme regret any extension of the present area of war and the consequent further deterioration of international relations. Without in any way becoming involved in the merits of the dispute, and limiting its interest to the solution of the dispute by peaceful processes only, this Government would, if agreeable to both parties, gladly extend its good offices." *Ibid.*, II, 384.

[55] In a midnight broadcast on November 29, 1939, Russian Foreign Minister Vyacheslav Molotov announced that diplomatic relations had been broken with Finland. He charged the Finnish leaders with bad faith, with an "irreconcilable attitude," and with "acting in the interests of foreign imperialistic war mongers." *Chicago Tribune*, November 30, 1939, p. 1.

Thursday, November 30, 1939.

A few minutes past nine this morning, the Secretary sent for Sumner Welles, Stanley Hornbeck, Jimmy Dunn, and myself, and said that we could not remain silent in the face of the Russian bombardment of Finland and that we should prepare a strong statement setting forth the views of this Government. Sumner Welles asked the Secretary if he did not feel that we should go much further and even consider the breaking of diplomatic relations with Russia. He argued that quite apart from the Finnish question, there was the chance of further German aggression, and still more, there was the chance of Russia and Japan coming to a working agreement to the detriment of China. He felt that a dramatic action of this sort would have a deterrent effect, would show the German public where we stood, and would give the extremists in Japan cause for a second thought. The Secretary was hesitant. He doubted whether a breach of relations accomplished its major purpose. He said that we would be riding high on the tide of popular emotion, that the action would be exceedingly popular at the time, but that the tide would recede and we would be left "holding the bag." The conference broke up as the Secretary and Sumner had to go to the station to meet the President, who was returning from Warm Springs.

Later in the morning, Sumner Welles sent for Stanley Hornbeck and myself to talk out his idea further. Stanley would not commit himself and rather annoyed Sumner because, whereas formerly he had said that a Russian-Japanese sticker was an impossibility, he had changed his mind without giving what Sumner thought were adequate reasons for the change. I told Sumner that I agreed with him that we were gaining very little from direct relations with Moscow at the moment, but I thought certain other angles should be thought through. In the first place, I did not favor encouraging the public impression that the maintenance of diplomatic relations with a nation was a sign of approval of its policies or even its form of government. On the contrary, I thought we needed diplomatic relations with nations "on the loose" even more than with the others. At least our Embassy in Moscow was giving us pretty good information as to what was occurring. If we broke relations, we would be in the same position as formerly where special pleaders, like Walter Duranty [Moscow correspondent of the *New York Times*] and others, had access to the White House and were able to give without fear of controversion a distorted picture of the situation. Further, if we should break with Russia now, the impulse would be almost irresistible to break with Germany and Japan at a later date, and soon we would find ourselves in a curious situation of quasi-isolation. I was in favor of giving Russia a pretty heavy jolt, but I was not sure that this was the best means to do it. Sumner, however, remained in favor of his original idea. . .

Sunday, December 31, 1939.

. . . Thus ends another decade. From the point of view of the world, it has been a pretty rotten one, starting with the financial smash and ending with a world war. From the point of view of the Pierrepont Moffat family, however, it has been a pretty good decade. We saved enough out of the wreckage to be able to live comfortably, even if careful budgeting is required. From the point of view of career, the advance up the ladder has been steady, and most of the time I have had exactly the work that I most coveted. From the point of view of health, we have all kept well, and the children have developed normally and happily. I might even say that they show signs of more than usual intelligence. There have been no losses in the family circle, except among the very old. May the next decade treat us as well. . .

Friday, January 5, 1940.

The Secretary sent for a few of us to discuss the attitude of the Department towards proposals for a loan to Finland. He took the position that on this count we should give no guidance to Congress. He felt that the isolationist group was lying low, waiting for the Administration to take a step which seemed at variance with the normal concepts of neutrality and would thereupon start attacking the Administration in full force. I gather from what Procopé tells me that the President feels otherwise, and if he does not actually take the initiative will personally encourage the leaders to do so. Two general schemes are afoot: the first, to reloan to Finland what she has repaid on her [World War I] loan, which would amount to about eight million dollars; the second is to loan her the sum she asks, which is sixty million dollars. As I don't anticipate we shall see the money again, I prefer the first, but suspect the second will go through.

The British have brought the *Mormacsun* into Kirkwall. The captain was under the following orders: if a British war vessel approached and its captain invited him to proceed to Kirkwall, he was to decline the invitation; if the captain thereupon ordered him to proceed to Kirkwall, he was again to decline, saying that it was against United States law to enter the combat zone; if, thereupon, his ship was boarded and a British officer took charge on the bridge, he was to offer no further resistance. We immediately telegraphed to Herschel Johnson [Counselor of the American Embassy at London] to make contact with the captain via the Consul at Edinburgh and get a full report of the facts. We then made public our note of December 14 in which we had warned the British that we would hold them responsible for loss or damage in case they forced one of our ships into the combat zone. . .[56]

Tuesday, January 16, 1940.

The Secretary sent for Feis, Pasvolsky [Leo Pasvolsky, Special Assistant to the Secretary of State], Dunn, and myself to tell us of his talk last night with Jesse Jones [Director of the Reconstruction Finance Corporation] and of the joint recommendations they were going to make to the President. The Secretary with his uncanny flair for political reactions, was convinced that even in a watered-down form a proposal to extend credits to Finland would meet with a very mixed reception in Congress. He felt that those who had been publicly advocating a loan were the vocal ones, but that the fear of becoming involved in the conflict through the extension of credit was very real, and he clearly did not want to give the opponents of the Administration a weapon on foreign policy with which to lead a political attack. After we left, he reluctantly agreed to see the Finnish Minister for a few minutes, and then went over to the White House to help draft a final text of the message with the President and Jesse Jones. It is clear that he does not like Procopé, whose ultra-emotional approach with the occasional "acts" he puts on annoys him.

The message went up to the House and Senate in a very diluted

[56] The text is in Jones and Myers, *Documents, 1940*, II, 710–711.

form — even more diluted than we gathered it would be — about noon, and immediately it unleashed a debate in the Senate which was exceedingly bitter.[57] About four o'clock Procopé came back, wringing his hands and pulling out his hair. He was in such a state of nerves that it was painful. He implied that the message was a great betrayal; he characterized it as a "tragic document"; he said that it could not have been written or even have had the approval of the President, et cetera. Calming down somewhat, he started off on another tack — "How can I explain this to my Government?" He said he must see the Secretary at once. The Secretary declined and asked me to give the pleasant message that as he had nothing further to contribute to the discussion he could not postpone any of his engagements to fit in the Minister. . .

Thursday, January 18, 1940.

. . . I asked the Soviet Ambassador to call this afternoon with reference to the questions he had put up to me on January 10. I began by reading him the memorandum I had prepared of our earlier talk, which he said represented the views he had expressed with complete accuracy.

I then told the Ambassador I had looked into the Wright Aeronautical Corporation's case.[58] I found that the request to exclude the Soviet engineers had originated in the War and Navy Departments.[59] It had nothing to do with the question of moral embargo, but arose

[57] President Roosevelt's letter of January 16 to the President of the Senate and the Speaker of the House said, in part, that "there is without doubt in the United States a great desire for some action to assist Finland to finance the purchase of agricultural surpluses and manufactured products, not including implements of war. There is at the same time undoubted opposition to the creation of precedents which might lead to large credits to nations in Europe, either belligerents or neutrals. No one desires a return to such a status.

"The facts in regard to Finland are just as fully in the possession of every Member of the Congress as they are in the Executive Branch of the Government. There is no hidden information; and the matter of credits to that Republic is wholly within the jurisdiction of the Congress." Jones and Myers, *Documents, 1940*, II, 390–391.

[58] In August 1939 the Soviet Government had signed a five-year contract with the Wright Aeronautical Company providing for the company's technical assistance in the construction of certain types of Soviet airplane engines. Fifteen Soviet engineers were to receive plans and survey construction in the Wright plant. The engines were to be manufactured in the Soviet Union. Moffat diary, January 10, 1940.

[59] Near the end of December 1939 the president of the Wright Company had informed the Soviet engineers that they would no longer be permitted to enter the Wright factory. *Ibid.*

from the fact that Soviet Russia was not in effect ordering engines from the plant while a large number of military engines were being produced in the plant for our own Army and Navy. I then read to the Ambassador the text of Articles XV and XIX of the Agreement between the Wright Aeronautical Corporation and the Stalin Plant of the U.S.S.R., according to which it was made abundantly clear that the United States Government reserved at all times the right to refuse to permit the technical representatives of the Russian firm to be stationed at or have access to the factories in question. The Ambassador argued that it was in effect destroying the value of the contract. I said that I agreed, but that the contract provided for this very contingency.

The Ambassador then said that it was clear that no legal right had been breached, but that it was destroying by that much more Soviet-American commercial relations.

He then inquired whether any *modus vivendi* had been worked out. I told him none, except that my understanding of the situation was that the Army and Navy might be prepared to grant day-to-day visits to foreigners to the factories which are made in connection with the actual purchase of American aircraft matériel. . .

The Ambassador then pointed out what he considered to be two glaring inconsistencies in American policy: (1) That while we were advocating a policy of nondiscrimination in all phases of international intercourse, we were at the very same time publicly advocating a policy based on discrimination. I replied that I admitted a certain inconsistency, but that we viewed the bombardment of civilians so seriously as to warrant a special attitude in regard thereto. (2) The second inconsistency alleged was that we were applying the moral embargo to the Soviet Union when in fact it was not engaged in bombarding civilian populations. The Ambassador went over the same ground as he had previously, to which I replied that this was purely a matter of opinion. We were guided by the reports from our own representatives in Finland, and I instanced the bombardment from Russian planes of the house at Grankulla previously occupied by Mr. Schoenfeld, the American Minister, which he alleged was nowhere near any conceivable military objectives.

The subject matter then veered to other matters. I told the Ambassador that whereas he had made various complaints against administrative practices in the United States, I had not at our last meeting brought up any complaints in return. However, there were four matters on which I did not feel that I could keep silent, as we regarded them all seriously:

(1) The first was the refusal of the Soviet authorities to allow Americans to travel from various parts of the interior of Russia to Moscow to consult the Embassy. He said this was the first he had heard of this and had difficulty in accrediting the report. I told him that it was only too true, and that I could at any time cite chapter and verse.

(2) The second complaint was a report received from the Ambassador that a formal censorship had been established and that open mail addressed to the Ambassador and members of his staff, in addition to being censored was now being withheld for approximately two weeks after its arrival at Moscow before being delivered.

(3) The third complaint was that on January 5, on trying to telephone Riga, Ambassador Steinhardt had been advised by the Director of the Telephone System that from now on only local calls would be accepted from the Embassy, and that long-distance might only be made on personal appearance in the central telephone station. I said that it was almost impossible to credit this news, and I did not believe for a moment that Soviet Russia would maintain this stand. I should hate to see the counsel of applying a tit-for-tat system prevail, and hoped accordingly that he could assure me shortly that the situation no longer held. On the other hand, it was clearly not the decision of an irresponsible subordinate, as the Ambassador had discussed the matter with the Director of the Telephone System. He promised to take up the matter at once.

(4) The fourth complaint I had to make was that despite our repeated inquiries he had not yet complied with our request to furnish the names of all Government employees in this country, including businessmen working for the Soviet Government under its special Government setup. The Ambassador made a long justification of his delay. . . He said that he would send us such of the list as was ready, and would complete it just as soon as was humanly possible. I said that we must ask for an immediate compliance with our request as we were already being subjected to considerable criticism and pressure.

The Ambassador then renewed his complaints about the treatment of Soviet citizens at the hands of our immigration authorities, which I assured him represented only a general tightening up rather than an anti-Soviet policy.

The Ambassador again said that he was not satisfied with our general policy and would return to this later. His parting shot was that whereas undoubtedly we had complaints against the Soviet authorities, he could match these with complaints against the American authorities; but that there was no discrimination against American business in the Soviet Union, whereas he maintained there was growing discrimination against Soviet business in the United States. . .

Friday, January 19, 1940.

The British action in stopping the Pan American Clipper and taking off foreign mail for censorship was under discussion most of the day. Judge Moore feels that no time should be lost in omitting Bermuda from the Clipper schedule. Sam Gates, the attorney of the Civil Aeronautics Authority, telephoned me to say that the Authority felt very much the same way, and that they were on the point of considering an amendment of the Pan American license to permit direct flights from New York to Horta and alternate flights on the way back. Of course, Gates pointed out, it would mean sacrifice of passengers as the pay load would have to be less on the longer flight. Juan Trippe [president of Pan American Airways] telephoned some time later from New York to say that his engineers had worked out a scheme for a return flight from the Azores to Puerto Rico. Trippe wants us to bargain with the British to obtain guarantees from them that they will not censor the westbound mail, in which case he would stop at Bermuda on the way back. My instinct is entirely against this, the more so as I don't believe the British would give such an undertaking. Still later in the day Burke [Thomas Burke, Chief of the Division of International Communications], who has been absent, returned, and thoroughly concurred in what was being done. Finally, I spoke to the Secretary, who gave his general approval and who, parenthetically, had thrown out the hint on his own in press conference that the omission of Bermuda would be the last resort. There thus seems pretty complete unanimity, and the great thing now is to obtain speed. . .

Saturday, January 20, 1940.

The report from London to the effect that the British are going to transfer their purchases of tobacco from the United States to Turkey is causing intense worry throughout the tobacco states. The Secretary has about reached a point where he wishes to call in the British Ambassador and say that while we have every appreciation of the fact that England at war must do certain things, none the less the extent to which she is diverting normal trade and the extent to which she is ignoring our American interests is disturbing to say the least and may create an adverse public opinion. After all, during the last war there was considerable bitterness of feeling which fortunately was eclipsed by a still stronger bitterness toward the Germans. Nearly everyone was in agreement along these lines except Herbert Feis who as usual spoke up in bitter opposition to any action on our part which would in any way embarrass England. His attitude is so extreme that Walter Hines Page [American Ambassador to Great Britain from 1913 to 1918] would have seemed a sturdy American by comparison. . .

Thursday, January 25, 1940.

. . . The press agitation against the British is growing steadily and has very much worried Lord Lothian. After appealing to Norman Davis for help — and Norman spent the better part of the day on the telephone urging an easing off of the pressure on the British, even though he agrees with our position — Lord Lothian came down to see Judge Moore and myself. The following is the memorandum of our talk:

The British Ambassador began by saying that he had been puzzled, if not somewhat hurt, by the recent publicity in the American papers indicating considerable irritation against the British on a variety of subjects. When the war broke out, Secretary Hull and he had agreed to try and deal informally with cases as they arose and, whenever possible, to dispose of them without the writing (and particularly without the publication) of notes.[60] The Ambassador had not been aware that so much irritation had existed, and he wondered if he

[60] On September 4, 1939, Secretary Hull had told Lord Lothian: "Let's simplify in every possible way the relations between our two countries as they may be affected by British interference with American commerce." Hull, I, 680.

had not been in some way at fault. Whatever the causes, "the heat had been turned on," and he was trying to see whether ways and means could not be found of easing the situation.

Judge Moore replied that there were, in fact, many causes of irritation, some justified and some growing out of an inadequate knowledge of the facts. A reading of the recent Senate debates, as well as conversations he had had with Congressmen, editors, et cetera, had convinced him that this feeling was widespread. Judge Moore instanced the feeling on tobacco where the North Carolina population was as pro-English as in any State of the Union, but where it felt its entire economic future to be jeopardized. He spoke of the situation in the south with regard to the purchases of lumber, where he felt that there had been considerable worry, but which was now being relieved by the sale of ships (specially earmarked) for its transportation.

Mr. Moffat stated that perhaps the Ambassador was asking for more fundamental reasons for the feeling that has grown up, not connected with individual commodities or individual disputes, but based on certain fears which, although not concretely expressed, were perhaps widely felt. In the first place, there was a general feeling that the United States had been particularly friendly to Great Britain, had even gone out of its way to give special forms of help, but that Great Britain had taken this friendship so much for granted, that she was giving more favorable treatment to countries which had not shown as friendly an attitude. A second cause was a fear that while Great Britain was bending all its energies toward pursuing a military war, it was at the same time entering into a series of commitments in its economic war which would have serious repercussions on American trade long after the war itself was over. Cases in point might be the agreements with Turkey, with the Argentine, et cetera. A third and more concrete fear was that in specific commodities there might be a change of taste on the part of the British consumer which would result in the permanent, not merely the temporary, loss of the British market.

The Ambassador said that this background was of real help to him. Of course, we knew the situation in which Great Britain found herself, struggling with all her resources against a powerful foe. The expenses of Britain's war efforts were rising by leaps and bounds. Everything that was not an immediate necessity to life or limb had to be subordinated to the purchase of direct war matériel. In fact, the greatest error which, in his opinion, the British and French were making was in not restricting much further the consumption on the part of their populations. For instance, he felt there should be severe rationing of food, clothing, and other forms of normal purchases. Total British purchases in the United States had risen sharply. Foreign exchange was limited, and every cent of it was being mobilized. Turkey, which was a necessary bastion in the east, had virtually blackmailed Great Britain. Most nonmilitary supplies which could be purchased elsewhere must be sought in alternative markets in order to save Britain's vital dollar exchange.

With this background, the Ambassador hoped that we would be more understanding of the failure of the British to come into the American market for nonessentials. He was thinking about setting forth this picture as cold-bloodedly as possible, and perhaps inviting the suggestions of the American Government as to how the British could proceed within the limits of their available exchange so as to cause the least damage to American economy. Judge Moore and Mr. Moffat both said that the more information this Government had available the better, but that no American Government official could choose between American products and assume the responsibility of robbing Peter to pay Paul.

The Ambassador then came back to the question of publishing notes, which he felt created a bad press, particularly as the Neutrality Bill had the paradoxical effect of removing counterbalancing causes of friction between the United States and Germany. Mr. Moffat said that in principle we agreed that publication was inadvisable, and it had only been when a number of problems were not settled that the different Divisions in the Department and the different Departments of the Government felt the time had come to make their stand public. At the same time, it was pointed out that while the British objected to the publication of our notes, the official spokesman in England had been commenting on the very points under discussion and not always in a way which had the happiest effect upon American psychology. A number of instances were mentioned. The Ambassador said that he was much impressed with the seriousness of the situation, and was already in telegraphic touch with his Government with a view to settling some of the points at issue.

Judge Moore said he thought that nothing would be more useful at the moment than for Britain to adopt a less rigid and more yielding attitude. On the matter of the censorship of Clipper mail at Bermuda, for instance, he wondered whether the advantages were worth the feeling that it had aroused. He feared that the British stand would even result in our having to route our Clippers by other routes, although it was very much to the interest of Britain to have speedy transatlantic mail service. The Ambassador agreed that the criterion should be: "Is a given course of action which is irritating to the United States absolutely necessary to win the war? If so, American public opinion cannot prevail; if it is merely a convenience and not a necessity, the British Government should definitely bear American reaction in mind". . .

Tuesday, January 30, 1940.

. . . Again most of the day was occupied with sale of Finnish arms. The Secretary has become more and more clear in his own mind that no surplus arms should be sold to Finland. This is going to be a body blow to the Finns, even though something *might* be salvaged by selling surplus arms to Sweden. At any rate, at the very moment the Secretary of State and the Secretary of War were agreeing that no surplus arms should be sold to any one, the President, through General Watson [Edwin M. Watson, secretary to the President], sent a message asking the War Department to hurry up in the matter of declaring some artillery surplus, and Secretary Morgenthau sent over word asking if the Army could not declare some seventy airplanes surplus in order that they might be sold to Sweden. The thing finally reached such a pitch that the Secretary of State telephoned the President, who agreed that arms could not, without danger, be sold to Finland, but suggested instead that there be inserted in legislation a provision that arms might be sold by the Government to "neutral European nations not engaged in hostilities." The Secretary thinks this was an addition the President would probably make to the Jesse Jones RFC Credit Bill; Joe Green [Chief of the Office of Arms and Munitions Control] and I think that he may have meant such an amendment to the bill authorizing the sale of arms and obsolete ships to Latin America. If the latter, Sumner Welles said he would fight it tooth and nail. Meanwhile, the Army doesn't want to sell supplies to anyone, and wants a conference between the President and the Secretaries of State, War, and Navy. To add to Finland's worries, Senator Harrison came out today opposing any form of credit to Finland and suggesting instead the floating of Finnish bonds on the public market. . .

The nations of Europe were now at war, but on either side of the Siegfried and Maginot lines the armies were immobile. This was the period of the "phony war."

It seemed to President Roosevelt that at this moment, before the fighting began in earnest, one last effort might be made to restore peace. With this in mind he suggested to Sumner Welles, in January 1940, that Welles go to Europe as the President's personal representative to discuss with the belligerents and Italy the possibilities of arranging a lasting peace.

On February 9, 1940, the country was informed that Mr. Welles was undertaking a mission to Europe:

> . . . This visit is solely for the purpose of advising the President and the Secretary of State as to present conditions in Europe.
> Mr. Welles will, of course, be authorized to make no proposals or commitments in the name of the Government of the United States. . .[61]

This diary is reconstructed on my return to Washington from very brief notes I jotted down at the time and from the few memoranda of conversations which I had time to dictate in full at our various Embassies.[62] It nowhere touches on Sumner Welles' conversations, which were and must in their nature remain secret.[63] But my own talks, for the most part with permanent officials of the countries visited, proved of more than passing interest. Moreover, there are few people during this war who have visited the belligerent capitals on both sides and have been able to make even superficial comparisons. So, for what it is worth, here goes.

[61] U.S. Department of State, *Department of State Bulletin*, II (February 10, 1940), 155.

[62] Mr. Moffat also wrote an acount, which he did not include in his diary, of the highly confidential aspects of the Welles Mission. Although a diligent search was made by the Moffat family and in the Department of State, no trace has been found of this second, more secret, manuscript.

[63] The substance of Mr. Welles' conversations with Count Ciano, Mussolini, Ribbentrop, Hitler, Goering, Chamberlain, Daladier, and others is given in Sumner Welles, *The Time for Decision* (New York: Harper & Bros., 1944), pp. 73–147.

We sailed February 17 on the "Rex." Our party consisted of Sumner Welles, as representative of the President; of myself, with the title of assistant; of Hartwell Johnson, as private secretary; and of Reekes, Sumner Welles' valet. . .

One sea voyage is much like another: it is time out in the march of life, and hence to be treasured. Suffice it to say here that there was no sense of strain, no feeling that war was being fought on the waters of the Atlantic, perhaps just beyond the horizon. We saw no ships from New York until within a few miles of Gibraltar.

February 23 [1940]. We were "invited" into Gibraltar, and the mails were removed. The passenger list was scanned, and one or two suspects were questioned, but none taken ashore. The cargo was covered by "navicerts" and was passed without trouble. In all, we were detained only three and one-half hours. The Italian Line "cooperates" with the British blockade, but the Italian Government resents the control, as we discovered later in Rome. The reaction of the Americans aboard varied from enthusiastic approval by Walter Lippmann (who is not only Anglophile, but an interventionist) to active rage on the part of others. It was the treatment of the mails that seemed to annoy more deeply than the treatment of passengers or cargo.

February 25 [1940]. Arrived at Naples — all the trappings of an official visit. Greetings by D'Ajeta the Secretary of Count Ciano. Correspondents and photographers. The red carpet. Three automobiles for a drive around the city and visits to one or two places of interest while waiting for our train. More red carpet. A private car on which a sumptuous tea was served. And finally a three hours' run through country of surpassing loveliness, past Gaeta (the port at which the Italian volunteers for Spain used to embark in the small hours of the morning), past the grim castle of Sermoneta, across the reclaimed Pontine marshes, and into Rome.

Bill Phillips, Ed Reed [Edward Reed, Counselor of the American Embassy at Rome], and Alan Rogers [Second Secretary of the American Embassy at Rome] had come to Naples to meet us. Their judgments about Italy on the whole coincided. They felt that the country was profiting to a reasonable degree from the war, but not so much as she had hoped. There was no shortage as yet of food, except for specialties like coffee and sugar. The key to the situation was coal. Clodius, for Germany, had put enough pressure on Italy to stop the delivery of war materials to England.[64] England was about to retaliate by stopping German exports of coal to Italy by sea. Italy needs more coal than can be supplied overland, and England could thus close down Italian industry. If this should happen, and hundreds of thousands should be thrown out of work, the feeling against England could grow very fast.[65] Meanwhile, however, the nation to a man wants to keep out of war. Mussolini, who had gained great popularity by preserving Italian neutrality, was again losing ground slightly. Mussolini was strongly pro-German; Ciano, anti-German, and believed by the English (I think wrongly) to be pro-Ally. Whatever happens, Italy sees dark days ahead: people are afraid of the currency, and are indulging in a buying orgy; gambling is rife, et cetera.[66]

At the hotel, we found messages from Kirk. He indicated that the Germans would talk to Sumner Welles more freely if he came to Berlin after London and Paris. The memory of Colonel House [Edward M. House, personal representative in Europe of President Wilson in 1914, 1915, and 1916] was still strong, and particularly his habit of repeating in London what he heard in Berlin. But the more we considered it, the less we liked the suggestion. Rumors are rife that Hitler will use Sumner Welles' visit to launch a peace plan. It will be bad enough if he does so while we are in Berlin; it would be far worse if he did so just after we had come from Paris and London.

February 29 [1940].

. . . We left for Germany at four o'clock. Switzerland was full of soldiers, but from the moment we got into Germany we no longer

[64] Karl Clodius, German economic expert for the southeast, had concluded a commercial agreement with Italy on February 24, 1940. Wiskemann, p. 193.
[65] On February 3, 1940, Great Britain had proposed the negotiation of a trade agreement with Italy. Italy had, however, refused to sell any war materials. The British in retaliation informed Italy that after March 1, 1940, they would confiscate the cargo of ships carrying German coal to Italy. Galeazzo Ciano, *Ciano's Diplomatic Papers*, ed. Malcolm Muggeridge, trans. Stuart Hood (London: Odhams Press, 1948), p. 335.
[66] For William Phillips' account of the Welles' visit to Italy see Phillips' book, *Ventures in Diplomacy*, pp. 261–262.

saw any troops. . . As dusk fell, not a house throughout the country-side lit up. It gave one at first the curious impression of a deserted countryside. . .

March 1 [1940]. Called on De With [Hendrik M. de With, Nether-lands Minister to Germany]. He is a changed man. Instead of the breezy, rather indiscreet friend of old times, I found a worried un-happy man. He sat in the middle of his drawing room and spoke to me in whispers. He trusts neither his servants nor the electricians who have examined his walls for dictaphones. He fears an attack on the low countries in the spring; he believes that all preparations are made, but that it will not come in March. He says that Germany is far stronger than the Allies realize; that she may be short on raw materials, but cannot be starved out. He doubts whether the régime will be overthrown, among other reasons because the opposition is made up of "amateurs." Nearly all the diplomats consort too much with the have-beens, the leftovers from the past. The result is false information and a false sense of values. Sir Nevile Henderson was particularly blameworthy in this respect. But though the Nazis are strong, they do want peace; if they don't get it, they will be willing to sacrifice two million men, conscious that the race can stand it, whereas they say the loss of a million Frenchmen would destroy France for all time. In conclusion, De With said that Hitler himself was not so bad, but that the men around him were *awful*.

I next went to see an old consular colleague of mine whom I had known in Australia, as I was anxious to have a talk with at least one representative from a typical middle-class milieu. It was not a cheery forty-five minutes. He, his wife, and I sat on straight chairs around a table in the middle of the room, directly beneath a chandelier; and after a few sentences of reminiscences, his talk became a gramophone record of German propaganda. This war, he claimed, was the war of the lower classes. The workman says, "We want peace, but we want to give the English a good kick first." Britain was the aggressor, et cetera. Then suddenly, "Why does America hate Germany so?" I told him as best I could that we didn't hate the Germans, but that our public opinion had been outraged by a policy whereby Germany merely took what she wanted from other nations by force or threat of force. He wanted to know if we would enter the war when (sic) the Allies were being beaten. I answered that no one could tell; we were an emotional people. Was the strongest influence in America still the international bankers? He went on with similar questions till I was able to get away. . .

March 4 [1940] — Monday.

The train passed through Karlsruhe about 8.30 A.M. and through Freiburg-im-Breisgau about 11. All morning we had been running well within the range of the French guns, but after Freiburg we ran for about fifteen miles right along the Rhine, looking across into France. For the most part, the tracks were laid along the slope of a hill, some 200 feet above the river, but in plain sight of the French trenches. Immediately below us, we could see the German communication trenches, artillery positions, camouflaged anti-aircraft guns, et cetera. Across the river we could clearly make out the advanced French positions, could see the strips of material placed alongside the roads to conceal the amount of traffic, et cetera. Not a gun was fired, not a disturbing sound broke the stillness. Men, women, and children were in the fields, or tying up the vines in the vineyards. Never have I had so strange a feeling of the unreality of this war. . .

March 5 [1940] — Tuesday.

At Lausanne. For the most part, rest and sleep. Arthur Sweetser [a director without section of the League of Nations] came over from Geneva to have tea with me. He is very depressed about the League. He says it is merely marking time. The belligerents are only interested in the war, and this is reflected in individual members of the Secretariat. The flavor (or was it pretense?) of an international outlook has disappeared. Morale in the Secretariat is at its lowest ebb. Avenol [Joseph Avenol, Secretary-General of the League of Nations] gives no leadership. Inspired by Bill Bullitt last December, he did strongly support the expulsion of Russia [67] and the extension of aid to Finland, but he has again lost interest and become utterly apathetic. Sweetser has no idea of his own future. He is living from day to day. He had just returned from England where he had seen Lord Perth, Lord Cecil, Sir Arthur Salter and other League enthusiasts. They had all

[67] The Union of Soviet Socialist Republics was expelled from the League on December 14, 1939.

grown hard and resented any limitation on Britain's "total war." "Let the neutrals beware" had become their policy. . .

March 7 [1940] — Thursday.

We reached Paris about ten o'clock, were welcomed by the appropriate officials at the station, and drove at once to the Ritz. At first blush, the city seemed its normal self. Traffic had not noticeably fallen off. Food was plentiful, and the French ideas of rationing made us smile: on meatless days, one can none the less eat duck, turkey, goose, birds, et cetera; on spiritless days, one cannot have a cocktail, but one can (and does) have a glass of champagne as an apéritif. Prices were high, but not in comparison with those in Berlin. The only outwardly visible signs of the war were the number of uniforms and the prevalence of sandbags.

While Sumner Welles was having his interviews with Lebrun [Albert Lebrun, President of the French Republic], Daladier, et cetera, I worked in the Chancery till six, and then went for a short walk. Ran into Walter Lippmann, who said that he had just completed a study of French finances and found them good. While we were walking, the extras appeared, announcing the tenor of the terms the Russians were offering Finland; and from then on for the next three days we heard of nothing but the northern war.[68]

Dinner at the Quai d'Orsay — just nine men in all: Daladier, Chautemps [Camille Chautemps, Vice Premier], Bonnet [Georges Bonnet, Minister of Justice], Champetier de Ribes [Auguste Champetier de Ribes, Under Secretary for Foreign Affairs], Léger [Alexis Léger, Secretary General of the Foreign Office], Coulondre [Robert Coulondre, former French Ambassador to Germany], Sumner Welles, Bob Murphy [Counselor of the American Embassy at Paris], and myself. Despite the fact that we all wore ordinary business clothes, we were met by footmen in knee breeches, and all the traditional formality and ceremony was observed.

The French talk freely, and for three hours they developed to us their immediate problems. Where they felt bitterness, they took no pains to conceal it. . .

---

[68] The Soviet Union had presented peace terms to Finland. A treaty of peace was signed between them on March 12, 1940. Jones and Myers, *Documents, 1940*, II, 392–397, contains the text of the treaty.

As to Finland, they all feared the game was up. The Russian terms, as published in the *Paris Soir*, were substantially accurate. The villain of the piece was Sweden. The French were all ready to send troops as soon as Finland sent out a final call for help. But now Sweden was pressing her not to issue such a call. The Allies had studied the possibility of landing an expeditionary force at Petsamo in Finland, but there were not enough docks. The troops must go through Norway and Sweden. But both countries were obsessed by fear of a German invasion and were not cooperating. They failed to realize that the Allies were fighting their battle. If the Finns capitulated, the French Government would be in danger; but even so, nothing could be done without the final call for help. At this point Léger intervened with a hymn of hate against neutrals in general. . .

With regard to Russia, all present felt that Stalinism had been on the verge of collapse and now had been saved by Hitler through the latter's pressure on Sweden, which in turn had been converted into Swedish pressure on Finland. Their estimate of Russian strength was as follows: troops good, matériel mediocre, officers bad, and organization deplorable. . .

March 10 [1940] — Sunday.

This morning we flew from France to England. The French authorities had put a large passenger plane at our disposal, and we were convoyed by three fast pursuit planes right up to the British coastline. The day was fair overhead, with a heavy ground mist; and as we rose into the blue, all we could see of Paris was the top of the Eiffel Tower rising above the clouds. A forty minute run brought us to Dieppe, where we received directions as to the course we should take and the height we should fly across the Channel. Another forty minutes and we were over Brighton, and then swung sharply to the west, and after a few miles straightened out and made for London. There Joe Kennedy, Cadogan [Alexander Cadogan, Permanent Under Secretary of State for Foreign Affairs], and a few others met us, and we rolled into London in comfortable time for lunch.

The afternoon was a warm spring day, and all London was spending its Sunday in the parks. There was a most noticeable absence of strain, and, apart from the prevalence of uniforms, little to remind me of the war. Joe Kennedy took us for a drive, showing us first the city and then motoring us to Kew Gardens where we took a walk. Meanwhile, Joe gave us his impressions, hastily garnered since his return [from the United States] four days ago. A recent by-election has given the Government great concern, inasmuch as an unknown candidate, unsupported by any political organization, won twenty-five per cent of the votes in his district running on a simple antiwar platform. The Government, however, is determined not only that it will not make peace with the present "gang" in Germany, but will not make peace on terms that would enable any German Government or the German people to say they had won the war. However, the English are honest enough to realize that a two-year war would bankrupt them, and the upper classes are bitterly worried. The lower classes are so convinced that war is not coming to them, that should there be an intensification, the effect on them would be even worse than had there been a "blitzkrieg" at the beginning. Anti-American feeling is growing fast. The press is becoming full of gibes, and our friends are growing sarcastic. Eden remarked to Kennedy, "We're going to be very polite to Sumner Welles; that will surely be appreciated in America." (Is this typical of his mentality?) They are resentful of our protests, partly because they don't like to be called down, and partly because they can't see why we aren't in this war with them. Joe Kennedy, who is as matter of fact as they make them, says, "For Christ's sake, stop trying to make this a holy war, because no one will believe you; you're fighting for your life as an Empire, and that's good enough."

March 11 [1940] — Monday
    . . . In the evening, R. A. Butler [Under Secretary of State for Foreign Affairs] (known as Rab Butler) gave me a dinner at "Claridge's." He tried to make it a cross-section of British officialdom, and had Dorman-Smith (Minister of Agriculture), R. S. Hudson (of the Board of Overseas Trade), the Duke of Devonshire (Under Secretary for the Dominions), Arthur Henderson (Labor M.P.), Admiral Godfrey (Chief of Naval Intelligence), Lord Dunglas (Private Secretary to the Prime Minister), et cetera. The dinner was excellent, and the talk good.
    Butler has an interesting mind. He is clever, quick, and intensely

ambitious. He is not afraid of expressing his own views, even when they are not orthodox. A good Parliamentarian. . .

As to the Great War, he said British public opinion was tending more and more to regard it as a struggle between Christianity and the forces of evil. He said the Christian revival was giving Halifax his chance, and that he alone could prevail against useless and unwarranted punishment of the German people, though it would probably be at the cost of his career.

R. S. Hudson, to whom I talked next, was a materialist of the most pronounced variety. He said categorically that no matter how much we might dislike it, England would not buy any quantities of American tobacco, and that any government that did would fall. If we were afraid of a change of taste on the part of the British smoker, we could buy the Turkish tobacco Britain had bought, provided this were additional to the purchases we normally made in Turkey. It might be cheap at the price for the American tobacco companies.

He then advanced a startling idea. He said that the debt question had done more to poison relations than any one other thing. He was therefore opposed in principle to further borrowing or even credits. On the other hand, Britain could not continue to finance the war alone, and when her exchange ran out, our economy would go bust. At that point, was there a possibility of our *giving* England and France a big sum, not because we loved them, not because we wanted them to win the war, but because only in that way could we protect our own economy? Wow, I'd like to see the reaction on Capitol Hill!. . .

About eleven o'clock the dinner broke up, and five of us went off for a while to "White's," the scene of the notorious gambling in the eighteenth century, and then still later to "Pratt's," where we drank beer and ate bacon sandwiches with the Duke of Devonshire and his son Hartington.

March 12 [1940] — Tuesday

. . . David Scott [British Assistant Under-Secretary of State] gave me a dinner at the Savoy to meet various Foreign Office officials and Lord Drogheda, of the Ministry of Economic Warfare. . .

It was not until a quarter to eleven that we got up from table. I then had my long-awaited chance for a talk with Lord Drogheda.

He is the type of Englishman who is outwardly polite, even friendly, but inwardly relentless and ruthless. He starts from the premise that what England wants is necessarily right, though out of amiability she can occasionally forego certain of her rights and privileges.

Lord Drogheda told me that he received nearly every day some seven or eight letters from the Embassy asking for the release of cargoes for American benefit, and that he had to reply in nearly every case that the request could not be granted and that no reasons could be given. I told him that this formula was causing a certain amount of resentment, and asked whether it was necessary to be as rigid in the type of reply given. He said that in ninety per cent of the cases reasons could be given with perfect propriety, but inasmuch as in the remaining ten per cent reasons could not be given, it was better to refrain from ever giving a reason. I asked him whether they could not at least say, when an application was refused, that the refusal had nothing to do with the standing of the American firm. He asked with a certain amount of astonishment whether I thought this would help. I replied that I did as there was an extraordinary fear throughout the United States that the British were using their contraband control to effect a disguised black list in the United States. Lord Drogheda replied that they were not doing this, although the temptation was exceedingly strong, and that it was very difficult not to be prejudiced against certain American firms.

We then got on the subject of "navicerts," and I told Lord Drogheda how upset we had been by the lack of candor on the part of certain members of the Embassy in Washington in putting into effect the "navicert" system, to which we said we would not object subject to four specified understandings, and only then turning around and telling us that they were not bound in any way by these understandings. Lord Drogheda said this was the first he had heard of the episode, and added that he could well see that this type of misunderstanding would create some bitterness. He regretted it enormously, as the last thing they wanted to do was "to hold out" on us. . .

I told him that the feeling on the mails went very deep. For instance, the censorship exercised by the British Government at

Bermuda was perfectly legal, as the planes voluntarily entered British jurisdiction; but was it wise? The British had used three reasons: (a) they said that information might thus reach the enemy; true, but anyone can radio-telephone freely to Germany; (b) the British said that money was being sent to Germany; true, but the amounts were small and, above all, Germany needed foreign exchange outside the country more than within; (c) the British talked of industrial diamonds; true, but these could easily be smuggled by individuals. In short, the question was not one of right, but of balancing the results against its effect on American public opinion. . .

Finally, I pointed out that in many matters the British were justifying their attitude by the phrase, "It is necessary to do this to end the war." Often this merely covered administrative conveniences. I was a little afraid that it was like raising the cry of "wolf, wolf," and that if it were used too frequently in a lighthearted sense it would not be listened to at some time when the British really meant it. . .

March 13 [1940] — Wednesday

. . . In the evening, I accompanied Sumner Welles to a small stag dinner given by Mr. Chamberlain at No. 10 Downing Street. Downing Street is at best unimpressive, but in the obscurity of a moonless blackout, it seemed like a sinister alley. The small doorway, and the long plain corridor leading toward the Cabinet Room do not prepare you for the delightful Georgian rooms upstairs. They are bright, spacious, and comfortable, and the dining room, with its heavy paneling and its portraits of Wellington, Nelson, Pitt, Fox, Salisbury, and others, is unquestionably one of the finest of its period.

There were only ten at dinner, five on each side of the table, with no one at the ends, which made conversation a trifle difficult as it always left one on each side to himself. Mr. Chamberlain sat in the middle with Joe Kennedy and Sir Archibald Sinclair (the Liberal leader) to his right, and Sumner Welles and Winston Churchill to his left. Opposite Mr. Chamberlain sat Sir Samuel Hoare [Secretary of State for Air], with R. A. Butler and me to his right, and Air Marshal Newall and Mr. Attlee (the Labor Party leader) to his left.

Conversation at table kept rigorously off the war. Sir Samuel Hoare reminisced about his days in Russia during the last war when he was British intelligence officer. We had many friends in common, chiefly among the Poles, and his comments on Slavic traits were in general well phrased and acute. He has a curious habit of repeating "yes, yes, . . . yes" in a low tone while you are speaking to him, which detracts from his impressiveness. He is still a potent force in the Conservative Party, but it is hard to envisage him as a leader in the House of Commons, much less throughout the electorate.

At coffee, the Prime Minister and Sir Samuel Hoare changed places at the table, which gave me a fifteen-minute chat with Mr. Chamberlain. We talked of Mrs. [Andrew] Carnegie and the Endicott family, the interplay of ideas and influence between England and New England and the like. He spoke of his old friend "Cotty" (Reverend Endicott Peabody), and was interested that he had been the schoolmaster of both Sumner and myself. Gradually the talk drifted to modern European history, to the mistakes that had been made after the last war, and, finally, to the personality of Hitler. At that point, Mr. Chamberlain described to me his flight and visit to Berchtesgaden. He said that Hitler throughout the talk was obsessed by one idea and one only: namely, the atrocities suffered by the Sudetens at the hands of the Czechs. Time was of the essence; speed imperative; hours counted. During the talk, an officer interrupted and handed Hitler a note (the episode was obviously prearranged) recording further atrocities. Hitler said he could hardly restrain action against Czechoslovakia long enough for Mr. Chamberlain to fly back to London to obtain approval of the plan he proposed. The man was dominated by one emotion: hurry. Yet, when they went out and Mr. Chamberlain admired the view of the countryside, Hitler's manner instantly changed. He wished Mr. Chamberlain might stay so that he could show him the beauties of the mountains thereabouts: a poetic note crept into his voice. Mr. Chamberlain said he had never forgotten the transition from one Hitler to the other.

After dinner I had a few words with Sinclair, and the conversation then became general. Everyone compared notes on how much sleep they needed, and it developed Winston Churchill gets into his pyjamas and goes to sleep for two hours every afternoon; as a result, he can do with about five and a half hours at night and is able to accomplish a vast amount of uninterrupted work after dinner and early in the morning. As to his writings, he says he always dictates his books; he has several people who prepare his material, which he reads in bed before getting up, and then puts what he has read into his words. On the other hand, he always writes his speeches. Mr. Chamberlain admitted he did the same.

Toward the end of the evening, Joe Kennedy brought the talk around to actualities, and under the cloak of horseplay was able to get across many unpalatable home-truths regarding Anglo-American relations. It was superlatively done. He made it very clear that certain things, such as taking our ships into the combat area, could not be done without risking a serious flare-up. Churchill protested, but in the end agreed. Sumner Welles had a chance to explain the background and the workings of the "chastity belt" around the Americas.[69]

Churchill kept doing more and more of the talking. He thought that no one understood better than he the mentality of the ordinary Britisher. "Take the workman, for instance. His back is up. He will stand for no pulling of punches against Germany. He's tough." "Well," replied Joe Kennedy, "if you can show me one Englishman that's tougher than you are, Winston, I'll eat my hat." And on this sally, the party broke up. . .

March 16 [1940] — Saturday.[70]

Sumner Welles saw the King and Ciano this morning. The latter suggested that we sail from Genoa the twentieth instead of from Naples the nineteenth, as he might by then have some further information of interest. Sumner Welles agreed, and we changed our plans accordingly.

Luncheon with the Phillipses at the Golf Club. This is the latest fad in Rome for the ultrasmart set. Ciano designed the clubhouse, and it is a great rendezvous for his immediate entourage. He is an open and rather disengaging snob. Countess Ciano refuses to set foot in the place, and the two of them are more and more pursuing their separate ways. . .

While Sumner Welles went to see Mussolini at six o'clock, I had a long talk with Myron Taylor [personal representative of the Presi-

[69] In the Declaration of Panama of October 3, 1939, the American Republics established a safety belt of from 300 to 1000 miles in width around Central and South America and North America south of Canada. In these waters the belligerents were warned against taking any naval action. Jones and Myers, *Documents, 1940*, II, 115–117.

[70] The Welles party had left England on March 14 and arrived in Rome two days later.

dent to the Vatican]. He told me that the Vatican did not believe the moment opportune for a peace conference. Reluctantly, it had come to the conclusion that there must first be a further trial of strength. Ribbentrop had given the impression that a vast German offensive on the western front was imminent, perhaps only a few days away; but this the Vatican discounted. It did look, however, for intensification of aerial and maritime war. Ribbentrop spoke with the assurance of final victory, but on this point had not carried conviction. The principal preoccupation of the Vatican at the moment was to keep Italy nonbelligerent: Italy stood a unit in wanting to keep out of war; but Mussolini firmly believed in the triumph of German might, and had neither forgotten nor forgiven the sanctions imposed on Italy by Great Britain. The essential was to keep Mussolini personally from losing his balance. . .[71]

[Washington] Tuesday, April 9, 1940.

As left off in my diary of yesterday, I was awakened by the telephone bell ringing at about half-past twelve to say that a message *en clair* had been received from Daisy Harriman [Florence Harriman, American Minister to Norway] that Koht [Halvdan Koht, Norwegian Minister of Foreign Affairs] had just told her that German ships were proceeding up the Oslo Fjord, were being fired on by the Norwegian batteries, and that Norway was now in a state of war with Germany. . .

At about half-past eleven, the Norwegian Minister called. He is not emotional like Procopé, and was consequently, if anything, a more tragic figure, and what he said carried more weight. He confirmed that the Germans had taken Bergen and other Atlantic ports, though how they were able to do so in the face of the British blockade and the presence of British warships he was unable to understand. He pointed out that Norway could at best put up merely a *pro forma* resistance. In the first place, the German troops were admirably prepared and equipped, and were not "inefficient" like the Russians. In the second place, the Norwegian army was small and incapable of a prolonged effort. . .

[71] Mr. Moffat and Mr. Welles sailed from Italy on March 20, 1940. They landed at New York eight days later. Moffat diary, March 20, 28, 1940.

Saturday and Sunday, April 27 and 28, 1940.

. . . In the late afternoon the Secretary telephoned me to say that the British Ambassador had been in to see him and had said that if, as was feared, the Allies would continue to suffer reverses in Norway, the psychologic effect on Mussolini would be very dangerous; if there was anything that the President could do to restrain Mussolini, or any message that he could send, the Allies would be enormously grateful. The Secretary had telephoned this to the President, who said that while he was not yet convinced, he hoped we would prepare some drafts for his consideration tomorrow. I tried my hand at a first draft, and then went to the annual Alibi [Club] spring dinner where we had an extremely amusing evening, preceded as usual with a bang-up meal. The high point came when the old Negress cook, now 86 years old, retired after 46 years' service and made the round of the table shaking each member by the hand.

Sunday morning we all met bright and early in the Secretary's office. Three or four drafts were produced, but Sumner's was far and away the best. However, both he and I argued very strongly that no message should be sent. After all, any message would imply that we disbelieved the assurances Mussolini had given Sumner Welles six weeks ago.[72] If he had lied, a new message would not have the slightest effect; if he had not lied, and were merely giving Hitler diplomatic support, he would bitterly resent a new message. In addition to the foregoing, I argued that whereas the Vatican was assuring Myron Taylor and the British Government was assuring us, via Lothian, that Mussolini was about to move our own Ambassador and our own local military and naval attachés did not believe so. Even if we decided to send a message, I felt it should not be sent at least and until our own people felt that the psychological moment had been reached. The upshot of two hours' palavering was that the Secretary would go down to the station, leave the President with a copy of Sumner's draft, but tell him that we all of us felt that we still had time.[73] Just as the Secretary was putting on his hat, Angus Malcolm [Second Secretary of the British Embassy at Washington] came rushing down with a

[72] Welles, pp. 84–89, 137–141. Ciano had also told Welles to tell Roosevelt "that so long as I [Ciano] remain Foreign Minister, Italy will not enter the war on the side of Germany." *Ibid.*, p. 145.

[73] The President had been at Warm Springs, Georgia.

further letter from Lord Lothian quoting a despatch from D'Arcy Osborne [British Minister to the Holy See] to the effect that well-informed Fascist circles believed that Mussolini was going to enter the war, against the protest of the Fascist Grand Council, some time this coming week, and that Malta and Gibraltar would be his objectives. The British, when they want us to do something, certainly know how to put on the pressure!

Sunday afternoon I took Peter and Henry (the butler's son) to their first professional baseball game, and saw Washington beat the New York Yankees in the tenth inning after a very exciting game. Incidentally, it was the first real day of spring we have had, and the crowd was correspondingly cheerful.

Monday, April 29, 1940.
    . . . The Secretary left for a week's vacation at Atlantic City. Fortunately, he was able to persuade the President not to send a further message to Mussolini. In fact, the President said, "I think we had better go a little slowly," to which Norman Davis replied that if the President felt that way, it must be three times justified.[74]

John Magruder [Chief of the Intelligence Branch of the War Department General Staff] came in for an hour's talk on the Norwegian situation. He is so pessimistic regarding the situation in which the Allies have found themselves south of Trondheim, that he says he has "mentally written off the whole expedition." Apart from poor preparation, the Allies have not been able to land enough mechanized equipment, as there are no docks on the fjords, and the work of unloading artillery from a ship to a lighter and from a lighter ashore can hardly be overestimated. He is inclined to fear a real disaster, and if this transpires no one can foresee the political effect in London. To hear Magruder, who is intensely pro-Ally, speak in these terms makes one more than ever indignant at the American press, which continues to print headline after headline of Allied victories in Norway. . .

Thursday, May 9, 1940.
    . . . Lilla and I dined at the 1925 F Street Club. . . Just as we were marching out, I was called to the telephone and found the Sec-

[74] The President altered his decision and sent a message to Mussolini on April 29 pointing to the dangers of "a further extension of the area of hostilities." Hull, I, 778–779; Moffat diary, April 30, 1940.

retary. He told me that Cudahy [John Cudahy, American Ambassador to Belgium] had just telephoned the President that the Belgian Cabinet believed the German troops would march before dawn. The Secretary asked me to get in touch with Jimmy Dunn, Berle, and others, and to stand by for a further call. At eleven o'clock I was again called to the phone. This time the Secretary said that Cudahy reported that planes were in the air overhead, border clashes had begun, and that invasion was imminent. He asked us to come to the Department, and we sat around with our numbers gradually growing. As a matter of fact, there was really nothing to do as all precautions had been taken well in advance; but, as Berle said, in times of crisis the key men should be at hand, and the public should know it. The Secretary tried telephoning to various capitals. He got hold of Kennedy, who was still in bed and knew nothing. He was never able to make a connection with either Bill Bullitt in Paris or with George Gordon [American Minister to the Netherlands], though curiously enough, we got Cudahy again about two o'clock. In time the press flashes came in, and the Secretary kept calling up the President on the White House phone.

The war has now begun in earnest. . .

Thursday, May 16, 1940.

The news this morning looked particularly black, with the reports of a German penetration of the little Maginot Line with armored cars. French officials were panicky, though they later recovered their equilibrium during the day. However, the situation looks exceedingly grave, and Hitler seems to have created a conflict of interest between England and France according to which the British want to keep their fighting planes at home to protect themselves from raids, and the French want the planes on the battle front.

The Secretary and Sumner Welles were particularly depressed all day.

Among the things worrying the Secretary was whether or not our policy of selling ships to foreigners was justified by events. At his request I called up Max Truitt [Member of the United States Maritime Commission] to find out the Maritime Commission's side of the story. Mr. Truitt said that he well understood the preoccupations which some of us undoubtedly felt, but explained, for our confidential information, that the Board was acting under direct White House inspiration. For instance, the President was behind the Buck Resolution in Congress,[75] the main purpose of which was to allow us to dispose of our over-age fleet. Mr. Truitt said that we had disposed of no ship that was not both old and slow. In every case the Board had satisfied itself regarding the good faith of the purchaser and had provided for replacement tonnage. He asked me to give the Secretary his assurance that the Board was not overlooking our national interests and would not weaken our position as a great mercantile marine power. . .

Tuesday, May 21, 1940.

This diary must grow shorter and shorter as we get busier and busier. We have reached a stage now where the main type of problem to be decided is to what degree we can help the Allies and to what degree we must conserve our inherent strength for our own defensive purposes. The news from the front looks increasingly bad so that we have to face the possibility that there may be a complete German victory as opposed to a negotiated peace. What this would mean in relation to the British fleet is the crux of the problem for ourselves.

We had several meetings in the Secretary's office in the course of the day. My outstanding impression is that there is not sufficient interdepartmental liaison or Cabinet unity. . .

[75] This resolution suspended the section of the Merchant Marine Act of 1936 which restricted the use of vessels in the "laid-up" fleet of the Maritime Commission. The resolution was passed by both the House and the Senate and sent to the President for approval on May 13, 1940. U.S. Congress, *Congressional Record*, 76 Cong., 3 Sess., LXXXVI, part V (Washington: Government Printing Office, 1940), 5233, 5599, 5613, 5620, 5748, 5635.

❧ V I I I ☙

OTTAWA

June 1940–December 1941

"To interpret government to government"

On May 27, 1940, Pierrepont Moffat wrote in his diary:

Now it can be told!

The night that the Germans marched into Belgium and Holland [May 9, 1940] the Secretary took me aside and said that he and Sumner Welles had been speaking to the President that day about the Canadian post [Minister to Canada], and that my name had been brought up and promptly approved by the President. In fact, the Secretary added generously, no other names were taken under consideration.

Two hours later I was summoned back to the Department, and sat up all night listening to the news of the beginning of the great offensive.

During the six weeks following the invasion of the Low Countries and France the world was stunned as with broad strokes Germany erased Allied resistance from the continent. On May 15 the army of The Netherlands capitulated, and thirteen days later Belgium under Leopold surrendered. The evacuation from Dunkirk began near the last of May. On June 10 Italy entered the war. And before the end of the month the armistice had been signed by representatives of France and Germany at Compiègne.

By the time Mr. Moffat arrived in Ottawa on June 12, 1940, the impact of these changes in Europe had transformed the character of the Canadian war effort. When Great Britain suddenly became the sole line of defense between Europe and America, the obligations of Canada as the arsenal for the mother country and, in event of British defeat, as the probable heir of power and responsibility increased. "Our Empire beyond the seas," as Churchill said, "would carry on the struggle, until, in God's good time, the New World, with all its power and might, steps forth to the rescue and the liberation of the Old." [1]

[1] Winston S. Churchill, *The Second World War*, vol. II, *Their Finest Hour* (Boston: Houghton Mifflin Co., 1949), pp. 115–118.

In this crisis Canada turned to the United States, whose concern for Canadian security had already been expressed by President Roosevelt.[2] The events of May and June, 1940, made it imperative to determine to what extent the interests of the two neighbors were identical and to evolve plans for furthering these common goals. When Mr. Moffat presented his credentials as Minister to Canada, he undertook a mission which witnessed the fruition of cooperative action between the United States and Canada.

Washington, June 10, 1940.

I called on the President this morning prior to leaving for Ottawa tomorrow.

He began the conversation by telling me of the visit of Mr. Keenleyside who had brought him the copy of a message from Mr. Churchill to Mr. Mackenzie King. This message had disturbed the President considerably, as Mr. Churchill had not given specific assurances that the British fleet would under no circumstances be surrendered. He seemed to envisage a possibility that in the event things went wrong, he might have to respond to the then will of the public, go to the Palace, and hand over office to a government more sympathetic than he to the Germans. However, added the President, this letter was written before Mr. Churchill's recent speech, and that speech was firmness itself.[3]

According to the President, no nation need ever surrender. There are occasions when a nation can no longer fight and must adopt

[2] In an address given at Queens University, Kingston, Ontario, Canada, on August 18, 1938, President Roosevelt said that "the people of the United States will not stand idly by if domination of Canadian soil is threatened by any other empire." Franklin D. Roosevelt, *The Public Papers and Addresses of Franklin D. Roosevelt*, 1938 vol., *The Continuing Struggle for Liberalism* (New York: The Macmillan Co., 1941), pp. 491–494.
[3] Dr. Hugh Keenleyside, First Secretary of the Department of External Affairs in Ottawa, had been sent to Washington to inform Mr. Roosevelt of Churchill's message of June 5. In this telegram Churchill had said that if the United States were at war and Britain defeated, the United States would naturally fall heir to the British fleet, but "if America continued neutral, and we were overpowered, I cannot tell what policy might be adopted by a pro-German administration such as would undoubtedly be set up." Churchill, *Their Finest Hour*, pp. 145–146. Later in June, 1940, in reply to a query from the President as to what would be done with the Fleet in case Britain were conquered, Churchill answered that the Navy would never be surrendered but would be sent to overseas bases. Robert Sherwood, *Roosevelt and Hopkins* (rev. ed.; New York: Harper & Bros., 1950), p. 146.

Mr. Churchill's speech of June 4 before the House of Commons, in which he promised "we shall never surrender," had impressed Mr. Roosevelt. Churchill, *Their Finest Hour*, pp. 115–118.

a policy of nonresistance. Even if Britain should be beaten down to
a policy of nonresistance, its Empire could still go on. How? First,
by dispersing the navy around the globe, centered on existing bases;
twenty percent only would be needed in Canada, ten percent would
do for South Africa, twenty percent for Bombay, and fifty percent
for Singapore. This would enable Britain to control the seas, carry
on a long-range blockade, and checkmate Japan. Second, by sailing
away from the British Isles all merchant shipping. Third, by destroying all shipping under construction or repair, whether naval or merchant, in shipbuilding yards or dockyards.

A long-range blockade could and would cut off Germany and
Italy from all essential raw materials and at the very least prevent
them from building up strong industrial economies. Where are the
main sources of raw materials? In America, in Africa, and in Russia.
None could come through a long-range blockade, with a patrol from
Greenland to Madeira, from the Americas; very little could be transported overland from Central and Southern Africa to the Mediterranean coast; and relatively little could be obtained from Russia in
its present state of disorder and inefficient transport system.

Even if only twenty percent of the British fleet came to Canada,
the Dominion could not service it alone. Although there was a lot
the United States as a neutral could *not* do, there was plenty she could.
For instance, a belligerent ship has a right to come into a neutral port
to repair damage. British ships could come into our navy yards alleging damage, and while our officers were looking for it, the ships' bot-
toms could be cleaned. Also, ships could be refueled once a month.

While talking to Canadian officials I was constantly to emphasize (a) that Canada should, for its own sake and not for ours, continue to seek assurances that the British fleet would never be surrendered, but be dispersed, with a part to North America, and (b)
that the United States could give almost as much help as a neutral
as if she became a belligerent. No one could tell if the United States
would become a belligerent; obviously she would not unless an overt
act were committed by Germany or Italy. Germany was clever and
would probably avoid an overt act; Italy was foolish and might commit one.

Mussolini was to speak in a few minutes. The President feared it
might mean a declaration of war. He, the President, was going to

make a speech that evening at Charlottesville, and it would be a "tough one" — one in which the issue between the democracies and the Fascist powers would be drawn as never before.[4]

He then said good-bye and good luck.

Ottawa, June 14, 1940.

The Prime Minister, Mr. Mackenzie King, asked me to come and see him late this afternoon.

He told me that he had just received a telegram from Mr. Winston Churchill describing his recent trip to France and his negotiations with the French.[5] Although it was not intended to be shown to anyone, he would read it to me and ask me to pass on its substance to the President and Mr. Hull, as he felt it of vital importance that Washington should be fully informed of every detail in Ottawa's possession during these critical days.

In brief, Mr. Churchill informed the Prime Minister that the French armies were at their last gasp. Even Weygand [General Maxime Weygand, French Commander in Chief] believed France would soon have to ask for an armistice. The French Ministers had instructed Reynaud to ask the British whether they would admit that France had done all she could and might enter into a separate peace. The British Government had answered that it could not consent to this. According to Reynaud, everything would now depend on the American reply to his appeals for aid.

A personal message from the President reached Reynaud at this point.[6] Churchill quoted it textually to Mr. Mackenzie King, and

[4] Mussolini did, in fact, bring Italy into the war against Great Britain and France on June 10, 1940. That evening at the University of Virginia President Roosevelt discussed the Italian action, which he described in the well-known sentence: "On this tenth day of June, 1940, the hand that held the dagger has struck it into the back of its neighbor." He also said that the sympathies of all the American nations were with the democracies in their struggle against the totalitarian powers, and he pledged material aid to the "opponents of force." Franklin D. Roosevelt, *The Public Papers and Addresses of Franklin D. Roosevelt*, 1940 vol., *War — and Aid to Democracies* (New York: The Macmillan Co., 1941), pp. 259–264. The attempts of the President and the Department of State to keep Italy from declaring war are described in Hull, I, 777–786.

[5] Churchill had gone to Tours on June 13. His account of meeting Premier Paul Reynaud appears in Churchill, *Their Finest Hour*, pp. 177–183. Reynaud's version is given in Paul Reynaud, *La France a sauvé l'Europe* (Paris: Flammarion, 1947), II, 318–322.

[6] President Roosevelt's message commended the French for the effort they were making in the fight for democracy. He expressed personal interest in the idea that

commented that it was an invitation to France to continue the war. While the President was unable to declare war without the assent of Congress, Mr. Churchill stated that the message "went to the very edge of such a step and seemed to give the assurance which Reynaud desired."

It was in these circumstances that Britain had just given France an unequivocal pledge of support. Now he appealed to Canada to give a similar pledge "more than ever now that Roosevelt has committed himself."

Mr. Mackenzie King told me he had just given this Canadian pledge to Parliament. He had added a sentence which he felt paraphrased the President's recent Charlottesville speech, yet which he felt did not cross the borderline and speak for the United States. "If I know the heart of the American people as I believe I do," said Mr. King, "and as I am certain I know the heart of the Canadian people, I believe I can say to Premier Reynaud, in this hour of [the] agony [of France] that the resources of the whole [of the] North American continent will be thrown into the struggle for liberty at the side of the European democracies ere this continent will see democracy itself trodden under the iron heel of nazism." [7]

The Prime Minister then began discussing the war and Canada's part therein. He referred to Keenleyside's talks with the President and the latter's worries as to some of Mr. Churchill's phraseology in a recent message to Mr. Mackenzie King.[8] He then went on to tell me that Canadian troops were now in France, that Canada had "stripped herself to the bone" to send munitions, artillery, planes, etc., abroad.

However, all evidence pointed to the fact that France, even if she does not capitulate and make a separate peace, no longer counts as a

---

France would continue to fight even, if necessary, outside the homeland in North Africa or other parts of the Empire. The importance of the mastery which the French and British possessed at sea was stressed. And, Roosevelt assured Reynaud, America was sending all the material possible to aid the Allies and would redouble its efforts in this regard. The text is printed in Gantenbein, pp. 201–202. A copy of this message reached Churchill on June 13 after his return to England. The Prime Minister thereupon telegraphed Reynaud commending to him "this magnificent document." Churchill, *Their Finest Hour*, pp. 183–186.

[7] Prime Minister King's speech is printed in Dominion of Canada, House of Commons, *Official Report of Debates*, vol. CCXXII (1940) (Ottawa: Edmond Cloutier, 1940), pp. 778–779. The words bracketed above were omitted in Mr. Moffat's quotation.

[8] See conversation of Jay Pierrepont Moffat with the President, June 10, 1940.

military force.[9] Her resistance will soon be limited to fleet action and colonial defense. This brings the inevitable attack on Great Britain much nearer. Mr. Mackenzie King believes this attack will be repelled, though at the cost of great punishment to the British population and the loss of the use of her southern and eastern ports to shipping.

However, supposing for the sake of argument that the attack were not repelled. Then the British fleet, in whole or in part, might come to Canada. In that event Canada would immediately be faced by many problems of a practical nature which could not be solved without American aid. Has not the time come for staff talks to begin between the two countries? There had been informal talks between our staffs three years ago about the Pacific.[10] Then both countries were at peace; now Canada was at war. Perhaps such a suggestion might embarrass the President; this was the last thing he wanted. On the other hand as no interests were involved, the President might welcome the suggestion. In the circumstances he asked me to feel out the situation and let him know. . .[11]

Ottawa, June 29, 1940.

The Prime Minister suggested that before going to Washington I have a talk with Mr. Ralston [J. L. Ralston, Minister of National Defence] and Mr. Power [C. G. Power, Minister of National Defence for Air] to see exactly what they had in mind in suggesting staff talks in Washington. They received me together in Mr. Ralston's office, and we spent approximately an hour running over the situation.

1. *Army*. Both Mr. Ralston and Mr. Power thought the time had come for high officers of the two armies to exchange impressions with

[9] The armistice between Germany and France was signed at Compiègne on June 22, 1940.

[10] These talks had taken place in January 1938.

[11] On June 17 the Canadian Chargé d'Affaires presented an *aide-mémoire* to Secretary Hull requesting Canadian-American staff talks about the defense of North America. Ten days later Mr. Moffat received a letter from Mr. Sumner Welles in which the Under Secretary suggested that Mr. Moffat determine in detail what the Canadians wanted to discuss in the staff meetings and come to Washington with this information. Stanley W. Dziuban, *U.S. Military Collaboration with Canada in World War II* (Washington: Office of the Chief of Military History, Department of the Army, 1954), pp. 28–29.

a view to helping the other to complete its appreciation of the situation. It was understood that no commitment would be asked for or given. I pointed out that the words "staff talk" had an unfortunate connotation and should be avoided if possible. The American public remembered only too well that the staff talks between the British and French in 1907 [12] were recalled by the French in 1914 as constituting a moral commitment on the part of Britain to action. Obviously neither one of us had anything of this sort in mind so although the term "staff talk" might be roughly used, what we really meant was "informal discussions on our respective problems of defence."

When the Canadians reach Washington they will tell our Army exactly what Canada has, what she has not, and will set forth with perfect frankness both her strength and her weakness.

The Canadians are definitely worried about the possibility of an air raid. They understand that Germany has a vessel capable of carrying about forty aircraft, and if this should escape the British blockade, particularly if accompanied by a cruiser, she could do great damage. The most important and vulnerable point is of course the great air field in Newfoundland.[13] The Canadians have troops there, but they have no artillery and no anti-aircraft guns. The communications are difficult as there are no roads and only a single narrow-track railway around the island. The Newfoundland Government is asking the Canadians with increasing urgency for assistance, notably in protecting her four main harbors. The Canadians will want to discuss the whole Newfoundland situation in Washington.

With regard to the island of St. Pierre–Miquelon Mr. Power said that if he had his way Canadian troops would occupy it.[14] Obviously, however, this raises so many political questions that there would be no move without the approval of the Department of External Affairs. If worse should come to worst the Canadians hope to find out what we have in mind with regard to preventing various places such as

---

[12] Staff talks were held intermittently between the British and the French from 1905 until the beginning of the First World War. Sidney B. Fay, *The Origins of the World War* (New York: The Macmillan Co., 1929), I, 192–213; G. P. Gooch, *Recent Revelations of European Diplomacy* (London: Longmans, Green & Co., 1940), pp. 314–318.

[13] A discussion of United States and Canadian defense efforts at the Gander airbase and in Newfoundland can be found in Dziuban, pp. 364–370, and R. A. MacKay (ed.), *Newfoundland* (Toronto: Oxford University Press, 1946), pp. 7–10, 492–497.

[14] St. Pierre and Miquelon are two islands off the southeast coast of Newfoundland.

Iceland, Greenland, the West Indies, etc., from being used as German bases.

The Canadians appreciate that the coastline of Nova Scotia is so long that they could not prevent the landing of a determined foe. Halifax is adequately guarded, but that is about all. Therefore they plan to concentrate their troops in the Maritimes and train them as a mobile unit.

There are about 100,000 men under arms in Canada today but of these by no means all have completed their training. 75,000 militia will be called up within the next six weeks. Canada has not enough equipment in the way of rifles or ammunition for these troops as she sent her surplus to France and Britain some time back to aid against German parachutists. Furthermore there is a great shortage of tents. The two battalions now in Iceland and Newfoundland have used 2000 Sell tents and 300 marquees. The Canadians are putting up modern barracks to house the new troops in approximately six weeks.

One suggestion that will be offered in Washington is that we put our summer training camps in New England all as near the Canadian border as possible. Perhaps the C.C.C. camp at Quoddy might be used.

They will also renew their plea for small arms and ammunition and for light artillery and ammunition.

2. *Navy.* The Canadian Navy Department wishes to exchange views with the American naval authorities on much the same terms. In addition they want to talk over the problems that would be raised if the British Fleet should fall back on Canada. There is only one adequate base, namely, at Halifax and two small repair stations on the St. Lawrence which is of course only navigable half the year. This raises all sorts of practical questions as to the extent of help which we could give (a) subject to strict neutrality, (b) subject to benevolent neutrality. The equipment of the British Fleet is so completely different from that of the American that there are no ready-made replacement parts, as the entire system even down to screws and nails is different. The problem is a big one. As to ammunition the Canadians did not know how much the British could bring with them. I said that I knew the British had not committed themselves about sending their Fleet to Canada in any contingency but I wondered if worse

came to the worst whether the Canadians anticipated that the whole Fleet might come or only a small part with the rest retreating to Singapore, Simonstown [South Africa], etc. Colonel Ralston said that he had never heard the suggestion even offered but saw some merit to it. I replied that in that way they could keep command of all the seas and would not overwhelm the facilities in any one place.

In Washington the Canadians will ask if we can give some moral help in showing our interest in the northwest Atlantic, as for instance by basing some fleet maneuvers off Boston. This, they felt, would have a discouraging effect on the Germans.

3. *Air*. Mr. Ralston and Mr. Power did not conceal that the air situation was unsatisfactory. The Air Training Scheme had broken down as a result of the failure of the British to supply the promised training planes and was just getting off to a new start.[15] So many of Canada's planes had been sent to England that they have not enough for domestic purposes. They have some patrol planes at Newfoundland but no fighters to protect them. They are not able to keep up an adequate air patrol off Nova Scotia. They want to purchase reconnaissance planes and flying boats with accompanying fighters. In addition to these immediate purchases they want to obtain the designs in order to continue manufacturing such types locally. They hope to get some of the planes ordered by the French and transferred to the British.

They then offered certain suggestions as to how we could help, admitting that these were ideas tossed out for examination rather than advanced as proposals. (1) Could we help by undertaking long reconnaissance flights, perhaps nominally to Greenland, with "forced stops" in Nova Scotia at Yarmouth, Sydney, Dartmouth, etc. (2) Could we rent, acquire, or purchase land in the West Indies or Newfoundland and develop them as American air bases. (3) Could we take a leaf out of the book of Hitler and Mussolini and send "volunteers" to Canada, *id est*, allowing American aviators to take leave with their planes and wink our eyes to the fact that they joined the Canadian forces. I told them that suggestion (3) was out of the question

[15] In 1939 Canada had signed the Commonwealth Air Training Plan with Great Britain, Australia, and New Zealand. It was hoped that when the plan was in full operation it would provide training for about 20,000 pilots and observers a year. Robert MacGregor Dawson, *Canada in World Affairs, Two Years of War 1939–1941* (London: Oxford University Press, 1943), pp. 20–21, 35–36.

legally and I thought would defeat its own purpose with public opinion if ever it were pressed.

4. Mr. Ralston and Mr. Power admitted that from this point on the question of priorities between the British and Canadians for American orders would assume greater importance. They recalled that some months back there had been a conflict of interest between France and England as to where equipment could most effectively be used. Now there is the mildest sort of conflict of interest between England and Canada. They are particularly anxious that there should never arise a conflict of interest between Canada and the United States. This is one reason they are so anxious to go to Washington.

They recognized that they had made a mistake in modeling their equipment so closely after the British. This, however, was water over the dam. Henceforth they would work closely with the Americans, not only industrially but strategically. The two countries were so close as to resemble parts of the same unit.

At one point in the conversation Mr. Power remarked that it was less than a month ago that he had suggested that the Canadians ask the British to write a testament leaving Canada her planes in the event of defeat. Mr. Ralston had bridled up at the time, but Mr. Power pressed his point and said that it might have been a good thing to do.

In conclusion Mr. Ralston said that he had perhaps gone into more detail than I desired but it was better to give too much than too little. I told him that I would report all this to General Marshall and Admiral Stark whom I would be seeing Tuesday or Wednesday and if the informal conversations were approved, the mere fact that our people knew what the Canadians had in mind would enable them to do some advanced thinking and thus save a great deal of time.

Ottawa, July 5, 1940.

I called on the Prime Minister this afternoon about half-past five to tell him the result of my talks in Washington.[16]

1. I explained that after consultations with the Chief of Staff, the Chief of Naval Operations, the Secretary of State and the Under

---

[16] In Washington on July 2 and 3 Mr. Moffat had met with General Marshall, Admiral Stark, Secretary Morgenthau, Secretary Hull, Under Secretary Welles, and other Department officials.

Secretary, the question the Prime Minister had raised of sending high-ranking Canadian officers to Washington for informal discussions had been laid before the President. I was glad to say that he had authorized such informal talks on matters of our respective interests in the field of defence.[17] Obviously no commitment would be asked or given. It might also be that the Canadians would feel that there were certain matters into which we could not go too deeply but I did not think that the Canadians would feel that this would rob the talks of their value. I also explained that we felt the Canadian officers should come secretly and offered the suggestion that if any explanation were needed or if any publicity should arise that they were going to Washington nominally to consult with Mr. Purvis [Arthur Purvis, head of the British Purchasing Commission]. The Prime Minister was delighted and asked me to thank the President and the Secretary of State for this new proof of their cooperation. He would let me know in a few days the names of the officers selected and the date when they would be traveling to Washington.[18]

2. I next told the Prime Minister that the Secretary of State had handed to the President the very full memorandum I had made of his message to Mr. Churchill of June 17th and the latter's reply.[19]

[17] Mr. Roosevelt gave authorization for the staff talks on July 3, 1940.

[18] Air Commodore A. A. L. Cuffe, Captain L. W. Murray, and Brigadier Kenneth Stuart, the Canadian staff officers, arrived in Washington on July 12, 1940.

[19] In a conversation on June 27, 1940, Mr. King had told Mr. Moffat about an exchange of messages which he had had with Churchill. Mr. Moffat's memorandum of this meeting reads:

"Mr. King then read me the telegram dated June 17th. It was a two-page message, the general purport of which was roughly as follows: Mr. King had noticed that in the last week or two that a certain feeling had grown up in the United States that the sending of the British Fleet to the Western Hemisphere, in case the British Isles could not be held was contingent on the previous entry of the United States into the war. He, Mackenzie King, felt that he knew enough both of the President's own feelings and of the reaction of the American public to realize that any belief, however unfounded, that Britain was trying to use the future of the Fleet as a lever would make it harder for the President to give aid to Britain in this hour of need. He thought as we must always envisage what would happen if anything went wrong, the time was nearly here for some concrete thought to be given to the practical questions that would arise if a large number of the surviving units of the British Fleet should suddenly arrive in Canada. Still more was this the case if it was desired that the United States should take over in one way or another the task of preventing the Germans from using certain territories as naval or air bases, such for instance, as Iceland, Greenland, Newfoundland or the West Indies. An attempt should be made to talk these things through by Great Britain, Canada and the United States, but these talks should be held independently and in no way related to the question of possible American participation in hostilities. Mr. King went on to emphasize that

Mr. Hull had told me that the President's comments were to the effect that Churchill was telling neither Americans nor Canadians of his ultimate intentions but that if worse should come to the worst he was convinced that Churchill would remember that the Fleet belonged to the entire British Empire, and that the Empire would remember it likewise. Mr. King said that despite Mr. Churchill's silence, his actions of late left no doubt that he would keep the Fleet intact even if it meant transferring its base.

3. The Prime Minister referred to the recent Fleet action at Oran when the large French units were sunk by the British Fleet.[20] I said that there was no doubt of the feeling of relief in the United States that the ships could never be used by the Axis Powers. My only regret was that one Ally had to shed the blood of another Ally. Mr. King said that he had to be extremely careful to prevent an adverse reaction among the French Canadians. Thus far he was perfectly satisfied and thought that with proper handling there would be no difficulty. After all, the French Canadian was Canadian first, last and always and his feelings for France were platonic. I suggested that the French Canadian would resent criticism of France by other Canadians but would not be unduly stirred up by criticism from third parties. He agreed.

Canada herself could not undertake this type of protection as she had sent most of her naval and aerial strength abroad in response to British requests and she was already very short in equipment.

"To this Mr. Churchill replied on June 24th in a 'most secret and personal telegram.' His reply was evidently based on a misreading of Mr. King's telegram as it was apparent that he thought Mr. King himself believed he was trying to bargain with the Fleet rather than that Mr. King was merely reporting his impressions of public opinion in the United States. He thanked Mr. Mackenzie King for his telegram of the 17th and said that if he would reread his telegram of June 5th he would note that Mr. Churchill had never referred to a bargain nor had he linked the question of the location of the Fleet with American participation in the war. This would be clear also to anyone who had read his messages to the President. Great Britain would successfully withstand the German attack which was about to break and he thought it would be a psychological mistake to consider in detail the consequences of a British defeat which he would not admit as a possibility. He himself would never discuss peace with Hitler but of course he could not bind future governments and if the United States deserted the British and they were defeated it was possible that a Quisling group might come into power representing the then existing public opinion. He closed with a tribute to the Canadian Division now in England." Churchill's reply is printed in full in *Their Finest Hour*, p. 227.

[20] On July 3, 1940, at Oran the British navy had blown up the French battleship *Bretagne*, the *Dunkerque* was run aground, and the *Provence* beached. An account of the operation against the French Fleet is given in *ibid.*, pp. 224–241.

4. With regard to equipment I told the Prime Minister that I had discussed his requests not only with our Army and Navy people but with the Secretary of the Treasury. The situation had materially changed on July 2nd when the President signed the bill which precluded the sale of any surplus equipment unless either the Chief of Staff or the Chief of Naval Operations personally certified that the matériel was not essential for United States defence. The wording of this bill made the certification difficult as it referred not to expediency but to our own need of the matériel.[21] Mr. King had not heard of this bill. I said, however, that his requests would be studied anew to see whether any part of them might be honored. Some of them obviously were impossible to give. We had heavy shortages of our own and had allowed the Allies to buy lavishly. Undoubtedly by the time the Canadian officers arrived in Washington our people would know more where they stood. Mr. Morgenthau had pointed out that they had never broken down British Empire requests into so much for Great Britain, so much for Canada. Henceforth this might be done.[22] The Prime Minister said that in the future the distinction would be made as he thought it would be easier for us to give certain things to Canada where they would have a direct bearing on United States defence than it would be to give them to England.

5. I then referred to a sentence that the Prime Minister had used with me last week when he said that we could be sure he would take no action in the Western Hemisphere without first talking it over with us. In particular, he had referred to the question of Aruba and

[21] In a memorandum of a conversation held in Washington on July 2 Mr. Moffat reported that General Marshall had said: "With regard to equipment, Congress had in the last day or two passed a bill which the President had signed forbidding the sale of any further surplus matériel unless the Chief of Staff or the Chief of Naval Operations personally certified that it was not 'essential' for our own national defence. The wording of this bill worried him greatly as had the adjective been 'expedient' he would feel far freer to make such certifications than he does today. There was no doubt in the world that we had sold so generously to the Allied powers that our own stocks were below the safety point. One could argue that by giving more aid to Britain or Canada we would be increasing our own defensive strength. That might be true but it was not provable, and if Britain were defeated the Army and the Administration could never justify to the American people the risk that they had taken."

The Act to Expedite National Defense was approved on June 28, 1940. Jones and Myers, *Documents, July 1939–June 1940*, II, 793–794.

[22] Mr. Morgenthau also told Mr. Moffat on July 3 that he was investigating the possibility of reallocating Norwegian, Swedish, and Belgian orders to the Allies, and particularly to Canada.

to the British request to Canada to land troops on the island. I said that I was going to tell him the way minds were running in Washington provided he would not assume that any decisions had been reached.[23] I said that we were contemplating working out with the American Republics at Havana a system whereby the American Republics would take over temporarily a trusteeship for those islands in the Western Hemisphere which the owners were not free to govern independently. Perhaps a small group of neighbors, always including ourselves, could exercise this temporary trusteeship.[24] Mr. King thought this an excellent idea and said that not only did he favor early action along these lines but that it would relieve him of many responsibilities. He felt that the Canadian troops, given the French defection, would have to go into Aruba, but if another satisfactory arrangement could be worked out their stay would not have to be too long.

6. I then raised the question of the islands of St. Pierre-Miquelon and expressed the hope, in view of what I had just told him, that Canada would undertake no unilateral occupation of the islands. He admitted that Newfoundland had been pressing him to do so but was categoric in his statement that he would not send any troops. He was planning to send a Canadian official, together with a Newfoundland official, to the island to talk over the disposition of a French armored sloop which was either at or near St. Pierre but he would be careful to avoid any untoward precedent. He might also have to send in a ship with relief supplies as the island which depended entirely for its subsistence on ships from France, and its

[23] Following the invasion of The Netherlands on May 9, the Dutch island of Aruba in the West Indies was occupied by French troops while the British sent forces to Dutch Curaçao. Secretary Hull protested this occupation and was assured by the British that their forces would be withdrawn when they were "satisfied" about conditions in the islands or Dutch defensive forces were available. After the fall of France the French were withdrawn from Aruba by Vichy, and the British proposed to send replacements. Secretary Hull in a talk with British Ambassador Lothian on July 8 objected to this plan and also to the suggestion that Canadian instead of British guards might be used. Mr. Hull stated that he "could not agree to any British guards going there, and said that ample plans would be worked out at the forthcoming Havana Conference to deal with the question." Hull, I, 814–816, 891.
[24] See Resolution 20 of the Act of Havana. U. S. Department of State, *Second Meeting of the Ministers of Foreign Affairs of the American Republics* (Washington: Government Printing Office, 1941), pp. 75–77. Cordell Hull in his *Memoirs*, I, 822–826, gives an account of the discussions and activities at the Havana Conference leading to the formulation of the resolution and convention.

ability to sell fish for these exports, would soon be in a desperate condition. . .

In the days of despair following the collapse of France when little more than faith seemed to keep England from the same fate, Canada was faced with the sobering prospect that the Allied front against Hitler might soon retreat to Canadian shores. Here, in the first line of defense, lay the province of Quebec, where the French Canadians were centered.

Comprising one third of the total population, the *Canadiens* were a force to be reckoned with in any political decision. Intensely loyal to Canada, history yet warned that the people of Quebec were less than enthusiastic participants in a war at Great Britain's side. Rural, religious, jealous of their peculiar heritage, they held aloof from other Canadians and were not moved by a feeling of kinship with Britain to bend every effort in her support.

The fall of France, which had touched the French Canadians deeply, made them willing to take measures within their own country to strengthen their defenses. But a divergence of opinion was quickly evident between Quebec and the rest of Canada toward the newly established Vichy Government. The Pétain regime with a conservative and clerical tone appealed to many of the French Canadians, while its collaboration with the Nazis made it anathema to English-speaking Canada.

Ottawa, July 24, 1940.

During the course of a conversation with Major Gladstone Murray [Head of the Canadian Broadcasting Corporation] we got to discussing the French Canadians. I remarked that I had been told during the day that the French Canadians were very favorable to General Pétain.[25] Major Gladstone Murray became very much worked up and said that he was faced with a very serious problem. The French Canadians were being subjected to hostile propaganda from French radios in German-controlled France. I suggested that very few French Canadians would have sufficiently powerful radio machines to receive on short wave. He replied that there were plenty and that what one heard he passed around. It would not be so bad if the propaganda was merely in favor of Pétain; it had, however, a distinctly anti-British tinge. The tenor of the broadcasts was that after a British defeat French Canada should be an independent republic going its own way without interference from without. Curiously

[25] Marshal Henri Philippe Pétain had been made Chief of State in the Vichy Government on July 11. See Dawson, pp. 261–263, for a discussion of the French Canadian attitude toward the Vichy Government.

enough, added Major Gladstone Murray, the French Canadians were being urged to join with Newfoundland where likewise there was discontent that the Germans were trying to exploit.[26] So seriously did the Canadian Broadcasting authorities take this anti-British propaganda among the French Canadians that there had been several proposals afoot to jam the air when the Paris station spoke. He resolutely opposed this as he felt that it would do more damage than good. I asked where the Catholic hierarchy stood in the matter. He said he thought the Cardinal [Villeneuve] was perfectly sound but that when he had spoken with the Cardinal he kept saying, "If only Britain would declare war on Russia, then all my people will follow the British Government like Crusaders."

A sudden climax to the staff talks came on August 17 and 18, 1940, in a private car on a railroad siding near Ogdensburg, New York, when two old friends met to discuss Canadian–American relations. The initiative in arranging the meeting rested, apparently, with President Roosevelt who had been led to take action in part because a message had reached him on August 16 from Mr. Moffat in which the insistent demand from all parts of Canada for a joint defense agreement with the United States was pointed out.[27] Since Mr. Roosevelt was to leave the next day to view army maneuvers in northern New York, he invited the Prime Minister to meet him at Ogdensburg.

Mackenzie King's acceptance reached the President a half-hour before his departure from Washington. Mr. Roosevelt had General Watson get in touch with Pierrepont Moffat immediately to ask him to accompany Mr. King on the trip. Mr. Moffat drove from Ottawa the next day with the Prime Minister, and he kept one of the two known accounts of this meeting[28] which resulted, Mr. King thought, in some of "the greatest developments of recent times."

August 17, 1940.

The Prime Minister and I reached Prescott about half-past six; a special ferry was awaiting to take us to Ogdensburg; there we were met by a motorcycle escort, which took us to the President's special train. He was seated in the observation room of the rear car with

[26] Because of financial difficulties representative government was suspended in Newfoundland in 1934, and a commission form of government was set up. The new government was not generally popular. John Parker, *Newfoundland* (London: Lincolns-Prager, Ltd., 1950), pp. 28–33.

[27] Dziuban, p. 45–48.

[28] The other record was kept by Mr. Stimson and is among his unpublished manuscript material.

Colonel Stimson [Secretary of War], Governor Lehman [of New York], and General Drum [Commander of the First Army]. The two latter left almost immediately.

The President had just come in from several hours inspecting troops in the field: he was tired but exhilarated. We all had long cooling drinks while he talked at random about whatever came into his head. His talk on the whole was brilliant and the charm of the man, a happy blend of Chief of State, man of the world, and host, was never more vivid. He wanted to get the text of the Willkie speech of acceptance,[29] but the only flash that came through was that Willkie had challenged him to a series of joint debates. "If that is true," he declared with emphasis, "Willkie is lost." He chuckled at "stealing half the show" because of the fact that his visit to Ogdensburg and his conference with Mackenzie King — although this was not on purpose — happened on the very day of Willkie's speech. He said that there were times when it was wiser and more effective not to campaign and this was one of them. He talked about Canadian politics and jollied Mackenzie King about interning Mayor Houde of Montreal.[30] He thought Grand Manan [31] with its high cliffs and icy waters would be an ideal spot for an internment camp. He criticized the British internment policy, with their mixing Nazis and anti-Nazis in the same camp without adequate investigation. He discussed British evacuated children and the availability of funds and homes to take care of those that Canada could not. He digressed with humorous anecdotes about the visit last year of the King and Queen. He told of . . . General Pakenham [Sir Edward Pakenham, English general who was killed in the Battle of New Orleans in 1815], whose body was sent back to England preserved in a cask of rum, and his horror at hearing the present day Pakenham say, "Yes, it's true, my great-grandfather arrived in a shocking condition as the sailors had discovered there was rum in the cask and had bored a hole, inserted a tube, and drunk it all!!" As to the war, the news he got from England was good. The English were well satisfied with the progress with the

[29] Wendell Willkie had given his acceptance speech of the Republican nomination for president at Elwood, Indiana, on August 17, 1940. Wendell Willkie, *This Is Wendell Willkie* (New York: Dodd, Mead & Co., 1940), pp. 259–280.

[30] Camillien Houde, Mayor of Montreal, had been sent to an internment camp, when he urged Canadians to refuse to participate in the national registration, which took place on August 19 and 20. Dawson, p. 47.

[31] Grand Manan is an island in the Bay of Fundy.

war in the air, but their men were getting tired and they wanted more pilots. As to the possibility of selling destroyers he was momentarily expecting a message from the Attorney General as to the law governing the situation.[32]

We broke up about 8, and the President asked Mr. King and Mr. Stimson to dine with him at 8.30, just the three of them. They dined and stayed in conference till after 11. Meanwhile, I had dinner with Pa Watson [Major General Edwin M. Watson, secretary to the President], Admiral Ross McIntire [White House physician], Captain Callaghan [Naval Aide to the President], and Gene Regnier [Military Aide to Secretary Stimson].

The conversation was boisterous and pleasantly Rabelaisian. Admiral McIntire from time to time introduced some serious talk, but not for long. However all four men seemed to believe: (a) that England would win the war, largely because of character; (b) that continental Europe was gone and not worth serious worry on our part; (c) that we had a holy duty to save England, almost irrespective of cost; (d) that we would probably be in the war before so very long (this last was implied rather than expressed); (e) that this might not be such a bad thing for the country; and (f) that the old world as we had known it was doomed no matter what happened.

As to the President, General Watson said his reëlection was certain. Willkie might carry 10 states, but he doubted it. The only bad situation was in New York and that only because Farley was so angry and upset at the way things had gone that he was sulking in his tent. Set a fox to catch a fox, and it was up to Flynn to clear up that situation.[33] Otherwise everything looked well.

Sunday, August 18th [1940].

I breakfasted with Colonel Stimson. He told me that he had gone to sleep easier as a result of the talk with Mr. King. This morning, in

---

[32] This agreement, by which the United States leased British bases in exchange for British acquisition of fifty overage American destroyers, was signed on September 2. See Hull, I, 831–843; U. S. Department of State, *The Department of State Bulletin*, September 7, 1940, pp. 201–207, contains the legal opinion of Attorney General Robert H. Jackson about the agreement.

[33] James A. Farley had resigned as Postmaster General on August 7, 1940, and he had previously given up the position of Chairman of the Democratic National Committee. Edward J. Flynn of New York had been chosen Farley's successor in the latter position. Farley gives a detailed account of his version of his break with Roosevelt in James A. Farley, *Jim Farley's Story* (New York: McGraw-Hill Book

the cold light of day, he felt that such progress had been made, that perhaps today would mark the turn in the tide of the war.[34]

He talked of his troubles in getting conscription through right away. Everyone wanted to postpone it till after election, some because of politics, some because they were "plain ornery." It must come, however, and at once.[35] The Willkie speech was a godsend, and Mr. Stimson characterized it as "able and courageous." [36] Sometimes he woke up at night in a sweat because of our poor defense posture. The world of invention had swept by and left us behind. We were moving now but not fast enough. The danger was very near, and only England was holding it off. We couldn't do enough for England. The old war horse smelled the smell of battle and rejoiced.

His start had been slow. His confirmation had had to wait for the end of the Republican Convention. He could not get rid of his chief assistant till after the Democratic Convention. The situation in the War Department was shocking. There were Woodring men and Johnson men and the Army had suffered deeply.[37] Judge Patterson [Assistant Secretary of War] was a trump. He had not known him well, but he knew that he was the ablest judge on the bench.

Personally Mr. Stimson rejoiced that he was a participant and not an onlooker in this great crisis affecting the world. It had given him a new zest in life.

At ten we all went to the review: the President, Mr. King, and Colonel Stimson in the first car; the Secret Service in the second; the three aides, Congressman Andrew J. May and myself in the third. First, the President inspected 113 planes of all makes and description lined up on a small flying field; then to an open-air church service for the 28th Division (at which Gov. James (Republican) succeeded in mixing a little politics with religion, much to Pa Watson's disgust).

Co., Inc., 1948), pp. 151–339. See also Edward J. Flynn, *You're the Boss* (New York: The Viking Press, 1947), pp. 154–169.

[34] In Stimson and Bundy, pp. 358–359, Stimson said about the meeting at Ogdensburg: "I felt that it was very possibly the turning point in the tide of the war, and that from now on we could hope for better things."

[35] The President signed the Selective Service Act on September 16, 1940. *Ibid.*, pp. 345–348.

[36] For Willkie's statements on foreign policy, see Willkie, pp. 263–270.

[37] Former Secretary of War Harry H. Woodring, who was isolationist in sentiment, had had disagreements with his Assistant Secretary, Louis Johnson, who favored greatly increasing armaments. Sherwood, pp. 136, 163.

Then back to the train where the President and Mackenzie King drafted a joint handout reading as follows:

> The Prime Minister and the President have discussed the mutual problems of defense in relation to the safety of Canada and the United States.
>
> It has been agreed that a Permanent Joint Board on Defense shall be set up at once by the two countries.
>
> This Permanent Joint Board on Defense shall commence immediate studies relating to sea, land and air problems including personnel and material.
>
> It will consider in the broad sense the defense of the north half of the Western Hemisphere.
>
> The Permanent Joint Board on Defense will consist of four or five members from each country, most of them from the services. It will meet shortly.[38]

While this last was going on I sat talking with Colonel Cornelius Wickensham, bellicist of the bellicists. Nearly every Easterner above 40 assumes as a matter of course that we shall and should enter the war to save England. Very few under 40 seem to agree.

About one o'clock Mr. King left the President's car and we motored back together to Ottawa. He gave me at great length the account of his talks with the President. . .

The essential features of the President's talks with Mr. Mackenzie King as given me by the latter were as follows:

A. The President will sell about 50 destroyers to the British. He will do this without submitting the matter to Congress.[39] His lawyers are working on the ways and means of doing it legally. Politically, the President believes that the public will accept it, given the fact that the United States is getting the naval bases it desires. Strategically, the President believes that the Navy will now favor it, since the new naval bases are a greater asset to our defense than 50 old destroyers. Churchill had said that they would be more valuable than rubies.

B. The President will announce the sale, probably within the week. The destroyers will be sent shortly thereafter to Halifax where

---

[38] This statement is also printed in U. S. Department of State, *The Department of State Bulletin*, August 24, 1940, p. 154.

[39] For a discussion of the destroyer deal see Langer and Gleason, pp. 742–776, Churchill, *Their Finest Hour*, pp. 398–416, and Hull, I, 831–843.

they will be turned over. Mr. King is telegraphing this very day to Mr. Churchill to send over crews to take them across. A skeleton crew of 75 men per ship should suffice. If more men can be spared they can learn about the ships during the crossing and save time. Canada has enough trained men to man about 5 destroyers. If, however, Canada wants these ships for convoy work, she will have to ask the British for them.

C. The President told Mr. King that Mr. Churchill had at last given a sufficient pledge that he would under no circumstances surrender the British Fleet to the Germans. Mr. King told the President that he thought Mr. Churchill, in hesitating during the month of June to give a satisfactory pledge, had been motivated by a desire to observe all the Constitutional niceties and not bind the hands of a possible successor. (Mr. King reminded me that he had cautioned Mr. Churchill not to try to use the British fleet to bargain with the United States. He had urged him to offer the United States naval bases in the Western Hemisphere. He regrets the two months lost, but now all was well.)

D. With regard to the naval bases to be leased to the United States on 99 year leases, these could be divided into three parts: the West Indian bases, which would be selected by the United States and Britain alone; the Newfoundland base, where Britain held title, but Canada had more immediate geographic and defense interests; and the Canadian base or bases, which would be selected by the United States and Canada alone.

E. The Canadian base or bases would be granted by the Government under its war powers without submission to Parliament. In effect, it would involve a limited free port where the United States could bring in its supplies and equipment, and install docks, drydocks, repair shops, etc. To prevent its wounding Canadian susceptibilities, there would be no objection to having Canadian artillery either on, or dominating, the bases.

F. There would be set up at once a Permanent Joint Board on Defense. The first meeting would be held in Ottawa probably this coming week. Although no final selections have been made, probably Mr. Forrestal will head the American group at the first meeting,[40] the others being the heads of the different services.

[40] James V. Forrestal, Under Secretary of the Navy, did not head the American

G. Among the problems to be worked out are the following: bases to select in Newfoundland and Canada; what supplies and equipment are needed; how an American army of 300,000 men could at need be sent into Nova Scotia without delay; what Canada could do in the event of a thrust toward Maine; what alterations should be made in Canadian railways, particularly with a view to strengthening bridges, enlarging tunnels, etc; what should be done about equipment, interchangeability of type, etc.

H. The President having grown eloquent about the Canadian-American frontier, was startled to have Mr. King declare that we were "creating a frontier" by our passport and visa requirements.[41] He explained the situation at some length, and found the President knew very little about it. He said he had been told, he thought by the State Department, that Canada desired the system as it would prevent men of military age from leaving the Dominion. He promised to speak to Mr. Hull about the matter without delay and try to get the system rescinded in so far as it relates to Canada.

Washington, October 6th to 10th [1940].

I spent four days in Washington and saw many old friends. The following are the highlights of my talks.

Secretary of State Hull.

Mr. Hull said that he had become increasingly worried this past week over the situation in the Far East. Every indication pointed to the fact that Japan was planning to advance in the southern Pacific. We were on the point of calling home our own citizens, of completing our naval mobilization in Hawaii, etc. We did not want, however, to become involved in the Pacific if it could be helped.[42] In a few days, when England has opened the Burma Road, there is a very real

---

delegation. Fiorella LaGuardia led the American group, which met with the Canadians in Ottawa on August 26.

[41] In June 1940 the exemption from passport and visa requirements for Canadians entering the United States was removed. Canadians who lived in the United States and went back to Canada for a visit were required to secure a reëntry permit before they could return to the United States. Dawson, pp. 238-239.

[42] For statements of official policy toward the Far East at this time, consult Hull, I, 906, 911-912. Grew, II, 1221-1375, contains an account of events in Japan and an analysis of American policy in 1940-1941.

chance that Japan will declare war on England.[43] If this should happen England wants us in the war with her. On the other hand, we must realize that the main theater where the war will be won or lost is in England itself and there must be no lessening of our supplies to England. Hornbeck views the problem as centering in the Far East. He is almost alone in advocating measures that almost certainly would bring us into war.[44] The British in the last three weeks have grown remarkably optimistic in Europe. They feel that the three key positions, Spain, Egypt, and Turkey, are all holding firm, and that even if Germany should join with Italy in a first-class attack on Egypt, it could be repelled.

The Secretary then asked me a few questions about Canada and notably about the United States–Alaska highway. His mind, however, was clearly on the Far East.

Under Secretary of State Sumner Welles.

Like the Secretary, Sumner Welles, after a few rather perfunctory questions about Canada, immediately launched into a discussion of the situation in the Far East. He said that for once he was less aggressive than the Secretary. He could never lose sight of the fact that Japan's aggression might well be a baited trap for us. If we went to war with Japan all our efforts would have to be directed toward supplying our ships and our troops in the field and England would correspondingly suffer. The British had been pressing us for a visit of the American Fleet to Australia and Singapore.[45] He was

[43] The Burma Road was reopened on October 18, after having been closed for three months. See Churchill, *Their Finest Hour*, pp. 497–498.

[44] The position of Stanley Hornbeck, Adviser on Political Relations in the Department, has been summed up by Langer and Gleason, p. 601, as that of proposing "greater aid to China and increased pressure on Japan." A memorandum prepared by Mr. Hornbeck and another attributed to him concerning American policy in the Far East are printed in U. S. Congress, *Pearl Harbor Attack*, Hearings before the Joint Committee on the Investigation of the Pearl Harbor Attack, 79 Cong., 1 Sess., Pursuant to S. Cong. Res. 7 (Washington: Government Printing Office, 1946), part 16, pp. 1987–2006.

[45] Lord Lothian, the British Ambassador at Washington, had presented an *aide-mémoire* on June 27, 1940, in which the suggestion was made that American warships should be sent to Singapore. On the next day Cordell Hull had answered that such action "would leave the entire Atlantic seaboard, north and south, exposed to possible European threats. Our main fleet is already well out in the Pacific, near Hawaii." The British proposal was repeated during the autumn of 1940. Hull, I, 897, 911; Churchill, *Their Finest Hour*, p. 498.

opposing it. Unless we were planning to go through with matters to the end this would merely be a gesture which would fool nobody. However, if Japan really wanted trouble, the initiative was always hers, and she herself could bring about a state of war.

I told Sumner Welles that Mr. Mackenzie King had confidentially and off the record told several of my friends that they might expect to see the United States take over the Singapore base any day. Sumner replied that Mr. King was badly informed. The British were trying their best to bring this about but certainly we were not agreeing to it. He urged me not to let the Canadians indulge in "wish thinking" about American participation in the Far Eastern crisis and told me as a matter of general policy to play down rather than to play up American contributions. . .[46]

Adolf Berle.

Adolf Berle said that we were fast moving into war and that he saw nothing to stop the prospect. As far as Canadian relations were concerned we ran over the whole gamut, and he gave me certain instructions. As for the situation in the Far East he too concurred with Sumner Welles and said that we should under no circumstances take over Singapore. After all, our relations with England now were incredibly close, but they would not remain so after the war and we must be sure not to take on anything which would ultimately be a source of embarrassment rather than strength.

Jimmy Dunn.

For many weeks now the Secretary has been telling his intimates that he will resign as Secretary of State at the end of the President's term. Partly this is because he does not believe in a third term,[47] partly because he feels his work is done, and partly because the President very obviously seeks Sumner Welles' advice in preference to his own.[48]

[46] Sumner Welles' comments on American foreign policy in the Far East in this period are given in Welles, pp. 286–288.

[47] Hull wrote in his *Memoirs*, I, 861: "I myself was strongly opposed to the third-term idea. I feared lest it set a precedent for some future President to abuse the power entrusted to him." The Secretary's discussion of the Democratic nomination in 1940 and the campaign can be found in *ibid.*, I, 855–869.

[48] Comments on the strained relations between the Secretary and the Under Secretary can be found in many places. Sherwood has written in *Roosevelt and Hopkins*, p. 135: "Roosevelt bypassed Hull to deal directly with Sumner Welles." He also

For a long time Jimmy Dunn, who is very close to the Secretary, thought that he would under no circumstances stay. Now, however, he is inclined to believe that if the President puts it up to Mr. Hull that it is his patriotic duty to stay on he will accept. At the moment the President is telling Mr. Hull he is indispensable; whether he will do so after the election is all important. If the Secretary goes, he, Jimmy Dunn, will resign. . .

Norman Davis.

Norman Davis considers that the chances are ten to one that we will be at war before the end of November. He said that the public thought that the President was anxious to get into war but that he had been impressed with the President's caution and hesitancy. The President was very tired and no longer showed his old-time punch and drive. In Norman Davis' point of view the British, even if victorious, will no longer be strong enough to preserve their whole Empire without assistance. We shall in effect be the heirs of the Empire and it is up to us to preserve its vital parts. What are these? Obviously there is some difference of opinion, but many in the Navy feel that Singapore is a key point which we could never let go. Of all the people in Washington with whom I talked Norman Davis was the one who would view a war with Japan with the greatest equanimity. . .

Loring Christie (Canadian Minister).

Upon comparing notes Loring Christie and I found that we both had the same conception of our job during wartime: namely, that we were at our posts to interpret government to government and not people to people. In happier days the latter role would again assume importance and there would be the question of representations, speeches, travel, and the like.

---

says that the relationship between Hull and Welles "became so ugly and so extremely dangerous that it eventually compelled the resignation of Welles." Churchill thought that in December 1941 Hull "did not seem to me to have full access at the moment to the President," and Farley quotes Hull in April 1941 as saying: "I don't see the President very often. Most of the details of the department are handled through Sumner Welles." Winston S. Churchill, *The Second World War*, vol. III, *The Grand Alliance* (Boston: Houghton Mifflin Co., 1950), p. 666; Farley, p. 341.

Secretary of War Stimson.

I spent an hour or two with Mr. Stimson bowling on the lawn with him, Herbert Feis, and Gene Regnier. He told me that as Secretary of State his main task was to prevent being pulled back by some intelligent young men who had their own ideas on policy. As Secretary of War he spent his energies in pulling forward several old Generals who lacked ideas but possesed inertia. In each case he was out in front and, he laughingly added, he was always right. He always quoted Mr. Dooley as saying there was a great difference between being Secretary of War and Secretary of a war.

General Strong [Chief of the War Plans Division of the War Department].

With General Strong I discussed the interior air route from the United States to Alaska and found that far more progress had been made than either Major Gullet or I had realized.[49] We discussed the work of the Permanent Joint Defense Board. General Strong felt that it had a tendency to work out strategic plans, which were beyond its competence, as well as to arrange for movement of troops which would later bring up vexing questions of command. General Strong makes no secret of the fact that he feels we are going to enter this war. In fact he said as much in his report on his trip to England which I was shown in the utmost confidence. . .

Stanley Hornbeck.

I had two talks with Stanley Hornbeck, the burden of which was that we were already at war though if we adopted a firm and uncompromising stand we might yet avoid being dragged into a "combat war." He considers Singapore a vital interest to the United States for which we should, if need be, fight. The general impression I had was that Stanley regarded Japan as the sun around which her satellites, Germany and Italy, were revolving.

---

[49] The Canadian Government had undertaken a survey of possible air routes to Alaska before the outbreak of war. After the Permanent Joint Board on Defense was established, the United States and Canada undertook cooperatively to develop air facilities between the United States and Canada. Dziuban, pp. 428–442, has a lengthy discussion of the Northwest Staging Route.

General observations.

Summing up my impressions I had the feeling that we were fast moving toward war, but doing so not because of reason but because of emotions which were becoming so highly involving that they would have to explode somewhere. There was less optimism regarding Britain's ultimate success than I had anticipated. Such help as can be given we shall give. Among other things we are trying to buy off Spain by supplying her with food. The best guess as to what took place at the Brenner conference between Hitler and Mussolini was that they decided upon a series of simultaneous attacks on the key points of the British Empire.[50]

As to the election nearly everybody thought that Mr. Roosevelt would win overwhelmingly — just a little less than he did over Landon. On the other hand, the Willkie workers are whistling to keep up their courage.

As to the Department, it is badly disorganized. In the field many of our men who have been separated for a long time from their wives are growing rather demoralized. We are going to adopt the policy of enforced leaves in the United States at Government expense for officers who have really been in the thick of things, such as London, Berlin, the occupied zones, etc. . .

The work of a Minister does not always have the excitement of Ogdensburg, the stimulation of talking to Mackenzie King or Franklin Roosevelt, the variety of trips to Washington. The day-by-day operation of a Legation is most often undramatic and routine.

In Ottawa in 1940 there were thirty-three people connected with the Legation who handled current business ranging from strictly confidential reports to granting a visa or passport, filling out invoices, or performing notorial services. There was a counselor, a secretary, a military, a naval, an agricultural, and a commercial attaché; there were assistant attachés, a consular section, an accounting department, typists, stenographers, and clerks.

All of these people to some extent aided Mr. Moffat in cleaning up during his first six months as Minister "a whole mass of outstanding questions — none of them of primary importance but a number that have caused a certain amount of bad feeling. Good will plus common sense has found one satisfactory compromise after another."

[50] Hitler and Mussolini met at the Brenner Pass on October 4, 1940. Ciano, pp. 298–299, and Wiskemann, pp. 236–237, shed some light on the discussions at the meeting.

In a letter to his father-in-law, Joseph C. Grew, on January 25, 1941, Pierrepont Moffat listed the nine major problems which the Legation had successfully concluded since he had arrived in Ottawa.

"(1) Arrangements for confidential staff talks between the Canadian and American armed services ending with the setting up of the Permanent Joint Defense Board.

"(2) Agreement with Canada exempting from seizure funds held outside of Canada by American residents in Canada, provided that the funds were not in Canada subsequent to September 1st, 1939.

"(3) Negotiations resulting in the allocation between Canada and the United States of civil aviation routes.

"(4) Arrangement for blanket permission for aircraft, coast guard cutters and the like to fly over certain specified portions of each other's territory or to sail through territorial waters.

"(5) An exchange of notes (confidential) further interpreting the Rush-Bagot Agreement to meet modern situations.

"(6) Persuading the Canadian authorities not to embargo, as was planned, the importation of American fresh fruits and vegetables.

"(7) Alleviation of the drastic visa requirements for Canadians which materially facilitated entry of visitors not planning to remain in the United States over twenty-nine days.

"(8) Acceptance by the United States of certain derogations by Canada from the Trade Agreement under the Wartime Escape Clause.

"(9) Arrangement whereby the United States issues a general license for exports to Canada in return for the Canadians making their list of exports subject to license coincide with our own."

In addition to settling these problems Mr. Moffat had given speeches at Ottawa, Toronto, and Montreal, seen a steady stream of visitors at the Legation, gone almost daily to the Department of External Affairs, and participated in the give and take of a heavy social schedule. Another responsibility of the Legation was the despatch of the weekly report to the State Department, which included not only analyses of current affairs, but also long-term reports on trade, business, defense, or anything which the Department had either called for or some official in the Legation had studied.

With the despatch of December 21, 1940, Mr. Moffat enclosed a discussion of the staple of Canadian political life — Prime Minister William Lyon Mackenzie King.

December 21, 1940.

Mackenzie King became leader of the Liberal Party in 1919 and has to his credit twenty-one years of continuous service in the post.[51]

---

[51] Mr. King was born in Berlin (Kitchener) in Western Ontario in 1874. He first entered politics in 1900 as Deputy Minister of Labour. Eight years later he was elected

This is, I believe, the record in a democratic state today. During those twenty-one years he has won five out of six general elections and has been Prime Minister a total of fourteen years. Time after time his leadership has been challenged within the Liberal Party, usually by some more colorful personality, but with unbroken regularity Mr. King has evaded the challenge, rather than met it head-on, and the challengers are today either forgotten men or else loyal lieutenants in Mr. King's government. For many years people were inclined to attribute his constant successes to mere luck; but when the long arm of coincidence could no longer explain these successes, people went to the other extreme and attributed them to Machiavellian cunning. Neither explanation is accurate. But it is a difficult task to analyze just why he has succeeded, for it calls into play his personality which is full of paradox.

He is no orator; he is no phrasemaker. As a speaker or even a writer, he is lacking in all three of the essential gifts of clarity, force, or ease. He is long winded and can rival Mr. Hoover in making a dramatic subject seem dull or statistical. When answering questions in the House of Commons he is a past master at evasion, or burying the kernel of truth, to which he does not wish to attract attention, in a haystack of extraneous detail. In the rough and tumble of debate, and particularly in the exchange of shafts with the leader of the Opposition, he will score many more points than he loses, though his shafts are apt to be so sugar-coated that it is only later their full sting is felt. But although his auditors are often bored by his presentation — which in addition to all else lacks wit or humor — they attach full weight to the opinion he is expressing, which they know is invariably a reasoned opinion, reached after considerable study and cogitation.

For Mr. King is primarily a student. It was more by accident than design that he elected to follow a political career, rather than to accept Professor Taussig's offer of a chair in the Department of Economics at Harvard.[52] He detests snap decisions and likes to weigh the

to Parliament as a Liberal. He was Prime Minister of Canada from 1921 to 1930, and he regained this office in 1935. Mr. King died on July 22, 1950. H. Reginald Hardy, *Mackenzie King of Canada* (London: Oxford University Press, 1949).

[52] Mackenzie King attended the Universty of Toronto, the University of Chicago, and Harvard University, from which he won a fellowship to study social conditions in Europe. In 1900 he was offered an instructorship in political economy at Harvard by Professor Frank W. Taussig.

pros and cons of a problem before finally committing himself. He has turned a lonely life into an asset, for he devotes a large part of his leisure, whether at Laurier House, or on his well-loved acres at Kingsmere, to reading and abstract thinking. In this he is the antithesis of President Roosevelt, who is impatient at reading documents and seeks to gain understanding by oral explanations coupled with searching cross-examination. Mr. King far prefers to take a problem home with him and dig out its intricacies from the typewritten memoranda before him. More than most political leaders he is "cursed with seeing two sides to a problem." But again, he has turned what is generally considered a political liability into an asset, for it has made him extremely careful to weigh the effect of any measure upon the many disparate — and often mutually hostile — elements that make up the body-politic in Canada, and above all it has taught him never to try for anything that he does not consider he has a reasonably sure chance of obtaining.

Thus Mr. King is not a Crusader, or at best not a tilter against the windmills of lost causes. But, if not a Crusader, he is at least a reformer, though unlike most reformers he has an almost infinite patience. From his early days when he spent a year at Hull House in Chicago, through his tenure of office as Minister of Labour in Ottawa, just as later on when investigating conditions in the Colorado coal industry for the Rockefeller Foundation,[53] he has shown a very rare comprehension of the underprivileged and of their needs and desires. Year by year he has ameliorated their lot in Canada, despite the fact that the two great parties are largely controlled by vested financial interests, and neither has ever committed itself to the task of real, as opposed to apparent, reform. Yet Canada has kept apace with changing methods and thought, and Mr. King has avoided much of the bitterness aroused in other countries by refusing to assault the resisting wall of reactionary capital with a battering ram, preferring to remove the wall brick by brick. Probably during the course of two decades approximately the same amount of debris would have been removed by either one of the two alternate systems.

Mr. King decided instead to accept the editorship of the *Labour Gazette* and the position of Deputy Minister of Labour. *Ibid.*, pp. 25–44.

[53] In 1896–97 Mr. King lived at Hull House Social Settlement in Chicago. He was Minister of Labour from 1909 to 1911 and directed industrial research for the Rockefeller Foundation from 1914 to 1917.

To Mr. King there is nothing inconsistent between reform and harmonizing, and in his leadership of his government and of his party, he always tries to get the essential part of what he wants through harmonizing. If he can gain the essence, he will willingly sacrifice the form if thereby he can achieve unity within the group. Few leaders have kept twelve or fifteen men of such diverse temperaments, origins, and interests as are inevitably found in a Canadian government more nearly in line than Mackenzie King. In the government, he is merely *primus inter pares*; the government makes a collective decision in which his voice is but one. Yet he has almost invariably had his own way; and if he saw that opinion was running against him he would as presiding officer postpone bringing a problem to the point of decision time after time until ultimately some change of circumstance would shift the balance of opinion to his side. He follows the same technique as far as he can in the party caucus, which during parliamentary sessions is held weekly. Given the strength of party discipline, plus the overwhelming present strength of the Liberal Party, the decisions reached in caucus are usually final. I am told that of all his many roles, that of leader in his party caucus is the one where his talents are the most outstanding.

But it is in a still larger field that Mr. King's harmonizing abilities are most vivid. To one unfamiliar with Canada the gulf between French Canadian and British Canadian is a constant source of wonder. The French Canadians are now about one third of the population, and a homogeneous group enjoying certain stipulated privileges in the matter of religion, language, and education. They have wisely refrained from forming a political party of their own but have always belonged to one or other of the two major parties. Of late they have been predominately liberal. The French Canadian regards himself as the truest Canadian, the descendant of the earliest settlers, vitally interested in Canada and interested not at all in the Empire; to him the British Canadian seems a colonial, willing to subordinate Canada's interests to those of Great Britain and ready to waste Canadian life and treasure in Britain's imperial wars. To the average British Canadian, the French Canadian is a member of a minority, inferior in culture, less loyal in outlook, who must be dealt with politely, humored, and endured. Alone among the outstanding British Canadian leaders today, Mr. Mackenzie King trusts, and consequently is trusted by, the French Canadian. He views national unity, not as a means but as an end. He will delay, he will compromise, he will travel only part of the road he would follow if he can travel with French and British Canadians pulling in double harness. For this he is often bitterly blamed by the Imperialists in Canada, but their criticism does not deflect him. He has seen the mistakes of the past, and what is rare, he has learned from them. When the time comes for him to leave office, he will leave a far more united Dominion than he found. What is more, he would not hesitate voluntarily to relinquish office rather than to break any pledge he has made to the French Canadians.

In this I acquit Mr. King of any self-interest, or political opportunism. His vision of a united Canada is a very genuine one, with almost a mystic tinge. It is one of the many things he *feels*, where his power of expression is less vivid than the feeling itself. This holds true of his religion, which is something very personal to him. He is constantly referring, but without carrying great conviction to others, to religious teachings, or even scraps of sermons heard decades ago, which have influenced his actions or his judgments. Above all, he believes that men and nations are subjected to all manner of trials with a view to testing their steel and giving them an opportunity better to temper it. He once told me his life's story, pointing out that on two or three occasions when he was at a crossroads and made an apparently wrong choice, it had nevertheless enabled him to gain experience in some new field, and develop into a bigger and better man. He similarly explained to me Winston Churchill's career. It was obvious that Churchill and he were mutually antipathetic, yet he recognized his peculiar genius for leadership in a desperate emergency and thought that Providence had reserved him for his present especial task.

Mr. King has been fortunate throughout his public life in having three well-defined goals constantly before him. The first was to win, and having won to maintain, recognition of Canada's independent status as a nation, bound to the other members of the British Commonwealth only by ties of loyalty to the Crown. The second was to support Great Britain and the Empire in bad days as well as in good, but to do so because it was in Canada's best interests. The third was to promote close friendship between Canada and the United States, partly because he felt that Canadian development would thereby be quickened, partly because he felt that it would bring the United

States and Great Britain into a closer understanding, which he believed to be the ultimate guarantee of peace.

Now that it is an accomplished fact, one is apt to overlook the resistance to Canada's independent status on the part of certain powerful moneyed groups in the Dominion. The Orangeman in Ontario, and the capitalist in Montreal have never lost their colonial outlook, their belief that Canada is too immature to stand alone, and that any move to cut adrift from British control was bound to speed an inevitable absorption of Canada by the United States. To Mr. King such an attitude was anathema. He had full confidence in Canada's ability, and in its duty, to stand on its own feet. He felt that Canada had come of age, and that it was time for the Dominion to be master in its own house. Family ties with the parents and sister would remain close, but there could be no compulsion in the relationship. He thus spent years in preaching self-confidence to his countrymen, and in telling [them] that they could and should decide their own destiny. The acid test lay in the answer to the question: could Canada remain neutral if Britain were at a war. The answer came in September 1939. Britain had been at war with Germany since September 3rd. The Canadian Parliament was only meeting on September 9th.[54] On one of the intervening days Mr. King's telephone rang, with the President of the United States desiring to speak to him. "Hello, Mackenzie," began Mr. Roosevelt (who parenthetically is the only man to call him thus; his intimates call him Billy or Rex), "we are about to issue our proclamation of neutrality and there is a difference of opinion in Cabinet as to Canada's legal status. The simplest way to settle the argument was to refer it to you. Is Canada at war with Germany, or is it not?" "No, Mr. President," was the answer, "until our Parliament acts Canada is not at war." The following Sunday [September 10] the King signed, on the advice of his Canadian Ministers, a declaration of war by Canada against Germany. The question which in theory had perplexed Canada for years had been finally settled.

Public opinion in Canada now recognizes that in his battle for independent status Mr. King was right. But having won the battle, he is accused of not having made full use of his victory. His critics allege, and with considerable justice, that he never tried to influence British foreign policy, which remained more absorbed by Great

[54] Parliament had been called to meet on September 7, 1939.

Britain's insular preoccupations than the interests of the Empire as a whole. Mr. King admitted the charge but said that it was due to his unwillingness to be put in a position where Canada might have to make a pledge of future conduct, whether expressed or implied. Complete freedom of action in all contingencies was what Mr. King desired. For better or worse the other members of the Canadian Government took little interest in foreign affairs, which thus came under the almost exclusive purview of Mr. King and his North-American-minded Under-Secretary Dr. Skelton. Both men recoiled from Canadian participation in a second world war; yet both men recognized that if Britain became engaged in a serious struggle Canada would again bleed and impoverish herself on Britain's behalf. The war, when it came, marked the crumbling of their hopes and their plans. But being realists, they did not waste a moment's time in regret for the collapse of their policies; they made an about-face and as a team are still guiding Canada's foreign policy, recognizing however that despite the outward trappings of independence, it is, at least for the duration of the war, a mere adjunct of British foreign policy as laid down from London. Even in matters of trade and economics, which with increasing government control have become closely tied in with foreign policy, Canada is tending to relinquish the preferred position she had given her own industries as against British competition. Whether or not Canada will recover and assert an independent foreign policy during the ultimate peace settlement is an open question.

But if some of Mr. King's castles have crumbled of late there is one to which he is coming to add stone upon stone and bastion upon bastion. Canadian-American friendship may well be the crowning and enduring work of his life. Again, I suspect that he has *felt* its importance more than he has rationalized it. The grandson of the old rebel, William Lyon Mackenzie, who sought refuge in the United States, Mackenzie King was brought up on the story as told him over and over again by his mother, whose memory remains today the most potent force in his life.[55] The idea of American friendship for Canada

---

[55] William Lyon Mackenzie was a Scotsman, who had immigrated to Canada in the eighteen-twenties. He became a successful journalist and printer and an influential politician in York County and Toronto. After his participation in the Rebellion of 1837 a price of 1000 pounds was put on his head, and his property was confiscated. Mackenzie escaped to the United States. In 1849 he was pardoned and returned to Toronto, where he lived until his death in 1861. Mackenzie's daughter Isabel was the mother of William Lyon Mackenzie King. Hardy, pp. 6–9, 12–13.

was bound to make an early appeal. It was enhanced by his experiences as a graduate student at the University of Chicago and at Harvard, where he made a group of friendships throughout our social strata, all the way from the very poor with whom he came in touch through settlement work, to the smart set in Newport whom he met at periodic visits he made to the Gerrys [Peter Goelet Gerry, Senator from Rhode Island]. With many Americans but particularly with various American women he met in his youth he has never allowed himself to lose touch, for his capacity for the friendly gesture, the kindly handwritten note, and the well-timed invitation is almost limitless. In his maturer years he has been greatly influenced by two men: John D. Rockefeller, Jr., and President Roosevelt. In Mr. Rockefeller, he found the story-book capitalist, who regarded his wealth merely as a trust to benefit others. Even in considering the ways and means of how this could best be done, he was humble in his judgments and sought the most objective advice he could find. In outlook and in temperament he and Mr. King were as one. In President Roosevelt he found the champion of all that he held most dear in the field of social reform. The President had the art of putting into telling phrases, which carried conviction to the most despondent, the injustices being suffered by the underprivileged, and the duty which had passed from the hands of capital into the hands of government to remedy them. Mr. King was a big enough man not to resent the success of the President in preëmpting the field, in which above all others he would most have liked to shine. Instead, he became a hero-worshipper and dedicated to Mr. Roosevelt a friendship, wherein the personal and the official are curiously blended. This friendship resulted in the cutting of red tape, the rounding of corners, and the smoothing of rough edges that were bound to crop up between the two countries in all manner of secondary problems. But by virtue of this, the ground was prepared for the seed to sprout, when the war impelled Canada and the United States to reëxamine their relationship.

With his capacity for infinite patience Mr. King had been content to see Canadian-American friendship ripen as a slow growth. Looking back over the twenty years of his active political life, he had seen the disappearance in Canada of any fear of American annexation or absorption as well as the gradual softening, under the healing influences of time, of the inherited grudge of the United Empire Loyalists.[56] In the United States, where the shadow of Canada had never loomed large, he had seen a growth of neighborly feeling to a point where not a dissenting voice was raised when the President pledged that "the people of the United States will not stand idly by if domination of Canadian soil is threatened by any other Empire." [57] But being content with slow progress, and relishing each forward step — he keeps, for instance, a scrapbook on Canadian-American relations, with texts of speeches, programs of commemoration events, and photographs of ceremonial occasions duly preserved for some ultimate historian — Mr. King never dared allow himself to hope for a public recognition that the defense of the two countries constituted a single problem, and the creation of a Joint Defense Board that would be reciprocal and that would be permanent. The famous meeting with the President at Ogdensburg, which was arranged by the President as a daring improvisation, and the understandings reached and announced there, constituted a fitting fruition for twenty years spent in preparing the ground. Yet no one was more surprised than Mr. King that his dream had suddenly come true. Six weeks before he had been cautiously suggesting staff talks, and Washington with equal caution wanted to know before answering just what Canada wished to discuss. But in those six weeks the world outlook had fundamentally changed, and the President changed with it. To his impulsive nature, Mr. King has always seemed overcautious, and apt to let opportunities slip by through unwillingness to take a risk. It is fair to say, however, that the present association of policies between the two countries could hardly have been achieved without the contribution of both authors, the one who with tireless zeal prepared the material, the other who conceived the brilliant climax.

In his conduct of the war, some critics charge Mr. King with having been slow to perceive the underlying issues of the struggle, and slow to throw Canada's effort into the high gear of total war. His answer is that prior to the black days of May 1940 he had provided

[56] During and after the American Revolution many Loyalists emigrated from the United States to the Maritime Provinces and Upper Canada. They and their descendants were know as the United Empire Loyalists. See George Bryce, *A Short History of the Canadian People* (London: Sampson Low, Marston & Co., 1914), pp. 455–456; Carl Wittke, *A History of Canada* (3rd ed.; New York: F. S. Crofts & Co., 1942), pp. 57–67.

[57] Roosevelt, *Papers and Addresses, 1938*, pp. 491–494.

everything that Britain had asked of Canada in men and in material; the British war effort was necessarily centralized in London and what was asked by London was given. He is criticized for having called a general election in wartime, and for having refused to form a coalition government.[58] His answer is that he needed a vote of confidence *ad hoc* for the prosecution of the war, and that party government, with a constructive opposition, brings the best results in a true democracy.

But when once Mr. King accepted the necessity for total war, and realized that Canada must think and plan and make decisions, if not independently at least as Britain's full war partner, he threw himself into his new role with surprising vigor. His sense of proportion, his energy, even a certain newborn ruthlessness have astonished his friends as well as his critics. Today he is at the very apex of his power, with full personal credit being paid him for the speed with which his government has geared up Canada's war effort since last June, for the closeness of Canadian-American relations, and for the large measure of unity between British and French Canadians which was conspicuously absent during the last war. There is no longer a trace of opposition to his leadership within his own party, and what opposition there might be from the Conservative party has been dissipated by several bad blunders on the part of its leaders.

Yet I doubt if any country has a leader with such powers and such an innate modesty. It approaches humility. He dislikes publicity, he never gives interviews, and in the occasional press conference he has to hold he is not only uninformative, but overpolite to the point of seeming disingenuous. His appearance is without distinction, and he possesses to a marked degree the faculty of losing himself in a crowd. But he has his little vanities. Being a man of few possessions he takes inordinate pride in those that he has acquired. Being a man of taste, he is more interested in the quality of his chattels than in their quantity. He is never happier than when dispensing hospitality, and the two roles he most enjoys are those of the scholar showing his guests his library when in town, and the squire exhibiting his skill in gardening when in the country. He loves a good dinner and alternates feasting and fasting. Though a bachelor he is no misogynist.

---

[58] Parliament had been dissolved on January 25, 1940, following an attack led by Mitchell Hepburn and the vote of censure of the Ontario legislature on Mr. King's conduct of the war. The election which was held on March 26 returned Mr. King and the Liberals with the largest majority in Canadian history. Dawson, pp. 21–26.

He gains real pleasure from the conversation of a congenial group of friends, but is quite ready when they leave to sit on for a while with his faithful terrier Pat and cogitate on some abstract subject. He is intensely loyal to his friends, though quite willing to laugh at their foibles. The only group of men to whom he is definitely unreasonable are his secretaries, whom he expects at his beck and call day or night, with utter disregard of their personal lives or convenience. But even they admit that Mr. King works longer hours than any one of them, and that his output of speeches, notes, memoranda, etc., is prodigious. He never dramatizes his premiership, but is content to appeal to his countrymen, and to history, not on the basis of his personality, but on the basis of his record.

The United States and Canada, separately and jointly, have planned to develop the potentialities of the great inland waterway lying between them — the St. Lawrence. Twice in the nineteen-thirties treaties were drafted which provided for harnessing the river's power and making it a waterway for ocean-going vessels. The first treaty died in the United States Senate in 1934 where it had run afoul of special interest groups. Opposition to this treaty had also arisen in Ontario and Quebec with the provincial premiers, Mitchell Hepburn and Maurice Duplessis, leading the denunciation.

In 1938 the United States redirected attention to the project by submitting new draft proposals which avoided many of the objectionable features of the old.[59] For two years the United States and Canada discussed and reworked these proposals, until a mutually satisfactory agreement was achieved. A few months before this agreement was signed Mr. Moffat was summoned to talk with Prime Minister King.

Ottawa, January 29, 1941.

The Prime Minister sent for me this afternoon. He said that he had postponed this talk because he had wished to confer with Colonel Ralston and Mr. Howe [C. D. Howe, Minister of Munitions and Supply] after their return from England in order to see exactly what it would be necessary for the Canadian Government to do in the way of intensifying the war effort. Mr. Howe and Colonel Ralston had come back full of enthusiasm for the bravery being displayed by the English people, but Mr. Howe in particular felt that the British Government was still underestimating the problem with which they

[59] F. H. Soward, *et al.*, *Canada in World Affairs* (London: Oxford University Press, 1941), pp. 229–230; Dawson, pp. 248–252, 313–315.

were faced and the terrible nature of the German attack which was expected in March or April. Reports reaching the Canadian Government were that the Germans were manufacturing gas in large quantities. Germany's military strength has suffered virtually no depletion thus far during the war.

In the circumstances Canada has reëxamined her war effort and is going to budget for $1,300,000,000 for direct war expenditures (not including the ordinary expenses of government) this year. This represents the cost of the maximum effort which Canada can exert. Her manpower and her industrial plant can do no more. But if on top of this the Canadian Government should bring in a Treaty or Agreement calling for the construction of the St. Lawrence seaway three questions would be asked: Where are you going to get the money? Where are you going to get the men? How do you reconcile this with your estimate of Canada's maximum war effort? Mr. King said he would have the utmost difficulty in answering.

Not much difficulty would arise if we limited ourselves at the present time to completing the works in the international section. This could be justified as a direct war effort in that it would provide the necessary additional power for Canadian industry.

The Province of Ontario is now in line, but the opposition to the seaway in the Province of Quebec is far more serious than Mr. King himself had realized. He spent the better part of three days canvassing the entire situation with Premier Godbout, who has the broadest grasp of statesmanship of any one coming from Quebec for a generation. Mr. Godbout told him that it was not merely the power interests and the financial interests that were opposed, but that there was great dissatisfaction among the plain people as well. If the work on the seaway could be postponed until after the war much of this opposition would disappear as the work would cushion the inevitable unemployment. Duplessis [former Premier of Quebec] was planning to attack Premier Godbout on the seaway and in Mr. King's judgment had a reasonable chance of ousting him.

If after all we should decide to proceed with the seaway, probably the only way in which it could be managed — and this Mr. King told us in the strictest confidence — would be for the Province of Quebec to take over the power interests and receive a contribution from the Federal Government for the work undertaken, much as in the case of the Ontario Hydro-Electric. In the first place this would start a battle royal in Quebec; in the second place it would be described as a bribe, and the other provinces would be tempted to seek similar bribes from the Dominion Government.

Mr. King thought that if Duplessis overthrew Godbout on this issue he and Hepburn would make common cause and seriously embarrass the Dominion Government. They were men in whose integrity he had very slight confidence. He would be willing to risk the overthrow of his government if he were completely satisfied that the President genuinely believed that the seaway were essential to national defense and personally asked him to proceed. He had, of course, read the President's message to Detroit [60] but he wished to assure himself once again that Mr. Roosevelt himself considered the seaway a necessary element in the war effort. Did the United States, for instance, have a concrete project to lay down ships in the Great Lakes shipyards within the near future, or was this merely a hope? Were those ships considered a necessity by Britain as well — in which case the seaway could be presented as a war measure desired by both the United States and Great Britain?

To conclude: If Mr. Roosevelt made a personal appeal he would go through with the project irrespective of cost, but in this case he would wish an exchange of letters which he could at the proper moment make public. He would write the first letter explaining his difficulties and the President would reply. His letter would then suggest, as an alternative to present plans, "a proposal to proceed with the development of the International Section but to postpone consideration of an obligation to develop the National Section for navigation until after the war when wide support could be obtained for this part of the project as a postwar reconstruction plan." The President's reply would set forth the necessity for the seaway as an immediate war need, with justificatory arguments. But he continued to hope that the President, after realizing his difficulties, would not press him to sign

[60] The President on December 5, 1940, had sent a message to the Great Lakes-St. Lawrence Seaway and Power Conference Meeting in Detroit in which he said:
"It is now a vital necessity.
"The United States needs the St. Lawrence Seaway for defense. . .
"The United States needs, tremendously needs, the power project." Roosevelt, *Papers and Addresses, 1940*, pp. 599–602; *New York Times*, December 6, 1940, p. 1.

an instrument specifically providing for the seaway, and in any event not at this time. . .

I made no observations during this long exposition of Mr. King's viewpoint other than to say it seemed to me as important to be able to transport the industrial output of Canada and the United States to England as to increase the output. That being the case, I felt that additional shipbuilding, and the moving of completed ships, was as much a war effort as any factory expansion, and could be so portrayed.

Washington, Friday, January 31st [1941].

Reached Washington about 1.15 and went straight to the Metropolitan Club where I lunched with Berle and Hickerson [John D. Hickerson, Assistant Chief of the Division of European Affairs]. I told them the story of my talk with Mackenzie King. . . They were both convinced that the President would ask him to keep the present seaway provisions in the draft but would agree to an exchange of letters in which he would take the responsibility of urging its early construction as a "war measure." On the other hand they agreed that as Mackenzie King had sent his message as a personal appeal to the President, and as it involved consideration of high policy, they should sit tight until the President had given his answer. Berle predicted that he would pick up the receiver and telephone Mackenzie King in person as soon as he heard the story. General Watson was at the next table and we made a tentative appointment with the President for tomorrow.

Berle thought we couldn't get a St. Lawrence Treaty through the House and Senate unless we had the votes of the Lake State members; these were only interested in the seaway.

Hickerson said that Mackenzie King always sheered off before taking a courageous decision, and that his attitude on the St. Lawrence today was essentially the same as it had been since 1925. He felt we should press Mackenzie King now and press him hard. He did not believe his Cabinet would be in danger, not even that Godbout would face real difficulties in Quebec. . .

Called on James C. Dunn. He was very unhappy over developments in the Department. Said the Secretary was used, but not consulted. He had only been shown the Lease-Lend Bill four hours before its introduction.[61] When it struck snags, his aid was enlisted to unsnarl them. He had not been told of the President's decision to go to the Chesapeake to meet Lord Halifax,[62] etc. The power behind the throne was [Supreme Court Justice] Felix Frankfurter. . .

[Washington], Saturday, February 1 [1941].

. . . I saw the President at 12.15, together with Adolf Berle and Leland Olds [Chairman of the Federal Power Commission]. He looked older and grayer than last summer, but surprisingly vigorous. . .

Steve Early [Secretary to President Roosevelt] left, and the President turned to me: "By the way," he began, "when am I going to send your name to the Senate as Minister to Luxemburg?" I thought he was joking in some way, but no — his intention is to accredit me near the Grand Duchess, who is living in Montreal, just as he is planning to accredit Tony Biddle [American Ambassador to Poland] near the exiled Chiefs of [the Polish] State now residing in London.

He then said, "Now tell me what is on your mind." I told him of my talk with Mackenzie King, and the latter's apprehensions about signing an agreement at the moment providing for the construction of the seaway, although he felt he could safely sign up for work on the International Section which he could justify as a war measure in that it would give additional and needed power for the expansion of Canadian and American war industries. I practically recited my memorandum of January 29th, merely adding a summary of recent political developments in Canada. . . He listened attentively without interruption, then said, "What Mackenzie King asks does not create too much of a problem. The great thing at the present time is to get the Barnhart Island Dam constructed. That is the key to both phases of the St. Lawrence problem — deep channel and power. If we can get that started right away, we can if need be meet Mackenzie King's wishes. I have never been didactic about method: if it is politically easier to sign up for a seaway, let's do that; if it is politically easier to sign up for power, let's do that. If Canada can't accept the seaway at the moment, let it go; we'll agree to proceed with work in the Inter-

[61] Hull, II, 923, and Edward R. Stettinius, Jr., *Lend-Lease* (New York: The Macmillan Co., 1944), p. 68.

[62] President Roosevelt went to Annapolis to meet the new British Ambassador, Lord Halifax.

national Section, and once the Dam is constructed, the completion of the seaway will follow as surely as day follows night. Personally, I think it will follow sooner than Mackenzie King thinks, as war developments may make it so obviously essential that we should be able to build ships in the Great Lakes that we'll be signing a supplementary agreement without political repercussions. But there's no point in forcing that issue now. We can't ask King to risk his Cabinet, and it wouldn't be in our interest to do so. King has his limitations, but he is in the war to the hilt now and mustn't be disturbed."

"Yes," I added, "and he's the only man I see who could keep French and British Canadians working together in alignment."

"Now as to our own situation," the President continued, "I think it would be just as useful to present the St. Lawrence agreement as primarily a power project, as it would to present it as power plus seaway. I think we might even pick up a few more votes. I have been dickering with the Lower Mississippi States and think I have them in line." He asked if Berle and Olds agreed with his diagnosis. They made no comment, even though I know that neither one agreed.

"All right," concluded the President, "you know the answer; we can manage things here. We shall have to encourage the Lake States as they are going to be disappointed, but they won't hurry up the seaway by rejecting an immediate development of the International Section."

"May I make one suggestion, Mr. President?" I asked. I then explained that we had exchanged notes with Canada "interpreting" the Rush-Bagot Agreement in the light of modern conditions so as to permit the construction of warships of any size on the Great Lakes, provided they were not left there, and provided the guns were not actually mounted until later.[63] "Could we not arrange at the psychological moment to publish this exchange of notes, which would then give you the opportunity publicly to hold out hopes of an eventual naval shipbuilding yard in the Great Lakes?"

[63] The Rush-Bagot Agreement of April 1817 placed limitations on the naval forces which the United States and Great Britain could maintain on the Great Lakes. The notes of June 9, 1939, June 10, 1939, October 30, 1940, and November 2, 1940, exchanged between the United States and Canada are printed in Canada, Department of External Affairs, *Exchange of Notes Relating to the Application and Interpretation of . . . (Rush-Bagot Agreement)* (Ottawa: Edmond Cloutier, 1941), pp. 1–10. These notes were made public in March 1941.

"A good idea," he said. "I'll look into that, and I think it's an idea that will improve with further acquaintance. Now go ahead, and get the best agreement we can which will let us start work on the Dam with the least possible delay". . .

Leland Olds and I then spent the latter part of the afternoon working on the St. Lawrence draft. Leland Olds was distinctly unhappy at the tenor of the President's instructions and feared that the Lake States would charge that we had "sold them down the river". . .[64]

After having spent a good part of his two years in Australia negotiating about economic matters, Pierrepont Moffat was acutely aware of the trials and the errors of the Commonwealth trading arrangement set up at Ottawa. In the Canadian capital in 1932 Great Britain and the Dominions had adopted the Imperial Preference system to meet the greatest of all depressions by building a closed economic unit, whose members could trade to mutual advantage. The Ottawa Agreements had effectively shut out many items of American trade. Canadian imports from the United States, which had been $875,000,000 at the peak of the boom in 1929, fell to $246,000,000 in the year of the Ottawa conference, and only rose to $463,000,000 by 1937.[65] Various modifications were made to the benefit of both the United States and Canada, particularly in the United States–Canada Trade Agreement of 1938.[66] And the changes brought about by the war, in trade and world economy, seemed to provide leverage by which the Department of State could encourage further alteration.

Washington, March 31st [1941].

Spent the entire day in the State Department. I had come to Washington to preach the gospel that unless we availed ourselves of the present situation to obtain a commitment from the members of the British Empire to modify the Ottawa Agreements after the war, we would ultimately be virtually shut out of our Dominion markets through a tendency on the part of them all to close the Empire further and further by means of increased Imperial preferences. Much to

[64] The agreement about the development of the Great Lakes–St. Lawrence Basin was signed on March 19, 1941. S. Shepard Jones and Denys P. Myers (eds.), *Documents on American Foreign Relations July 1940–June 1941* (Boston: World Peace Foundation, 1944), III, 179–203.

[65] Frank A. Knox, "Trade and the World Economy," *Canada*, ed. George W. Brown (Berkeley: University of California Press, 1950), p. 527. Part of this decline was due, of course, to the world depression, which began in 1929 and hung on into the late thirties. But Canadian trade with Great Britain increased much more rapidly from 1932 to 1937 than did United States–Canadian trade.

[66] Soward *et al.*, pp. 195–199, 212–224.

my delight I found that people had begun to think along these lines, largely because the Treasury had set up for the State Department's approval an agreement with the British regarding repayment under the Lease-Lend Bill.[67] The Treasury had set it up as an account against which the return of equipment would be debited. Look at it as you will it was creating a new war debt and war debt psychology. There were, therefore, held three conferences on Monday, Tuesday, and Wednesday, at which I was asked to be present, when we were trying to formulate our collective State Department opinion.

We felt in general that the problem should be subdivided into three heads: (a) Matériel such as shells, bombs, etc., which was meant to be destroyed in use and which obviously could not be returned. This, we felt, should be written off completely as a contribution to the British cause. (b) Matériel which could be returned, such as guns, planes, etc. This should be returned and no depreciation for use or deterioration charged. (c) Nonmilitary supplies, such as foodstuffs, merchant shipping, etc., as well as information services, etc. Here we felt that repayment should be made. However, we recognized that cash repayment was extremely unlikely and that in lieu of cash we could get certain advantages from England which she could readily give.

What were those advantages: in the first place there were a number of islands in the Pacific, both those to which England and America each claimed title and a few others which our navy wanted for strategic considerations. We thought Britain could readily give us these, though it would be better to do so as an apparently unilateral offering rather than as part of a bargain. Then too there were British investments in Latin America which could be transferred to us. Here, curiously enough, the Latin American experts were distinctly uninterested. They said that these investments were for the most part in utilities, that the trend was toward confiscation or at least expropriation with minimum compensation, that they would be the source of constant disputes throughout the next decades and that we were better off without. The third and most important *quid pro quo* was the Ottawa Agreements.

We all agreed that something should be done here and for a wonder Welles, Acheson [Dean Acheson, Assistant Secretary of

[67] Stettinius, pp. 57–85.

State] and Berle agreed completely. Curiously enough the Secretary thought that a general statement of policy from the British was all we could ask for at the time.[68] The rest of us took the view that there should be something far more concrete and that we should obtain definite commitments now. It also was clear that owing to rising agricultural prices in the United States we would probably be able to negotiate a real trade agreement with the Empire, provided we would be willing to give concessions on the vexed products of wool, butter and possibly meat. Curiously enough the Department of Agriculture was in favor of our doing so. The Secretary, however, was curiously unconvinced. I could not make out his attitude and his apparent indifference towards striving for what would be the biggest success in his particular program. The only explanation I could give was fatigue. Everyone from highest to lowest is so tired that the quality of the work and the quality of thinking is not up to its usual standard.

The conferences were, as usual, inconclusive but I understand that both sides will be put up to the White House.[69] The two predominant influences there for the moment are Harry Hopkins and Mr. Justice Frankfurter. Harry Hopkins is sound in his ideas and, while tremendously impressed with the need for haste in sending aid to Britain, is under no illusions that we can postpone indefinitely obtaining what we want and trusting to ultimate British generosity. Mr. Justice Frankfurter on the other hand has, I am told, virtually become the lawyer for the British case and argues for them on all occasions, even against the State Department which is the guardian of American interests. . .

Ottawa, October 8, 1941.

I called on Mr. Robertson [Norman Robertson, Under-Secretary of State for External Affairs] this afternoon to talk over a number of pending problems with him. I was not successful, however, in

[68] Apparently Mr. Roosevelt agreed with Mr. Hull, because the Secretary has written that the President instructed that "the *quid pro quo* for our Lend-Lease supplies and facilities should be deferred until a final settlement were reached, and that it should then be framed within certain broad principles relating to world peace and international economic relations." Hull, II, 1151–1152. See also Sherwood, pp. 360–361, 506–507.

[69] Canadian-American economic matters had been under discussion for some time in Washington, particularly in the talks of Mr. Berle with Mr. Keenleyside. These discussions were considerably speeded along, when President Roosevelt and Prime

making a satisfactory beginning, as his mind was filled with worries over what he called our "assault on the preferential system." He was so exercised over this that he talked about it for fifty minutes.

He asked me whether I had seen the draft note regarding lease-lend which we had submitted to Lord Halifax a week or ten days ago. I told him that I had not. He said that in essence it suggested a reciprocal undertaking that after the war neither country would impose or maintain any form of discrimination against the trade of the other country. He said that he did not feel that the British would be able to accept this formula but would reply that while they could not give so broad a commitment at the moment, the two Governments might start informal conversations on this phase of their relationships. I told Mr. Robertson that such a reply would be a serious disappointment, to put it mildly, to our officials. He countered by saying that both the American formula and the British formula (if in fact London decided to reply in this sense) would be a bitter disappointment to Canada. The disappointment and the resentment would be based on the fact that in the last analysis it would not be Britain but the Dominions which would be making the sacrifices.

At this point Mr. Robertson went into a long-term discussion of the 1938 agreements and the fallacy of considering that the country which accorded a preference was making any concession when it abandoned its position. It was the other country, the one which benefited by the preference, that did all the paying. To suggest that Britain give up all forms of discrimination against the United States was in effect penalizing the Dominions, upsetting their economies, and facing Canada with a squeeze play.

Mr. Robertson said that he was not objecting to our trying to modify the Ottawa system; he felt that we had already made two successful modifications and that a further and greater modification was probably in order.[70] What he did object to was our assumption that this was purely an Anglo-American problem. I argued that the attitude of Messrs. Keynes [John Maynard Keynes, member of the Chancellor of the Exchequer's Consultative Council], Geoffrey Crowther [editor of *The Economist*], and others, made it clear to us

Minister King met at Hyde Park in April 1941 and announced their own personal plans for economic cooperation. William L. Langer and S. Everett Gleason, *The Undeclared War 1940–1941* (New York: Harper & Bros., 1953), pp. 431–432.

[70] See Soward, *et al.*, pp. 175–224.

that there was a strong school of thought in England that wished to adopt either a closed Empire system or to pursue a cutthroat policy of straight bilateralism. Mr. Robertson said that the former was utterly impossible, that it would be contrary to Canadian interests to belong to a closed Empire; that she was not even in the sterling block, etc. Canada would help us work out an adjustment, but in his opinion we were oversimplifying the problem. He did not feel that it was enough to talk of discriminations only. Discriminations were one side of a picture, of which the other side was the absolute height of tariffs. He did not feel that we could solve the problem unless we faced both phases simultaneously. The worst thing possible for Canada would be a cutthroat competition between two self-sufficient economies, British and American. Canada could not afford to join either one of them, and she was not strong enough to play that game independently.

But meantime, he wished to iterate and reiterate the hope that we were not going to leave Canada on the sidelines and discuss with Britain problems which are vital to Canada for both her financial and economic future.

In the sixteen months I have worked closely with Mr. Robertson I have never seen him as perturbed as he was today.

◆ IX ◆

OTTAWA

December 1941–January 1943

"The state of Canadian-American relations . . . should serve as a model for other countries"

On December 7, 1941, shortly after Pierrepont Moffat learned of the Japanese attack on Pearl Harbor, he went to the Foreign Office. Here he found Norman Robertson, with whom he discussed "loose ends" — putting into operation Joint Plan Number 2, concerting policy about interning Japanese citizens, and transferring United States citizens who had been serving with the RCAF but now wished to join the U. S. Air Corps. The absence of major problems was a tribute to the efficiency of the joint planning operations in the year and four months since Ogdensburg. Although new situations had to be prepared for, often only the implementation of plans already made and the acceleration of operations begun was necessary.

Before either the United States or Canada had adjusted to their roles as cobelligerents, a controversy arose which involved not only their interests but those of Great Britain, Vichy France, and the Free French. Although called a "footnote" to history, a "fleabite," "a departmental point," this incident nonetheless had a continuing influence on decisions made before and after D-Day.[1]

After the defeat of France by Germany the United States continued relations with Vichy. At first it seemed reasonable to do so because the Pétain government was the legally constituted authority and the trend of French reaction to defeat was not yet apparent. It later seemed necessary to maintain relations because the possible rewards were so great — the prevention of the French fleet, colonies, and bases being used by the Germans.[2]

[1] William L. Langer, *Our Vichy Gamble* (New York: Alfred A. Knopf, 1947), pp. 212–226, discusses the St. Pierre–Miquelon incident. He concludes that the episode's major importance lay in its influence on our policy toward De Gaulle and the Free French, because De Gaulle had put the "United States in a most embarrassing position and had thereby built up a resentment in official circles that it was almost impossible to overcome."

[2] Although this was the major objective of our Vichy relations, there were others

Off the south coast of Newfoundland lay a small residue of French power near this continent. The islands of St. Pierre and Miquelon passed with the fall of France under control of Vichy. This was a source of concern to the United States, Canada, and Great Britain, because on St. Pierre was a powerful wireless and cable station.

As soon after his arrival in Ottawa as July 5, 1940, Pierrepont Moffat had mentioned to Mr. King American interest in the status of the islands.[3] He cautioned against a unilateral occupation of the islands by Canada, since the United States desired to work out with the other American republics a system of joint action and trusteeship of colonial possessions in this hemisphere.

As the war progressed the Canadians became increasingly worried that the wireless station might forward information to France about Canadian shipping and might serve as a guide to enemy submarines.[4] On November 3, 1941, Norman Robertson, the Under-Secretary of State for External Affairs, told Mr. Moffat of the plan to send Canadian "monitors" to the island to check on the messages transmitted. When Mr. Moffat protested that such action might involve Canada in trouble with Vichy and violate the agreements reached by the Pan-American nations at Havana, the Under-Secretary asked if the United States would prefer to see the island taken over by the Free French.

This query, when communicated to Washington, brought a definite negative reply, because as Secretary Hull has written: "I looked with something like horror on any action that would bring conflict between the Vichy French and the Free French or the British."[5] To allay Canadian fears the Department of State agreed that the "monitors" might be sent.

This was about where the story rested when Admiral Emile Muselier of the Free French arrived in Ottawa on December 15, 1941. In the afternoon of the day of his arrival he visited the American Minister.

Ottawa, December 15, 1941.

I received this afternoon Admiral Muselier, Commander in Chief of the Free French Naval Forces. Admiral Muselier was introduced

---

such as combating Axis propaganda, trying to prevent further French collaboration in any sphere, and aiding refugees. William D. Leahy, *I Was There* (New York: Whittlesey House, 1950), pp. 8–9, gives a summary of the purpose of his mission as Ambassador to Vichy as explained by President Roosevelt. See, also, Welles, pp. 156–158.

[3] See the conversation of Jay Pierrepont Moffat with Mackenzie King, July 5, 1940.

[4] Mr. Moffat, for instance, reported a conversation of June 3, 1941, with Mr. Thomas Stone of the Department of External Affairs, who was "terrified" about "the danger of St. Pierre–Miquelon to the Canadian-British convoy routes. Stone said a fishing smack sailing one hundred miles from St. Pierre could bring back and put on the wireless vital information." Moffat diary, June 3, 1941.

[5] Hull, II, 1128.

by Vice Admiral Percy Nelles, Chief of Staff of the Canadian Navy.

1. Admiral Muselier told me that he had been authorized by General de Gaulle to sail to St. Pierre–Miquelon with the Free French corvettes under his command and to take over the islands.[6] He said that the population was entirely favorable to General de Gaulle, that the operation would take place without bloodshed and that the threat of the wireless station on the flank of the convoy routes would thus be permanently removed. He had not been willing to carry out this mission until he had satisfied himself that the project was agreeable to the Governments of Newfoundland, Canada and the United States.

2. He next told me that he would shortly get in touch with the Free French representative at New York with a view to his persuading the American Government to put into service as quickly as possible the "Normandie" and other French merchant ships which the United States had taken over.[7] He said that the British Government in the past had made some bad mistakes in its treatment of the French crews but that with wise handling it should be possible for the United States or the Allies, as the case might be, safely to use a large part of the French crews on the commandeered ships.

3. The third problem which he had on his mind and which General de Gaulle had instructed him to present to the American authorities was the conviction that any seizure by the United States of Martinique or other French possessions in the West Indies would provoke a strong anti-American reaction in occupied and unoccupied France. In the belief that action would ultimately have to be taken and that there was less danger of unfortunate repercussions if these islands were taken over by the Free French rather than by the United States, he stood ready, if we so desired, to sail down to Martinique in the hope of obtaining control. He was not as certain, however, that the operation in the Antilles would be without resistance as he was in the case of St. Pierre–Miquelon.

4. He said that he would either await in Ottawa for some indication in reply to this question from the Department of State, or if

[6] Such action had been considered by General Charles de Gaulle, leader of the Free French, as early as July 1940. Emile Muselier, *De Gaulle contre le Gaullisme* (Paris: Editions du Chêne, 1946), pp. 247, 252.

[7] Fourteen French freighters, tankers, and passenger ships which were in American ports were seized by the United States on December 12, 1941. *New York Times*, December 13, 1941, p. 1.

desired he would proceed to Washington to present his ideas and those of General de Gaulle informally and in greater detail to the competent authorities in Washington. . .[8]

Ottawa, December 17, 1941.

I called on Admiral Muselier by appointment this morning. I explained to him that we were equally anxious to achieve the same goal, namely, the defeat of Hitlerism, but that we sometimes differed on methods of bringing this about.

Specifically, he had asked me what was the opinion of the United States Government about an occupation by the Free French Forces of the islands of St. Pierre–Miquelon. He had told me that he had the authorization from General de Gaulle to stop by with his three corvettes [9] and that the islands could be taken over without the slightest possibility of bloodshed. About the same time that I had reported his request the matter had likewise been brought up in Washington by the British. After careful study by our authorities it had been referred to the President who felt that it would be a mistake for such an occupation to take place.[10] On the other hand, he agreed strongly that the wireless station (and, added Admiral Muselier, the cable) constituted a source of possible danger to North Atlantic convoys and that it was in everyone's interest to bring this method of communication under control.

We had been discussing for some time the ways and means of doing this with the Canadians, and the President felt that there would be fewer adverse repercussions if the Canadians took control of the communications from the island, by suasion, if possible, but otherwise by stronger means, and assured themselves, the United States and the Allied Powers that no communications of a deleterious nature left the islands.

[8] When General de Gaulle read in a newspaper that Muselier was planning to go to Washington, he sent the Admiral a telegram telling him to return to London because the projected trip to the American capital was entirely contrary to the General's instructions. In explaining his intentions at this time Admiral Muselier wrote in *De Gaulle contre le Gaullisme*, p. 263: "Il m'avait été question pour moi d'aller à Washington m'occuper de la situation dans le Pacifique, ou de la reconnaissance du général par le gouvernement américain."

[9] There were three Free French corvettes, the *Mimosa*, the *Alysse*, and the *Aconit*, based at St. John's, Newfoundland. Admiral Muselier had, with the permission of the Canadian Commodore who commanded the French ships, taken them to sea for an inspection tour. *Ibid.*, p. 256.

[10] Hull, II, 1129.

Admiral Muselier replied that in this event he would of course not proceed to the occupation. He questioned very much whether Canadian control would be effective and asked what we proposed in the event that this should transpire. I replied that I did not see why the control could not be made a hundred percent effective the moment it was taken over. He then asked whether we had considered the precedent we were creating. Admiral Darlan [Jean François Darlan, Vichy French Minister of Marine], who was eaten by ambition and driven by hatred for the British on account of Oran to seek full-fledged collaboration with the Germans, would say a control of communications in St. Pierre by a foreign power will give him a good excuse to give control of communications in North Africa to Germany, likewise a foreign power. I said that we recognized that no course of action was entirely without possible adverse repercussions. It was a question, however, of balancing which course would have the more serious repercussions and being guided accordingly. On balance, the United States Government believed that action by the Canadians, limited to protecting communications, was the wiser course. In addition to my informing him of this we had likewise informed the British.

The second question he had raised with me was the possibility of his going down to the West Indies. Here our feeling was that the question of occupation of Martinique and other French territory had not even arisen. Somewhat to my surprise, the Admiral did not press this point further. . .

Acting on Atherton's [Ray Atherton, Chief of the Division of European Affairs] instructions to discourage the visit [to Washington] in every possible way, I told him that there was so much interest in the United States and so much publicity if he were to come to the United States, that we thought his ends could be met if one of his friends came up from the United States to see him in Canada. He demurred a little and finally said that he would personally give up the idea of going but that he hoped we would give a visa for one of his staff to go down and talk to the Free French representatives in New York. I said I would gladly try and obtain authorization to give him a visa but that it might take a day or two.

The Admiral then asked what he should do. Here he was with his three corvettes in Halifax and in an embarrassing position. I suggested that he work out this problem with the Canadians. His idea at the moment is to remain in Canada more or less indefinitely, confident that the Canadian control of St. Pierre will not work and that he, or he and the British in conjunction, can persuade Washington to change its official mind.[11]

Summing up, the Admiral said that he was intensely disappointed with our conversation, not so much in relation to St. Pierre–Miquelon which, while important, was not perhaps vital, but because it indicated that the thinking in Washington was still revolving around the idea of playing ball with the Vichy Government. He was rather bitter in his comments of the leaders in Vichy France at the moment. He said that for six months he had been playing the role of Cassandra and telling us that collaboration on our part with Vichy would merely result in one body blow after another. Had we, for instance, encouraged the Free French to take over Indo-China there would have been no agreement with Japan and no war in the Pacific today. Our policy in North Africa had not worked out. . . Sooner or later we would find that our attitude toward St. Pierre–Miquelon and Martinique was a wrong one, but by then much damage would have been done. I suggested that even admitting the ultimate failure of our policy, nevertheless each day's delay was a precious gain. He did not agree. He said that his compatriots were far more pro-American than they were either pro-English or pro–Free French (for, he added, there were many in France who did not uphold General de Gaulle or his movement), and that a strong stand by the United States would electrify the French.

Ottawa, December 25, 1941.

Shortly after I awoke on Christmas Day I heard the radio announcing that the Free French forces under Admiral Muselier had occupied the islands of St. Pierre–Miquelon.[12] This was contrary to the undertakings he had given us last week.

1. I immediately called up Mr. Stone of the Department of Ex-

[11] The Admiral on this same day received a telegram from General de Gaulle ordering him to return to London as soon as his inspection of the ships was completed. Muselier made reservations on a flight to England for the following week. Muselier, pp. 263–264.

[12] The Admiral's forces had landed on St. Pierre at about 3 A.M. on December 24, 1941, and on Miquelon during the afternoon of the same day. Ibid., pp. 267–268.

ternal Affairs and asked him what he knew about the report. He said it was true but had come as a complete surprise to the Canadians. Admiral Muselier had left announcing that he had been recalled to London by De Gaulle, had indicated that he would take his three corvettes straight back from Halifax to St. John's, Newfoundland, and would take a bomber across the Atlantic.[13] He had not given a single indication that he had not accepted the veto given by the United States and Canada. The facts, in so far as the Canadian Government knew, were very simple. The wireless station at Newfoundland reported that no signals were received the previous day from St. Pierre–Miquelon until about 5 in the afternoon. At that time the station began to operate again and the following message came through:

Please ask no questions but transmit the following three telegrams.

The first was to the Secretary of State for Dominion Affairs in London. The second was for General de Gaulle, and the third was a one-line message to the Canadian Government.[14] Mr. Eberts, the Canadian Consul, announced that the occupation had taken place peacefully. Mr. Stone said that the matter was extremely embarrassing, though personally he thought it a good thing that the blister had broken, even if in an irregular fashion.

2. Some fifteen or twenty minutes later I called up Norman Robertson, who repeated Mr. Stone's expression of surprise and embarrassment. He said he had not telephoned me last night as he had been in a personal jam which he had to straighten out before anything else. Yesterday afternoon Mr. Ristelhueber, the Vichy Minister, had called on him and said that he had heard two rumors: the first, that Admiral Muselier was going to take over the islands, the second that the Canadians were going to take over the islands or the communications. Mr. Robertson had taken the occasion to talk to him more frankly than he had for a long time past. He said it was not true that Admiral Muselier was going to take over the islands but pointed out the constant potential menace to Allied security of the

[13] Admiral Muselier apparently intended to return to England up to the time, when he received General de Gaulle's message of December 18, which said, in part: "Les Canadiens ont l'intention de faire eux mêmes destruction du poste de T.S.F. de Saint-Pierre-et-Miquelon. Dans ces conditions je vous prescris de procéder au ralliement de Saint-Pierre-et-Miquelon." *Ibid.*, p. 264.

[14] *Ibid.*, pp. 281–284.

wireless station which was emitting code messages so close to the convoy routes. From the despatches which came in last night it seemed that when Mr. Robertson had given the assurances that the Free French would not take over the islands, they were already in occupation. Mr. Robertson had accordingly gone right around to call on Mr. Ristelhueber to explain that Admiral Muselier's action was a complete surprise, et cetera. The French Minister said he would report the facts to his Government and did, in fact, send off a long cipher message shortly after midnight. He did not give the impression that he felt the occupation would be the straw that broke the camel's back in Franco-Canadian relations. Mr. Robertson added that Mr. King was particularly upset, that the episode would prove an embarrassment to him in Washington tomorrow, but that he planned to talk it over with the President and Mr. Churchill shortly after his arrival.[15]

3. Having satisfied myself that there was no possible collusion between the Canadians and Admiral Muselier, I sent a brief telegram to the Department outlining the facts.

4. Shortly after 12, I had a few words with Malcolm MacDonald [High Commissioner for the United Kingdom], who said he was upset by the news from St. Pierre, that he belonged to the school of thought that we must not give Vichy or the Nazis an excuse to justify (however illogically) further measures of collaboration, et cetera. He did not understand what had gotten into Admiral Muselier, as he had been told at Ottawa of the veto by the Canadian authorities, by the United States Legation, and by the British High Commission.

5. At half-past one, Ottawa time, Mr. Hull called me up from the Department by long distance. He asked me for the facts about Admiral Muselier and the understandings reached with him, and then said that nothing could have been more unfortunate or more embarrassing to the United States Government. He had to be guarded in his language over the telephone but he could say that he and his colleagues regarded the situation as of the utmost delicacy, as involving not only our agreement with Admiral Robert (under whose jurisdiction St. Pierre–Miquelon lies),[16] but our understanding with

---

[15] Mr. Churchill had arrived in Washington on December 22, 1941.

[16] An agreement had just been renewed with Admiral Georges Robert about

Vichy and all that we were playing for (North Africa and the fleet) by means of our policy. He wanted me to persuade the Canadians that very afternoon to take steps to restore the status quo. I told the Secretary that although the Canadians were extremely embarrassed by what had taken place, I feared they would be reluctant to restore the situation, particularly in the event that the plebiscite which was being held at the moment we were talking went favorably to De Gaulle. Mr. King planned to discuss the matter when he arrived in Washington tomorrow. The Secretary said that that was not quick enough, that the situation was so urgent that the Canadians should start steps this very afternoon. He referred to Canadian pledges. I pointed out that there had been no pledges but merely an understanding as to policy. He replied that in the first place Mr. Wrong's [Hume Wrong, Counselor of Canadian Legation at Washington] conversation with Mr. Atherton virtually involved a pledge,[17] that in the second place whether it was a pledge or an understanding was merely a quibble, that in the third place, on the basis of our meeting of minds, the United States had reached an agreement with Admiral Robert which had now been breached. Unless the status quo were immediately restored, Admiral Robert could make the accusation, and with considerable justice, that the agreement had been violated from our side, and Vichy, the Nazis, et cetera, could play that up to a damaging degree.[18] Canada had perhaps greater responsibilities than anybody else, partly because of geography, partly because of her understandings with Admiral Muselier. In any event we must ask Canada to repair the damage and to do so at once.

The Secretary then brought up the question of publicity and said that he was thinking of issuing a statement to the effect that Admiral Muselier's action was an arbitrary one contrary to agreements, and that the United States was asking Canada what steps she was prepared to take to restore the status quo. I asked the Secretary if he could not withhold any statement until after I had seen the Cana-

---

French colonial possessions in the Western Hemisphere, and President Roosevelt had, eleven days before Muselier's action, sent a message to Pétain in which he recognized the agreement between the two countries "involving the maintenance of the status quo of the French possessions in the Western Hemisphere." Hull, II, 1130.

[17] *Ibid.*, p. 1129.

[18] Admiral Robert did tell Mr. Hull that he thought the United States was "obligated to obtain the reestablishment of French sovereignty over Saint-Pierre-Miquelon." *Ibid.*, p. 1130.

dians. I said that I appreciated the pressure he was under but two or three hours would not make much difference for tomorrow's papers. The Secretary evidently did not understand me for he did not repeat this remark to the others in the room, although to my observations he answered "Yes, yes." I arranged to speak to Dunn or Atherton after I had seen the Canadians.

6. I found Mr. Robertson at Mr. Stone's house just getting ready to go on to his Christmas dinner. I gave him the Secretary's message which he said involved asking Canada in great urgency to take a very serious step. While he was trying to get hold of Mr. King, who was also out eating a Christmas dinner, we discussed various possible steps that could be taken, or at least could be started in the course of the day. He called up Mr. Hume Wrong in Washington, who reported, however, that he had not yet been approached by anyone in the State Department. He called up Mr. Malcolm MacDonald and asked him to get in telephonic touch with Lord Halifax so that the three governments would beyond peradventure of doubt be marching in alignment. There was no doubt that Mr. Robertson's mind was running along the lines of trying to find a formula that would save De Gaulle's face. He appreciated all the dangers that this unwarranted step on De Gaulle's part might provoke. On the other hand, he felt that we must think twice before taking any step to disavow him or his Movement, as the repercussions of this disavowal might be most unfortunate in France. Again I explained that I thought he was putting too much emphasis on an entirely subsidiary point, that the main point to bear in mind was the threat to North Africa and the French fleet, that my Government, which had been working on this problem closely for months and months, felt that there was a chance of losing out, and that we must put first things first and not delay while trying to work out subsidiary points. Finally he got hold of Prime Minister King, whose reaction was about as follows: If the British and the United States jointly asked Canada to take action, Canada will of course do so. Thus far, however, Britain had not expressed herself at all, and the American request is certainly far from concrete. He was leaving in less than two hours and would feel much happier deferring action until he could talk it over at greater length with the President and Mr. Churchill. Meanwhile, he wanted Robertson to come to Washington with him, even though

he would not take him to the White House talks. Mr. Robertson should continue searching for a possible formula or recommendation of action. As soon as something concrete were put before him he would study it. Until then he hoped there would be no publicity.

7. By this time it was approaching three and Norman Robertson had not had a bite of Christmas dinner. He therefore sat down at Stone's house to some while I went home. Some fifteen minutes later he called up in great perturbation to say that Washington had released a statement containing the phrase which of all others they objected to saying that the United States had approached Canada to inquire "as to the steps that Government is prepared to take to restore the status quo of these islands." [19] The press was now after Mr. King and himself for comment, the fat was in the fire, and they did not consider that the United States had played the game. In a word, his whole attitude had changed from one of helpful cooperation to one of most reluctant cooperation.

8. A few minutes later Mr. Dunn telephoned me. I explained the damage done by the communiqué. He said the Secretary had not understood my plea for a delay in the issuance of any publicity until after I had spoken to the Canadians. Mr. Dunn said it was too bad but couldn't be helped. Muselier would have to get out of the islands, the status quo would have to be restored, although the Canadians after restoring it might leave their monitors to control the wireless station. I explained that some of the Canadian reluctance was due to their inability to see why they should be the whipping boy, acting apparently on their own. Mr. Dunn replied it was because the islands lay so close to their territory that they had an especial interest. I explained that a second cause of reluctance was the failure of the British as yet to have joined us in making this request of the Canadians. Mr. Dunn said that they had had no intention of bringing the British in at all; that we had only discussed the status of the islands with the Canadians and that it was essentially a North American problem. I

---

[19] Mr. Hull's full statement was: "Our preliminary reports show that the action taken by the so-called Free French ships at St. Pierre–Miquelon was an arbitrary action contrary to the agreement of all parties concerned and certainly without the prior knowledge or consent in any sense of the United States Government.

"This Government has inquired of the Canadian Government as to the steps that government is prepared to take to restore the status quo of these islands." Leland M. Goodrich (ed.), *Documents on American Foreign Relations July 1941–June 1942* (Boston: World Peace Foundation, 1942), IV, 466.

pointed out that this was not correct, that Atherton had discussed it with the British Embassy and so informed me, and that most certainly we should bring in the British at once. As a matter of fact, MacDonald was at this moment telephoning Lord Halifax and if he was not primed about our viewpoint the situation would become more difficult than ever. Mr. Dunn said that if Canada wouldn't act then we would have to pursue a sharply divergent policy. I asked if we were prepared to act ourselves in the event that Canada didn't. He said we would be reluctant to do so as it would be so much resented in Canada. I said I was not sure but that the Canadians would prefer to see us take action than to have the onus thrust upon them. I concluded by saying that as Canada was trying to keep in step with both Britain and the United States they had better lose no time in seeing that Britain and the United States were in step together. Mr. Dunn indicated that he considered the Canadian objections as obstructive and of doubtful validity. He concluded by saying that Muselier must go, and go shortly.

9. I telephoned Mr. Robertson, explained the misunderstanding about the press release in Washington, and urged him to draft out a first formula we had agreed on, namely, that Muselier's occupation having undoubtedly been taken under a misapprehension, the Canadian Government was taking steps to inform him of this by sending an official to St. Pierre in the very near future. He said he would try and call me back if he had time before leaving on the train with the Prime Minister but that now he only had forty-five minutes.

10. At half-past six Mr. Stone came to my house for Christmas eggnog. We were having a Christmas party for the staff and some seventy American aviators stationed in Ottawa. Robertson would discuss the problem with Mr. King and the three Defence Ministers on the train between Ottawa and Montreal and would telephone from Montreal in the course of the evening. Meantime, he showed me a first draft prepared by Hugh Keenleyside of a statement. It was so bad and so completely divergent from all we were asking that I pled with him to issue nothing at all rather than a statement which placed our positions further and further apart. Mr. Stone argued that our policy was a shortsighted one and made a long plea for De Gaulle — in fact, all the "Free Movements," which he felt we were discouraging. He said that the United States talked about Canadian collabora-

tion, but was giving very little collaboration in the form of advance consultation, in return. There had been a whole series of incidents of late where we had either left Canada out in the cold, or told her after the event, or at best informed her of our intention to act a few hours only before we acted. What, in fact, did we mean by restoring the status quo? I answered in the terms given me by Mr. Dunn. He said that this meant, in effect, that we were asking Canada to put out De Gaulle after a plebiscite had been taken in his favor, that we were thereby impugning the honesty or value of the plebiscite,[20] that we were disavowing and discouraging the Free French and that we were asking Canada to run the risk of coming to physical blows in the event that Admiral Muselier should offer forcible resistance.

I replied that he was completely ignoring the essence of the problem, which was keeping the fleet and North Africa out of Axis hands, that he was ignoring the question of keeping faith, explicitly or implicitly, with Admiral Robert, that he was forgetting the responsibilities that fell upon Canada as a result of the long conversations held here with Admiral Muselier and as a result of geographical propinquity of the islands, et cetera.

Neither convinced the other.

The only further development was his showing me a signal from Admiral Muselier announcing that he had occupied the islands "under new instructions received from General de Gaulle and in response to the wishes of the inhabitants" . . .

12. At 10.15 Mr. Pearson [Lester Pearson, Assistant Under-Secretary of State for External Affairs] telephoned and read me the following message from Mr. King and his colleagues, which he asked me to pass on to Washington:

Canada is in no way responsible for the Free French occupation of St. Pierre. We have kept in close touch with both the United Kingdom and the United States on this question and have always been ready to cooperate in carrying out an agreed policy. We decline to commit ourselves to any action or to take any action pending such agreement. In the circumstances and until we have had an opportunity of considering action with the Presi-

[20] The plebiscite which Admiral Muselier took in St. Pierre showed 98 per cent of the voters in favor of Free France. The Admiral's description of the vote and its counting is given in Muselier, pp. 288–289, 298–299; see, also, the despatches of Ira Wolfert to New York Times, December 26, 1941, p. 1, and December 29, 1941, p. 5.

dent and Mr. Churchill, the Canadian Government cannot take the steps requested to expel the Free French and restore the status quo in the islands.

Mr. Pearson explained that despite a great deal of pressure there would be no statement issued at Ottawa tonight and that the situation would thus be left completely liquefied, to be handled in Washington tomorrow. . .

Ottawa, January 2, 1942.

I called on Mr. Robertson this afternoon to confirm the information I had given him yesterday of developments in Washington on St. Pierre–Miquelon. I had told him that according to Mr. Dunn the French Ambassador called on Mr. Hull on December 30th. He had started to read some notes based on a telegram from his Foreign Office. The Secretary, after noting that there were many references to sovereignty and status quo without any indication about accommodating us in the matter of the wireless station, stopped him short and said: "If that is all you have, it will be difficult to work out a solution." [21] The Ambassador had not, accordingly, been able to finish his presentation but had said, presumably with regard to the wireless, that his Government was expecting Admiral Robert to settle the matter. Mr. Dunn was not certain what that meant but thought it might be a way of keeping the conversations open in the event that the Ambassador's first approach was not successful. The Secretary had then told the Ambassador to hurry up and obtain assurances about Allied control of communications. The upshot is that the Secretary did not accept the Ambassador's representations, nor did he entirely close the door. The situation was growing worse because Admiral Leahy was reporting that the Germans were already using this as an excuse to demand the right to send troops to North Africa to prevent "a repetition of the incident". . .[22]

I asked Mr. Robertson how he explained Mr. Churchill's speech

[21] Hull's account of his meeting with the French Ambassador, Gaston Henry-Haye, is given in Hull, II, 1131–1132. The Secretary said: "Soon it will be too late to handle this matter on its merits and in a proper spirit because of its explosive possibilities."

[22] William D. Leahy has written in *I Was There*, p. 75, that "Darlan told me early in January that already he had heard from the Germans that the latter proposed to send troops to North Africa to prevent any similar attempt there by the Free French." The substance of this statement was included in Hull's memorandum for the President of December 31, 1941. Sherwood, pp. 484–485.

to the House of Commons which had given the general impression that he was for De Gaulle in all circumstances. Mr. Robertson said that Mr. Churchill in four or five days had boxed the compass. At the White House he had indicated that it would be easy to put pressure, and he could take part in it, to make General de Gaulle toe the line and evacuate the islands.[23] In Ottawa he had made his speech before Parliament, presumably to prevent the Free French movement from falling to pieces under Allied criticism.[24] I remarked that he had not differentiated between the Free French on the one hand and General de Gaulle personally on the other, to which Mr. Robertson replied that apparently the Free French had no other possible leader. Following his speech he had told the editors of the Canadian newspapers off the record that he hoped Canada would keep Mr. Ristelhueber as Minister from Vichy and not sever relations and again used the phrase, "St. Pierre is a small problem which we can easily adjust." [25] Everyone in Canada is utterly confused.

I then asked whether he had any ideas of his own about adjustment other than putting pressure on De Gaulle to withdraw his forces after being thanked by the Allies for having taken care of the communications system. He said that he did not have many other suggestions to offer. The President had thrown out the idea of letting the islands manage themselves until the end of the war without control by either Vichy or De Gaulle. In this event Canada and the United States would at once strengthen their consular representation. . .

Mr. Robertson said that he was awaiting further news from Washington, and meantime would not allow himself to be drawn into any negotiations with the French as he felt these must be concentrated in Mr. Hull's hands. However, he said that Mr. Hull and Mr. King had looked at each other sympathetically at the White House, when the President and Mr. Churchill had turned to them and said: "Now

[23] Hull, I, 1132–1133.
[24] The text of Churchill's speech before the Canadian Parliament on December 30, 1941, is printed in the *New York Times*, December 31, 1941, p. 6. He had said, in part, in regard to the French situation: "Some Frenchmen there were who would not bow their knees and who like their General De Gaulle have continued to fight at the side of the Allies. . . their names will be held and are being held in increasing respect by nine Frenchmen out of every ten. . ."
[25] Churchill in *The Grand Alliance*, pp. 666–667, writes of Mr. Hull and the St. Pierre–Miquelon incident: "Mr. Hull . . . pushed what was little more than a departmental point far beyond its proportions. The President in our daily talks seemed to me to shrug his shoulders over the whole affair."

that you know our general ideas you two will have no trouble at all in working out a satisfactory practical solution."

Ottawa, January 9, 1942.

Mr. King came to dine with Lilla and myself at a quarter to eight last night. He had hardly gotten into the house when the President called him up by long distance and later in the evening Harry Hopkins [adviser and assistant to President Roosevelt] telephoned him. He looked tired and worried, due I think to the fact that the Government has not yet satisfactorily worked out the solution to Canada's manpower problem.

Mr. King had been intensely interested in seeing Churchill and Roosevelt together in Washington Christmas week. He thought that whereas in many respects they were like each other, yet where their characters differ instead of grating they supplemented each other. Their plan of covering virtually every phase of the war effort by themselves without advisers at hand to tell them what to do has both advantages and disadvantages.

One of the disadvantages is evidenced in the St. Pierre–Miquelon business. After a good deal of rather painful thrashing around, during which the President and Mr. Churchill took a somewhat divergent view, and Mr. Hull and Mr. King together had to tell Mr. Churchill he was wrong, an agreement was reached on principle. Yet when it came to putting that agreement on paper it was found that practical questions arose which had not been adequately thrashed out by means of this informal type of conversation. He thought there was a danger that this same result would occur in many other problems thought to have been finally settled by the President and Mr. Churchill themselves.

Speaking in greater detail regarding St. Pierre–Miquelon, he said that he was still struck with the importance of regarding the larger issues involved rather than the status of the islands by itself. He was bitter about De Gaulle and said that when he was in England even a few months ago the British were pretty well fed up with him as a leader. . . Mr. King went on to say that this was the only problem on which he and Robertson had materially differed. Robertson and Stone had cooked up a plan of sending Stone to the islands in a corvette to take over the radio. He had approved Stone's going but had absolutely vetoed the corvette. He felt that if Robertson and Stone had had their way they, rather than Admiral Muselier, might have upset the equilibrium with repercussions all over the world. He thought that the realization of this had sobered them and that they had learned a valuable lesson without cost.

He thought that the group in the Department of External Affairs was peculiarly able and deserving of all praise. Robertson and Pearson were obviously his two favorites. He said, however, that they always wanted to go a little too fast. For instance, they were pressing him to establish Canadian Legations all over the place.[26] He was inclined to think that a Legation would soon be opened in Moscow,[27] and I suggested that Mexico might have some merits.[28] He said yes, but he had no intention of spreading too fast, particularly as he did not have the men to fill these posts. . .

This gave me my opportunity and I set forth all the reasons why a working collaboration between Canada and the twenty-one American Republics would be more effective than an agitation for joining the Pan American Union.[29] I skirted the British issue but he brought it up himself and said that he saw very well why it might be inadvisable to allow any of the twenty-one American Republics to get the impression (however erroneous) that the British Empire was trying to join their hemispheric councils.

But although he was critical of the Department of External Affairs for moving too fast on some of these problems and recognized that in many strategic directives the decision would have to be made

[26] The inauguration of a separate Canadian diplomatic service from the British took place in 1927 with the exchange of representatives between Canada and the United States. H. Gordon Skilling, *Canadian Representation Abroad* (Toronto: The Ryerson Press, 1945), pp. 184–218.

[27] Although the exchange of Ministers between Canada and the Soviet Union was announced in November 1942, the Canadian legation was not established until April 1943. *Ibid.*, pp. 252–254.

[28] In January 1944 Canada and Mexico announced the exchange of Ministers.

[29] Because Canadian foreign policy had been directed by the British for so long a time, there was opposition to admitting Canada to the Pan American Union. In August 1942 King stated that "there have been times quite recently when we might have expected invitations but were given reasons why it would not be advisable to have an invitation extended." He seemed to suggest that the reasons were related to the wariness of Latin America and the United States about discussing economic and other matters before a member of the close-knit British Empire. Skilling, pp. 218–224. On December 16, 1941, Mr. King told Mr. Moffat that "he had made soundings" and "the President had now told him that he felt it would be a mistake to bring in any member of the British Commonwealth of Nations at this time."

by Mr. Roosevelt and Mr. Churchill alone, Mr. King was very critical of the attitude of many of our technicians, particularly in the Army and Navy, for trying to settle in two-way discussions matters that directly affected Canada and should be carried on in a three-way discussion.[30]

The conversation wandered to war aims and peace aims, and he said that Mr. Churchill was so concentrated on the war that he could not see that settling certain broad problems of the peace now would in effect help the actual war effort. I said that I assumed among others he was referring to trade matters and explained the importance we all attached to making certain that Britain did not choose after the war to adopt a closed economy rather than a nondiscriminatory open economy. I again explained that if the wrong choice would be made, England and the United States could undoubtedly get along, though with a somewhat lowered standard of living, but that I did not see how Canada could. She would be ground between the upper and nether millstone. He agreed, but I could not gather that he felt that Canada should put pressure on Britain in the circumstances. He said that of course Churchill himself was by instinct a free trader but that as leader of the Conservative Party he was bound to a large degree by their policy. Mr. King had told him that unless certain very big decisions were made there might be no Party. I said that equally potent with the Party attitude was the attitude of the civil servants, notably of the Treasury. As far as I could make out they were definitely in the saddle where economics and finance were concerned. Mr. King said he agreed that they were in the saddle but that the saddle was on a rather hollow horse. Even before the war England was not as strong economically or financially as the world at large thought, and he feared that after the war many signs of weakness would become evident. . .

Ottawa, February 7, 1942.

Mr. Atherton telephoned this morning to say that not only have there been no new developments recently with regard to St. Pierre,

[30] On January 7, 1942, a telegram from the American Legation in Ottawa reported that "there is widespread resentment, directed in equal measure against Great Britain and the United States, because as Canada sees it, military and economic planning, even in fields where Canada has a direct interest, is confined to the United States and the United Kingdom, with the Canadians only invited in 'for the photograph.'" Department of State, MS, 851.A/40.

but that the matter was more and more disappearing from the public eye.[31] He said that someone had well described the situation by saying that the St. Pierre incident and our relationship thereto had served the purposes which were considered essential at the time, but which today had far less application.

This cryptic statement is in line with another point received from Washington, that our relations with Vichy were rapidly deteriorating.

Perhaps Churchill's hope that the islands would sink back into the obscurity from which for a day they emerged may come true.

In the months before the Canadian Parliament met on January 22, 1942, the issue of conscription assumed ominous proportions. The Conservative Party, led by Mr. Arthur Meighen and his supporters in Toronto and on the West Coast, attacked the King government for the "inadequacy of its war programme" and particularly its failure to bring Canada's total resources in manpower to bear on the world crisis by conscripting men for armed service overseas. They declared that Mr. King's fears that such action would alienate French Canada were unfounded, for if the problem were "clearly and fairly" laid before French Canadians they would agree to the necessity of the measure.[32]

On the day when Parliament opened it was announced in the Speech from the Throne that a plebiscite would be taken through which the people would have an opportunity to indicate whether or not they wished Mr. King and his government to be held to or released from the promise of March, 1939,[33] that conscription for overseas service would not be adopted in case of conflict.

Before April 27, 1942, when the plebiscite was to be held, party, group, and sectional disagreements over the issue were given a thorough airing. In Quebec where the opposition to conscription centered, Mr. Maxime Raymond of the Bloc Populaire, the nationalist party, declared that in the struggle over this question the weapons were being forged which would "stay national unity and possibly confederation as well."[34]

[31] Secretary Hull in a memorandum of February 2, 1942, to the President suggested the matter be dropped until the war had ended. Hull, I, 1137.

[32] C. Cecil Lingard and Reginald G. Trotter, *Canada in World Affairs* (Toronto: Oxford University Press, 1950), pp. 87–94.

[33] In a speech before the Canadian House of Commons on March 30, 1939, Mr. King had promised in speaking of conscription for overseas service "that so long as this government is in power no such measure will be enacted." Dominion of Canada, House of Commons, *Official Report of Debates*, vol. CCXX (1939) (Ottawa: J. O. Patenaude, 1939), pp. 2408–2428.

[34] Mr. Raymond's speech of February 5, 1942, is printed in *ibid.*, vol. CCXXIX (1942) (Ottawa: Edmond Cloutier, 1942), p. 365.

Quebec, February 17, 1942.

While in Quebec today I paid a short courtesy call on Premier Godbout in his office and later had a long talk with him after dinner at Spencerwood.

I asked Mr. Godbout whether he felt that tactically Mr. King was right or wrong in delaying the holding of the plebiscite for several months. Mr. Godbout said that from his point of view Mr. King was unquestionably right. The situation in Quebec was so confused, there were so many cross-currents, that to get a large "yes" vote such as was needed would take a real campaign of education. If the plebiscite were held now he implied that it would result in a "no" vote of large proportions.

There was no doubt that virtually the entire French Canadian population of Quebec was opposed to conscription for overseas service. He thought this was due to several causes: first, to resentment over the way similar conscription was voted and carried out during the last war;[35] secondly, to the prevalence of a belief, which the Government has not yet been able to eradicate, that this is not basically Canada's war but a struggle between British imperialism and German imperialism in Europe and between the United States and Japan in Asia; thirdly, to an inherent anti-British complex due in part to historic memories, in part to faulty textbooks, and in part to "superior" British manners; and, finally, to resentment at the anti-French Canadian campaign carried on by such organs as the Toronto *Globe and Mail*, Montreal *Gazette*, etc. All but the last of these are susceptible to treatment by education. But that is a very slow process.

The political situation within the Province is a further complicating factor. For a while it appeared that the Quebec Cabinet might not be a unit in supporting Mr. St. Laurent, the new Minister of Justice, who was contesting the East Quebec riding. In fact, the situation became so acute at one stage that he, Mr. Godbout, had to dash back from Montreal and spend all one night and part of the next day in bringing his Ministers into line. The result was that the Quebec Cabinet was present in the St. Laurent campaign, but the effect was

[35] The passing of the conscription law of August 1917 and the attempt to enforce it were the occasions for rioting and violence in many parts of Quebec. See Wittke, pp. 299–303.

considerably weakened by the fact that not one of the French Canadian Federal Cabinet Ministers came down to Quebec.

On the plebiscite, again the division between the Quebec Provincial Government on the one hand and the members of the Federal Parliament from the Province of Quebec on the other hand will be very pronounced. If the members of the Federal Parliament remained a virtual unit in voting for the plebiscite bill when it is brought down his task would be much easier.[36] Irrespective of the final vote in Parliament on the reply to the address to the Throne, he thought that more than half of the Federal members would vote against the Government's plebiscite bill and would go out urging their constituents to vote "no" in the plebiscite itself. . .

I asked him about the sentiment in the province vis-à-vis the Vichy Government and General de Gaulle. He said that the active Vichy supporters, although noisier, were very few. Similarly, the active supporters of General de Gaulle were few and, incidentally, less noisy. The great bulk of the French Canadian population was not really deeply interested. Its feelings toward France were platonic, and the thing to remember was that the average French Canadian sympathized with one side or another in the French situation more as a reflection of his beliefs and interests in the Province of Quebec than as a barometer of his judgment on the actual issues abroad. Mr. Godbout himself still believed that Pétain personally was a sincere and honest patriot, but he feared that he was aging fast and that there was little honesty or patriotism in his colleagues who seemed to be gaining the upper hand.

Mr. Godbout's worries in the Province of Quebec were by no means confined to the present. He was very fearful of the postwar situation, particularly with the prospect of Russia emerging very strong. I said I had been surprised that there had been no outburst against the establishment of Canadian diplomatic relations with Soviet Russia; he said that he, too, had been surprised. In any event, in the confusion and disillusionment of the postwar era when in many places outside Quebec there would probably be near communist manifesta-

---

[36] The French Canadian members of the Federal Parliament campaigned in favor of releasing the government from the pledge of March 1939. They suggested that such a "Yes" vote on the plebiscite did not mean that conscription must follow but only that the government would be free in the future to conscript if it should become necessary. Lingard and Trotter, p. 94.

tions, it might well be that all the discontented elements in Quebec might make common cause and take over the Government. . .

After all, I must remember that while the extremists in Quebec were noisy and had a great voting strength, they were probably neither noisier nor proportionately more numerous than were the extremist elements in Ontario. . . I would see the same thing in Quebec, namely, that when the great mass of the voters saw the blind alley down which the extreme nationalists were leading them, they would continue to vote soundly. But I should not forget, moreover, that voluntary enlistments in Quebec were at the moment entirely satisfactory and that Quebec's contributions to the war loans were magnificent. But I should equally not forget that the whole Province of Quebec was at one and the same time opposed to conscription for overseas service and in favor of the Mackenzie King Government. Hence all the confusion throughout the Province.

Washington, March 2, 3, 4, 1942.

. . . Norman Davis [Chairman of the American Red Cross and unofficial adviser to the Department of State] has been far from well this winter and poor Mrs. Davis is desperately ill. In addition to these worries, he has been upset over the Secretary of State. The latter has been hurt to the quick by several episodes. The first was the unfounded accusation in the press that he had failed to tip off the Army and Navy as to the seriousness of the situation with Japan. The second was the St. Pierre–Miquelon issue, where he felt that Churchill had double-crossed him and that the President had supported Churchill. The third was when Sumner Welles changed his instructions without consulting Washington and agreed to a weakening of the wording of the Conference Resolution in order to obtain unanimity, rather than to have forced a vote and pushed Argentina and Chile out on a limb.[37]

[37] At the Rio de Janeiro Conference, January 15–28, 1942, the United States tried to persuade the other American Republics to sign a declaration committing them to break off relations with the Axis. Due to the opposition of Argentina and Chile, Sumner Welles, Under Secretary of State and the head of the American delegation, agreed to a modified declaration in which only a "recommendation" was made that relations be severed. Secretary Hull has written: "I was frankly very angry that Welles had acted as he had. He had not only acted without consulting me; worse, he had committed his Government to an unwise agreement." Hull, II, 1143–1150. Mr. Welles, in commenting on the attitude that the United States viewpoint should have prevailed, even if unanimity with the other Republics was sacrificed, has said that

In addition to that the Secretary was upset at the way members of the Department were pursuing individual policies; he was not able to keep them in order. Actually he had resolved to resign and had cleared out his desk of the accumulation of eight years of papers which were stacked on it. Norman Davis had prevailed upon him not to resign in anger and, above all, not to resign on the St. Pierre–Miquelon issue. Finally the Secretary decided to resign on the ground of ill health. He went through every known test and the Doctor pronounced him absolutely fit, merely suffering from nervous exhaustion. He has therefore gone to Florida and will be away about two months. Already his spirits are rising and his fighting mood is returning.[38]

Actually the Secretary is under attack from two groups. The first centers around Harry Hopkins and the extreme New Dealers; the second centers around Justice Frankfurter. The upshot is that the Secretary will stay just as long as he feels the President wants him. The President knows that the Secretary and Mr. Churchill got on each other's nerves. Each is the complete antithesis of the other and it was a case of mutual distrust and dislike at first sight. The President feels that he has backed up Mr. Hull through thick and thin and that he [Hull] has made only one mistake and that was the Christmas Day communiqué about St. Pierre–Miquelon with its reference to "so-called Free French ships". . .[39]

Jimmy Dunn. Jimmy Dunn gave me much the same story about the Secretary as had Norman Davis. Like everyone else I ran into in Washington he is unhappy, but it is because the Department in the first instance and the Government as a whole can not work as a unit. Old grudges are borne, old feuds are continued, the Spanish Civil

"such a course would be inexpedient from the long range point of view, and highly unwise from the practical and immediate standpoint." Welles, pp. 220–234.

[38] Secretary Hull wrote in his *Memoirs*, II, 1137–1138, that he actually made a first draft of his resignation. He stated that the St. Pierre and Miquelon controversy was "one of several factors" which brought about his desire to give up the secretaryship, the most important of which was the state of his health. But, he wrote: "After thinking this over very intensively, I decided that I could not give up at this moment when disaster after disaster was overtaking the United Nations in the Far East, even if it meant the total collapse of my health."

[39] See above, p. 367n. for the text of this statement of December 25, 1941. The phrase "so-called Free French ships" was interpreted to mean that Hull questioned the existence of the Free French movement. This aroused adverse comment in the press, and in protest letters were sent to the "so-called Secretary of State." Secretary Hull points out that he only meant by this phrase: "three ships supposedly of the Free French." Hull, II, 1130–1131; Sherwood, pp. 482–483.

War is still viewed by the extreme left as the test of a man's patriotism, etc. . .

Loy Henderson [Assistant Chief of the Division of European Affairs] . . . The great difficulty with Russia at the moment is Stalin's demands that Britain and the United States make a commitment guaranteeing Russia's 1941 frontiers, including the absorption of Estonia, Latvia, and Lithuania. Before his trip to Moscow Eden agreed with us that there should be no commitments regarding the eventual peace. Eden, however, weakened under Stalin's insistence and agreed to come back and try and persuade the United States to agree to Stalin's terms.[40] The Government is widely split, one group, headed by the State Department, Bill Bullitt and others, maintaining that if we make a single commitment regarding the peace we have lost the chance of being free agents; that the acid test of our good faith in Russia is whether we deliver the supplies we promise, etc.[41] Litvinov [Maxim Litvinov, Soviet Ambassador to the United States] is not pushing the matter but is allowing it to go through Maisky [Ivan M. Maisky, Soviet Ambassador to Great Britain] and Winant [John G. Winant, American Ambassador to Great Britain]. The latter has been taken completely into camp and has sold Stalin's ideas to Harry Hopkins. Winant is actually on his way home to the United States to make this an issue. There is intense bitterness and meanwhile Stalin in his recent speech tried to hurry matters by throwing out the possibility of a treaty with Germany.[42] Actually no one thinks that he could do this, that the wounds are too deep and that it is purely maneuver on his part. . .

Ottawa, April 13, 1942.

In the course of a conversation with Mr. Robertson the subject came up of relations between the Allies and Russia. Mr. Robertson

[40] Anthony Eden, British Foreign Secretary, went to Moscow in December 1941. His account of the territorial demands made by Stalin is given in Churchill, *The Grand Alliance*, pp. 628–629. Eden stated that he promised Stalin to "consult" his government and that of the United States about these proposals. Eden's speech upon his return is given in Anthony Eden, *Freedom and Order* (London: Faber & Faber Ltd., 1947), pp. 143–147.

[41] In a letter of February 4, 1942, to the President, Secretary Hull had said that the opinion of the Department was that not "our willingness to agree to the recognition of extended Soviet frontiers at this time, but rather the degree of determination which we show loyally to carry out our promises to aid the Soviet Government with equipment and supplies" should be the proof of our good faith. Hull, II, 1168.

[42] The Stalin speech of February 23, 1942, is printed in Joseph Stalin, *The Great*

told me that General Sikorsky [43] had come back highly satisfied with the President's assurance that the United States would not make any commitments about Russia's postwar frontiers. On the other hand, the British, notwithstanding the President's attitude, felt that they must go ahead and reassure Russia on this point. He said that, of course, the Polish frontiers would be reserved, that nobody worried about Finland, and that Estonia, Latvia, and Lithuania was a small price to pay to convince Russia of Britain's trust and earnestness. I remarked that a divergence in policy between Great Britain and the United States would from my personal point of view be unfortunate. What the British Government was suggesting and what he (Mr. Robertson) was endorsing could certainly not be reconciled with the Atlantic Charter and would certainly be resented by the small states in Europe. As a matter of fact, I heard in Washington that the publication of Sir Stafford Cripps' article in *Fortune* [44] wherein he advocated "strategic frontiers" for Russia irrespective of the wishes of the local inhabitants had produced violent repercussions in Sweden and, above all, Turkey. Mr. Robertson admitted that he had heard this about Turkey, in fact, General Sikorsky characterized the alienation of Turkey's friendship as among the most serious blunders of the war, but even so there were considerations which made it necessary for Britain to act. Russia was demanding more and more supplies and refusing to show Britain and the United States enough for them to judge whether those supplies could be put to better use in other theatres of the war. If Britain, by underwriting Soviet Russia's 1941 frontiers, can reëstablish a relationship of mutual trust with Russia, it may mean a great saving in supplies for the common good. Mr. Robertson concluded by referring to Stalin's speech in February, wherein he talked of "liberating" Russian territory, and characterized it as a pressure move against Britain and secondarily the United States. Actually it constituted pressure which could not be resisted in England on either strategic or on political grounds. I remarked that the

---

Patriotic War of the Soviet Union (New York: International Publishers, 1945), pp. 39–46.

[43] General Wladyslaw Sikorski, Prime Minister of the Polish Government in exile, had been on an official visit in the United States and Canada.

[44] Sir Stafford Cripps, British Ambassador to Russia, in answering "Twenty Russian Questions" in *Life*, March 9, 1942, said on p. 87 that "judging by the strategic necessities of the situation, the Soviet Government must ask for boundaries which it has fought to defend against Germany — the boundaries of June 1941."

public in England had seemed to anchor all its hopes on Soviet successes and that if any disaster should occur to Russian arms the consequence on British morale might be serious. Mr. Robertson agreed and said this was an additional reason why England had to meet Russia's wishes on her frontiers irrespective of other considerations.

On April 27, 1942, the people of Canada voted by about a two to one majority to release the government from its pledge not to conscript men for overseas service. But the victory was in reality a defeat for Mr. King's hopes to achieve national unity on the manpower problem. Ninety per cent of the French Canadians voted against conscription.[45]

Ottawa, April 29, 1942.

Having lunched yesterday at the Rideau Club where I got no comments on the recent plebiscite more interesting than a choice of epithets against the French Canadians, I tried my luck at the cafeteria today and lunched with Jack Pickersgill (Private Secretary to the Prime Minister), Jim Coyne (Assistant to Donald Gordon in Price Control), Saul Rae and Escott Reid of the Department of External Affairs.

Pickersgill indicated that the Prime Minister was bitterly disappointed with the results of the plebiscite. He had believed that a far larger segment of the French Canadian population would vote to release him from his commitments than was in fact the case. The more the vote was examined by precincts the more clearly it appeared that it was a racial division from beginning to end. Roughly, nine out of ten French Canadians voted "no" and about the same proportion of British Canadians voted "yes." Even in small districts in the Prairie Provinces where there was a material French Canadian population, the "no" vote was immediately evident. Despite all the efforts of the Government to make the people understand the situation, they got nowhere against what Pickersgill called the brilliant propaganda work done by the League for the Defense of Canada.[46] The League was obviously in funds but their source was not determined; some of the more partisan politicians saying that the money had been put up

---

[45] Lingard and Trotter, pp. 94–95; Hardy, pp. 198–204.

[46] The League for the Defense of Canada was led by French nationalist leaders such as Maxime Raymond. The League held anticonscription meetings and distributed literature opposing conscription. William Henry Chamberlin, *Canada Today and Tomorrow* (Boston: Little, Brown & Co., 1942), pp. 104–105.

by the Toronto magnates solely to embarrass Mr. King. Be that as it may, the feeling was general that if one wanted to forget the war one had only to go to rural Quebec.

The vote having been taken the next question to arise was what should be done about it. Pickersgill made it quite clear that he thought nothing would be done in a hurry, and certainly that no general election would be called. He mentioned Ralston's statement of last February which was that so long as recruits came in adequately the Government preferred the system of reinforcing a volunteer army by volunteers. Only in the event that the flow of recruits dried up would it have to consider changing the system. Escott Reid took the ground that the Government would have to bring down conscription for overseas service and bring it down quickly as the country was "raring-to-go." Pickersgill doubted this assertion, and Coyne took the middle ground that one could both conscript and keep the volunteer system going at the same time, reinforcing volunteer units with volunteers and conscript units with conscripts.

Escott Reid said that he thought the French Canadians would bolt the Liberal Party if Mr. King should bring in conscription. Not being able to join the Conservatives, they would set up a National Party of their own. Pickersgill was inclined to doubt this, if for no other reason than because of the interplay between Federal and Provincial patronage. Besides, he said the French Canadians at the moment had no statesmen who could lead them. Reid, Rae, and Coyne all felt that the vote proved once and for all the extent of French Canadian determination. Pickersgill denied this, claiming that if conscription were to be imposed today the Province would revolt, but if Mr. King held off until something else happened it would be glad to accept the will of the majority. He felt that with few exceptions the French Canadians were not really happy in their isolation, the more so as it was not merely isolation from British Canadian Tories but from the whole trend of North American thought. It struck me, however, that he spoke without great conviction. . .

[Ottawa], July 29, 1942.

I have been told that a while back the Ottawa *Journal* tried an experiment. For one week they had the headlines accurately reflect the news in the articles, neither smearing over nor mitigating the bad war news. As a result the circulation of the Ottawa *Journal* dropped 1500 within the week.

The following week was known in the paper as "Cheerful Week" and the policy was to put cheerful headlines, even if they bore only the most tenuous relations to the articles they headed. The result was not only a regaining of the lost circulation and a slight increase, but the highlight came when toward the end of the week a Major General in the Ministry of National Defense told the Editor how comforted he had been at the greatly improved war news.

Ottawa, October 1, 1942.

I went to the meeting of the Canadian Chamber of Commerce at the Seigniory Club with Clifford Clark [Deputy Minister of Finance] and Dana Wilgress [Deputy Minister of Trade and Commerce] and had the opportunity for a long uninterrupted talk with them.

Clifford Clark told me that in view of the delay in starting the U.S.–U.K. talks on implementing Article 7 of the Lease-Lend Agreement the British were putting out feelers for a preliminary session with the Dominions.[47] Neither Clark nor Wilgress liked the idea for two reasons: (a) that psychologically it might look as though the Empire were ganging up against the United States, and (b) because Britain has a tendency to allege that she is speaking on behalf of

[47] Article VII in the lend-lease agreement with Great Britain read as follows: "In the final determination of the benefits to be provided to the United States of America by the Government of the United Kingdom in return for aid furnished under the act of Congress of March 11, 1941, the terms and conditions thereof shall be such as not to burden commerce between the two countries, but to promote mutually advantageous economic relations between them and the betterment of world-wide economic relations. To that end, they shall include provision for agreed action by the United States of America and the United Kingdom, open to participation by all other countries of like mind, directed to the expansion, by appropriate international and domestic measures, of production, employment, and the exchange and consumption of goods, which are the material foundations of the liberty and welfare of all peoples; to the elimination of all forms of discriminatory treatment in international commerce, and to the reduction of tariffs and other trade barriers; and, in general, to the attainment of all the economic objectives set forth in the joint declaration made on August 14, 1941, by the President of the United States of America and the Prime Minister of the United Kingdom.

"At an early convenient date, conversations shall be begun between the two Governments with a view to determining, in the light of governing economic conditions, the best means of attaining the above-stated objectives by their own agreed action and of seeking the agreed action of other like-minded Governments." Leland M. Goodrich and Marie J. Carroll (eds.), *Documents on American Foreign Relations July 1942–June 1943* (Boston: World Peace Foundation, 1944), V, 112.

Canada when in fact she isn't. But if Clark and Wilgress dislike the idea of a preliminary Empire discussion, they equally dislike the idea of U.S.–U.K. talks on this subject from which they are entirely excluded. Clark in particular objected to the trend which he said was growing in political, economic, financial and social matters for the U.S. and U.K. to make decisions and announce them. He said that Canada for one would be found far more cooperative if more attention were given to consulting her and letting her feel that she had some share, even if not a major one, of responsibility in decisions.

I asked why Canada had not yet given us an answer on our suggestion of signing Article 7 of the Lease-Lend Agreement by itself without relation to lease-lend. I pointed out (a) that if later they wished to negotiate a reciprocal lease-lend agreement it would not in any way prejudice their position, and (b) that by standing alone outside the framework of Article 7 (at least as far as the public is concerned) they were losing a tactical position in connection with future talks on implementing this article. I said that our people in Washington just could not understand the delay in giving an answer to what they considered a suggestion of major importance, and the preliminary oral observations had certainly not carried conviction.

Dana Wilgress replied that of course the Canadian Government having agreed to Britain's signing the article was committed, but that the Canadian public would be extremely critical at an open endorsement which in appearance placed more emphasis on the removal of discriminations (which to them means Imperial preference) than it did on the removal of tariff barriers which they consider equally stifling to international cooperation. He said that he could notice a great change in Canadian opinion and that the country almost to a man would support the freest possible trade, provided there were a world movement in that direction in which the United States would play its part. There was still considerable suspicion that the United States would stop where she is and not make further tariff concessions. The present Imperial preferences will be held onto zealously until the United States makes a move such as, for instance, obtaining authority to reduce duties — at least the higher duties — by more than the present fifty per cent. Smoot-Hawley [48] and Ottawa in Canada's

[48] The Hawley-Smoot tariff bill, setting very high tariffs, was signed by President Hoover in June 1930.

mind balance themselves, and as our tariffs go down lower so will Imperial preferences become lesser but not a day before.

I replied that even admitting the justice of this thesis, it still did not explain why Canada would not by signing Article 7 join in the procession of the United Nations toward trade liberalizations.

Dana Wilgress then got on to the British position and said that he had had a series of talks with Leith-Ross [Chief Economic Adviser to the British Government], with Sir Frederick Phillips [Joint Secretary of the Treasury], with Mr. Richard Law [Parliamentary Under Secretary of State, Foreign Office], with Mr. Clement Attlee [Deputy Prime Minister], with Mr. Arthur Jenkins [Parliamentary Private Secretary to Mr. Attlee], M.P., etc. He had also read the brochures gotten out by the Federation of British Industries, and four other large trade organizations. His conclusions, based on his talks and his reading, were discouraging. He found that the central point in British thinking was a determination to retain many, if not all, trade controls now in existence. The motivation would be to regard the restoration of United Kingdom prosperity and the solution of the United Kingdom payments problem as the center around which the other phases of world revival must rotate. The political prognostication is that the British public will accept these controls, including rationing, long after the war because they have resulted in greater equalization and a better break for the British lower classes. The result of the continuation of these controls would obviously be the canalization of trade, particularly foreign trade, which comes perilously close to a closed economy.

Leith-Ross was not willing to go as far as the others in advocating the retention of controls, but even he gave Wilgress the impression that the advantages of bulk buying had proved so great that they would be retained in essential commodities, notably wheat. Wilgress pointed out that Britain by buying or not buying great bulks of wheat from Canada had a leverage on Canadian national economy for which she could extract almost any amount of concession. Attlee and Jenkins were talking of what amounted to a socialized State. They would allow the continuance of free enterprise in nonessentials but the great mass industries, such as iron and steel, textiles, shipbuilding, etc., would be definitely a government matter and free enterprise squeezed out.

All of the Britishers, but Jenkins in particular, evinced considerable worry over the extent of Canadian industrialization during the war. They wanted to know what Canada would do with its new factories after the war, and were told that they would be converted to peacetime production. They then wanted to know if Canada would set up a high tariff wall. The Canadians had replied that there was still a great deal of low tariff sentiment in the country, finding its center in the agricultural west, plus a belief that in a world of free or relatively free economies Canada could successfully survive as an industrial nation. The answer they invariably got was that Britain could only maintain a free economy if the United States made it possible.

I suggested that from a psychological point of view it would be very important for postwar public opinion in the United States not to feel that Britain was closing the ranks against her or indulging in a closed economy. I said public opinion was a fragile thing and while it was all right at the moment it could react violently if it felt that Britain was not playing fair. Wilgress agreed to this extent. He said he thought the prime decision after the war would have to be made by Britain, but that meantime we could make a gesture during the war, such as the passage of an enlarged trade agreement, which would make it very much easier for Britain to be liberal after the war. . .

From all the foregoing Wilgress drew the conclusion that in interest and in sentiment Canada was more in sympathy with the American position than the British and that on balance we should find Canada an ally if we drew her into economic discussions. . .

On the night of November 7–8, 1942, the amphibious landing of American and British forces along hundreds of miles of the North African coast took place. The elation and optimism following the invasion in North Africa led the minds of many people to think beyond the war and speculate upon the new peace-time order.

Ottawa, December 9, 1942.

Mr. Mackenzie King dined with us last night. I only had time for a relatively short conversation with him but it was clear that he came back from his trip to Washington "with his batteries recharged." He told me that he had found Mr. Hull in far better shape than last year and obviously pleased over the justification of his North African policy.[49]

[49] By maintaining relations with Vichy we had been permitted to keep American

Almost his entire time, however, had been spent in the White House chatting with the President. The latter, he told me, was quite satisfied with events in North Africa and inclined to believe that General Eisenhower had done well in obtaining all the advantages deriving from an association with Darlan, to whom the Army and Navy were personally loyal.[50] On the other hand, he was worried at the political implications and was sending the General's brother over to North Africa by airplane to tell him to make it clear to all and sundry that he, Eisenhower, was commanding and giving orders in North Africa and that Darlan was working under his authority rather than the reverse. The President thought that with this shift in emphasis the matter would clear up soon.

Mr. King said that Mr. Roosevelt's ideas as to the future peace were crystallizing. He took the point of view that in big lines at least the United Nations should come to an agreement during the fighting (in this respect diverging from Mr. Hull's views),[51] that much remained to be done and that it might be that there would be little time in which to do it. The essence of the President's idea is that there should be few boundary changes and that the main emphasis should be placed on the complete disarmament of Germany, the constant and thorough inspection of their industry, coupled with an international police force, particularly an aviation bombardment police force of the four big Allied Powers, U.K., U.S., Russia and China. He was toying with the idea of breaking up Germany into its component states, though I did not gather that he was even mentally committed.

Mr. King said that the President was delighted at the state of

---

consuls in North Africa, who had supplied valuable military information for the African operation. The fact that the lives lost were much fewer than in the case of the British and French operations in Syria, Secretary Hull thought was a vindication of his Vichy policy. Hull, II, 1193.

[50] Admiral Darlan had by chance been visiting his son, who was ill in Algiers, when the Allied invasion occurred. General Dwight Eisenhower conducted negotiations with him, which led to his being made supreme French leader in North Africa. Winston S. Churchill, *The Second World War*, vol. IV, *The Hinge of Fate* (Boston: Houghton Mifflin Co., 1950), pp. 629–647; Hull, II, 1195–1210; Dwight D. Eisenhower, *Crusade in Europe* (Garden City, N.Y.: Doubleday & Co., 1948), pp. 99ff.

[51] In a visit to Washington in November 1942 Mr. Moffat had noted in a memorandum of a conversation with Mr. Norman Davis: "He, the Secretary, is inclined not to discuss any postwar matters in concrete terms and to resent any speeches. Sumner Welles, on the other hand, says that the President has commissioned him to keep the issue before the public and to educate it now instead of confronting it, as was done last time, with a *fait accompli*." Moffat diary, November 13–17, 1942.

Canadian-American relations, feeling it was one of the bright spots and that it should serve as a model for other countries.

As to domestic postwar plans, he said that the President had been immensely impressed with the Beveridge scheme, which he felt coincided with his own philosophy of "security from the cradle to the grave."

This was among the last memorandums which Pierrepont Moffat dictated. In mid-December an illness confined him to his home, and his sudden death on January 24, 1943, ended his notable career and record of twenty-five years in the American Foreign Service.

INDEX

Abbott, Edwin, 143
Abyssinia, 126n., 127, 128, 155n., 157n., 176, 180
Acheson, Dean, 353
Aconit, 360n.
Adams, Charles Francis, 51
Advisory Committee on Far East, *see* Far East Advisory Committee
Africa: U.S. policy toward Vichy territory, 361, 362, 365, 366, 369; German attitude toward, 370; Allied landing, 387–388; mentioned, 195, 311, 312n. *See also* Abyssinia; Liberia; Union of South Africa
Air bases, *see* Bases
Airplanes, *see* Aviation
Alaska, 331, 334
Albania, 242, 247
Aldrovandi-Marescotti, Luigi, 166–167, 181
Alsop, Joseph, 227
Alysse, 360n.
Anschluss, see Austria
Anti-Comintern Pact, 146
Aranha, Oswaldo, 229
Argentina, 115, 223, 288, 378
Arms and ammunition, control of the trade: U.S. and 1925 Convention for supervision, 80; Nye Committee investigates, 113–114, 114–115. *See also* Embargo; Neutrality policy
Army, U.S.: and disarmament proposals, 47, 49–53, 60, 62–64, 68, 91–92, 94–95; sale of material to foreign countries, 283–284, 290, 318–319, 321; Selective Service Act, 327; coordination with Canadian army, 374; mentioned, 316, 378. *See also* War, Department of
Arnold, Thurman, 248
Arsène-Henry, Charles, 160
Artillery: proposals for reduction and abolition, 61n., 63, 92, 94; Canada appeals to U.S. for, 316; mentioned, 290, 306, 313, 315, 329
Aruba, 321
Atherton, Ray, 361, 365, 368, 374–375
Atlantic Charter, 381
Attlee, Clement, 301, 386
Aubert, Ludvig, 179–180
Australia: anti-American feeling, 124, 125, 128–130, 134; trade situation (1918–

1935), 125; U.S. refuses trade agreement, 125; reaction to the Abyssinian crisis, 126–127, 128; British policy, 126, 127, 128, 129, 132, 133–134, 139, 140, 141, 143; representation at Washington, 127, 139; idea of Pacific Pact, 128; view of U.S. trade, 129, 130–131, 132–137, 139–141; relations with Japan, 129–130, 139, 141n.; trade diversion program, 132, 134–138, 143–145; trade with Canada, 137, 140, 144; U.S. suspends trade concessions, 137–138; position on Czech crisis, 208–209; enters World War II, 261; mentioned, 1, 4, 181, 294, 317n., 331, 352
Austria: and the MacDonald Plan, 92; the *Anschluss*, 4, 189, 191–192, 193, 195; mentioned, 9, 12, 13n., 30, 45
Avenol, Joseph, 295
Aviation: disarmament plans, 49, 52, 53, 56, 60, 61, 62–64, 69–70, 91, 92; use in Nicaragua and Honduras, 70; inferiority of French, 206; rights of neutrals, 260; U.S. shipments of planes to belligerents, 262, 263, 290, 317–318; censorship of airmail at Bermuda, 286, 290, 300–301; Soviet plane orders at Wright plant, 283–284; France and Great Britain disagree, 307; U.S.-Canadian coordination, 317–318, 336; air routes to Alaska, 334; civilian air routes, 336; Roosevelt suggests, as police force, 388; mentioned, 249, 313. *See also* Bases; Bombing; Kosciuszko squadron
Axis powers, *see* Germany; Italy
Azores, 286

Bacteriological warfare, 56, 58, 92n.
Baldwin, Stanley, 73n.
Balkans, 190, 192. *See also individual countries*
Ballantine, Arthur, 77
Ballantine, Joseph, 264
Baltic states, 241, 269. *See also individual countries*
Barclay, Edwin, 83, 87
Barnhart Island Dam, 350
Bases, U.S.: air, in Canada, 315, 317, 319n.; naval, leased from British, 326n., 328, 329, 353; rumored, at Singapore, 331, 332, 333, 334; mentioned, 319n.